D0907034

TALES OF NARCISSUS - THE LOOKING GLASS OF ECONOMIC SCIENCE

TALES OF NARCISSUS - THE LOOKING GLASS OF ECONOMIC SCIENCE

CRAIG FREEDMAN AND RICK SZOSTAK
EDITORS

Nova Science Publishers, Inc.
New York

Senior Editors: Susan Boriotti and Donna Dennis
Coordinating Editor: Tatiana Shohov
Office Manager: Annette Hellinger
Graphics: Wanda Serrano
Editorial Production: Matthew Kozlowski and Maya Columbus
Circulation: Ave Maria Gonzalez, Raymond Davis and Vladimir Klestov
Communications and Acquisitions: Serge P. Shohov
Marketing: Cathy DeGregory

Library of Congress Cataloging-in-Publication Data

Tales of narcissus : the looking glass of economic science / Craig Freedman and Rick Szostak, editors.
  p. cm.
  Includes bibliographical refernces and index.
    ISBN 1-56072-855-8
    1. Economics--Philosophy. 2. Economists. I. Freedman, Craig, 1950- II. Szostak, Rick, 1959-
HB72.T274   2000
330--dc21   00-049003

Copyright © 2003 by Nova Science Publishers, Inc.
      400 Oser Ave, Suite 1600
      Hauppauge, New York 11788-3619
      Tele. 631-231-7269   Fax 631-231-8175
      e-mail: Novascience@earthlink.net
      Web Site: http://www.novapublishers.com

Printed in the United States of America

CONTENTS

Preface   vii

Acknowledgments   ix

More of a Contradiction than an Introduction

The Narcissistic Science   3
    Craig Freedman

Are Economists by Nature a Social Animal?

Life Among the Econ   17
    Axel Leijonhufvud

Does Studying Economics Inhibit Cooperation?   29
    Robert H. Frank, Thomas Gilovich, and Dennis T. Regan

Do Economists Have a Sense of Humour?

Towards a Deeper Economics of Sleeping   45
    Theodore C. Bergstrom

The Economics of Brushing Teeth   47
    Allan S. Blinder

A Theory of Extramarital Affairs   53
    Ray C. Fair

Can Economists Tell the Difference between Rigor and Rigor Mortis?

Economics Science: A Search Through the Hyperspace of Assumptions?   73
    Donald N. McCloskey

In Defense of Formalization in Economics   85
Donald W. Katzner

Comment: Has Formalization Gone Too Far?   93
Edward E. Leamer

Economics as Dentistry   95
Martin Bronfenbrenner

Are Economists Accountable?

Why Economists Can't Read   105
Craig Freedman

Mirowski's Screed: A Review of Philip Mirowski's
More Heat than Light: Economics as Social Physics,
Physics as Nature's Economics   123
Kevin D. Hoover

Economic Nostrums and Economic Practices - Accountability
in Economic Journals   131
Craig Freedman

Economic Textbooks: Missing and Misplaced Incentives   159
Craig Freedman

Is Economics a Useful Science?

The Whimsical Science   175
Richard A. Levins

Why I am No Longer a Positivist   189
Donald N. McCloskey

The History of Art and the Art in Economics   203
Rick Szostak

The Glass Shattered

Confessions of an Ex-Beauty Queen: Some Simple Lessons For the Profession   237
Rick Szostak

Index   247

PREFACE

And only I was left to tell the tale - Herman Melville

Plato, as some scholars would have it, slept with a copy of the works of Aristophanes by his side to remind him of the potential futility of his own objectives. He knew that only serious people are able to laugh at themselves. Being solemn, is simply not the same as being seriously engaged in one's work. It is here that even the best economists, like George Stigler, get it wrong. In his published memoirs he states that 'economists are unable to laugh'.[1] Stigler had one of the quickest and sharpest wits in the economics profession. But, he carefully avoided turning that weapon upon himself. Self-examination, whether amused or not, was never a dominant characteristic. He doesn't of course mean that they can't tell a joke or get the point of one (though after one too many conferences some may begin to doubt even this). He means that economists can't allow themselves the luxury of laughing at themselves, that this undermines an economist's expressed objectives. But this is more than curious, since it seems to indicate the extreme fragility of the discipline's enterprise, a house of straw that can collapse if faced with a strong gale of laughter. Economists are implicitly urged to suppress legitimate doubts and to instead blindly forge ahead. Such a closed-minded approach surely can't be healthy. It is a pity that Stigler and all other economists were not raised on Hillaire Belloc's *Algernon and Other Cautionary Tales*[2], an irreverent take on child raising and moral rectitude.

This book of edited articles is offered then as a mature age substitute for Belloc. We recommend it as required bedside reading to all economists clinging tightly to an illusion of certainty, having somehow missed out on the fact that one of our enduring sources of merriment is our own foibles and absurdities, especially those that touch our work-a-day lives. The editors take great pleasure in dedicating this volume to all those economists who find the line between rigour and rigour mortis difficult to locate.

As always we must admit that in any academic endeavour there are casualties. Apologies must go to our all too patient wives for our many absences both physical and mental. Our small children in particular could see no justice in the choices we made and had limited recourse to amend our errant behaviour. We expect to hear from their attorneys in the years to come.

REFERENCES

Belloc, Hillaire (1991) *Algernon and Other Cautionary Tales*. London: Jonathan Cape.
Stigler, George J. (1988) *Memoirs of an Unregulated Economist*. New York: Basic Books.

NOTES

[1]   Some of these traits of intellectual leaders are caught in the statement that they lack a sense of humor. I mean by this, not the inability to laugh at the right point when hearing a joke, but the ability to view oneself with detached candor. Ridicule is a common weapon of attack but amused self-examination is a form of disarmament; one so endowed cannot declaim his beliefs with massive certainty and view opposing opinions as error uncontaminated by truth (Stigler 1988:213-214)

[2]   Now available with charming illustrations by Quentin Blake (1991), it is not too late for deprived economists to recreate some of their missed childhood.

ACKNOWLEDGMENTS

The editors and publishers wish to thank the authors and the following publishers who have kindly given permission for the use of copyright material.

American Economic Association for the article: Frank, Robert, Thomas Gilovich and Dennis Regan (1993) "Does Studying Economics Inhibit Cooperation," *The Journal of Economic Perspectives*. 7(2): 159-171.

Association for Social Economics for the article: McCloskey, Donald (1989) "Why I Am No Longer a Positivist," *Review of Social Economy*. 47(3): 225-239.

Copyright Clearance Center and the American Agricultural Economics Association for the article: Levins, Richard (1992) "The Whimsical Science," *Review of Agricultural Economics*. 14(3): 139-151.

History of Economic Theory Society of Australia for the article: Szostak, Rick (1992) "The History of Art and the Art in Economics," *History of Economics Review*: 18 (Summer): 70-107.

International Network for Economic Methodology for the articles: Freedman, Craig (1993) "Why Economists Can't Read," *Methodus* 5(1): 6-23. Hoover, Kevin (1991) Mirowski's Screed: A Review of Philip Mirowski's *More Heat than Light: Economics as Social Physics, Physics as Nature's Economics,"* Methodus 3(1): 139-145. Katzner, Donald (1991) "In Defense of Formalization in Economics," *Methodus* 3(1): 17-24. Leamer, Edward (1991) "Comment: Has Formalization Gone Too Far?" *Methodus* 3(1): 25-26. McCloskey, Donald (1991) "Economics Science: A Search Through the Hyperspace of Assumptions?" *Methodus* 3(1): 6-16.

Oxford University Press and the Western Economic Association for the article: Leijonhufvud, Axel (1973) "Life Among the Econ," *Western Economic Journal*. 15(2): 327-337.

Southern Economic Association for the article: Bronfenbrenner, Martin (1991) "Economics as Dentistry," *The Southern Economic Journal*. 57(3): 599-605.

University of Chicago Press for the articles: Bergstrom, Theodore (1976) "Toward a Deeper Economics of Sleeping," *The Journal of Political Economy*. 84(2): 411-412. Blinder, Allan (1974) "The Economics of Brushing Teeth," *The Journal of Political Economy*. 82(4): 887-892. Fair, Ray (1978) "A Theory of Extramarital Affairs," *The Journal of Political Economy*. 86(1): 45-61.

The editors and publishers would also like to thank Pluto Press for reprinting parts of Szostak, Rick (1999) *Econ Art*.

Extraordinary efforts have been made to trace all the copyright holders but if any have been inadvertently overlooked the publishers will be pleased to make the necessary arrangement at the very first opportunity.

The editors would also like to express their thanks and indebtedness to Therese Smith for making this publication possible.

More of a Contradiction than an Introduction

... luckily Owl kept his head and told us that the Opposite of an Introduction my dear Pooh, was a Contradiction; and, as he is very good at long words, I am sure that that's what it is (A.A. Milne).

THE NARCISSISTIC SCIENCE

Craig Freedman

... he fell in love with his reflection. At first he tried to embrace and kiss the beautiful boy who confronted him, but presently recognized himself, and lay gazing enraptured into the pool, hour after hour. How could he endure both to possess and yet not to possess? Grief was destroying him, yet he rejoiced in his torments; knowing at least that his other self would remain true to Him, whatever happened (Graves 1960:287).

'We tell ourselves stories in order to live.' Though Joan Didion (1979:11) never intended to speak directly to economists, they as much as anyone else are addicted to story telling. Some of us, hearing the same stories repeated time and time again, may come to believe them. Still others are so moonstruck by these tales that they become creatures fashioned after their own bedtime stories. When an economist looks into the mirror of his soul (and let's admit it, most of these gazers are male) he sees a rational economic man looking back at him. Economists have not only fallen in love with their own creation, but like some deranged Henry Higgins, they have also become the very image of that which they have laboured so long to create. By talking mostly to each other, economists have crossed that fine line which distinguishes their own heuristic models from the reality in which they supposedly live.

That this state of affairs exists in a profession that arose out of the perceived need to solve policy issues is curious. Even more so since surprisingly, economists, as a group, seem to be a particularly introspective lot. That is, if we measure introspection by the extent to which they poke and probe into their own group behaviour. There is no aspect of an economist's life that hasn't been examined using the full analytic artillery of the profession to do it. Yet each new exploration is read with at least a certain degree of avidity and finds a place in some of the profession's most distinguished journals. Despite this spate of articles, a corresponding degree of self awareness is mostly absent. The reason for this apparent paradox easily suggests itself. These articles are more an indication of a narcissistic fascination with ourselves rather than any desire for self knowledge. Economists seem to have cultivated a Lear-like blindness to their own motivations without having this lack of insight counterbalanced by the remnants of grandeur which makes the old king a tragic figure.

The story of Narcissus, like any other Greek myth, represents a lesson to be learned on our journey through life: a lesson that when properly applied will help us lead a better life. If contemporary economists have implicitly rejected the Greek abjuration to *'know thyself'*, then perhaps it is time that these modern day Narcissi were educated into moderation by employing a new book of fables. Perversely, economists have grown more confident with each failure of their own discipline, operating in this sense more like a cult than a science. We need to translate the advice of the Delphic Oracle, *'everything in moderation',* into terms that can guide the self-regarding economist towards a more balanced perspective. Thus *'everything in moderation'* might become *'don't over promise because we don't really know very much'*. Our new ***Tales of Narcissus*** take direct aim at an economist's arrogant pride in knowing nothing but a method, yet scorning all else as irrelevant, a mere matter of anecdotal details.

The profession is currently in need of an antidote to curb the ever growing infestation of a priori formalism. Such a priori models are churned out in the almost blind hope that sheer numbers alone will produce something of significance. This hope is sadly mistaken. Even a billion monkeys chained to keyboards will still fail to produce a copy of ***Pride and Prejudice***. Economists churning out variations on existing formal models too often succeed only in avoiding any attempt at introspection. Formalism remains an easier path to pursue than dealing directly with urgent economic problems. The imperative then becomes to ignore specifics in order to grasp empty generalities.

What these new tales for aspiring economists represent, is above all not an attack on mathematical economics. It is far from accidental that discussions of the role of pure formalism in economics are so often transmuted into debates which weigh the benefits of applying mathematical tools to the study of economics. This obscures the issue. The problem is not whether economics has become a sheltered workshop for second rate mathematicians, but if the profession's unthinking pursuit of formalism detached from any concrete relevance is slowly, but surely, trivialising the work that economists do.

Fifty years of pursuing the holy grail of undiluted formalism has left the profession inhabited by uni-dimensional figures. Graduate schools are churning out humourless young fogies who are taught to harumph at any work presented outside a strictly formalistic canonical mode. The discipline has become an umbrella stand of academic Lady Bracknells. While economists continue to laud markets for providing ongoing diversity to economic life, they have come to abhor it in their own profession. As a result, economists are rapidly becoming the sole consumers of their own work.

Each chapter of this collection represents an attempt to create a dialogue with a profession that has become increasingly hard of hearing, distracted by the beauty of its own creations. The very first step in pulling our gaze away from that mirror of our own creation is to stop being so defensive and instead accept criticism. We all need to recognise that we share this fatal weakness for formalism to the point that it has made us arrogant and scornful of anything else. The aim must be not to defend this proclivity by making it into a virtue. Instead, we must maintain a sense of humour about the limitations of our own endeavours. As long as we continue to confuse solemnity with seriousness, there will be no hope for the profession.

"Life Among the Econ" by Leijonhufved (1973), which leads off our collection, has never ceased to amuse struggling young graduate students. Amongst the strange tribes he depicts, the model (or modl) has become a totem. Formalism is worshipped as an exotic, but powerful, deity that must be appeased if one is to become an elder of the tribe. By adopting a pseudo anthropological tone, the distance achieved points out the absurdity of the tribe's practices. Since its initial publication in 1973, nothing has occurred to weaken the relevance of this absurdity.

> The dominant feature, which makes status relations among the Econ of unique interest to the serious student, is the way that status is tied to the manufacture of certain types of implements, called "modls."The status of the adult male is determined by his skill at making the "modl"of his "field." The facts (a) that the Econ are highly status-motivated, (b) that status is only to be achieved by making "modls," and (c) that most of these "modls" seem to be of little or no practical use, probably accounts for the backwardness and abject cultural poverty of the tribe (Leijonhufvud 1973:328).

This description of the backward Econ is not far removed from a recent confession of a Harvard graduate student:

> We are being socialized into something, but nobody in the faculty seems to know what that is, except they were socialized themselves five years ago ... You end up in the middle of the semester completely malleable. You write down whatever you can and try to understand it. If you get you head above water, you survive ... The way I feel now is that I try to float with the current (Klamer and Colander 1990:94).

Instead, as the research by Frank, Gilovich and Regan (1993) point out (chapter 2), we have become our own creation. The study of economics seems to transform its acolytes into increasingly stunted specimens, to such a degree that one wonders why the subject isn't offered with a mandatory warning label attached. Economics, in purveying its academic goods, may be closely akin to the tobacco industry's morally ambiguous marketing of its own wares. In the future, economists and tobacco barons alike may be charged with corrupting the young. Will the general public as a reflexive response soon be given to saying, *'Some of my best friends are economists but I wouldn't want my daughter to marry one'*.

We recognise this last line as a rather feeble attempt to raise a smile while making a point. This strategy is common to a number of authors in this collection. It stands out due only to its relative rarity in most economic literature. Punch lines to jokes seldom find their way into economic discourse. Humour is the one unobtainable scarce resource in the profession. What few jokes, or even attempts at light heartedness exist, tend to be rather heavy handed. The cause of this deficiency probably lies in the pervading, near-obsession with formalism.

As a result, deliberate attempts at humour or satire tend to be overstated, rather Germanic, when trying to poke fun. It is difficult to satirise that which is almost a self parody. Devotional attention to a priori theorising, makes it nearly impossible to locate the proximity of tongue to cheek of any economics author.

> At an abstract level, love, and other emotional attachments, such as sexual activity or frequent close contact with a particular person can be considered particular nonmarketable household commodities, and nothing much needs to be added to the analysis (Becker 1976:223).

Included in this collection are a couple of short pieces by Blinder (1974) and Bergstrom (1976) that attempt to satirise the work of Becker in an amusing but necessary obvious way. However in a manner which strongly evokes Becker, Fair (1978), in the included piece, is dead serious in providing us with a blinding glimpse of the obvious dressed up in formal attire. He applies similar techniques and standard statistical analysis to explicate adultery as a leisure activity. In its own way, Fair (1978) is much more adept at unintentionally satirising Becker's work than the deliberate but less telling attempts by Blinder (1974) and Bergstrom (1976). Keeping a straight face, he employs data from a **Redbook Magazine** survey to conclude that increased time spent in adulterous affairs reduces the time spent with one's legal spouse.[1]

Becker's attempt to extend the assumptions and formal a priori analysis of economics to all human (and biological functions) is presented with all seriousness, lacking the least element of self doubt. These methods should strike most readers outside the charmed circle of the profession as belonging to the theatre of the absurd rather than to any serious academic endeavour. Formalism merges into near Dadaist absurdity. How else to explain Becker's (1991) attempt to account for restaurant pricing (not included in this collection). His interest is piqued by the way two very similar restaurants, facing each other across the street, one very popular and one not, adopt nearly identical pricing policies despite the obvious differences in demand. The naive approach to answering this anomaly would be to simply ask the owners of the restaurants in question, or at least to ask questions of people knowledgeable about the business. This is not the route chosen by Becker and most other practising economists. Becker isn't really interested in restaurant pricing. If he were, he would have compared the answers available by using survey techniques with those supplied by standard price theory. Instead he falls guilty of the sin of a priori hypothesising. Restaurants become an occasion for economic theorising, not a problem to be solved. Becker constructs an interesting pricing model (interesting to other economists) but totally unrelated to the way restaurant owners think and operate[2].

The problem underlying Becker's analysis is clear. We as a profession have regard for and talk to ourselves alone. The stories we tell are stories of interest only to sheltered academics because all these stories are self referential.

> The only characters in academic stories are academic economists themselves ... they are invariably about economists who are troubled by some anomaly or another, go through some complicated technical analysis and end up happily with a result (Klamer and Leonard 2000:16).

Klamer and Leonard (1992 article not included in this collection) have pointed out that the incommensurable difference between academic and everyday narratives emphasises a cavalier disregard for how economic actors think. This approach underlies the core of the work done by Becker and others. Academic stories are devoid of drama for two reasons: 1) academics are convinced that they have nothing to learn from economic actors, 2) academics already know the conclusions to their stories before they even begin to tell them.

> After all, if ideas do not matter, ideas about the economy (and its inhabitants) do not matter either, and therefore producers and advocates of economic thought, i.e. professional economists, lack a *raison d être*. When agents are assumed to be optimizing automatons, as they are in conventional theorizing, economists are left with no

opportunity to improve on what those agents do, nor could we, since we, too, are economic agents without cognition (Klamer and Leonard 1992:2).

The difference between the way people think about economic issues in everyday life and how academic economists think about their subject professionally is thus divided by an unbridgeable gap[3]. But is this a worry to these inwards looking academics? Not a bit, since that difference must by definition be inconsequential. Though thought should inform action, the a priori assumptions of the working economists turn economic actors into economic calculators that merely react in a predictable way to outside stimuli. Economists not only do not expect that the general public will understand the stories they tell, they take great pride in this lack of communication[4].

> Our map of the world differs from that of the layman. Perhaps our map will never be a best seller. But a discipline like economics has a logic and validity of its own. We believe in our map because we cannot help doing so. In Frank Ramsey's beautiful quotation from William Blake: *'Truth can never be told so as to be understood and not believed'* (Samuelson 1962:6).

Our pride encourages a peculiar desire to converse with professional mathematicians. At heart, these two groups have relatively little to say to each other. By pursuing this tack we end up valuing the form and denigrating the content of our studies. It is thus not enough for us to support Katzner (1991) in his stand against bad formalisation or even to agree with Leamer (1991) that:

> We should value the content of the message communicated by a model, not the mathematical form and technique. The model should not be pushed too far - it is only a metaphor (Leamer 1991:25).

The real issue here is whether we have headed down the road of formal irrelevance by caring more for the aesthetics of the approach than the economic problem at stake. Should we pursue the implication of our assumptions regardless of other considerations? In which case, we are becoming self absorbed with solving formal puzzles of our own devising and care little for the content contained. We are left once again, talking only with ourselves.

Few civilians care to associate with these high priests of formalism because according to Martin Bronfenbrenner (1991) in a piece included in this collection, the discipline in the postwar period has transformed itself into the trivial science, using models and language that lack any relevance to those outside the pale of economic theorising. The confirmed formalist trivialises himself by spending all his time staring into a mirror, pleased by what he sees.

> Ultra-quantitative, ultra-rigorous economics may indeed become the Greek and Sanskrit, or perhaps the *"belles-lettres* and orthoepy" of the 21st century. The burgeoning of "business" or "managerial" economics on our ideological Right, the burgeoning of "political economy" and "economic sociology" on our ideological Left, and the compression of economics to a few snippets in "Social Science" surveys are three straws in the wind (Bronfenbrenner 1991: 605).

The result of fifty years of formalism, as Freedman claims (1993), is that not only are economists proud of their lack of specific knowledge, they are also proud of their inability to communicate. We are mutes perversely given to wearing mittens. In fact, the formalist approach is used to cut off attempts at conversation - to erect barriers to entry. Like Edith Wharton's *Age of Innocence* (1966), language and behaviour can become stylised to such a degree that it loses the ability of conveying any information. The onus is thrown back on the reader or the listener. All becomes guesswork. The profession claims to be erecting standards to keep the profession from lapsing into the anarchy of *anything goes*. We waste so much of our time and energy fearing barbarians, that we cease to realise that the true barbarians are those on the walls looking out.

> The barbarians are surely at the gate. The only question is: Are the barbarians the ones outside the gate, or are we inside it? (Sen 1993).

Formalism in rhetoric, with style narcissistically overwhelming content, has become a tool to exclude, to limit conversation. In this way we successfully reject all that is truly novel, that hasn't been said before. Seminal articles have been met with stony silence, forced to remain homeless as myopic reviewers lacking real ability to read and analyse failed to judge their value (Gans and Shepherd 1994). Freedman (2003a) urges us to improve the profession by opening those gates erected against change. Are we so insecure that our self-appointed guardians must stamp out any deviation as heresy? Economists seem unable to grasp the irony of extolling markets for their creation of diversity while maintaining within the profession itself a complete intolerance for alternative views and especially alternative formal approaches. One can sin against doctrine but formal sins remain unforgivable.

Kevin Hoover, in just such a non-reading mode, unintentionally demonstrates in his review of Phillip Mirowski's (1990) controversial book (*More Heat Than Light*), why economists are the sort of frivolous tribe described in Leijonhufvud's anthropological stroll. The problem inherent in Hoover's review has little to do with Mirowski's thesis. Economists are unable to swallow strong writing, unable to digest anything which deviates greatly from the canonical form. In this ongoing inversion of standards, pabulum becomes the benchmark for haute cuisine. As a profession we will overcome our penchant for the frivolous only when we can recognise the underlying folly of our positions and understanding. In what can only be termed a spiteful review, Hoover takes Mirowski to task by committing the same sort of ungenerous behaviour that he describes as characteristic of Mirowski. Leaving aside the content of the work, *More Heat Than Light* is deliberately provocative. The author intends to stir the profession much as Keynes did in 1936. The results are depressingly similar. Misunderstanding this rhetorical device leads to a rather peculiar ad hominem attack. Hoover harumphs like a Victorian matron. At the height of his outrage he could pass himself off as the reincarnation of Wilde's (1986) Lady Bracknell. What in fact upsets him most of all is the rhetorical strategy adopted by Mirowski. For Kevin Hoover, it is a case of the importance of not being sufficiently earnest[5].

> Taken as a whole, it is an outrageous book: neither the history or the methodology are persuasive; the scholarship is often slapdash; the tone is intemperate; and the style is often obnoxious. Mirowski's hatred of neoclassical economics borders on the pathological; one sometimes wonders if his mother didn't run off with a neoclassical economist, leaving little Phil bereft in the cradle. Mirowski strikes a flashy, bullying tone throughout the book, patronizing the reader, economists and physicists (Hoover 1991:139).

Reviews that combine an ungenerous spirit to a carefully contentious attitude might be said to exemplify the Chicago School of discussion typified by George Stigler's slash and burn approach to debate[6]. The purpose is not to communicate but to confine discussion to carefully regulated channels.

This meanness of spirit is perhaps what makes economics the Ebenezer Scrooge of the social sciences (prior to any dramatic Christmas Eve conversion). Though it may be that performers in seminars or journals sometimes let their desire for self-display override their obligation to play the scholar, the same explanation of human weakness won't in a parallel fashion extend to the performance of the journal referee. These are the self-appointed guardians already mentioned, the shock troops of the profession's ongoing cultural revolution. In the words of Walt Kelley's comic creation Pogo, *"We have met the enemy and they are us.* Given the current refereeing process, it is not surprising that narrowness of education and vision may sometimes triumph over original ideas. Refusing to maintain the preferred standard of formalism is judged to be undignified behaviour. The associated host of referees in this sense seems the last redoubt of the Victorian matron. Like those matrons, referees tend to bristle at the impropriety of material being presented in a form other than that already enshrined in current literature[7].

Ultimately, journal editors are in the best position to reform the profession. By demanding that articles be well written rather than merely formally correct, the tenor of the profession would surely change. In the same way, only editors can scold those referees that nitpick, or merely quibble. Unless there are sanctions against poor or indifferent refereeing, nothing will change. We may need to find the courage to throw the baby out with the bathwater if it turns out that the baby is stillborn. Fortunately there is an underlying, if unexpressed, demand for better writing within the profession. The birth of *The Journal of Economic Perspectives* in 1987 was proof of this need for a journal that could appeal to a wide cross section of the profession. Might we even say a journal whose articles were read by more than just the authors and the relevant referees?

> We cannot help but wonder whether the strong market showing (popularity) of the *Journal of Economic Perspectives*, with its emphasis on presentation of arguments and findings in essay form, reflects a widespread reaction within the profession to the mathematical/statistical emphasis of the 1970s and 1980s. If so, we would expect some fraction of new entrants, as well as current editors, in the 1990s to follow the *JEP's* example with respect to style (Laband and Salisbury quoted in Shapiro and Krueger 1994: 485).

Again we note the unintended irony. A profession that bases its theories on consumer sovereignty is characterised by an authoritarian rather than market response to its readership. Ideally the question of which style will dominate should not need to be raised. The lurking admission here is that the profession itself is not responsive to its membership.

Even if we accept that economics has given up reason in pursuit of rhyme, many in the profession have retained a hidden belief that no matter how much we may have declined in pursuing form over content, our cousins over at ag econ were still doing good empirical work. The brigade that introduced statistics into the discipline surely would continue to get its hands dirty in pursuit of worthwhile causes. They remained the Medècins Sans Frontiers of our profession. Levins (1992) in his article included in this collection, disabuses us of any such illusions. Whimsy has become the byword amongst agricultural economists. Levins takes a journey through the looking glass in the vain hope of discovering underlying meaning beneath a sometimes impenetrable approach. He ends up wondering whether research in his field consists only of mathematical erotica, a familiar triumph of formalism over practicality.

According to Donald (now Deirdre) McCloskey (1989), formalism explains why economics has remained the last bastion of modernism, characterized philosophically by logical positivism. Narcissistically we are more enraptured by our formal methods, too often observed only in the breach, than with the more pragmatic way in which much of the work in the field gets done. McCloskey here is at the confessional, explaining like Augustine how he was able to turn away from the paths of methodological self delusion.

We have already seen that McCloskey (1991) views much of the profession as unconscious as well as unlicensed poets in its quest to develop aesthetically pleasing models. In many ways this obsession with formalism, with process rather than content or context is reminiscent of the late-Victorian hot house flourishing of the aesthete. It would seem curious that economics should have anything to do with the pale and desperately sensitive poets lampooned by Gilbert and Sullivan in their operetta, **Patience**. Certainly Alfred Marshall with his emphasis on communicating with the business world would never have fit this pattern. Yet somehow economists have come to adopt the Victorian vestments of the English aesthete. Producing fin de siecle poetry would ostensibly have little to do with today's thoroughly modern economist. But if economists are to be seen as poets, perhaps they have more to do with this movement or even that of the French imagists than with the epic poetry of Homer or the sonnets of Shakespeare. The unifying thread is that they all seem to live by the same simple creed *'art for art's sake'*, a purity of goal and intention. A need to communicate is absent. Accordingly, the danger of self indulgence is ever present.

> Not for us is the limelight and the applause. But that doesn't mean the game is not worth
> the candle or that we do not in the end win the game. In the long run, the economic
> scholar works for the only coin worth having ... our own applause (Samuelson 1962: 18).

If we are not poets than Szostak (1992) may be right in comparing economists with avant garde artists. Economics as a profession in love with its own formalism is a decorative art. Which art movement best exemplifies the current state of economics? Economists seem to have much in common with the early surrealists. Both certainly take a childlike glee in proclaiming their overly ambitious manifestos. It was the arbiter and promoter of that movement, Andre Breton, who best summed up the aim and spirit of those kindred spirits, (*épater le bourgeoisie'*). Equivalently, economists are increasingly enchanted with models demonstrating the dominant role of unintended consequences in economic relations. They continue to take great pride in informing the public that everything it thinks it knows is wrong.

> The extraordinary achievement of the classical theory was to overcome the beliefs of the
> 'natural man' and, at the same time, to be wrong (Keynes 1960: 350).

This is nothing but an old conjurer's trick (the surrealists at least were conscious that they were using visual tricks to shock their audience). The aim is to distract the audience through a display of cleverness. In this way your potential critics are left to fume in confused silence.

I remember Bonar Law's mingled rage and perplexity in face of the economists, because they were denying what was obvious. He was deeply troubled for an explanation. One recurs to the analogy between the sway of the classical school of economic theory and that of certain religions. For it is a far greater exercise of the potency of an idea to exorcise the obvious than to introduce into men's common notions the recondite and the remote (Keynes 1960: 350-51).

If then as many of our authors claim, economics has become a discipline self absorbed by its own workings, what is to be done? We need to wean economics away from its narcissism, its tendency to exclude all those who don't share its own passions for formalism. Making virtues out of our own shortcomings won't do the trick. Economics as a profession, best serves itself and its community by becoming an inclusive science that stresses an ability to communicate rather than putting the onus for understanding on those outside our professional gates. This would also have the unintended consequence of limiting the articles churned out each year. It is unarguably more difficult to turn out a well-written piece than to simply pursue formalism by rote[8]. In Martin Bronfenbrenner's words we need to stop offering *'techniques in search of an application'* (1991: 604). We may not all aspire to the rhetorical heights of Keynes but we can endeavour to become a useful profession.

But chiefly, do not let us overestimate the importance of the economic problem, or sacrifice to its supposed necessities other matters of greater and more permanent significance. It should be a matter for specialists - like dentistry. If economists could manage to get themselves thought of as humble, competent people, on a level with dentists, that would be splendid! (Keynes 1963: 373).

REFERENCES

Becker, Gary (1991) "A Note on Restaurant Pricing and Other Examples of Social Influences on Price," *The Journal of Political Economy.* 99(5): 1109-1116.

Becker, Gary (1976) *The Economic Approach to Human Behavior.* Chicago: University of Chicago Press.

Bergstrom, Thomas (1976) "Toward a Deeper Economics of Sleeping," *Journal of Political Economy.* 84(2): 411-412.

Blinder, Allan (1974) "The Economics of Brushing Teeth," *The Journal of Political Economy.* 82(4): 887-892.

Bronfenbrenner, Martin (1991) "Economics as Dentistry," *The Southern Economic Journal.* 57(3): 599-605.

Didion, Joan (1979) *The White Album.* London: Weidenfeld and Nicolson.

Fair, Ray (1978) "A Theory of Extramarital Affairs," *The Journal of Political Economy.* 86(1): 45-61.

Frank, Robert, Thomas Gilovich and Dennis Regan (1993) "Does Studying Economics Inhibit Cooperation," *The Journal of Economic Perspectives.* 7(2): 159-171.

Freedman, Craig (1993) "Why Economists Can't Read", *Methodus.* 5(1): 6-23.

Freedman, Craig (2003a) "Economic Nostrums and Economic Practices- Accountability in Economic Journals", in Freedman, Craig and Rick Szostak (eds.) *Tales of Narcissus - A*

Journey Through the Soul of an Economist. Armonk New York: Nova Science Publishers.

Freedman, Craig (2003b) "Economic Textbooks: Missing and Misplace Incentives," in Freedman, Craig and Rick Szostak (eds.) *Tales of Narcissus - A Journey Through the Soul of an Economist*. Armonk New York: Nova Science Publishers.

Friedman, David (1986) *Price Theory: An Intermediate Text*. Cincinnati: South-Western.

Gans, Joshua and George B. Shepherd (1994) "How Are the Mighty Fallen: Rejected Classic Articles by Leading Economist," *The Journal of Economic Perspectives*. 8(1): 165-180.

Graves, Robert (1960) *The Greek Myths - Volume I*. Harmondsworth: Penguin Books.

Hoover, Kevin (1991) "Mirowski's Screed: A Review of Philip Mirowski's *More Heat than Light: Economics as Social Physics, Physics as Nature's Economics,*" *Methodus* 3(1): 139-145.

Katzner, Donald (1991) "In Defense of Formalization in Economics," *Methodus* 3(1): 17-24.

Keynes, John Maynard (1960) *The General Theory of Employment, Interest and Money*. London: Macmillan.

Keynes, John Maynard (1963) *Essays in Persuasion*. New York: W.W.Norton.

Klamer, Arjo and David Colander (1990) *The Making of an Economist*. Boulder: Westview Press.

Klamer, Arjo and Thomas Leonard (1992) "Everyday versus Academic rhetoric in Economics," Unpublished Manuscript.

Leamer, Edward (1991) "Comment: Has Formalization Gone Too Far?" *Methodus* 3(1): 25-26.

Leijonhufvud, Axel (1973) "Life Among the Econ," *Western Economic Journal* 15(2): 327-337.

Levins, Richard (1992) "The Whimsical Science," *Review of Agricultural Economics*. 14(3): 139-151.

McCloskey, Donald (1989) "Why I Am No Longer a Positivist," *Review of Social Economy*. 47(3): 225-239.

McCloskey, Donald (1991) "Economics Science: A Search Through the Hyperspace of Assumptions?" *Methodus* 3(1): 6-16.

Mirowski, Phillip (1960) *More Heat Than Light*. Cambridge: Cambridge University Press.

Samuelson, Paul (1962) "Economists and The History of Ideas," *The American Economic Review*. 52(1): 1-18.

Sen, Amartya (1993) Back cover, of Marianne Ferber and Julie Nelson eds. *Beyond Economic Man: Feminist Theory and Economics*. Chicago: University of Chicago Press.

Shapiro, Carl and Alan Krueger (1994) "Report of the Editor *Journal of Economic Perspectives,*" *The American Economic Review*. 84(2): 484-486.

Snow, Charles Percy (1959) *The Two Cultures and the Scientific Revolution*. Cambridge: Cambridge University Press.

Snow, Charles Percy (1964) *The Two Cultures, and a Second Look: An Expanded Version of the Two Cultures and the Scientific Revolution*. Cambridge: Cambridge University Press.

Szostak, Rick (1992) "The History of Art and the Art in Economics," *History of Economics Review*. 18(Summer): 70-107.

Wharton, Edith (1996) *The Age of Innocence*. London: Constable.

Wilde, Oscar (1986) *The Importance of Being Ernest and Other Plays*. Harmondsworth: Penguin Books.

NOTES

[1] It is necessary to point out that the author regards this particular work as something of an anomaly. Ray Fair's significant contribution to economics is not questioned by anyone familiar with his work. My remarks extend only to a particular article not to an individual or his work as a whole.

[2] This point does need some clarification. Over the years I have come to believe that though you can strongly disagree with Gary Becker it is difficult, if not impossible, to dismiss him out of hand. He is far too intelligent and careful for that sort of approach to work. The model he actually develops in his restaurant article (1991) is intriguing and not without potentially important implications. It's just that it doesn't seem to be the best explanation for his original specific pricing question. I did once have the opportunity in October 1997 of asking him why he simply didn't raise the issue with the owner or manager of that particular restaurant. He replied that he had done that. However the important problem at hand for Becker, is not what restaurant owners think they're doing or their strategy. What is crucial is the dominance of market competition. Economic agents are best understood as responding to competitive demands. If taken to the extreme, this attitude becomes almost a Chicago version of the base and superstructure distinction beloved by ersatz Marxists. In the Marxian alternative, material relations are the key to unlocking any mystery, while all else belongs to the epi-phenomena known as the superstructure, a mere reflection of the underlying reality. We need only to substitute market relations to complete the analogy. The real issue then becomes the degree to which you are willing to accept such a large measure of market dominance. Unfortunately, this underlying point of contention is seldom made explicit in so many of the models constructed.

[3] This discussion is somewhat reminiscent of C.P. Snow's discussion of the *Two Cultures* (1959, 1964) more than three decades ago.

[4] As Klamar and Leonard (1995) point out, even economists are human. Most operate by straddling both worlds, playing a different role and telling different stories depending on whether they are at work or at home. This is what these authors refer to as toggling. But it might be well to remind ourselves of all too many of our colleagues whose toggle switches have somehow become frozen. The gradual encroachment of the professional into everyday life becomes total. The compleat Narcissus raises his or her children according to strict marginal precepts (see David Friedman's (1986) tale of family life with Milton and Rose).

[5] Hoover (1991) may have a legitimate case to make. However, etiquette, if nothing else, proscribes allowing personal elements to slip into what should be zoned as a strictly professional neighbourhood. In the most famous of Greek myths, Oedipus makes a similar mistake. Fortunately, there is little likelihood that Hoover's slip will entail similar consequences.

[6] George Stigler's attacks on opposing theories attempted to eliminate rather than investigate alternative economic approaches. It was not that Stigler's intuitions were necessarily incorrect, but that he saw debate in terms of a zero sum game. This is an attitude that is better confined to adversarial legal proceedings rather than animating economic discussion.

[7] Nor should this be surprising given their sheltered education and upbringing. A diet of introductory textbooks does not yield strong bones or shiny, clear-eyed faces. Though it is widely suspected that our teaching texts are decidedly second-rate and our students left unsatisfied, incentives work against either good teaching or the writing of such texts as would support it. (See Freedman (2003b) included in this volume.)

[8] An alternative would be to award each economist upon receipt of a PhD., a page publication limit. It would then be up to each of these academics how he or she chose to distribute their publication efforts over his or her lifetime career. Squandering a quota on too many mediocre early efforts would leave them deprived of any publication vehicle for the remainder of their

working years. Economists might start to think deeply and carefully before setting fingertips to keyboard.

Are Economists by Nature a Social Animal?

He who is unable to live in society, or who has no need because he is sufficient for himself, must be either a beast or a god (Aristotle).

LIFE AMONG THE ECON[*]

AXEL LEIJONHUFVUD
University of California, Los Angeles

The Econ tribe occupies a vast territory in the far North. Their land appears bleak and dismal to the outsider, and travelling through it makes for rough sledding; but the Econ, through a long period of adaptation, have learned to wrest a living of sorts from it. They are not without some genuine and sometimes even fierce attachment to their ancestral grounds, and their young are brought up to feel contempt for the softer living in the warmer lands of their neighbours, such as the Polscis and the Sociogs. Despite a common genetical heritage, relations with these tribes are strained - the distrust and contempt that the average Econ feels for these neighbours being heartily reciprocated by the latter - and social intercourse with them is inhibited by numerous taboos. The extreme clannishness, not to say xenophobia, - of the Econ makes life among them difficult and perhaps even somewhat dangerous for the outsider. This probably accounts for the fact that the Econ have so far not been systematically studied. Information about their social structure and ways of life is fragmentary and not well validated. More research on this interesting tribe is badly needed.

CASTE AND STATUS

The information that we do have indicates that, for such a primitive people, the social structure is quite complex. The two main dimensions of their social structure are those of caste and status. The basic division of the tribe is seemingly into castes; within each caste, one finds an elaborate network of status relationships.

An extremely interesting aspect of status among the Econ, if it can be verified, is that status relationships do not seem to form a simple hierarchical "pecking-order," as one is used to expect. Thus, for example, one may find that A pecks B, B pecks C, and *then C pecks A!* This non-transitivity of status may account for the continual strife among the Econ which makes their social life seem so singularly insufferable to the visitor.

---

[*] *Editor's Note:* Since many of our younger readers are, with the idealism so characteristic of contemporary youth, planning to launch themselves on a career of good deeds by going to live and work among the Econ, the editor felt that it would be desirable to invite an Econologist of some experience to write an account of this little known tribe. Diligent inquiry eventually turned up the author of the present paper. Dr. Leijonhufvud was deemed an almost perfect candidate for the assignment, for he was exiled nearly a decade ago to one of the outlying Econ villages (Ucla) and since then has not only been continuously resident there but has even managed to get himself named an elder (under what pretenses - other than the growth of a grey beard - the editor has been unable to determine).

Almost all of the travellers' reports that we have comment on the Econ as a "quarrelsome race" who "talk ill of their fellow behind his back," and so forth. Social cohesion is apparently maintained chiefly through shared distrust of outsiders. In societies with a transitive pecking-order, on the other hand, we find as a rule that an equilibrium develops in which little actual pecking ever takes place. The uncivilized anomaly that we find among the Econ poses a riddle the resolution of which must be given high priority in Econological research at this time.

What seems at first to be a further complication obstructing our understanding of the situation in the Econ tribe may, in the last analysis, contain the vital clue to this theoretical problem. Pecking between castes is traditionally not supposed to take place, but this rule is not without exceptions either. Members of high castes are not infrequently found to peck those of lower castes. While such behavior is regarded as in questionable taste, it carries no formal sanctions. A member of a low caste who attempts to peck someone in a higher caste runs more concrete risks - at the extreme, he may be ostracized and lose the privilege of being heard at the tribal midwinter councils.

In order to bring out the relevance of this observation, a few more things need to be said about caste and status in the tribe. The Econ word for caste is "field." Caste is extremely important to the self-image and sense of identity of the Econ, and the adult male meeting a stranger will always introduce himself with the phrase "Such-and-such is my field." The English root of this term is interesting because of the aversion that the Econ normally have to the use of plain English. The English words that have crept into their language are often used in senses that we would not recourse. Thus, in this case, the territorial connotation of "field" is entirely misleading for the castes do not live apart. The basic social unit is the village, or "dept." The depts of the Econ always comprise members of several "fields." In some cases, nearly every caste may be represented in a single dept.

A comparison of status relationships in the different "fields" shows a definite common pattern. The dominant feature, which makes status relations among the Econ of unique interest to the serious student, is the way that status is tied to the manufacture of certain types of implements, called "modls." The status of the adult male is determined by his skill at making the "modl" of his "field." The facts (a) that the Econ are highly status-motivated, (b) that status is only to be achieved by making "modls" and (c) that most of these "modls" seem to be of little or no practical use, probably accounts for the backwardness and abject cultural poverty of the tribe. Both the tight linkage between status in the tribe and modl-making and the trend toward making modls more for ceremonial than for practical purposes appear, moreover, to be fairly recent developments, something which has led many observers to express pessimism for the viability of the Econ culture.

Whatever may have been the case in earlier times the "fields" of the Econ apparently do not now form a strong rank-ordering. This may be the clue to the problem of the non-transitivity of individual status. First, the ordering of two castes will sometimes be indeterminate. Thus, while the Micro assert their superiority over the Macro, so do the Macro theirs over the Micro, and third parties are found to have no very determined, or at least no unanimous, opinion on the matter. Thus the perceived prestige of one caste relative to another is a non-reflexive relation. In other instances, however, the ranking is quite clear. The priestly caste (the Math-Econ) for example, is a higher "field" than either Micro or Macro, while the Devlops just as definitely rank lower. Second, we know that these caste-rankings (where they can be made) are not permanent but may change over time. There is evidence, for example, that both the high rank assigned to the Math-Econ and the low rank of the Devlops are, historically speaking, rather recent phenomenon. The rise of the Math-Econ seems to be associated with the previously noted trend among all the Econ towards more ornate, ceremonial modls, while the low rank of the Devlops is due to the fact that this caste, in recent times, has not strictly enforced the taboos against association with the Polscis, Sociogs, and other tribes. Other Econ look upon this with considerable apprehension as endangering the moral fiber of the tribe and suspect the Devlops even of relinquishing modl-making.

If the non-transitivity of Econ status seems at first anomalous, here at least we have a phenomenon with known parallels.[1] It may be that what we are observing among the Econ is simply the decay of a once orderly social structure that possessed a strong ranking of castes and, within each caste a perfectly unambiguous transitive status ordering.

GRADS, ADULTS, AND ELDERS

The young Econ, or "grad," is not admitted to adulthood until he has made a "modl" exhibiting a degree of workmanship acceptable to the elders of the "dept" in which he serves his apprenticeship. Adulthood is conferred in an intricate ceremony the particulars of which vary from village to village. In the more important villages,

---

[1] Cf., e.g., the observations concerning the Indian jajmani-system in Manning Nash, *Primitive and Peasant Economic Systems,* Scranton, Pa., 1966, pp. 93 ff, esp. p. 94: "For example, goldsmiths give polluting services to potters, and the potters receive pollution from herders, who in turn give polluting services to goldsmiths. In this exchange of ritually crucial interaction the goldsmiths see themselves above the potters and below the herders, but the herders are below the potters, yet above the goldsmith caste." Precisely.

furthermore, (the practice in some outlying villages is unclear) the young adult must continue to demonstrate his ability at manufacturing these artifacts. If he fails to do so, he is turned out of the "dept" to perish in the wilderness.

This practice may seem heartless, but the Econ regard it as a manhood rite sanctioned by tradition and defend it as vital to the strength and welfare of the dept. If life is hard on the young, the Econ show their compassion in the way that they take care of the elderly. Once elected an elder, the member need do nothing and will still be well taken care of.

TOTEMS AND SOCIAL STRUCTURE

While in origin the word "modl" is simply a term for a concrete implement, looking at it only in these terms will blind the student to key aspects of Econ social structure. "Modl" has evolved into an abstract concept which dominates the Econ's perception of virtually all social relationships - whether these be relations to other tribes, to other castes, or status relations within his caste. Thus, in explaining to a stranger, for example, why he holds the Sociogs or the Polscis in such low regard, the Econ will say that "they do not make modls" and leave it at that.

The dominant role of "modl" is perhaps best illustrated by the (unfortunately very incomplete) accounts we have of relationships between the two largest of the Econ castes, the "Micro" and the "Macro." Each caste has a basic modl of simple pattern and the modls made by individual members will be variations on the theme set by the basic modl of the caste. Again, one finds that the Econ define the social relationship, in this instance between two castes, in terms of the respective modl. Thus if a Micro-Econ is asked why the Micro do not intermarry with the Macro, he will answer: "They make a different modl," or "They do not know the Micro modl." (In this, moreover, he would be perfectly correct, but then neither, of course, would he know the Macro modl.)

Several observers have commented on the seeming impossibility of eliciting from the member of a "field" a coherent and intelligible account of what distinguishes his caste from another caste which does not, in the final analysis, reduce to the mere assertion that the modls are different. Although more research on this question is certainly needed, this would seem to lend considerable support to those who refer to the basic modl as the *totem* of the caste. It should be noted that the difficulty of settling this controversial question does not arise from any taboo against discussing caste with strangers. Far from being reticent, the Econ will as a rule be quite voluble on the subject. The problem is that what they have to say consists almost entirely of expressions of caste-prejudices of the most elemental sort.[2]

---

[2] This observation is far from new. One finds it recorded, for example, in Machluyp's *Voyages* in the account of "The Voyage of H.M.S. Semantick to the Coast of England."

To the untrained eye, the totems of major castes will often look wellnigh identical. It is the great social significance attached to these minor differences by the Econ themselves that have made Econography (the study of Econ arts and handicrafts) the central field of modern Econology. As an illustration, consider the totems of the Micro and the Macro. Both could be roughly described as formed by two carved sticks joined together in the middle somewhat in the form of a pair of scissors (cf. Figure 1).

Certain ceremonies connected with these totems are of great interest to us because of the indications that they give about the origin of modl-making among the Econ. Unfortunately, we have only fragmentary accounts by various travellers of these ceremonies and the interpretations of what they have seen that these untrained observers essay are often in conflict. Here, a systematic study is very much needed.

The following sketchy account of the "prospecting" - ceremony among the Macro brings out several of the riddles that currently perplex Econologists working in this area:

**Figure 1-A. Totem of
the Micro**

**Figure 1-B. Totem of
the Macro**

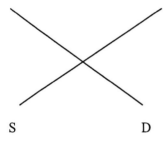

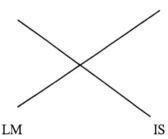

S   D   LM   IS

The elder grasps the LM with his left hand and the IS with his right and, holding the totem out in front of himself with elbows slightly bent, proceeds in a straight line -'gazing neither left nor right'[3] in the words of their ritual - out over the chosen terrain. The grads of the village skip gaily around him at first, falling silent as the trek grows longer and more wearisome. On this occasion, it was long indeed and the terrain difficult ... the grads were strung out in a long, morose and bedraggled chain behind their leader who, sweat pearling his brow, face cast in grim determination,

---

[3] The same wording appears in the corresponding Micro-ritual. It is reported that the Macro belittle the prospecting of the Micro among themselves saying that the Micro "can't keep from gazing right." The Micro, on their side, claim the Macro "gaze left." No one has offered a sensible hypothesis to account for this particular piece of lithurgical controversy. Chances are that far-fetched explanations are out of place and that this should simply be accepted as just another humdrum example of the continual bickering among the Econ.

stumbled onward over the obstacles in his path ... At long last, the totem vibrates, then oscillates more and more; finally, it points, quivering straight down. The elder waits for the grads to gather round and then pronounces, with great solemnity: "Behold, the Truth and Power of the Macro."

It is surely evident from an account such as this why such a major controversy has sprung up around the main thesis of the 'Implementarist' School. This influential Econographic School argues that the art of modl-carving has its historical origin in the making of tools and useful "implements," and that ceremonies such as the one described above reflect, in ritual form, the actual uses to which these implements were at one time put.

Fanciful as the 'Implementarist' hypothesis may seem, it would be injudicious to dismiss it out of hand. Whether the Macro-modl can be regarded as originally a "useful implement" would seem to hinge in the first place on whether the type of "prospecting" ritualized in the described ceremony produces actual results. The Macro themselves maintain that they strike gold this way. Some travellers and investigators support the contention, others dismiss it as mere folklore. The issues are much the same as those connected with attempts to appraise the divining-rod method of finding water. Numerous people argue that it works - but no scientific explanation of why it would has ever been advanced.

We do have some, apparently reliable, eyewitness' reports of gold actually being struck by the Macro. While not disputing the veracity of all such reports, skeptical critics argue that they must be heavily discounted. It is said, for example, that the Econ word for "gold" refers to any yellowish mineral however worthless. Some Econologists maintain, moreover, that the prospecting ceremony is seldom, if ever, conducted over unknown ground and that what the eyewitnesses have reported, therefore, is only the "discovery" of veins that have been known to the Macro for generations.

One might ask how the practice manages to survive if there is nothing to it. The answer is simple and will not be unexpected to those acquainted with earlier studies of the belief-systems of primitive peoples. Instances are known when the ceremony has not produced any concrete results. When this happens, the Macro will take either of two positions. Either he will accuse the member performing the ceremony of having failed to follow ritual in some detail or other, or else defend the man's claim that the gold is there by arguing that the digging for it has not gone deep enough.[4]

It is clear enough that, whichever position is taken, the "phenomena are saved" in the sense that the role of the totem in the belief-system of the caste remains unassailed.

MYTHS AND MODLS

In recent years, interest in controversies about whether certain Econ modls "work" or not (or in what sense they may be said to "work") has dwindled. This is certainly not because the issue has been settled - it is fair to say that we are today less certain than ever of what the answers to the questions raised by the Implementarists would be. It is rather that our methodological perspective has changed so that the Implementarist issue is no longer seen as productive of "good" questions. The "New Econology," as it is known, stresses *Verstehen* and, correspondingly, rejects attempts to appraise Econ belief-systems according to rationalistic criteria purloined from modern natural science.[5]

It has become increasingly clear that the Econ associate certain, to them significant, beliefs with every modl, whether or not they also claim that modl to be a "useful tool." That taking "usefulness" as the point of departure in seeking to understand the totemic culture of this people leads us into a blind alley is particularly clear when we consider the Math-Econ caste.

The Math-Econ are in many ways the most fascinating, and certainly the most colorful, of Econ castes. There is today considerable uncertainty whether the "priest" label is really appropriate for this caste, but it is at least easy to understand why the early travellers came to regard them in this way. In addition to the deeply respectful attitude evidenced by the average Econ towards them, the Math-Econ themselves show many cultural patterns that we are wont to associate with religious orders or sects among other peoples. Thus they affect a poverty that is abject even by Econ standards, and it seems clear that this is by choice rather than necessity. It is told that, to harden themselves, they periodically

---

[4] The latter rationalization is the more palatable since it puts the blame on a different caste namely the O'Maitres or O'Metrs (transcriptions vary) who do the digging work of both the Macro and the Micro.

The "diggers" caste is of special interest to those concerned with the underdevelopment of the Econ. Traditionally the lowest Econ caste, the O'Metrs, were allowed to perform only the dirtiest manual tasks and - more significant in Econ eyes - lacked a totem of their own. In more recent times, however, it is through this caste that industrialization has begun to make some inroads among the Econ. Free from the prejudices instilled through an education concentrating on modl-carving and the associated totemic beliefs, the O'Metrs take willingly to modern machinery and have become quite proficient for example, at handling power shovels and power mills. The attitude of the rest of the tribe towards these erstwhile untouchables taking the lead in industrialization is, as one would expect, one of mingled scorn and envy.

[5] C. Levi-Strauss, *The Savage Mind* should be mentioned here as essential reading for anyone with a serious interest in the belief-system of the Econ.

venture stark naked out into the chill winds of abstraction that prevail in those parts. Among the rest of the Econ, who ordinarily perambulate thickly bundled in wooly clothing, they are much admired for this practice. Furthermore, glossolalia - the ability to say the same thing in several different tongues[6] - is a highly esteemed talent among them.

The Math-Econ make exquisite modls finely carved from bones of walras. Specimens made by their best masters[7] are judged unequalled in both workmanship and raw material by a unanimous Econographic opinion. If some of these are "useful" - and even Econ testimony is divided on this point - it is clear that this is purely coincidental in the motivation for their manufacture.

There has been a great deal of debate in recent years over whether certain Econ modls and the associated belief-systems are best to be regarded as religious, folklore and mythology, philosophical and "scientific," or as sports and games. Each category has its vocal proponents among Econologists of repute but very little headway has been made in the debate. The ceremonial use of modls (see above) and the richness of the general Econ culture in rituals has long been taken as evidence for the religious interpretation. But, as one commentator puts it, "If these beliefs are religious, it is a religion seemingly without faith." This interpretation seems to have stranded on this contradiction in terms and presently is not much in favor. More interesting are the arguments of those who have come to view certain Econ belief-systems as a form of quasi-scientific cosmological speculation. As an illustration, Mrs. Robinson's description of what she terms the "Doctrine of K," which is found prevalent among the members of the powerful Charles River villages, inevitably brings to mind the debates of the ancient Ionian philosophers over whether water, air, or fire was the "basic stuff" of the universe. The Doctrine of K bears, in fact, striking resemblances to the teachings of Anaximander.[8] It is known, moreover, that in some other depts a "Doctrine of M" is taught but we do not as yet have an understandable account of it and know, in fact little about it except that it is spurned (as heresy?) by the

---

[6] I.e., in several Math tongues - the Indo-European languages, for example, do not count.

[7] The budding collector of Econographica should know that most of the work found on the market today is imitative and done by apprentices. Much of it is nonetheless aesthetically superior to, say, the crudely carved totems of the Macro and certainly to the outsized, machine-made modls nowadays exported by the O'Metrs who have no artistic tradition to fall back on.

[8] Arthur Koestler, *The Sleepwalkers,* New York 1968, pp. 22-23, aptly summarizes Anaximander's teachings: "The raw material (of the universe) is none of the familiar forms of matter, but a substance without definite properties except for being indestructible and everlasting. Out of this stuff all things are developed, and into it they return; before this our world, infinite multitudes of other universes have already existed, and been dissolved again into the amorphous mass."

If one were to dignify this primitive doctrine with modern terminology, one would have to put Anaximander in the "putty-putty, bang-bang" category.

Charles River Econ. Spokesmen for the cosmology view buttress their arguments by pointing out the similarities between the Math-Econ and the Pythagorean brotherhood. Whether the Math-Econ know it or not, they point out, they do obey the ancient Pythagorean principle that "philosophy must be pursued in such a way that its inner secrets are reserved for learned men, trained in Math."

The sports and games interpretation has gained a certain currency due to accounts of the modl-ceremonies of the Intern caste.[9] But even here it is found that, though the ceremony has all the outward manifestations of a game, it has to the participants something of the character of a morality play which in essential respects shapes their basic perception of the world.

THE ECON AND THE FUTURE

It would be to fail in one's responsibility to the Econ people to end this brief sketch of life in their society without a few words about their future. The prospect for the Econ is bleak. Their social structure and culture should be studied now before it is gone forever. Even a superficial account of their immediate and most pressing problems reads like a veritable catalogue of the woes of primitive peoples in the present day and age.

They are poor - except for a tiny minority, miserably poor. Their population growth rate is among the highest in the world. Their land is fairly rich, but much of the natural resources that are their birth-right has been sold off to foreign interests for little more than a mess of pottage. Many of their young are turning to pot and message. In their poverty, they are not even saved from the problems of richer nations - travellers tell of villages half-buried in the refuse of unchecked modl-making and of the eye-sores left on the once pastoral landscape by the random strip-mining of the O'Metrs. It is said that even their famous Well Springs of Inspiration are now polluted.

In the midst of their troubles, the Econ remain as of old a proud and warlike race. But they seem entirely incapable of "creative response" to their problems. It is plain to see what is in store for them if they do not receive outside aid.

One may feel some optimism that the poverty problems *can* be solved. While population growth may slow down in time, one can have little hope that the ongoing disintegration of Econ culture will be halted or

---

[9] One observer casts his account of this ceremony explicitly in parlour-game terms: "Each player gets 2 countries, 2 goods, 2 factors, and a so-called Bowley Box ..." etc., etc., and also compares the intern game, in terms of intellectual difficulty, with checkers.

could be reversed. Here the sad and familiar story of a primitive people's encounter with "modern times" is repeating itself once again. The list of symptoms is long and we will touch only on a few.

Econ political organization is weakening. The basic political unit remains the dept and the political power in the dept is lodged in the council of elders. The foundations of this power of the elders has been eroding for some time, however. Respect for one's elders is no more the fashion among the young Econ than among young people anywhere else. Authority based on age and experience has weakened as recognized status has come increasingly to be tied to cleverness in modl-making. (As noted before, many elders will be inactive as modl-makers.) Although dept establishments have responded to these developments by cooptation of often very young modl-makers as "elders," the legitimacy of the political structure in the eyes of the Econ people is obviously threatened - and the chances of a constructive political response to the tribe's problems correspondingly lessened.

The Econ adult used to regard himself as a lifelong member of his dept. This is no longer true -migration between depts is nowadays exceedingly common and not even elders of a village necessarily regard themselves as permanent members. While this mobility may help them to cope with the poverty problem, it obviously tends further to weaken political organization. Urbanization should be noted as a related problem - many villages are today three or four times as large as only a generation or two ago. Big conurbations, with large transient populations, and weak and ineffective political machinery - we are all familiar with the social ills that this combination breeds.

Under circumstances such as these, we expect alienation, disorientation, and a general loss of spiritual values. And this is what we find. A typical phenomenon indicative of the break-up of a culture is the loss of a sense of history and growing disrespect for tradition. Contrary to the normal case in primitive societies, the Econ priesthood does not maintain and teach the history of the tribe. In some Econ villages, one can still find the occasional elder who takes care of the modls made by some long-gone hero of the tribe and is eager to tell the legends associated with each. But few of the adults or grads, noting what they regard as the crude workmanship of these dusty old relics, care to listen to such rambling fairytales. Among the younger generations, it is now rare to find an individual with any conception of the history of the Econ. Having lost their past, the Econ are without confidence in the present and without purpose and direction for the future.

Some Econographers disagree with the bleak picture of cultural disintegration just given, pointing to the present as the greatest age of Econ Art. It is true that virtually all Econographers agree that present modl-making has reached aesthetic heights not heretofore attained. But it is doubtful that this gives cause for much optimism. It is not unusual to find some particular art form flowering in the midst of the decay of a culture. It may be that such decay of society induces this kind of cultural "displacement activity" among talented members who despair of coping with the decline of their civilization. The present burst of sophisticated modl-carving among the Econ should probably be regarded in this light.

DOES STUDYING ECONOMICS INHIBIT COOPERATION?

Robert H. Frank, Thomas Gilovich, and Dennis T. Regan[*]

From the perspective of many economists, motives other than self-interest are peripheral to the main thrust of human endeavor, and we indulge them at our peril. In Gordon Tullock's (1976) words (as quoted by Mansbridge, 1990, P. 12), "the average human being is about 95% selfish in the narrow sense of the term."

In this paper we investigate whether exposure to the self-interest model commonly used in economics alters the extent to which people behave in self-interested ways. The paper is organized into two parts. In the first, we report the results of several empirical studies-some of our own, some by others - that suggest economists behave in more self-interested ways. By itself, this evidence does not demonstrate that exposure to the self-interest model *causes* more self-interested behavior, since it may be that economists were simply self-interested to begin with, and this difference was one reason they chose to study economics. In the second part of the paper, we present preliminary evidence that exposure to the self-interest model does in fact encourage self-interested behavior.

Do Economists Behave Differently?

Free-Rider Experiments

A study by Gerald Marwell and Ruth Ames (1981) found that first-year graduate students in economics are much more likely than others to free-ride in experiments that called for

---

[*] *Robert H. Frank is Goldwin Smith Professor of Economics, Ethics, and Public Policy, Department of Economics; and Professor of Economics, Johnson Graduate School of Management, both at Cornell University, Ithaca, New York. Thomas Gilovich and Dennis T. Regan are Associate Professors of Psychology, Cornell University, Ithaca New York.*

private contributions to public goods. In their experiments, groups of subjects were given initial endowments of money, which they were to allocate between two accounts, one "public," the other "private." Money deposited in the subject's private account was returned dollar-for-dollar to the subject at the end of the experiment. Money deposited in the public account was pooled, multiplied by some factor greater than one, and then distributed equally among all subjects. Under these circumstances, the socially optimal behavior is for all subjects to put their entire endowment in the public account. But from an individual perspective, the most advantageous strategy is to put everything in the private account. Marwell and Ames found that economics students contributed an average of only 20 percent of their endowments to the public account, significantly less than the 49 percent average for all other subjects.

To explore the reasons for this difference, the authors asked their subjects two follow-up questions. First, what is a "fair" investment in the public good? Of the noneconomists, 75 percent answered "half or more" of the endowment, and 25 percent answered "all." Second, are you concerned about "fairness" in making your investment decision? Almost all noneconomists answered "Yes." The corresponding responses of the economics graduate students were more difficult to summarize. As Marwell and Ames wrote,

> More than one-third of the economists either refused to answer the question regarding what is fair, or gave very complex, uncodable responses. It seems that the meaning of 'fairness' in this context was somewhat alien for this group. Those who did respond were much more likely to say that little or no contribution was 'fair.' in addition, the economics graduate students were about half as likely as other subjects to indicate that they were 'concerned with fairness' in making their decisions.

The Marwell and Ames study can be criticized on the grounds that their noneconomist control groups consisted of high school students and college undergraduates, who differ in a variety of ways from first-year graduate students in any discipline. Perhaps the most obvious difference is age. As we will see, however, criticism based on the age difference is blunted by our own evidence that older students generally give greater weight to social concerns like the ones that arise in free-rider experiments. It remains possible, however, that more mature students might have had a more sophisticated understanding of the nuances and ambiguities inherent in concepts like fairness, and for that reason gave less easily coded responses to the follow-up questions.

Yet another concern with the Marwell and Ames experiments is not easily dismissed. Although the authors' do not report the sex composition of their group of economics graduate students, such groups are almost always preponderantly male. The authors, control groups of high school and undergraduate students, by contrast, consisted equally of males and females.[1]

---

[1] This was the case, in any event, for the groups whose sex composition the authors reported.

As our own evidence will later show, there is a sharp tendency for males to behave less cooperatively in experiments of this sort. So while the Marwell and Ames findings are suggestive, they do not clearly establish that economists behave differently.

Economists and the Ultimatum Bargaining Game

Another study of whether economists behave differently from members of other disciplines is by John Carter and Michael Irons (1991). These authors measured self-interestedness by examining behavior in an ultimatum bargaining game. This simple game has two players, an "allocator" and a "receiver." The allocator is given a sum of money (in these experiments, $10), and must then propose a division of this sum between herself and the receiver. Once the allocator makes this proposal, the receiver has two choices: (1) he may accept, in which case each player gets the amount proposed by the allocator; or (2) he may refuse, in which case each player gets zero. The game is played only once by the same partners.

Assuming the money cannot be divided into units smaller than one cent, the self-interest model unequivocally predicts that the allocator will propose $9.99 for herself and the remaining $0.01 for the receiver, and that the receiver will accept on the grounds that a penny is better than nothing. Since the game will not be repeated, there is no point in the receiver turning down a low offer in the hope of generating a better offer in the future.

Other researchers have shown that the strategy predicted by the self-interest model is almost never followed in practice: 50-50 splits are the most common proposal, and most highly one-sided offers are rejected in the name of fairness (Guth, et al., 1982; Kahneman, et al., 1986). Carter and Irons found that in both roles (allocator and receiver) economics majors performed significantly more in accord with the predictions of the self-interest model than did nonmajors.[2]

As always, questions can be raised about experimental design. In this case, for example, Carter and Irons assigned the allocator and receiver roles by choosing as allocators those who achieved higher scores on a preliminary word game.[3] Allocators trained in the marginal productivity theory of wages (that is, economics majors) might thus be more likely than others to reason that they were entitled to a greater share of the surplus on the strength of their earlier performance. But while not conclusive, the Carter and Irons results are again suggestive.

---

[2] Kahneman, Knetsch, and Thaler (1986) report findings similar to those of Carter and Irons: commerce students (the term used to describe business students in Canadian universities) were more likely than psychology students to make one-sided offers in ultimatum bargaining games.

[3] This allocation procedure is described in a longer, unpublished version of the Carter and Irons paper (1990).

Survey Data on Charitable Giving

The free-rider hypothesis suggests that economists might be less likely than others to donate to private charities. To explore this possibility, we mailed questionnaires to 1245 college professors randomly chosen from the professional directories of 23 disciplines, asking them to report the annual dollar amounts they gave to a variety of private charities. We received 576 responses with sufficient detail for inclusion in our study. Respondents were grouped into the following disciplines: economics (N = 75); other social sciences (N = 106); math, computer science, and engineering (N = 48); natural sciences (N = 98); humanities (N = 94); architecture, art, and music (N = 68); and professional (N = 87).[4] The proportion of pure free riders among economists - that is, those who reported giving no money to any charity - was 9.3 percent. By contrast, only 1.1 percent of the professional school respondents gave no money to charity, and the share of those in the other five disciplines who reported zero donations ranged between 2.9 and 4.2 percent.[5] Despite their generally higher incomes, economists were also among the least generous in terms of their median gifts to large charities like viewer-supported television and the United Way.[6]

On a number of other dimensions covered in our survey, the behavior of economists was little different from the behavior of members of other disciplines. For example, economists were only marginally less likely than members of other disciplines to report that they would take costly administrative action to prosecute a student suspected of cheating. Economists were slightly above average for the entire sample in terms of the numbers of hours they reported spending in "volunteer activities." And in terms of their reported

---

[4] The "other social sciences" category includes psychology, sociology, political science, and anthropology; "natural sciences" includes physics, chemistry, biology, and geology; "humanities" includes philosophy, history, English, foreign languages, and religion; and "professional" includes education, business, and nursing.

[5] Although we do not have data on the gender of each survey respondent, gender differences by discipline do not appear to account for the observed pattern of free-ridership. For example, the natural sciences, which are also preponderantly male, had only one-third as many free riders as did economics.

[6] The annual median gift of economists to charities is actually slightly larger, in absolute terms, than the median for all disciplines taken as a whole. But because economists have significantly higher salaries than do the members of most other disciplines, the median gift overstates the relative generosity of economists. To correct for income differences by discipline, we proceeded as follows: First, we estimated earnings functions (salary vs. years of experience) for each discipline using data from a large private university. We then applied the estimated coefficients from these earnings functions to the experience data from our survey to impute an income for each respondent in our survey. Using these imputed income figures, together with our respondents' reports of their total charitable giving, we estimated the relationship between income and total giving. (In the latter exercise, all economists were dropped from the sample on the grounds that our object was to see whether the giving pattern of economists deviates from the pattern we see for other disciplines.) We then calculated our measure of a discipline's generosity as the ratio of the average value of gifts actually reported by members of the discipline to the average value of gifts expected on the basis of the members' imputed incomes. The computed ratio for economists was 0.91, which means that economists in our sample gave 91 percent as much as they would have been expected to give on the basis of their imputed incomes.

Figure 1

Monetary Payoffs for a Prisoner's Dilemma Game

	Player X	
	Cooperate	Defect
You Cooperate	2 for X 2 for Y	3 for X 0 for Y
You Defect	0 for X 3 for Y	1 for X 1 for Y

frequency of voting in presidential elections, economists were only slightly below the sample average.[7]

Economists and the Prisoner's Dilemma

One of the most celebrated and controversial predictions of the self-interest model is that people will always defect in a one-shot prisoner's dilemma game. Figure 1 shows the monetary payoffs in dollars to two players, X and Y, in a standard prisoner's dilemma. The key feature of such a game is that for each player, defection has a higher payoff irrespective of the choice made by the other player. Yet if both players follow this self-interested logic and defect, both end up with a lower payoff than if each cooperates. The game thus provides a rich opportunity to examine self-interested behavior.

We conducted a prisoner's dilemma experiment involving both economics majors and nonmajors. All groups were given an extensive briefing on the prisoner's dilemma at the start of the experiment and each subject was required to complete a questionnaire at the end to verify that he or she had indeed understood the consequences of different combinations of choices; in addition, many of our subjects were students recruited from courses in which the prisoner's dilemma is an item on the syllabus. Our subjects met in groups of three and each was told that he or she would play the game once only with each of the other two subjects.

---

[7] In fairness to the self-interest model, we should note that there may be self-interested reasons for volunteering or contributing even in the case of charities like the United Way and public television. United Way campaigns, for example, are usually organized in the workplace and there is often considerable social pressure to contribute. Public television fund drives often make on-the-air announcements of donors' names and economists stand to benefit just as much as the members of any other discipline from being hailed as community-minded citizens. In the case of smaller, more personal charitable organizations, there are often even more compelling self-interested reasons for giving or volunteering. After all, failure to contribute in accordance with one's financial ability may mean outright exclusion from the substantial private benefits associated with membership in religious groups, fraternal organizations, and the like.

The payoff matrix, shown in Figure 1, was the same for each play of the game. Subjects were told that the games would be played for real money, and that confidentiality would be maintained so that none of the players would learn how their partners had responded in any play of the game.

Following a period in which subjects were given an opportunity to get to know one another, each subject was taken to a separate room and asked to fill out a form indicating a response (cooperate or defect) to each of the other two players in the group. After the subjects had filled out their forms, the results were tallied and the payments disbursed. Each subject received a single payment that was the sum of three separate amounts: the payoff from the game with the first partner; the payoff from the game with the second partner; and a term that was drawn at random from a large list of positive and negative values. None of these three elements could be observed separately, only their sum. The purpose of this procedure was to prevent subjects from inferring both individual and group patterns of choice. Thus, unlike earlier prisoner's dilemma experiments,[8] ours did not enable the subject to infer what happened even when each (or neither) of the other players defected.

In one version of the experiment (the "unlimited" version), subjects were told that they could make promises not to defect during the time they were getting to know each other, but they were also told that the anonymity of the responses would render such promises unenforceable. In two other versions the experiment (the "intermediate" and "limited" versions), subjects were not permitted to make promises about their strategies. The latter two versions differed from one another in terms of the length of pre-game interaction, with up to 30 minutes permitted for the intermediate groups and no more than ten minutes for the limited groups.

For the sample as a whole there were a total of 267 games, which means a total of 534 choices between cooperation and defection. For these choices, the defection rate for economics majors was 60.4 percent, as compared to only 38 percent for nonmajors. This pattern of differences strongly supports the hypothesis that economics majors are more likely than nonmajors to behave self-interestedly ($p < .005$).[9]

One possible explanation for the observed differences between economic students and others is that economics students are more likely to be male, and males have lower cooperation rates. To control for possible influences of sex, age, and experimental condition, we performed the ordinary least squares regression reported in Figure 2.[10] Because each

---

[8] For an extensive survey, see Dawes (1980).

[9] Because each subject responded twice, the 534 choices are not statistically independent, and so the most direct test of statistical significance, the chi-square test, is inappropriate for the sample as a whole. To overcome this problem, we performed a chi-square test on the number of subjects who made the same choice-cooperate or defect-in both of their games. There were 207 such subjects (78 percent of the sample). The pattern of results observed in this restricted sample is essentially the same as the one observed for the sample as a whole.

[10] Because the conventional assumptions regarding the distribution of the error term are not satisfied in the case of linear models with dichotomous dependent variables, the standard ordinary least squares significance tests are not valid. In an appendix available on request from the authors, we report the results of models based on the probit and logit transformations. The statistical significance patterns shown by the coefficients from these transformed models are the same as for the ordinary least squares model. Because the coefficients of the ordinary least squares model are more easily interpreted, we report the remainder of our results in that format only.

Figure 2

Whole Sample Regression

	Dependent variable: cooperate (0) or defect (1)		
Variable	Coefficient	s.e.	t-ratio
Constant	0.579127	0.1041	5.57
econ	0.168835	0.0780	2.16
limited	0.00	-	-
intermediate	-0.091189	0.0806	-1.13
unlimited	-0.329572	0.0728	-4.53
sex	0.239944	0.0642	3.74
class	-0.065363	0.0303	-2.16
$R^2 = 22.2\%$		R^2 (adjusted) = 20.3%	
s = 0.4402 with 207 - 6 = 201 degrees of freedom			
Source	Sum of Squares	df	Mean Square	F-ratio
Regression	11.1426	5	2.229	11.5
Residual	38.9540	201	0.193801	

subject played the game twice, the individual responses are not statistically independent. To get around this problem, we limited our sample to the 207 subjects who either cooperated with, or defected from, each of their two partners. The 60 subjects who cooperated with one partner and defected on the other were deleted from the sample. The dependent variable is the subject's choice of strategy, coded as 0 for "cooperate" and 1 for "defect." The independent variables are "econ" which takes the value 1 for economics majors, 0 for all others; "unlimited," which is 1 for subjects in the unlimited version of the experiment, 0 for all others; "intermediate," which is 1 for subjects in the intermediate version, 0 for all others; "limited," which is the reference category; "sex," coded as 1 for males, 0 for females; and "class," coded as 1 for freshmen, 2 for sophomores, 3 for juniors, and 4 for seniors.

Consistent with a variety of other findings on sex differences in cooperation,[11] we estimate that, other factors the same, the probability of a male defecting is almost 0.24 higher than the corresponding probability for a female. But even after controlling for the influence of gender, we see that the probability of an economics major defecting is almost

---

[11] See, for example, the studies cited in Gilligan (1982).

0.17 higher than the corresponding probability for a nonmajor.

The coefficients for the unlimited and intermediate experimental categories represent effects relative to the defection rate for the limited category. As expected, the defection rate is smaller in the intermediate category (where subjects have more time to interact than in the limited category), and falls sharply further in the unlimited category (where subjects are permitted to make promises to cooperate).[12]

Note, finally, that the overall defection rate declines significantly as students progress through school. The class coefficient is interpreted to mean that with the passage of each year the probability of defection declines, on the average, by almost 0.07. This pattern will prove important when we take up the question of whether training in economics is the cause of higher defection rates for economics majors.

For subjects in the unlimited subsample, we found that the difference between economics majors and nonmajors virtually disappears once subjects are permitted to make promises to cooperate. For this subsample, the defection rate for economics majors is 28.6 percent, compared to 25.9 percent for nonmajors. Because the higher defection rates for economics majors are largely attributable to the no-promises conditions of the experiment, the remainder of our analysis focuses on subjects in the limited and intermediate groups. The conditions encountered by these groups are of special significance, because they come closest to approximating the conditions that characterize social dilemmas encountered in practice. After all, people rarely have an opportunity to look one another in the eye and promise not to litter on deserted beaches or disconnect the smog control devices on their cars.

When the choices are pooled for the limited and intermediate groups, both economics majors and nonmajors defect more often, but the effect is considerably larger for economists. In those groups, the defection rate was 71.8 percent for economics majors and just 47.3 percent for nonmajors, levels that differ significantly at the .01 level.

As part of the exit questionnaire that tested understanding of the payoffs associated with different combinations of choices, we also asked subjects to state reasons for their choices. We hypothesized that economists would be more inclined to construe the objective of the game in self-interested terms, and therefore more likely to refer exclusively to features of the game itself, while noneconomists would be more open to alternative ways of interpreting the game, and would refer more often to their feelings about their partners, aspects of human nature, and so on. Indeed, among the sample of economics students, 31 percent referred only to features of the

---

[12] With the permission of subjects, we tape-recorded the conversations of several of the unlimited groups, and invariably each person promised each partner to cooperate. There would be little point, after all, in promising to defect.

game itself in explaining their chosen strategies, compared with only 17 percent of the noneconomists. The probability of obtaining such divergent responses by chance is less than .05.

Another possible explanation for the economists' higher defection rates is that economists may be more likely to expect their partners to defect. The self-interest model, after all, encourages such an expectation, and we know from other experiments that most subjects defect if they are told that their partners are going to defect. To investigate this possibility, we asked students in an upper division public finance course in Cornell's economics department whether they would cooperate or defect in a one-shot prisoner's dilemma if they knew with certainty that their partner was going to cooperate. Most of these students were economics majors in their junior and senior years. Of the 31 students returning our questionnaires, 18 (58 percent) reported that they would defect, only 13 that they would cooperate. By contrast, just 34 percent of noneconomics Cornell undergraduates who were given the same questionnaire reported that they would defect from a partner they knew would cooperate (p < .05). For the same two groups of subjects, almost all respondents (30 of 31 economics students and 36 of 41 noneconomics students) said they would defect if they knew their partner would defect. From these responses, we conclude that while expectations of partner performance play a strong role in predicting behavior, defection rates would remain significantly higher for economists than for noneconomists even if both groups held identical expectations about partner performance.

Why Do Economists Behave Differently?

Economists appear to behave less cooperatively than noneconomists along a variety of dimensions. This difference in behavior might result from training in economics; alternatively, it might exist because people who chose to major in economics were different initially; or it might be some combination of these two effects. We now report evidence on whether training in economics plays a causal role.

Comparing Upperclassmen and Underclassmen

If economics training causes uncooperative behavior, then defection rates in the prisoner's dilemma should rise with exposure to training in economics, all other factors held constant. Recalling our earlier finding that defection rates for the sample as a whole fall steadily between the freshman and senior years, the question is thus whether defection rates fall to the same degree over time for economists as for noneconomists. We found that the pattern of falling defection rates holds more strongly for noneconomics majors than for economics majors in the no-promises subsample. For noneconomics underclassmen in this group (freshmen and sophomores), the defection rate is 53.7 percent, compared to only 40.2 percent for upperclassmen. By contrast, the trend toward lower defection rates is virtually absent from economics majors in the no-promises subsample (73.7 percent for underclassmen, 70.0 percent for upperclassmen). In other words, students generally show a pronounced tendency toward more cooperative behavior with movement toward graduation, but this trend is conspicuously absent for economics majors.[13]

Naturally, we are in no position to say whether the trend for noneconomists reflects something about the content of noneconomics courses. But the fact that this trend is not present for economists is at least consistent with the hypothesis that training in economics plays some causal role in the lower observed cooperation rates of economists.

Honesty Surveys

In a further attempt to assess whether training in economics inhibits cooperation, we posed a pair of ethical dilemmas to students in two introductory microeconomics courses at Cornell University and to a control group of students in an introductory astronomy course, also at Cornell. In one dilemma, the owner of a small business is shipped ten microcomputers but is billed for only nine; the question is whether the owner will inform the computer company of the error. Subjects are first asked to estimate the likelihood that the owner would point out the mistake; and then, on the same response scale, to indicate how likely they would be to point out the error if they were the owner. The second dilemma concerns whether a lost envelope containing $100 and bearing the owner's name and address is likely to be returned by the person who finds it. Subjects are first asked to imagine that they have lost the envelope and to estimate the likelihood that a stranger would return it. They are then asked to assume that the roles are reversed and to indicate the likelihood that they would return the money to a stranger.

Students in each class completed the questionnaire on two occasions: during the initial week of class in September, and then during the final week of class in December. For each of the four questions, each student was coded as being "more honest" if the probability checked for that question rose between September and December; "less honest" if it fell during that period; and "no change" if it remained the same.

The first introductory microeconomics instructor (instructor A) whose students we surveyed is a mainstream economist with research interests in industrial organization and game theory. In class lectures, this instructor placed heavy emphasis on the prisoner's dilemma and related illustrations of how survival imperatives often militate against cooperation. The second microeconomics instructor (instructor B) is a specialist in economic development in Maoist China who did not emphasize such material to the same degree, but did assign a mainstream introductory text. On the basis of these differences, we expected that any observed effects of

---

[13] A regression similar to the one shown in Figure 2 confirms that this pattern continues to hold even when controlling for other factors that might influence defection rates.

Figure 3
Freshmen Honesty Survey Results

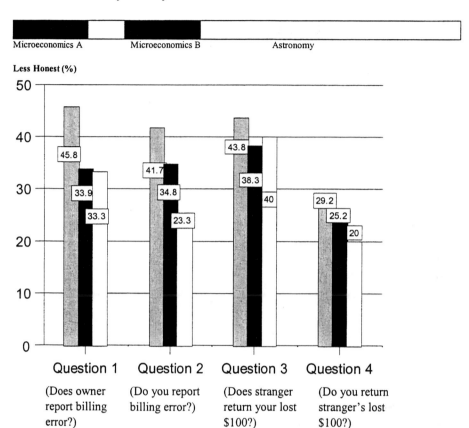

economics training should be stronger in instructor A's class than in instructor B's.

The results for these two classes, plus the class of noneconomists, are summarized in Figure 3, which shows the proportion of each class reporting a "less honest" result at the end of the semester than at the beginning. As the figure indicates, one semester's training was accompanied by greater movement toward more cynical ("less honest") responses in instructor A's introductory economics class than in instructor B's. Subjects in instructor B's class, in turn, showed greater movement toward less honest responses than did those in our control group of introductory astronomy students.

It may seem natural to wonder whether some of the differences between the two economics classes might stem from the fact that students chose their instructors rather than being randomly assigned. Perhaps the ideological reputations of the two professors were known in advance to many students, with the result that a disproportionate number of less cynical students chose to take instructor B's course. However, the average values of the initial responses to the four questions were virtually the same for both classes. Moreover, even if students had differed across the two classes, this would not alter the interpretation of our findings, since the entries in Figure 3 record not the level of cynicism but the change in that level between the beginning and end of the course. Even if the students in Microeconomics A were more cynical to begin with, they became still more so during the course of the semester. This finding is consistent with the hypothesis that emphasis on the self-interest model tends to inhibit cooperation.

Discussion

A variety of evidence suggests a large difference in the extent to which economists and noneconomists behave self-interestedly. We believe our survey of charitable giving and our prisoner's dilemma results lend additional support to the hypothesis that economists are more likely than others to free-ride.

Both of these exercises, however, also produced evidence that economists behave in traditionally communitarian ways under at least some circumstances. For example, economists reported spending as much time as others in volunteer activities, and were only marginally less likely than others to vote in presidential elections. Moreover, in the unlimited version of our prisoner's dilemma experiments, where subjects were allowed to promise to cooperate, economists were almost as likely to cooperate as noneconomists.

We also found evidence consistent with the view that differences in cooperativeness are caused in part by training in economics. This evidence is clearly less compelling than the evidence for a difference in cooperativeness. But it would be remarkable indeed if none of the observed differences in behavior were the result of repeated and intensive exposure to a model whose unequivocal prediction is that people will defect whenever self-interest dictates.

Should we be concerned that economics training may inhibit cooperation? Some might respond that while society would benefit if more people cooperated in social dilemmas, economists cannot be faulted for pointing out the unpleasant truth that self-interest dictates defection. One difficulty with this response is that it may be wrong. Several researchers have recently suggested that the ultimate victims of noncooperative behavior may be the very people who practice it (see, for example, Akerlof, 1983; Hirshleifer, 1987; Frank, 1988; and the essays in Mansbridge, 1990). Suppose, by way of illustration, that some people always cooperate in one-shot prisoner's dilemmas while others always follow the seemingly dominant strategy of defecting. If people are free to interact with others of their own choosing, and if there are cues that distinguish cooperators from defectors, then cooperators will interact selectively with one another and earn higher payoffs than defectors. Elsewhere we have shown that even on the basis of brief encounters involving strangers, experimental subjects are adept at predicting who will cooperate and who will defect in prisoner's dilemma games (Frank, 1988, ch. 7; Frank, Gilovich, and Regan, 1992). If people are even better at predicting the behavior of people they know well - a reasonable enough presumption - then the direct pursuit of material self-interest may indeed often be self-defeating.

In an ever more interdependent world, social cooperation has become increasingly important-and yet increasingly fragile. With an eye toward both the social good and the well-being of their own students, economists may wish to stress a broader view of human motivation in their teaching.

References

Akerlof, George, "Loyalty Filters," *American Economic Review*, March, 1983, 73:1, 54-63.

Carter, John, and Michael Irons, "Are Economists Different, and If So, Why?" *Journal of Economic Perspectives*, Spring 1991, 5:2, 171-77.

Carter, John, and Michael Irons, "Are Economists Different, and If So, Why?," working paper, College of the Holy Cross, December 1990.

Dawes, Robyn, "Social Dilemma" *Annual Review of Psychology*, 1980, 31, 163-93.

Frank, Robert H., *Passions Within Reason.* New York: W. W. Norton, 1988.

Frank, Robert H., Thomas Gilovich, and Dennis T. Regan, "The Evolution of Hardcore Cooperation," In *Ethology and Sociobiology*, forthcoming 1993.

Gilligan, Carol, *In a Different Voice.* Cambridge: Harvard University Press, 1982.

Guth, Werner, Rolf Schmittberger, and Bernd Schwarze, "An Experimental Analysis of Ultimatum Bargaining," *Journal of Economic Behavior and Organization*, December 1982, 3:4, 367-88.

Hirshleifer, Jack, "On the Emotions as Guarantors of Threats and Promises." In Dupre, John, ed., *The Latest and the Best: Essays on Evolution and Optimality.* Cambridge: The MIT Press, 1987, 307-26.

Kahneman, Daniel, Jack Knetsch, and Richard Thaler, "Fairness and the Assumptions of Economics," *Journal of Business*, Part 2, October 1986, 59, S285-S300.

Mansbridge, Jane J., *Beyond Self-Interest.* Chicago: University of Chicago Press, 1990.

Marwell, Gerald, and Ruth Ames, "Economists Free Ride, Does Anyone Else?: Experiments on the Provision of Public Goods, IV," *Journal of Public Economics*, June 1981, 15:3, 295-310.

Tullock, Gordon, *The Vote Motive.* London: Institute for Economic Affairs, 1976.

Do Economists Have a Sense of Humour?

Some of these traits of intellectual leaders are caught in the statement that they lack a sense of humor... Ridicule is a common weapon of attack but amused self-examination is a form of disarmament; one so endowed cannot declaim his beliefs with massive certainty and view opposing opinions as error uncontaminated by truth (George Stigler).

Miscellany

Toward a Deeper Economics of Sleeping

Exhaustive study of Professor M. A. El Hodiri's tedious, yet curiously superficial analysis of the economics of sleeping has led to a powerful and remarkably boring reformulation of Hodiri theory.[1]

As Hodiri astutely observes, it is difficult to deny that a sensible man would seek to maximize $U(x,y) = x^2y$ where x is daily consumption and y is the fraction of the day spent in bed. Hodiri supposes that daily consumption equals daily income, which in turn equals the daily wage rate, w, times the fraction of the day one spends out of bed.[2] Hence $x = w(1 - y)$. But then $U = w^2(1 - y)^2y$. By substituting all real numbers between zero and one into this expression, the reader will quickly verify that U is maximized when $y = 1/3$. Thus Hodiri asserts that, regardless of the wage rate he receives, a sensible man will sleep $1/3 \times 24 = 8$ hours per day. Had Hodiri been more deeply embedded in the profundities of economic literature, he could hardly have closed his eyes to the abundance of platitudinous evidence that some reap who do not sow. This fertile observation makes two things obvious. One is that the Hodiri equation, $x = w(1 - y)$, must be replaced by $x = w[(1 - y) + (R/w)]$ where R is daily earnings from nonlabor sources. The proper substitution for $U = x^2y$ is then $U = w^2[1 - y + (R/w)]^2y$. Consequently, U is maximized when $y = [1 + (R/w)]$. This inescapable truth would appear to rend Hodiri theory all to pieces. How can it be that sensible men have always slept 8 hours unless R/w has always been both constant and zero?

---

[1] It would be difficult to underestimate the importance of El Hodiri's contribution in enabling the author to achieve these heights of pedantry. Historians of thought could no doubt find many wearisome parallels in the advance of science. Though I do not presume to have mounted the shoulders of a giant, I hope that I have trod gently on the toes of El Hodiri.

[2] Professor J. T. Little of Washington University, St. Louis, in an unpublished note, maintains that not all time out of bed is spent in productive labor. However, there is reason to suppose that Little's observations have been confined to a pathological sample of the labor force.

Resolution of this fearsome paradox will display once again to the jaded reader the beauty and the mystery of Economic Fairyland. Observe that the source of nonwage income is called "capital." Where r is the daily interest rate, K is the stock of capital, and N is the size of the labor force, the average daily nonwage income is $R = rK/N$. Then $R/w = (1 - y)rK/(1 - y)wN$. Since total daily labor income is $(1 - y)wN$, $rK/(1 - y)wN$ is the ratio of capital's share to labor's share of national income, which is well known to have been remarkably constant over time and is in fact equal to ¼. Hence in all historical epochs, the average value of R/w has been $(1 - y)¼$. Recalling that $y = 1/3[1 +(R/w)]$, making the appropriate substitution, and solving for y, we have $y = \dfrac{5}{13}$. Now $\dfrac{5}{13}$ x 24 = 9.231 hours. Thus have we elegantly vindicated Hodiri's tiresome "first law of soporifics," namely, "In all epochs the average man has spent the same amount of time in bed."

There remains a yawning chasm between Hodiri's banal "second law of soporifics" which is "most people sleep 8 hours a day" and our unassailable demonstration that the average man has always spent 9.231 hours per day in bed. As in the science of astronomy, the existence of the planet Pluto was first conjectured as a consequence of a remarkable deviation of planetary orbits from those predicted by pure theory, so must we conjecture that the average man spends 1.231 hours per day in bed doing something other than sleeping. I eagerly await the announcement that some penetrating theorist or tireless data-massager has actually discovered Activity X.

T. C. BERGSTROM

Washington University

Reference

El Hodiri, M. A. "The Economics of Sleeping." Unpublished manuscript, University of Kansas, 1973.

Miscellany

The Economics of Brushing Teeth

The ever-growing literature on human capital has long recognized that the scope of the theory extends well beyond the traditional analysis of schooling and on-the-job training. Migration, maintenance of health, crime and punishment, even marriage and suicide, are all decisions which can usefully be considered from the human capital point of view. Yet economists have ignored the analysis of an important class of activities which can and should be brought within the purview of the theory. A prime example of this class is brushing teeth.[1]

The conventional analysis of toothbrushing has centered around two basic models. The "bad taste in one's mouth" model is based on the notion that each person has a "taste for brushing," and the fact that brushing frequencies differ is "explained" by differences in tastes. Since any pattern of human behavior can be rationalized by such implicit theorizing, this model is devoid of empirically testable predictions, and hence uninteresting.

The "mother told me so" theory is based on differences in cultural upbringing. Here it is argued, for example, that thrice-a-day brushers brush three times daily because their mothers forced them to do so as children. Of course, this is hardly a complete explanation. Like most psychological theories, it leaves open the question of why mothers should want their children to brush after every meal. But it does at least have one testable implication: that individuals from higher social classes will brush more frequently.

In these pages I describe a new model which is firmly grounded in economic theory and which generates a large number of empirically testable hypotheses. I then show that the predictions of the model are supported by the data.

The basic assumption is common to all human capital theory: that individuals seek to maximize their incomes. It follows immediately that each individual does whatever amount of toothbrushing will maximize his income. The "mother told me so'' model can be considered as a special case where the offspring only does as he or she is told, but the mother's decisions are governed by income maximization for the child. Thus, offspring will behave *as if* they maximized income.

EDITOR'S NOTE -This paper derives from the Princeton oral tradition.
  I wish to thank my dentist for filling in some important gaps in the analysis, and my colleague, Michael Rothschild, for insightful kibitzing. Support for this research is graciously solicited.
[1] The analysis to follow can also be applied to such important problems as combing hair, washing hands, and cutting fingernails, as I hope to show in a series of future papers.

An example will illustrate the usefulness of the model. Consider the toothbrushing decisions of chefs and waiters working in the same establishments. Since chefs generally come from higher socioeconomic strata, the "mother told me so" model predicts that they will brush more frequently than waiters. In fact, it has been shown that the reverse is true (Barnard and Smith 1941). Of course, the human capital model predicts precisely this behavior. On the benefits side, chefs are rarely seen by customers and work on straight salary. Waiters, by contrast, are in constant touch with the public and rely on tips for most of their income. Bad breath and/or yellow teeth could have deleterious effects on their earnings. On the cost side, since wages for chefs are higher, the opportunity cost of brushing is correspondingly higher. Thus, the theory predicts unambiguously that chefs will brush less. It is instructive to compare this rather tight theoretical deduction with Barnard and Smith's glib attribution of the observed differences to the different hygiene standards in the birthplaces of the individuals. (The chefs were born mostly in France, while the waiters were largely Brooklynites.)

I. Review of the Literature

A substantial literature on dental hygienics exists. It is ironic that economists are almost completely unaware of these studies, despite the fact that most economists brush their teeth.

The best empirical study was conducted by a team of researchers at the University of Chicago Medical Center in 1967. They compared toothbrushing habits of a scientifically selected sample of 27 sets of twins who had appeared in Wrigley's chewing gum commercials with a random sample of 54 longshoremen. The twins brushed their teeth an average of 3.17 times per day, while the longshoremen brushed only 0.76 times daily. The difference was significant at the 1 percent level. As noneconomists, the doctors advanced two possible explanations for this finding: either twins had a higher "taste for brushing" than nontwins, or the Wrigley Company deliberately set out to hire people with clean teeth. Further study, they concluded, would be needed to discriminate between these two hypotheses (Baker, Dooley, and Spock 1968). The human capital viewpoint makes the true explanation clear enough. Earnings of models depend strongly on the whiteness of their teeth. On the other hand, no direct connection has ever been established between the income of longshoremen and the quality of their breath. Another recent contribution was a survey of professors in a leading Eastern university. It was found that assistant professors brushed 2.14 times daily on average, while associate professors brushed only 1.89 times and full professors only 1.47 times daily. The author, a sociologist, mistakenly attributed this finding to the fact that the higher-ranking professors were older and that hygiene standard's in America had advanced steadily over time (Persons 1971). To a human capital theorist, of course, this pattern is exactly what would be expected from the higher wages received in the higher professorial ranks, and from the fact that younger professors, looking for promotions, cannot afford to have bad breath.

II. A Theoretical Model of Toothbrushing

Let w be the wage rate of an individual; let J be an index of his job; and let B be the time spent brushing his teeth. With no loss of generality, I can reorder the jobs so that jobs with higher J are the jobs where clean teeth are more important. The assumed wage function is therefore

$$w = w(J, B), \; w_B \geq 0, \; w_{BJ} = w_{JB} \geq 0 \qquad (1)$$

Since jobs have been reordered, there is no a priori presumption about the sign of w_j. It is also assumed that w(.) is continuous, twice differentiable, and semistrictly quasi-concave in the nonnegative orthant.

Each individual is assumed to maximize his income:

$$Y = w\,(J, B)(\,T - B) + P, \tag{2}$$

where T is the fixed amount of time per period available for working or brushing[2] and P is the (exogenously determined) amount of unearned income.[3] That is, each individual selects a value of B to maximize (2). The necessary condition for a maximum is[4]

$$w_B\,(J, B)(T - B) - w\,(J, B) = 0. \tag{3}$$

Several important implications follow from (3). First, since both w and w_B are presumptively positive, (3) implies that T - B must be positive. In words, the theory predicts that no person will spend every waking hour brushing his teeth-an empirically testable proposition not derivable from either the "bad taste" or "mother told me" models.

Second, (3) can be rewritten

$$\frac{B}{T-B} = \frac{Bw_B}{w} \tag{4}$$

In words, the ratio of brushing to nonbrushing time is equated to the partial elasticity of the wage with respect to brushing time. So individuals in jobs where wages are highly sensitive to brushing will devote more time to brushing than will others-as indicated in the verbal discussion. Also, for any two jobs with equal w_B's but unequal w's, (3) implies that the higher-wage person will brush less due to his greater opportunity cost.

Finally, consider the important case where (1) is linear in B (though possibly nonlinear in J):

$$w = \alpha(J) + \beta\,(J)B, \ \alpha \geq 0, \ \beta \geq 0. \tag{1'}$$

Substituting into (3) and solving yields

$$B = \frac{T}{2} - \frac{\alpha}{2\beta} \tag{5}$$

In jobs where brushing is immaterial to success, $\beta \rightarrow 0$, so (5) calls for a corner maximum with B = 0. Thus, we have a second strong prediction from the model: such persons will never brush. At the other extreme, as the ratio α/β approaches zero, (5) implies B $\rightarrow$ T/2. In words, individuals whose wages depend almost exclusively on the whiteness of their teeth (M.C.'s of television quiz shows are a good example) will spend approximately half their lives brushing. Again, no sociological theory can generate predictions as strong as this.

---

[2] It is assumed, for simplicity, that these are the only possible uses of time. The model can easily be extended to accommodate an arbitrary number of uses of time, as is not shown in an appendix.

[3] A more general model would allow for the possibility that cleaner teeth can lead to a larger inheritance, that is, $P(B)$ with $P'(B) > 0$. For evidence of this, see "Toothpaste Heir Disinherited for Having Bad Breath," *Wall Sireet Journal,* April 1, 1972, p. 1.

[4] Since w is assumed semistrictly quasi-concave, this is also sufficient for a weak maximum.

III. A Regression Model

The implications of the model can be put to an empirical test thanks to a recent cross-section study of American adults in the civilian labor force conducted by the Federal Brushing Institute. In its Survey of Brushing, the institute collected data on toothbrushing frequency and many socio-economic characteristics of 17,684 adults in 1972. From these data, the following regression model was formulated:

$$NBRUSH = a_o + a_1 AGE + a_2 WAGE + a_3 NTEETH + a_4 S + a_5 EXP + \qquad (6)$$
$$a_6 FDUM + a_7 Y + u.$$

The dependent variable is the number of times teeth were brushed during the year. *AGE* is included as a proxy for the number of years remaining before the individual's teeth fall out. Viewing brushing as a human investment clearly implies that $a_1 < 0$. *WAGE*, of course, measures the opportunity cost of time; so $a_2 < 0$. *NTEETH* is the number of teeth in the person's mouth. Since brushing time is nearly independent of the number of teeth brushed, having more teeth should certainly encourage more brushing. *S* and *EXP* are, respectively, years of schooling and work experience. They are included because this is a human capital model; although there are no a priori expectations about the signs of a_4 and a_5, both should have high t-ratios. *FDUM* is a dummy for persons who live in an area with fluoridated water supply, included since there is some substitution in the production function for good teeth between brushing and fluoridating the water. Finally, Y is nonlabor income, which enables us to estimate the income effect on toothbrushing frequency.

Since I have argued above that *WAGE* should depend on *NBRUSH*, equation (6) was estimated by the instrumental-variables technique. Denture wearers were included in the sample, but 189 people with no teeth at all were omitted from the analysis. The empirical results are reported below, with standard errors in parentheses:

NBRUSH =   2.04 - *0.006 AGE* - *0.096 WAGE* + *0.054 NTEETH* + 0.0043 *S* - 0.0022 *EXP* -
            (0.63) (0.001)   (0.001)   (0.009)   (0.0002)   (0.0001)

            0. 146 *FDUM* + 0.0006 *Y*,
            (9.027)   (0.0002)

$$R = .79, \quad SE \ 0.056.$$

By any standards the results are very good. The R^2 is very high for cross-section work indicating that the data have been successfully mined. All the variables suggested by the theoretical model are highly significant and, wherever the theory implied a priori sign restrictions, they are satisfied.

In summary, the survey data strikingly confirm the predictions of the theoretical model of toothbrushing presented here. Of course, this is only one of many possible tests of the theory. But it does point out the usefulness of human capital concepts in understanding dental hygiene. Hopefully, these results will stimulate renewed interest in such questions on the part of economists.

ALAN S. BLINDER
Princeton University

References

Baker, M. D.; Dooley, C.; and Spock, B. "Brushing by Longshoremen and Twins: A Case Study."
  Q. *J. Orthodontics* 3 (1968): 377-462.
Barnard, C., and Smith, L. "Brushing Proclivities of Restaurant Employees in New York City."
  Rev. Periodontics and Dentistics 7 (1941): i-2.
Persons, T. "Dental Hygiene and Age: A Sociological View." *J. Dental Soc.* 11 (1971): 1-243.

A Theory of Extramarital Affairs

Ray C. Fair
Yale University

In this paper a model is developed that explains the allocation of an individual's time among work and two types of leisure activities: time spent with spouse, and time spent with paramour. Data from two recent magazine surveys are available that can be used to test the predictions of the model regarding the determinants of time spent with paramour. The results of estimating the equation explaining time spent with paramour, by the Tobit estimator, are generally supportive of the model, although more evidence is needed before any definitive conclusions can be drawn. The model can also be applied to the allocation of time among other types of leisure activities.

I. Introduction

Relationships with other people are generally an important part of a person's life. The key relationship for most adults is, of course, that with one's spouse and children. The fact that most adults are married and have children has undoubtedly been an important reason for the emphasis in the literature on the household as a basic decision unit. Because of this emphasis, little consideration has been given to the question of the allocation of a person's leisure time[1] between activities with household members and activities with nonhousehold members. Even Becker's (1973) pioneering work on marriage, which as he points out (p. 816) does not require that different members of the household have the same preference function, concentrates on the allocation of a person's time between time spent in household

---

I would like to thank Sharon Oster for many helpful comments on this paper. I am also indebted to George Stigler and an anonymous referee for useful suggestions, to the editors of *Psychology Today* and *Redbook* for permission to use data from two recent surveys, and to Robert Athanasiou, Shirley Glass, and Susan Sadd for help in supplying me with the data. I assume responsibility for all errors.
[1] By "leisure time" in this paper is meant any time spent in nonmarket activities.

activities and time spent in market activities. For many people, leisure time spent with nonhousehold members plays an important role in their lives, and it is unfortunate that this fact has received so little attention by economists.

The purpose of this paper is to consider the determinants of leisure time spent in one particular type of activity with nonhousehold members: extramarital affairs. The extent of such activity is by no means small. In one of the two surveys used for the empirical work in this study, 27.2 percent of the first-time-married working men and 22.9 percent of the first-time-married working women were having an extramarital affair at the time of the survey. In the other survey (of women only), 32.2 percent of the first-time-married working women had had at least one affair during their married lives. Given the apparent frequency of extramarital affairs, it is of some interest to see if economic analysis can help to predict their incidence.

In Section II a theoretical model is presented that explains the allocation of a married person's time among work, spouse, and paramour. Time spent with paramour is seen to be a function of the person's wage rate, the price level, the person's nonlabor income, the time spent by the spouse in the marriage, the value of goods supplied by the spouse to the marriage, the time spent by the paramour in the affair, the value of goods supplied by the paramour to the affair, and any other variables that have an effect on the utility received from the marriage or on the utility received from the affair.

Some data are available from two recent magazine surveys, conducted respectively by *Psychology Today* and *Redbook,* that can be used to test the model. The variables that were constructed from these surveys for use in this study are discussed in Section III. The results of estimating the model, by the Tobit estimator (Tobin 1958), are presented and discussed in Section IV. Although the data are far from ideal for testing the model, the results presented in Section IV are generally supportive of it. The results clearly appear to be good enough to warrant further tests of the model in the future if more data become available.

Although the theoretical model developed in the next section is concerned with two specific types of leisure activities, time spent with spouse and time spent with paramour, it should be fairly clear that the model has wider applicability than this. Many types of leisure activities with nonhousehold members are covered by the theory. Participation in a men's club or a women's auxiliary, for example, is clearly a type of leisure activity that is covered by the theory; the theory is not limited merely to sexual activities. The model in the next section could have been formulated in more general terms first and then applied to the extramarital affairs case, but there seemed little point in doing this. The model is easier to present by means of a particular case, and once presented in this way it can be applied easily to other cases.

II. The Theoretical Model

The primary motivation for the model is the idea that people like variety in their lives. This idea is hardly novel in economics, since it is presumably one of the main motivations for the inclusion of more than one type of good in the utility function in classical demand theory. This same idea has not however, generally been applied to leisure activities - in particular, for present purposes, to leisure activities with different people. All leisure activities are generally grouped together into one variable called "leisure."

Outside of economics it is easy to find defenses for the idea that variety is important in people's lives. They range from the cliché, "variety is the spice of life," to the poetry of John Donne (1967 ed.):

> The heavens rejoyce in motion, why should I
> Abjure my so much lov'd variety,
> And not with many youth and love divide?
> Pleasure is none, if not diversifi'd.

Since it is clear that variety is important in life, and since this idea is already one of the main motivations for the inclusion of more than one good in the utility function, there is ample justification for applying it to leisure activities. This will now be done for two particular types of leisure activities.

Consider a married individual i and assume that there are three types of activities that he or she can engage in: time spent with spouse (t_1), with paramour (t_2), and working (t_3). Let U_1 and U_2 denote the utility that i derives from the spouse and paramour relationships, respectively. Variety with respect to relationships is assumed to be important to i, and, as mentioned above this is the main justification for postulating more than one type of relationship. For simplicity, there is assumed to be only one possible paramour and only one type of good in existence. This latter assumption means that variety with respect to goods is ruled out of the analysis, an omission that is of little consequence for purposes of the present study.

Now, U_1 is postulated to be a function of t_1, of the time spent by the spouse in the relationship (t_s), of the number of units of the good consumed in the relationship (x_1), and of a vector of other variables (E_1):

$$U_1 = f(t_1, t_s, x_1, E_1). \tag{1}$$

The vector E_1 is taken to include all variables that have an effect on U_1 other than t_1, t_s, and x_1. The function f is similar to what Becker (1973) calls the household production function. Variables such as the times spent by the children in the household which are included in Becker's household production function, are assumed here to be included in E_1.

Similarly, U_2 is postulated to be a function of t_2, of the time spent by the paramour in the affair (t_p), of the number of units of the good consumed in the affair (x_2), and of a vector of other variables $(E_2,)$:

$$U_2 = g\,(t_2,\, t_p,\, x_2,\, E_2). \tag{2}$$

The vector E_2 is taken to include all variables that have an effect on U_2 other than t_2, t_p, and x_2.

The total utility of i (U) is postulated to be the sum of U_1 and U_2:

$$U = U_1 + U_2. \tag{3}$$

The functions f and g are assumed to be strictly concave.

The variable x_1 consists of units of the good supplied by $i(x_{1i})$ and of units of the good supplied by the spouse (x_{1s}):

$$x_1 = x_{1i} + x_{1s}. \tag{4}$$

Similarly, x_2 consists of units of the good supplied by $i(x_{2i})$ and of units of the good supplied by the paramour (x_{2p}):

$$x_2 = x_{2\,i} + x_{2p}. \tag{5}$$

t_1, t_2, and t_3 are assumed to sum to the total available time in the period (T):

$$T = t_1 + t_2 + t_3. \tag{6}$$

The decision problem for i is to choose t_1, t_2, x_{1i}, and x_{2i} so as to maximize U, subject to the budget constraint:

$$w(T - t_1 - t_2) + V = p(x_{1i} + x_{2i}), \tag{7}$$

where p is the price of the good, w is i's wage rate, and V is i's nonlabor income. The problem is also restricted in that t_1, t_2, x_{1i} and x_{2i} cannot be negative. Taken as given for purposes of this problem are t_s, t_p, x_{1s}, x_{2p}, p, w, V, E_1 and E_2. Note that the budget constraint (7) is not the household budget constraint but is rather i's individual budget constraint. The decision problem analyzed here is an individual decision problem, not a household decision problem. Note also that the treatment of t_s and x_{1s}, as exogenous means that no consideration is given to possible effects of i's decisions on the spouse's decisions.[2]

---

[2] The assumption that t_s, and x_{1s} are exogenous is clearly a strong one in the present context, and, as mentioned below, it might be of interest in future work to relax it. If the spouse is unaware of i's affair, then the assumption is, of course, less restrictive than otherwise. The assumption would also be less restrictive if the other leisure activity were something like participation in a club or auxiliary. It should also be noted that the model could be easily modified to the case in which the paramour is a prostitute. In this case t_p would be purchased by i at some rate w_p; t_p would now be a decision variable for i, rather than being

Likewise, the treatment of t_p and x_{2p} as exogenous means that no consideration is given to possible effects of i's decisions on the paramour's decisions.

The decision problem for i can be solved in the standard way by setting up the Lagrangian,

$$\mathscr{L} = U + \lambda[w(T - t_1 - t_2) + V - p(x_{1i} + x_{2i})], \tag{8}$$

and differentiating $\mathscr{L}$ with respect to the four decision variables and λ. The first-order conditions are:

$$\frac{\partial f}{dt_1} - \lambda w = 0, \tag{9a}$$

$$\frac{\partial g}{dt_2} - \lambda w = 0, \tag{9b}$$

$$\frac{\partial f}{dx_{1i}} - \lambda p = 0, \tag{9c}$$

$$\frac{dg}{dx_{2i}} - \lambda p = 0, \tag{9d}$$

$$w(T - t_1 - t_2) + V - p(x_{1i} + x_{2i}) = 0. \tag{9e}$$

These conditions hold if the solution is an interior one; they do not necessarily hold if, for example, the optimum value of t_2 is zero. For purposes of the rest of the discussion in this section, however, the solution is assumed to be an interior one.

The first-order conditions can be interpreted in the usual way. At the optimum, the marginal utility of time spent in the marriage is equal to the marginal utility of time spent in the affair ($\partial f/\partial t_1 = \partial g/\partial t_2$). Similarly, the marginal utility of consumption of the good in the marriage is equal to the marginal utility of consumption of the good in the affair ($\partial f/\partial x_{1i} = \partial g/\partial x_{2i}$). Finally, the marginal rate of substitution between time spent in the marriage (affair) and consumption of the good in the marriage (affair) is equal to the real wage ($\partial f/\partial t_1 \div \partial f/\partial x_{1i} = w/p$ and $\partial g/\partial t_2 \div \partial g/\partial x_{2i} = w/p$).

The main concern of this paper is to trace the effects of changes in the various exogenous variables on t_2. This can be done by taking the total of equations (9a)-(9e) and then solving, using Cramer's Rule, for the derivative of t_2 with respect to each exogenous variable (all other exogenous variables assumed to remain unchanged). The results from this exercise will now be summarized. The following discussion of signs is based on the assumption that all first derivatives of f and g are positive, that all cross partial derivatives of f and g are positive, and that all second derivatives of f and g are negative.

---

exogenous, and w_p would be exogenous. The budget constraint in this case would be: $w(T - t_1 - t_2) + V = p(x_{1i} + x_{2i}) + w_p t_p$.

The determinant of the bordered Hessian is positive because of the strict concavity of f and g. The following derivatives relating to t_2 are unambiguous in sign:

$$\frac{dt_2}{dV} \rangle 0; \frac{dt_2}{dx_{1s}} = \frac{dt_2}{dx_{2p}} = p\frac{dt_2}{dV} \rangle 0; \frac{dt_2}{dt_s} \langle 0; \frac{dt_2}{dE_1} \langle 0. \tag{10}$$

The first term is the income effect on t_2; it is positive as expected. An increase in V, i's nonlabor income, causes i to work less and to increase both t_1 and t_2 (dt_1 / dV is also positive). The next two derivatives in (10) are, respectively, the effect on t_2 of a change in units of the good supplied by the spouse to the marriage and by the paramour to the affair. Both derivatives are equal to the price of the good times the income effect. Since there are no restrictions on the allocation of units of the good that i purchases between the marriage and the affair, an increase in x_{1s} or x_{2p} has the same effect as an equivalent increase in i's nonlabor income which is in this case merely the price of the good times the increase in x_{1s} or x_{2p}. (An increase in x_{1s} or x_{2p} also has a positive effect on t_1, the effect being p times dt_1/dV.)

The second-to-last derivative in (10) is the effect on t_2 of a change in the time spent by the spouse in the marriage. The effect is negative. If the spouse spends more time in the marriage, this increases the utility that i derives from the marriage and causes the time spent in the affair to fall. This negative effect of the spouse on t_2 is to be contrasted with the effect on t_2 of an increase in units of the good supplied by the spouse to the marriage, which, as just discussed, is equivalent to an income effect and is positive. The last derivative in (10) is the effect on t_2 of a change in E_1, any variable that has a positive effect on the utility from the marriage. This effect is negative as expected.

The following derivatives relating to t_2 are ambiguous in sign:

$$\frac{dt_2}{dw}, \frac{dt_2}{dp}, \frac{dt_2}{dt_p}, \frac{dt_2}{dE_2}. \tag{11}$$

The ambiguity of the wage and price effects comes from the usual ambiguity due to income and substitution effects. The income effect of an increase in w on t_2 is positive, and the substitution effect is negative. Conversely, the income effect of an increase in p on t_2 is negative, and the substitution effect is positive.

Consider now the third term in (11), the effect on t_2 of a change in the time spent by the paramour in the affair. An increase in t_p increases the utility that i derives from the affair, which leads, other things being equal, to an increase in t. An increase in t_p also, however, affects the division of i's time between work and leisure, and it is from this effect that the ambiguity in the sign of dt_2/dt_p arises. In particular, an increase in t_p increases the marginal utility that i derives from consuming the good in the affair. This, other things being equal, induces some increase in working time. If this effect of a decrease in leisure time is very large, it may swamp the substitution effect and cause an overall fall in t_2. In most cases, this seems unlikely, so in general it is likely that dt_2/dt_p is positive. A similar argument holds for dt_2/dE_2; in general it is likely to be positive.

This completes the presentation of the formal model. A summary of it is presented in the first half of table 2. Before concluding this section, however, mention should be made of other ways that one might model behavior concerning extramarital affairs. One way would be to borrow from the literature on the economics of crime (see, e.g., Becker 1968) and consider the decision on whether or not to have an affair to be analogous to the decision on whether or not to commit a crime. The individual in making the decision would weigh the gains from the affair against the expected loss, where the expected loss is the probability of being caught times the cost if caught. In this framework one would consider the factors that influence the gain from the affair, the factors that influence the probability of getting caught, and the factors that influence the cost if caught.

A second way would be to set the decision problem up as a multiperiod optimization problem, where each period the individual would choose paths of the decision variables. The range of the paths would be from the initial period (the period in which the decision was made) to the end of the person's life. This treatment would allow one to consider in an explicit way the effects of future events (or expected future events) on current decisions. A third approach would be to drop the assumption that i's decisions have no effect on the spouse's decisions, and either set up the problem as a game-theory problem or else postulate explicitly how i's decisions affect the spouse's decisions. Finally, one might borrow from the job-search literature and interpret extramarital affairs as a form of search for an alternative spouse. Many of the same types of factors that induce a worker to search for an alternative job could be postulated as inducing a person to search for an alternative spouse.[3] In future work it may be of interest to pursue one or more of these approaches, but for purposes of this paper the analysis is limited to the above model.

---

[3] Much of the theory in Kelley (1976) can be interpreted as a theory of search for a spouse. Kelley's theory implies (p. 22) that, other things being equal, length of marriage should have a negative effect on time spent in extramarital affairs (search for an alternative spouse). This implication is consistent with the theory of job search, where search for an alternative job is a negative function of the length of the present job. The empirical results reported in Section IV of this paper are, however, contrary to this conclusion: length of marriage has a positive effect on time spent in extramarital affairs. It is somewhat unclear whether Kelley's theory can be modified to fit this result or not. In this paper the result is interpreted to mean that utility from marriage declines with length of marriage. Kelley's discussion (pp. 23-24) of the effects of income on time spent in extramarital affairs is not very convincing because he does not appear to be aware of the difference between income and substitution effects.

III. The Data and Estimation Technique

It is possible from two recent magazine surveys to gather data that can be used to estimate the above model. As with a lot of data, they are not the best that one might hope for, but they do appear to be at least of some use for present purposes. The first survey was conducted in 1969 by *Psychology Today* (*PT*). A questionnaire on sex was published in the July 1969 issue of *PT,* and readers were asked to mail in their answers. About 20,000 replies were received, of which about 2,000 were coded onto tape. The second survey, of women only, was conducted in 1974 by *Redbook* (*RB*). A questionnaire on sex was published in the October issue of *RB,* and readers were asked to mail in their answers. About 100,000 replies were received, of which about 18,000 were coded onto tape. The questionnaires included questions about extramarital affairs as well as about many other aspects of sexual behavior and about various demographic and economic characteristics of the individual. The *PT* and *RB* questionnaires included 101 and 81 questions, respectively. The discussion of the answers to the *PT* survey can be found in the July 1970 issue of *PT.*

It should be noted that neither of these two surveys is likely to be a random sample of the U.S. population. For present purposes, of course, a random sample is unnecessary. What is needed here is the condition that the samples have not been selected on the basis of the size of the dependent variables used in the estimation work, that is, on the basis of the amount of time spent in extramarital affairs. Although this requirement is much less strong than the requirement that the sample be random, there is no guarantee that it is met in the present case. There may thus be some bias in the following results due to the sampling procedure, although, at least to the author this bias does not seem likely to be very large.

Table 1 contains a list of the variables that were constructed from the data on the two tapes. Only people who were married and married for the first time were included in the sample from each tape. People who were married but married more than once were excluded because of lack of information on some of the variables for these people. The questions regarding the number of years married and the number or existence of children, for example, pertain to all marriages, and it is not possible if a person has been married more than once to determine the length of the current marriage and the number or existence of children from the current marriage. Also, only employed people were included in the sample from each tape. For unemployed people, t_3 in the above model is zero, and the solutions to their maximization problems are not interior ones. The first order conditions, therefore, do not necessarily hold for unemployed people, and so these people must be excluded from the samples. Also excluded from the samples were people who failed to answer all the relevant questions. The size of the usable sample from the *PT* tape was 601

TABLE 1
VARIABLES CONSTRUCTED FROM THE DATA ON THE *PT* AND *RB* TAPES

Question No.	Notation for Variable	Description of Variable	Values of Variable	Mean Value
			PT Tape	
75	y_{PT}	How often engaged in extramarital sexual intercourse during the past year	0 = none, 1 = once, 2 = twice, 3 = 3 times, 7 = 4 -10 times, 12 = monthly, 12 = weekly, 12 = daily	1.46
42	z_1	Sex	0 = female, 1 = male	0.476
43	z_2	Age	17.5 = under 20, 22.0 = 20-24, 27.0 = 25-29, 32.0 = 30=34, 37.0 = 35-39, 42.0 = 40-44, 47.0 = 45-49, 52.0 = 50-54, 57.0 = 55 or over	32.5
47	z_3	No. of years married	.125 = 3 months or less, .417 = 4-6 months, .75 = 6 months-1 year, 1.5 = 1-2 years, 4.0 = 3-5 years, 7.0 = 6-8 years, 10.0 = 9-11 years, 15.0 = 12 or more years	8.18
50	z_4	Children	0 = no, 1 = yes	0.715
56	z_5	How religious	5 = very, 4 = somewhat, 3 = slightly, 2 = not at all, 1 = anti	3.12
60	z_6	Level of education	9.0 = grade school, 12.0 = high school graduate, 14.0 = some college, 16.0 = college graduate, 17.0 = some graduate work, 18.0 = master's degree, 20.0 = Ph.D., M.D., or other advanced degree	16.2
64	z_7	Occupation	1-7, according to Hollingshead classification (reverse numbering)	4.19
66	z_8	How rate marriage	5 = very happy, 4 = happier than average, 3 = average, 2 = somewhat unhappy, 1 = very unhappy	3.93
			RB Tape	
.	y_{RB}	Measure of time spent in extra-marital affairs (=.0 or = $q_1 q_2 / v_3$)	.0-57.6	.705

Question No.	Notation for Variable	Description of Variable	Values of Variable	Mean Value
			RB Tape	
49	q_1	If since marriage have had sexual relations with man other than husband, with how many different men	1.0 = 1, 3.5 = 2-5, 8.0 = 6-10, 12.0 = more than 10	
50	q_2	Continuing from question 49, approximate number of times had sexual relations with each man	1.0 = once, 3.5 = 2-5, 8.0 = 6-10, 12.0 = more than 10, 5.6 = it varied greatly from partner to partner	
2	v_1	How rate marriage	5 = very good, 4 = good, 3 = fair, 2 = poor, 1 = very poor	4.11
61	v_2	Age	17.5 = under 20, 22.0 = 20-24, 27.0 = 25-29, 32.0 = 30-34, 37.0 = 35-39, 42.0 = 40 or over	29.1
63	v_3	No. years married	.5 = less than 1 year, 2.5 = 1-4 years, 6.0 = 5-7 years, 9.0 = 8-10 years, 13.0 if more than 10 years and oldest child under 12 years of age, 16.5 if more than 10 years and oldest child between 12 and 17 years of age, 23.0 if more than 10 years and oldest child 18 years of age or over	9.01
66	v_4	No. children	.0 = none, 1.0 = 1, 2.0 = 2, 3.0 = 3, 4.0 = 4, 5.5 = 5 or more	1.40
70	v_5	How religious	4 = strongly, 3 = fairly, 2 = mildly, 1 = not	2.43
72	v_6	Level of education	9.0 = grade school, 12.0 = high school, 14.0 = some college, 16.0 = college graduate, 17.0 = some graduate school, 20.0 = advanced degree	14.2
75	v_7	Occupation	6 = professional with advanced degree, 5 = managerial administrative, business, 4 = teacher, counselor, social worker, nurse; artist, writer; technician, skilled worker, 3 = white collar (sales, clerical, secretarial), 2 = farming, agriculture; semi-skilled or unskilled worker; other, 1 = student	3.42
77	v_8	Husband's occupation	Same as v_7	3.85

observations, and the size of the usable sample from the *RB* tape was 6,366 observations.

Table 1 is self-explanatory, and only a few remarks about it will be presented here. In the column "Values of Variable" the items to the right of the equal signs are the answers that were allowed on the questionnaires. The number to the left of each equal sign is the value chosen by the author to represent that answer. A number of questions were open-ended in the upper range and fairly arbitrary values for the largest value of the variables had to be used in these cases (see z_2, z_3, v_2, v_3, and v_4). The 5.6 value used for the last answer pertaining to q_2 is the average of values of the other answers weighted by the number of people who chose each answer.

The largest value of y_{PT}, was taken to be 12, even though larger values could have been used for people who answered that they engaged in extramarital sexual intercourse weekly or daily. This means that t_2 was assumed to be the same for monthly, weekly, and daily people. As discussed below, a linear specification was used for the estimated equation, and it did not seem reasonable in this case, given the range of values of the explanatory variables, to have a dependent variable that ranged from, say, 0 to 365.

The *RB* questionnaire did not ask if the person was currently having an affair, and y_{RB} as defined in table 1 was the best that could be done regarding a measure of t_2. The implicit assumption here in the use of y_{RB} as a measure of t_2 is that the current value of t_2 is highly correlated with past values of t_2. The occupation variable z_7 was coded onto the tape according to the Hollingshead (1957) classification, a classification that is meant to correspond in at least some rough way to social position.

Table 1 includes all variables from the two tapes that appeared to be relevant for purposes of this study.[4] Table 2 contains a matching of these variables with the variables from the theoretical model. The first half of table 2 contains a list of the explanatory variables in the theoretical model and their expected effects on t_2. The second half of the table contains a list of the observed explanatory variables, their likely correlation with the explanatory variables in the theoretical model, and their likely effects on the dependent variable. The following is a brief discussion of the second half of table 2.

The occupation variables (v_7 and z_7) are likely to be positively correlated with the wage rate (w). The correlation may not, however, be very large for z_7, since the Hollingshead classification used in the coding of the variable is more a classification by social position than it is by wage rate.

---

[4] Both surveys included a question about the size of family income, but this variable is unfortunately of no use here. Family income is, among other things, a function of t_3, which is itself a decision variable ($t_3 = T - t_1 - t_2$). It would be inappropriate to use as an explanatory variable for t_2 a variable that is directly related to t_3 in this way.

TABLE 2

MATCHING OF THE VARIABLES IN THE THEORETICAL MODEL WITH OBSERVED VARIABLES

A. THEORETICAL MODEL*

		Explanatory Variables	Effect on t_2
t_s	=	time spent by spouse in marriage	-
x_{1s}	=	no. units of the good supplied by the spouse to the marriage	+
x_{2p}	=	no. units of the good supplied by the paramour to the affair	+
V	=	nonlabor income	+
E_1	=	any variable that has a positive effect on the utility from the marriage	-
p	=	price of the good	Ambiguous
w	=	wage rate	Ambiguous
t_p	=	time spent by paramour in affair	Ambiguous but likely to be +
E_2	=	any variable that has a positive effect on the utility from the affair	Ambiguous, but likely to be +

B. EMPIRICAL WORK†

OBSERVED EXPLANATORY VARIABLES			LIKELY TO BE CORRELATED WITH (SIGN)	LIKELY EFFECT ON DEPENDENT VARIABLE
PT	RB	Variable		
z_7	v_7	Occupation	w (+)	Ambiguous
z_6	v_6	Education	w (+)	Ambiguous
	v_8	Husband's occupation	x_{1s} (+)	+
z_8	v_1	Marital happiness	E_1 (+)	-
z_2	v_2	Age	E_2 (-) (or none)	Ambiguous, but likely to be - (or none)
z_3	v_3	No. years married	E_1 (-) (or none)	+ (or none)
z_4	v_4	Children	E_1 (-) (or none)	- (or none)
z_5	v_5	Degree of religiosity	E_2 (-)	Ambiguous, but likely to be -
z_1	...	Sex	none	none

* Dependent variable : t_2 = time spent in affair.
† Observed dependent variables: y_{PT} and y_{RB} (see table 1).

Even if z_7 and v_7 are positively correlated with w, their effect on the dependent variables is ambiguous because the effect of w on t_2 is ambiguous. The effect of the education variables (z_6 and v_6) on the dependent variables is likewise ambiguous, even though z_6 and v_6 are likely to be positively correlated with w.

With respect to the husband's occupation variable (v_8), to the extent that it is positively correlated with the husband's wage rate, it is likely to be positively correlated with x_{1s}, the value of goods supplied by the husband to the marriage. The effect of v_8 on the dependent variable is thus expected to be positive.

The variables z_8 and v_1, measure marital happiness, which in the present context means that they are positively correlated with E_1. They are thus expected to have a negative effect on the dependent variables. These two variables are quite unusual and useful variables to have in a study of this kind. There are clearly many factors that have an effect on the utility from a marriage that are not observed, and variables like z_8 and v_1 are likely to capture the effects of a number of these factors.

If age has a negative effect on the enjoyment of sexual activity, something which may or may not be true, and if affairs are primarily sexual, then age will have a negative effect on the utility from an affair. The age variables (z_2 and v_2) may thus be negatively correlated with E_2, in which case they are likely to have a negative effect on the dependent variables. If the number of years married has a negative effect on the utility from the marriage because of boredom, something which again may or may not be true, then the variables z_3 and v_3 will be negatively correlated with E_1 and will thus have a positive effect on the dependent variables. If the existence or number of children has a positive effect on the utility from the marriage because of time spent by the children in the household, then the variables z_4 and v_4 will be positively correlated with E_1 and will thus have a negative effect on the dependent variables.

The degree of religiosity of a person may have a negative effect on the utility from an affair to the extent that it is related to concerns about divine or moral disapprobations from engaging in an affair. The religious variables z_5 and z_5 may thus be negatively correlated with E_2, and if they are they are then likely to have a negative effect on the dependent variables.[5] The last variable in table 2, the sex of the person (z_1), is not expected from the theoretical model to have any effect on t_2. No behavioral differences between men and women were postulated in the model; i in Section II can be either a man or a woman.

This completes the discussion of table 2. While it would be useful to have access to more data, the data from the two tapes do allow enough variables to be constructed to provide at least a rudimentary test of the model. The last item to be discussed in this section is the estimation technique used.

When the dependent variable t_2 is zero, the first-order conditions do not necessarily hold. Because of this and because many values of y_{PT} and y_{RB} are zero, it would clearly be incorrect to use ordinary least squares to estimate the equations. The obvious technique to use in this case is the Tobit estimator (Tobin 1958). Let $\bar{z}_i$ and $\bar{v}_i$ denote row vectors of observations on the explanatory variables for individual i from the PT and RB tapes,

---

[5] If as discussed at the end of Section II, the person's decision problem were set up as a multiperiod optimization problem, the effects of concern about divine or moral disapprobations could be handled in a more explicit way. In this framework, the person could be considered as weighing the current utility from the affair against possible loss of utility in the future (perhaps in a future life) from divine or moral disapprobations.

respectively. Let α and β denote the corresponding column vectors of unknown coefficients. The stochastic specification of the model is then:

$$y_{PTi} \quad = \quad \bar{z}_i \alpha + u_{PTi} \quad \text{if RHS} > 0 \qquad i = 1, 2, \ldots, 601, \qquad (12a)$$
$$\quad = \quad 0 \qquad\qquad \text{if RHS } 0,$$

$$y_{RBi} \quad = \quad \bar{v}_i \beta + u_{RBi} \quad \text{if RHS} > 0 \qquad i = 1, 2, \ldots, 6{,}366, \qquad (12b)$$
$$\quad = \quad 0 \qquad\qquad \text{if RHS } 0,$$

where u_{PTi} and u_{RBi} are independently distributed error terms with distributions $N(0, \sigma^2_{PT})$ and $N(0, \sigma^2_{RB})$, respectively (RHS = right-hand side). This specification is consistent with the theoretical model in the sense that the variables in $\bar{z}_i$ and $\bar{v}_i$ have an effect y_{PTi} and y_{RBi} if the latter two are nonzero (no corner solutions), but not otherwise.

Tobit estimates are generally computed by some version of Newton's method, but with 6,366 observations this can be expensive. Tobit estimates can, however, as discussed in Fair (1977), be computed by a much simpler procedure and this is the procedure that was used for the work in this study. Some initial experimentation indicated that considerable computer time could be saved by the use of this procedure over Newton's method.

IV. The Results

The results of estimating equations (12a) and (12b) by the Tobit estimator are presented in table 3. Two sets of coefficient estimates are presented for each equation. For the first set all of the z_j or v_j variables in table 1 were used as explanatory variables; for the second set some of these variables were excluded.

The PT and RB results are in fairly close agreement. Variables that are clearly significant[6] are marital happiness (-), age (-), number of years married (+), and degree of religiosity (-). The signs of the coefficient estimates are as expected from table 2. The sex dummy variable, z_1, is not significant, which is also as expected from the discussion in the previous section. The fact that the coefficient estimates of age and length of marriage are significantly negative and positive, respectively, is interpreted from the theory to mean that utility from affairs declines with age and that utility from marriage declines with length of marriage. The negative significance of the religiosity variable means from the theory that utility from affairs declines with the degree of religiosity of the person. Finally, the high negative significance of the marital happiness variable indicates that it is a good proxy for a number of unobserved factors that have an effect on the utility from marriage.

---

[6] In what follows a variable will be said to be "significant" if its t-statistic in table 3 is greater than 1.65 in absolute value, 1.65 being the critical value of the t distribution with infinite degrees of freedom at the 95 percent confidence level for a one-tailed test.

TABLE 3
THE RESULTS

Variable		PT DATA*					RB DATA†			
		Coeff. Est.	t-Stat	Coeff. Est.	t-Stat		Coeff. Est.	t-Stat	Coeff. Est.	t-Stat
Constant	...	7.60	1.92	8.17	2.96	...	7.85	11.10	7.18	11.39
Occupation	z_7	.213	.67	.326	1.29	v_7	.314	3.77	.255	3.30
Education	z_6	.0252	.11	...	...	v_6	-.0853	-2.24	...	...
Husband's occupation	...	...	...	...	...	v_8	.0151	.27	...	...
Marital happiness	z_8	-2.27	-5.48	-2.28	-5.61	v_1	-1.53	-20.68	-1.53	-20.82
Age	z_2	-.193	-2.37	-.179	-2.26	v_2	-.107	-4.24	-.120	-4.91
No. years married	z_3	.533	3.63	.554	4.13	v_3	.130	4.82	.140	6.11
Children	z_4	1.02	.79	...	...	v_4	-.0285	-.36	...	...
Degree of religiosity	z_5	-1.70	-4.15	-1.69	-4.14	v_5	-.944	-11.03	-.950	-11.14
Sex	z_1	.945	.88	...	...	...	...	...	...	...
	$\hat{\sigma}^2_{PT}$	8.26	...	8.25	...	$\hat{\sigma}^2_{RB}$	4.50	...	4.50	...
No. observations		601‡		601‡			6,366§		6,366§	

NOTE. - "t-Stat." = ratio of coefficient estimate to estimated standard error of coefficient estimate.

*y_{PT} is dependent variable

† y_{RB} is dependent variable

‡ 150 nonzero

§ 2,053 nonzero

The results regarding the occupation and education variables are mixed. For the *PT* results neither variable is significant. For the *RB* results the estimates of the coefficients of the two variables are significant but of opposite signs, which is not as expected if both variables are positively correlated with the wage rate. The occupation variable had a higher *t*-statistic associated with it than did the education variable in each case in table 3, and so for the second set of estimates in each case the education variable was excluded from the equation. In both cases the sign of the estimate of the coefficient of the occupation variable is positive, which if the variable is a proxy for the wage rate implies from the analysis in Section II that the income effect of a change in the wage rate on the time spent in the affair is larger than the substitution effect. It is not clear, however, that much confidence should be placed on this result because of the overall mixed results regarding the occupation and education variables. It may be that neither variable is a good proxy for the wage rate.

For the *RB* results the estimate of the coefficient of the husband's occupation variable is of the expected positive sign, but it is not significant. It may also be that this variable is not a good proxy for the husband's wage rate (and thus for the value of goods supplied by the husband to the marriage), which would explain its lack of significance. For both the *PT* and *RB* results the children variable is insignificant. This means from the theory that children have no independent effect on the utility from the marriage. Any positive effects of children must be offset by a sufficient number of negative ones. This is not necessarily as expected, but it does seem to be what both the *PT* and *RB* data indicate.

V. Conclusion

The primary purpose of this paper has been to develop a model to explain the allocation of an individual's time among spouse, paramour, and work. The model can, however, be fairly easily applied to other types of leisure activities. The main motivation in this paper for considering leisure activities with more than one person is the same motivation that lies behind the postulation of more than one good in the utility function in classical demand theory, namely, that variety is important in life. Given this, it is of some interest to see if economic analysis can help explain the allocation of an individual's leisure time among various activities.

Although the data used in this study are far from ideal for testing the model as applied to extramarital affairs, the results in table 3 do lend some support to it. At the least, the results suggest that further tests of the model would be of interest. It is clear for any future tests of the model that better data on wage rates are needed. A better test of the model could also be performed if data on nonlabor income were available.

References

Becker, Gary S. "Crime and Punishment: An Economic Approach." *J.P.E.* 76, no. 2 (March/April 1968): 169-217.

_____ "A Theory of Marriage: Part I." *J.P.E.* 81, no. 4 (July/August 1973): 813-46.

Donne, John. "Elegie XVII. Variety." In *John Donne: Poetry and Prose,* edited by Frank J. Warnke. New York: Random House, 1967.

Fair, Ray C. "A Note on the Computation of the Tobit Estimator." *Econometrica* 45 (1977): 1723-27.

Hollingshead, August B. "Two-Factor Index of Social Position." Mimeographed. Yale Univ., 1957.

Kelley, Jonathan. "Sex and Social Bonds: A Theory." Mimeographed. Yale Univ., 1976.

Tobin, James. "Estimation of Relationships for Limited Dependent Variables." *Econometrica* 26 (January 1958): 24-36.

Can Economists Tell the Difference between Rigor and Rigor Mortis?

Let us remember the unfortunate econometrician who, in one of the major functions of his system, had to use a proxy for risk and a dummy for sex (Fritz Machlup).

"Has Formalization in Economics Gone too Far?"

The following five papers by Professors McCloskey, Katzner, Leamer, Caldwell, and Solow respectively were presented at the joint session of the International Network for Economic Method and the American Economic Association at the Annual Meeting of the latter in Washington, D.C., 28-30 December, 1990. The session was chaired by Professor Daniel R. Fusfeld.

Economics Science: A Search Through the Hyperspace of Assumptions?

Donald N. McCloskey
University of Iowa

It would of course be silly to object to the mere existence of mathematics in economics. No one wants to return to the time, not so distant, in which economists could not keep straight the difference between the movement of a curve and a movement along it.[1] Economics made progress without mathematics, but has made faster progress with it. Mathematics has brought transparency to many hundreds of economic arguments. The metaphor of the production function, the story of economic growth, the logic of competition, the facts of labor force participation would rapidly become muddled without mathematical expression. In fact muddled they once were. Most economists and I agree with Léon Walras, who wrote in 1900, "As for those economists who do not know any mathematics, who do not even know what is meant by mathematics and yet have taken the stand that mathematics cannot possibly serve to elucidate economic principles, let them go their way repeating that 'human liberty will *never* allow itself to be cast into equations' or that 'mathematics ignores frictions which are *everything* in social science" [p. 47].

But economists know that a qualitative argument for something does not automatically fix its optimal quantity. When America has market power in some exportable, and takes a selfish view, the economist can assert qualitatively that some tariff would improve on free trade. But an argument for the existence of an optimal tariff does not automatically tell how large the tariff should be, quantitatively speaking. Likewise, if some industries are monopolized, then forcing other industries to price exactly at marginal cost may be a bad idea, as a matter of qualitative, logical, on-off, what-might-possibly-happen truth. But the scientific question is quantitative. How far from competitive is the economy? What closeness to marginal cost would trigger the second best? How much marginal cost pricing can the economy stand?

In other words, economists do not need more existence theorems about the role of mathematics in economics - "there does not exist a mathematical economics that can take account of human liberty" or "there does not exist a rigorous economic argument unless in Bourbaki-style mathematics." To answer the quantitative question about the role of mathematical formalism in economics we need quantitative standards.

Comparison provides a quantitative standard. On several grounds, physics is a good standard for comparison. For one thing, economists share some human qualities with physicists. Economists like to think of themselves as the physicists of the social sciences, and they are. Like physicists they are political animals, in love with conferences and competition. They are hedgehogs, not foxes; they know one bit thing (F = ma;

$e = mc^2$; P=MC; MV = PT) not a large number of little things. They like to colonize other fields, the way biology was colonized after the War by physicists ashamed of making bombs. And economists are approximately as arrogant about the neighboring fields as physicists are.[2] The jokes that economists tell about sociologists and political scientists, without knowing anything about sociology or political science, are matched in physics by jokes about chemists and engineers. The chemist in the Manhattan Project who made the trigger for the bomb (a brilliant trick, without which no bomb) was praised by one of the physicists: "George, you're an absolutely first-rate chemist – which is to say, a good third-rate physicist!" Very funny.

For another, economists admire physicists and judge themselves, as do most people in our culture, to be intellectually inferior to the physicists. Like philology in the centuries of Scaliger, Erasmus, and Bentley, physics nowadays is at the top. Physicists have the most prestige among intellectual workers. The peculiarly English word "Science" (all other languages use the word to mean "systematic inquiry") has come to mean "a field of study close to what non-physicists imagine physics is like." The first-rate economists imagine themselves to be good third-rate physicists. Comparisons with sociology, then, would not be to the point, since economists, without knowing any sociologists, imagine sociologists to be inferior to economists. The standard of comparison should be the field we look up to rather than the one we look down upon.

Robert Solow has a good story on the matter. He was complaining at lunch one day to the Nobel laureate Victor Weisskopf about the dearth of really bright people in economics, "unlike physics," said Solow, in a bit of ill-advised humility. Weisskopf replied that such a situation did not sound like an equilibrium: if there were too few bright people in economics, then some of the marginally bright in physics could move over into economics and make their intellectual fortunes. So in equilibrium the marginal person would be equally bright. Solow was stunned and embarrassed. Here was a physicist inventing on the spot the economist's favorite argument and using it better than Solow himself to show that self-deprecation was not in order. The story says either that physicists are brighter than economists or, at another level, that they are not, and likewise for sociology. It's that way in the human sciences.

Most economists would accept physics as a standard for the use of mathematics. The empirical result of applying it is this: physics is less mathematical than modern economics.

The proposition sounds crazy. The average economist knows a lot less mathematics than the average physicist, as is apparent from the courses both take in college. Walk the aisles of the college bookstore and open some of the upper-division undergraduate books in physics (or in the much-despised civil engineering, for that matter). It makes the hair stand on end. Even the mathematically more sophisticated economists know less math than comparable physicists, if by "knowing math" one means "knowing about Bessel functions" or "knowing six ways to solve an ordinary differential equation" or even "knowing a lot about the theory of groups."

The proposition, however, does not say that economics *uses* more math; it says that economics is "more mathematical." In the Economics Department the Spirit of the Math Department reigns. The spirit is different over in the Physics Department. The great theoretical physicist Richard Feynman, for example, introduced a few simple theorems in matrix algebra into his first-year class at Cal Tech with considerable embarrassment [1963, Vol. I, 22-1]: "What is mathematics doing in a physics lecture? ... Mathematicians are mainly interested in how various mathematical facts are demonstrated ... They are not so interested in the result of what they prove." Feynman's rhetorical question startles an economist. In most first-year graduate programs in economics it would be rather "What else but mathematics should be in an economics lecture?" In physics the familiar spirit is Archimedes the experimenter. But in economics, as in mathematics, it is theorem-proving Euclid who paces the halls.

Economists know little about how physics operates as a field, and the physicists are amazed at the math-department character of economics. The new Santa Fe Institute, which brings the two groups together for the betterment of economics, has made the cultural differences plain. In 1989 *Science* described the physical scientists there as "flabbergasted to discover how mathematically rigorous theoretical economists are. Physics is generally considered to be the most mathematical of all the sciences, but modern economics has it beat" [Pool, p. 701]. The physicists do not regard the mathematical rigor as something to be admired. To the seminar question asked by an economist, "where are your proofs?", the physicist replies, "You can whip up theorems, but I leave that to the mathematicians" [701]. A physicist at the Institute solved a problem with a computer simulation, approximately, while the economist found an analytic solution. Who is the more mathematical?

Economists think that science involves axiomatic proofs of theorems and then econometric tests of the QED, which therefore will test the axioms. In truth the physicists could care less about mathematical proofs. Even the theoreticians in physics spend much of their time reading the physical equivalent of agricultural economists or economic historians. Pencil-and-paper guys are uncommon in physics departments. Physics is finding driven. Economics is theorem driven. Ask your local physicist what he thinks about proofs. He'll say, "Well, I prefer to depend on an existence theorem about existence theorems: if the mathematicians tell me they exist, fine; I reckon they know, but it ain't physics."

The economists, to put it another way, have adopted the intellectual values of the Math Department - not the values of the Departments of Physics or Electrical Engineering or Biochemistry they admire from afar. The situation is odd on its face. Philip Anderson, the distinguished physicist who brought the Sante Fe Institute together, explained the differences with "the differences in the amount of data available to the two fields" [701]. But economists are drenched in data, as hard as they want them to be. Odd.

No one would make the absurd claim, of course, that axiom and proof have no place of honor in economic reasoning. They do, and should, though economists might be more sensitive to Alfred Marshall's remark long ago that "the function then of analysis and deduction in economics is not to forge a few long chains of reasoning, but to forge rightly many short chains and single connecting links" [1920, p. 773]. We had better know that assumption A leads to conclusion C, although it would be a poor economics that only knew this.

But at the heart of axiom and proof as practiced in economics is a rhetorical problem, a failure to ask how large is large. As our own William Brock put it in 1988:

We remark, parenthetically, that when studying the natural science literature in this area it is important for the economics reader, especially the economic theorist brought up on the tradition of abstract general equilibrium theory, to realize that many natural scientists are not impressed by mathematical arguments showing that "anything can happen" in a system loosely disciplined by general axioms. Just showing existence of logical possibilities is not enough for such skeptics. The parameters of the system needed to get the erratic behavior must conform to parameter values established by empirical studies or the behavior must actually be documented in nature (p. 2 of typescript).

The problem, to put it formally, is that economists have fallen in love with existence theorems, the beloved also of the Math Department. There *exists* a canopener, somewhere. The most famous of these theorems is of course Arrow-Debreu, though I intend the word "existence theorem" to apply to all the qualitative theorems with which economists wile away their hours between 8:00 and quitting time. Significantly, what are commonly regarded as the first formal proofs of the existence of a competitive equilibrium, advanced during the 1920s and 1930s, were devised by professional mathematicians, John von Neumann and Abraham Wald. (Equally significantly, one could plausibly claim that Edgeworth had already proven the theorem, for merely N = 2, of course, but so what?)

From everywhere outside of economics except the Department of Mathematics the proofs of existence of competitive equilibrium, just to take them as concrete examples, will seem strange. They do not claim to show that an actual existing economy is in equilibrium, or that the equilibrium of an existing economy is desirable. The blackboard problem thus solved derives more or less vaguely from Adam Smith's assertion that capitalism is self-regulating and good. But the proofs of existence do not prove or disprove Smith's assertion. They show that certain equations describing a certain blackboard economy have a solution, but they do not give the solution to the blackboard problem, much less to an extant economy. Indeed, the problem is framed in such general terms that no specific solution even to the toy economy on the blackboard could reasonably be expected. The general statement that people buy less of something when its price goes up cannot yield specific answers, such as $4598 billion.[3] The proofs state that somewhere in the mathematical universe there exists a solution. Lord knows what it is; we humans only know that it exists.

The usual way the quest for existence is justified is to say that, after all, we had better know that solutions exist before we go looking for them. Ask an economist why she's so interested in existence theorems and this is the answer you will get. Of course, the economist giving it does not then go out and look for parameterized and empirical solutions. But nobody's perfect. The answer anyway sounds reasonable: if you can't actually find it, nonetheless know that what you're looking for exists. Judging again from physics, however, it is not reasonable. Physicists have happily used the Schrödinger equation since 1926 without knowing whether it has solutions in general. The three-body problem in Newtonian physics does not possess known solutions in general. Yet astronomers can tell you with sufficient accuracy for most of the questions they ask where the moon will be next year. For that matter, poets can write particular *terza rima* poems without knowing whether the form has in general a solution possessing optimal properties. Whether a solution under assumption A exists in general is irrelevant if the physical or economic or poetic question has to do with a particular finite case under assumption A' merely close to A.

The way the mathematical rhetoric has been transformed into economic rhetoric has been to *define* the economic problem as dealing with a certain kind of (easily manipulable) mathematics. One searches under the lamppost because the light there is good. The notions of "equilibrium" and "maximization" in economics have been treated in such a way [Weintraub 1991; Mirowski 1990]. Many economists have claimed that Adam Smith's question *is* the mathematical one of existence. The move is doubtful as intellectual history. Smith used the phrase "the invisible hand" only once (albeit in each of his books) and it is not until the coming of mathematical values in economics that the matter of existence was considered to be important.

But what is more unhappy is that a proof of existence leaves every concrete question unresolved, while enticing some of the best minds in the business into perfecting the proofs. With certain assumptions about preferences and technology one can write down equations which can be shown to have somewhere out there a solution (and sometimes, more to the point, even a stable solution, insensitive to trembling hands). Naturally the result, which is about the equations, not about the economy, depends on the assumptions. The task has been to vary the assumptions and see what happens. Unsurprisingly, under some assumptions the equilibrium does exist and under others it does not; under some assumptions the equilibrium is efficient and under others it is not.

Well, so what? Sometimes it rains and sometimes it does not. In some universes the moon is made of green cheese and in others it is not. None of the theorems and counter theorems of general equilibrium theory has been surprising in a qualitative sense. *But this is the only sense they have.* They are not quantitative theorems. They are mathematics without numbers, of great and proper interest inside the Department of Mathematics, but of little interest to quantitative intellectuals.

The problem is that the general theorem does not relate to anything an economist would actually want to know. We already know for example that if the world is not perfect the outcomes of the world cannot be expected to be perfect. This much we know by being adults. But economists arguing over the federal budget next year or the stability of capitalism forever want to know *how big* a particular badness or offsetting goodness will be. Will the distribution of income be radically changed by the abandonment of interest? Will free trade raise American national income? It is useless to be told that if there is not a complete market in every commodity down to and including chewing gum then there is no presumption that capitalism will work efficiently. Yet that is a typical piece of information from the mathematical front lines. It does not provide the economic scientist with a scale against which to judge the significance of the necessary deviations from completeness. Chewing gum or all investment goods: it does not matter for the proof.

Practical people, including most economists, understand Adam Smith's optimism about the economy as asserting something like this: economies that are approximately competitive are approximately efficient, if approximate externalities and approximate monopolies and approximate ignorance do not significantly intervene;

and anyway they are approximately progressive in a way that the static assertion does not pretend to deal with, even approximately. The claim has analogies to the theorems of general equilibrium theory (say: similar fuzzy but highly relevant claims are made in other parts of economics). But except on the knife edge of exact results, where a set of measure zero lives, the theorems are not rigorously relevant. If we are going to be rigorous we should be rigorous, not rigorous about the proof and extremely sloppy about its range of application.[4] The theorems are exact results, containing no definition of the neighborhood in which they are approximately correct.

The exact existence theorems may be worth having, though why exactly it is worth having needs to be argued more rigorously than it has been so far – a matter of rhetorical, not mathematical, rigor, but rigor all the same. Mathematical economics has not been sufficiently rigorous about its arguments.

To put it rigorously, the procedure of modern economics is too much a search through the hyperspace of conceivable assumptions. In the second of his *Three Essays on the State of Economic Science* (1957) Tjalling Koopmans argued for precisely such a program of research, referring to a "card file" of logical results connecting a sequence of assumptions A, A', A", A'", ... A^N to the corresponding conclusions C, C', C", and so forth. He specifically wished to separate blackboard economics from empirical economics, "for the health of both." Economists should have a theoretical branch and an empirical branch (which he thought was going to result in an imitation of physics). The theoretical branch should devote itself to "a sequence of models".

Koopmans' program has been widely accepted. In 1984, for example, Frank Hahn thought he was answering the objection that anything can happen in general theorising by saying: "It is true that often many things can be the case in a general theory but not that anything can be. Everyone who knows the textbooks can confirm that" (p.6). What he means is that the textbooks line up the sequence of assumptions A, A', A", ... with the conclusions C, C', C", ... True enough. But of course it is not an answer to the objection that in economic theorizing, contrary to its declared love of rigor, in fact anything goes. I conjecture the following important:

Metatheorem on Hyperspaces of Assumptions

For each and every assumption A implying a conclusion C and for each alternative conclusion C' arbitrarily far from C (for example, disjoint with C), there exists an alternative assumption A' arbitrarily close to the original assumption A, such that A' implies C'.

I have not been able to devise a proof, but you can whip one up; anyway, as an empirical scientist, I leave that to the mathematicians. The empirical evidence is overwhelming. Name a conclusion, C, in recent but not last year's formal economics – say, that rational expectations obviates government policy or that interaction in many different markets makes for closer collusion of oligopolists. Observe that by now there have appeared numerous proofs that alternative assumptions A' or A", which for most purposes look awfully close to the original A, result in C' or C" – that government policy outwits rational expectations or that the oligopolists are nonetheless unable to achieve collusion.[5]

The problem, to repeat, is a rhetorical one. The prestige of mathematical argument led economists to believe, contrary to their discipline, that the economist could get something intellectually for nothing, proving or disproving great social truths by writing on a blackboard. Programs of research since the 1940s that focused on existence theorems have for a time been rhetorically successful, until the economists have realized once again that after all nothing has been concluded. Besides the general equilibrium program itself, one can mention the 2 x 2 x 2 program of international trade, the theory of international finance, and the rational expectations revolution in macroeconomics. The economists responsible for these excellent ideas have wandered off into a discussion of whether or not an equilibrium exists for this or that "setting" and what its character might be, qualitatively speaking.

They have seldom asked in ways that would persuade other economists how large the effects were. They have not asked how large is large. Eventually they have gotten bored with the formal tool of the day and have walked off to develop a new one. For example, game theory is beginning (for the third time in its brief history) to bore economists; evolutionary theory stands enticingly ready to fuel careers and then to be abandoned in its turn. The economists, though they talk about it quite a lot, and sneer at lesser breeds without the law such as lawyers and sociologists, have not taken the rhetoric of science seriously, and have retreated from the library and laboratory to the blackboard. The research in many fields of economics does not cumulate. It circles.

The problem was brought into focus by the philosopher Allan Gibbard and the mathematical economist Hal Varian some time ago. "Much of economic theorizing," they noted (without intent to damn it), "consists not ... of forming explicit hypotheses about situations and testing them, but of investigating economic models" [1978, p. 676]. That's right. Economic literature is largely speculative, an apparently inconclusive exploration of possible worlds. In defending the excess of speculation over testing in economics journals Gibbard and Varian use a phrase heard a lot in the hallways: "When we vary the assumptions of a model in this way to see how the conclusions change, we might say we are *examining the robustness of the model*" [same page]. Economists commonly defend their chief activity by saying that running through every conceivable model will show them the crucial assumptions. They have embarked so to speak on a fishing expedition in the hyperspace of possible worlds.

The trouble is that they have not caught any fish with the theoretical line. The activity works as science only when it gets actual numbers to fish in. But economic speculation does not use actual numbers. It makes qualitative arguments, such as existence theorems. (Paul Samuelson, who founded the present paradigm in economics, spent a good deal of time in his book of marvels published in 1947 trying to derive *qualitative* theorems; he did not show the way to empirical work. Maybe for all his astounding excellences Samuelson in this respect set economics off in the wrong direction.)

What economics needs, say Gibbard and Varian, is a quantitative rhetoric, telling how large is large:

> When a model is applied to a situation as an approximation, an aspiration level epsilon is set for the degree of approximation of the conclusions. What is hypothesized is this: there is a delta such that (i) the assumptions of the applied model are true to a degree of approximation delta, and (ii) in any possible situation to which the model could be applied, if the assumption of that applied model

were true to degree of approximation delta, its conclusions would be true to degree epsilon. [pp. 671-72]

That sounds good. Yet they realize that the degree of approximation of this desirable, physical, engineering rhetoric to economics is poor. In the next sentence they concede that "Of course ... few if any of the degrees of approximation involved are characterized numerically" [p. 672]. Oh, oh. Wasn't that the point? If the literature of economics consists largely of *qualitative* explorations of possible models, what indeed *is* its point? Don't we already know that there exist an unbounded number of solutions to an unbounded number of equations? Where, one might ask will it end?

Gibbard and Varian are uneasily aware of how crushing their remark is. They conclude lamely "but the pattern of explanation is, we think, the one we have given" [same page]. Well, be quantitative. Within what neighborhood of radius epsilon does economic theory, high-brow - or low, approximate the quantitative procedures that are routine in physics, applied math, labor economics, or quantitative economic history?

Varying the assumptions of economic models with no rhetorical plan in mind because "it's interesting to see what happens" when assumption A is replaced by assumption A', – is not science but mathematics. It is the search through the hyperspace of assumptions. A long time ago I helped interview a young man who had written a thesis weakening one of the assumptions in Arrow's Impossibility Theorem. We asked him mildly what the scientific uses of such a result might be. The youth waxed wroth: "What! Don't you understand? I have *weakened* an assumption in *Arrow's Impossibility Theorem!*" Here was someone from the Math Department, at least in spirit.

Scientists think differently. When the economic historian Robert Fogel varies an assumption he plans to strengthen his economic case by biasing the findings against himself. When Richard Feynman cut the safety seals of the space shuttle engine with a kitchen knife he also had an *a fortiori* plan in mind. The most prestigious research method in modern economics, imitated at all levels of mathematical competence in the field, has no such rhetorical plan.

The rhetorical problem, to repeat, is that economists have taken over the intellectual values of the wrong subjects. It is not that the values or the subjects are intrinsically bad. No reasonable person could object to such values flourishing within the Department of Mathematics. Splendid. Some of all our best friends are mathematicians. Capital. The problem comes when the economists abandon an economic question in favor of a mathematical one, and then forget to come back to the Department of Economics. Questions of existence or questions that ring the changes on the mathematical object itself might be of interest to mathematics, regardless of how remote. Unless they can be shown to bear directly on a dispute in economic science, however, they are not of interest to economics.

The problem lies in the sort of mathematics used, which is to say the details of the formal methods. Physicists and engineers routinely state the bounds within which their assertions hold approximately true and then they tell how true. Listen to page 3 of one of the leading textbooks, in engineering mechanics:

> In mechanics models or idealizations are used in order to simplify application of the theory ... A *particle* has a mass but a size that can be neglected. For example, the size of the earth is insignificant compared to the size of its orbit ... *Rigid Body* ... In most cases, the actual deformations occurring in structures ... are relatively small ... *Concentrated Force* ... We can represent the effect of the loading by a concentrated force, providing the area ... is *small* compared to the overall size of the body. (Hibbeler, 1989, p. 3)

Such talk about magnitudes is foreign in economics. It is surprising to both their students and to their colleagues in physics and engineering that in what economists regard as their chief scientific work they do not talk about magnitudes at all. Of course, when they come to advise on policy or reconstruct past economies the bounds of error must be stated, and often are, with wonderful skill. On the blackboard, where they spend most of their time, however, economists routinely forget to say how large is large. They have taken over unawares the intellectual ideals of that admirable, excellent department where existence is all important and magnitude is irrelevant. The economists are in love with the wrong mathematics, the pure rather than the applied.

It is not fair, in other words, to blame the Department of Mathematics for the economist's love of existence theorems. In fact, it is not fair to blame the mathematical economists themselves. Even non-mathematical economists have always loved existence theorems. It is said that economists would have had to reinvent the calculus for their own lovely marginal analysis if it had not already been invented; likewise they would have had to reinvent fixed point lemmas.

It's not a matter of the use of mathematical notation. A mathematical spirit pervades the works of David Ricardo (Schumpeter called the spirit The Ricardian Vice), who used no mathematics. The physiocrats, too, were attempting to solve great social questions by manipulating definitions. The Ricardian Vice has little or nothing to do with the use of *mathematical* formalism. It is formalism, whether of words or statistics or mathematics, that creates the false hope that the blackboard is all we need. The wholly verbal Austrian economists are as much in love with their own sort of formalism, and hostile to the notion that science might have to come off the blackboard, as is the most math-besotted graduate of Berkeley or Minnesota. The older sort of Marxian economists are, too. System is what people want, as Francis Bacon promised in sounding the bell that gathered the wits, "the business done as if by machine."

Among the oldest questions in economics, after all, is a theorem about whether, as Bernard Mandeville put it in the early 18th century, private vice can be a public benefit: "Thus every Part was full of Vice. Yet the whole Mass a Paradise." Are social systems automatically virtuous as well as automatically stable? No numbers are expected in the answer, which is a tip-off that social philosophy, not social physics, is in question. It is to be done at the blackboard or the lecture podium, not in the world of measurement. A modern student of the matter, known as the Hobbes Problem, is the non-mathematical but Nobel economist James Buchanan; and another the philosopher Robert Nozick; and another the lawyer and judge Richard Posner; and scores of lesser lights, none of whom can be accused of making a fetish out of mathematics. The non-mathematical existence theorems are as peculiar as the mathematical ones. Why would it matter for a worldly philosophy whether or not a knife-edge existence theorem could be proven? Unless it concerns the relevant quantitative questions *how* full of vice, *how* paradisical – the theorem will not enlighten economics.

The problem, again, is not the presence of logic or mathematics – plainly, systematic imagination will often need them. The problem, as one can see clearly in these non-mathematical cases, is the strange rhetoric of existence theorems.

The classic definition of economics is Marshall's: "a study of mankind in the ordinary business of life" (p. 1). The literary critic Northrup Frye would extend the definition: "The fundamental job of the imagination in ordinary life ... is to produce, out of the society we have to live in, a vision of the society we want to live in" (1964, p. 140). Mathematical economics, and indeed theory generally, should be viewed as poetry in this act of imagination. Poets are not mere luxuries. We need their constructs – although it should be noted that we do not need large numbers of third-rate constructs any more than we need lots of third-rate poetry. The third rate in empirical work is still useful, something on which one can build. The third rate in theoretical work is perfectly useless, even bad for one's soul, the way that Edgar Guest or even Robert Bridges is.

The advantage of looking at theorists this way is that they are cut off from their false claim of physics-mimicking scientificity. They are bards, imaginaries, mathematicians. One of them, Brock again, speaks of his work explicitly in such terms, as for example (1989, p. 443), "chaos theory unfetters our imagination ... [L]ike much of abstract economic theory, it may give us a hint of how to formulate better empirical models even though the guidance is still rather limited".

The intellectual values of poets are not to be taken as a guide to science. The rhetoric of existence theorems elevates consistency to the only intellectual virtue – not merely the most important or the one necessary, but the only one. "A foolish consistency," the American philosopher said, "is the hobgoblin of little minds, adored by little statesmen and philosophers and divines." The singleminded pursuit of consistency is the Math Department's value. In economics it is too often a foolish consistency.

Alan Turing, the great mathematician, had a good-natured debate in 1939 with Ludwig Wittgenstein, the still greater philosopher (who was trained, not incidentally, as an aeronautical engineer):

Wittgenstein: the question is: Why are people afraid of contradictions? It is easy to understand why they should be afraid of contradictions in orders, descriptions, etc., *outside* mathematics. The question is: Why should they be afraid of contradictions inside mathematics? Turing says. "Because something may go wrong with the application." But nothing need go wrong. [D.N. Mc.: the word "need" in the sentence should probably be emphasized; cf. Friedman's methodology.] And if something does go wrong – if the bridge breaks down – then your mistake was of the kind of using a wrong natural law ...
Turing: You cannot be confident about applying your calculus until you know that there is no hidden contradiction in it.
Wittgenstein: There seems to be an enormous mistake there ... Suppose I convince Rhees of the paradox of Liar, and he says, "I lie, therefore I do not lie, therefore I lie and I do not lie, therefore we have a contradiction, therefore 2 x 2 = 369." [D.N.Mc.: Wittgenstein here refers to the logical proposition that an accepted contradiction allows one formally to prove any false proposition whatever.] Well, we should not call this "multiplication," that is all ...
Turing: Although you do not know that the bridge will fall if there are no contradictions, yet it is almost certain that if there are contradictions it will go wrong somewhere.
Wittgenstein: But nothing has ever gone wrong that way yet ...

Andrew Hodges, a mathematical physicist and the biographer of Turing, writes of this exchange:

But Alan would not be convinced. For any pure mathematician, it would remain the beauty of the subject, that argue as one might about its meaning, the system stood serene, self-consistent, self-contained. Dear love of mathematics! Safe, secure world in which nothing could go wrong, no trouble arise, no bridges collapse! So different from the world of 1939 (p. 154)

The mathematician's mad pursuit of consistency (for which in the 1920s and 1930s the gods rewarded him, in part through this very Alan Turing, with rigorous proofs of its ultimate impossibility) is aesthetic, not practical. The poet's values surface again. Whatever may be its merits in mathematics (and there are doubters even there; Kline 1980, p. 352), the aestheticization of science is bad. The main argument that economists appear to have in favor of an argument is that it is "deep" or "elegant," as against "ad hoc." I would suggest that the reason they have such a non-rigorous vocabulary of persuasion is that they are not aware they are persuading. In any event, taking over the persuasive rhetoric of the Math Department is not a good idea. Economics is a science, not a branch of mathematics.

In the end the engineer's criterion is what matters: does it work? Quantitatively speaking, has the formalism of economics resulted in good science? The question is complicated, but by now, after forty years of rigorous trial it is fair to ask what has been learned. It is not fair to claim in answer simply the number of theorems or papers. The mathematician Stanislaw Ulam calculates that some 200,000 theorems are proven annually in mathematics (1976, p. 288). The NSF reckons that some 2,000,000 articles are published each year in science, from 20,000 journals. Such figures suggest the question whether much of it matters. What ideas that matter have come out of the formalization of economics?

In 1965 one could stand back from the program of formalization in economics and remark wisely that economics needed to invest a little in searching the hyperspace of assumptions, because perhaps in 50 years one of the theorems will become empirically relevant. We should tolerate the mathematical economists for a while. After all, said the tolerant sages, non-Euclidean geometry was useless at its birth but proved to be just what Einstein needed.

There are three practical problems with such tolerance. First, it is no longer 1965. It is 25 years on, and we have still yet to see the payoff. In the meantime the empirical parts of economics have taught us all manner of things, that we now will always know, about how economies actually work. The second problem is that economists think that being a social physicist means not having to read anything that is older than the last round of xerox preprints. So economists reinvent the wheel, and the claim that old theorems will come back into use is undermined. Monopolistic competition, for example,

example, keeps getting reinvented. Likewise, economists reinvent every few years the point that pure bargaining, being language (which always can be trumped by itself, has no solution. There is no point piling up theorems whose half-life is six month. Or more exactly, to recur to the quantitative theme, the number of them we presently produce seems grossly non-optimal. Wassily Leontief recently categorized the articles in the leading journals in physics, chemistry, economics, and sociology. In physics and chemistry the theoretical papers were about 10 or 15 percent of the total. In economics (and sociology, perish the thought) the figure was about 50 percent.

I hesitate to articulate the third practical problem with continuing to tolerate the large scale of formalization in economics, because it will seem mean spirited. It probably is. I feel mean about it. But someone has to say it, because everyone knows it is true: A dominant coalition of the formalizers are not themselves tolerant of science. It is an open secret that they want economics to become a branch of the Math Department. What is most objectionable about their want is that they are willing to act as *homines economici* in a rigorous sense to achieve it. One economics department after another has been seized by the formalists and marched off to a Gulag of hyperspace searching. Few graduate programs in economics teach economics, especially to first-year students. They teach "tools," tools which become obsolete every five years or so.

Partly this is because of the vocabulary we use. The leading middle-aged economists laugh when Gary Becker is described as a "theorist" and the leading young economists do not even think it is funny. The way first-year graduate programs are structured is a direct result of such terminological confusion. If you do not know anything about any actual economy, the argument goes, perhaps you had better be assigned to the "theory" sequence. "Theory" will at least be your comparative advantage.

Whatever the merits of the argument for static allocation, it has had dismal effects dynamically speaking. It has resulted in graduate students who believe (until experience drives the madness out) that economics is about certain mathematical objects called "economies". The students have no incentive to learn about the economy. When Arjo Klamer and David Colander asked graduate students whether having a thorough knowledge of the economy was a very important thing to have for academic success in economics only 3.4 percent said it was [1990, p. 18]. Nor do the students have an incentive to learn about economic theory beyond that embodied in certain mathematical books (only 10 percent said it was very important to have a knowledge of the literature of economics). Such students become teachers and practitioners who do not understand economics: micro teachers, say, who do not grasp opportunity cost and cannot think about entry; macroeconomists who have not read Keynes; policymakers who do not know the history of their section of the economy.

Their ignorance is commonly defended by saying that, well, they certainly did acquire in their education a lot of "tools". But the tool kit turns out to be filled mainly with bits of mathematics that in five years will become unfashionable again (in favor of other "tools": witness the history of linear programming in economics). Broken power routers and defective power jigsaws have crowded out the hammers and nails.

The problem of a training in technique that does not deal with life appears to be a widespread modern problem. Look at modern art, School of Manhattan, if you can, or modern architecture, from Bauhaus to our house. In a recent essay the critic John Aldridge attacks what is known in English departments as "the workshop writer," that is, the product of one of the numerous programs that teach writing in imitation of the University of Iowa's original Workshop. His description of "that odd species of bloodless fiction so cherished by the editors of *the New Yorker*" would fit most graduate programs in economics. Try substituting "academic economists " for "writers," "economic research" for "writing," and "economics" for "literature":

> [W]hat finally counts ... is not the quality of the work produced but the continued existence and promotion of writers. Any question raised about quality would surely be considered a form of treason or self-sabotage [I]t is entirely possible for a young writer to be graduated from one of these programs in almost total ignorance of the traditions of his craft and, for that matter, with only superficial knowledge of literature ... [O]ften the promise they show is the variety most young people show up to the age of about twenty-five,

> while other qualities more essential to the continued productivity of writers are not so immediately detectable ... [T]hese writers are not only estranged from their culture but seem to have no impressions of, or relations to it at all. In fact, they show no symptoms of having vital social and intellectual interests of any kind or any sense of belonging to a literary tradition ... [A]ny of their novels and stories might conceivably have been written by almost any one of them. (pp. 31, 32, 33, 37)

The benefits, I claim, have been meagre. The physics standard shows that something is wrong. Another standard is the scale of promised and then boldly claimed accomplishments. To hear mathematical economists say it, you would think that mathematical economics would bring us to a Newtonian stage in the science. In a review of Kenneth Arrow's collected works Frank Hahn made the following assertion: "The theory which Arrow and his coevals and successors have built is all we have of honest and powerful thinking on the subject." "The subject" appears to be economics. Suppose, to be generous, that Hahn means rather "the subject" to be the narrower matter of thinking about the desirability of capitalism since Adam Smith. Even so, his claim that general equilibrium has afforded "that precise formulation which would allow [Adam Smith's arguments] to be evaluated and their range of applicability discussed" will seem unreasonable to many economists. It is similarly unreasonable to say that "the case for modern economics" rests on the achievements of one who "has only concerned himself with establishing what it is that can be claimed as true if certain assumptions are made," when the " assumptions" are formal only, the product of the blackboard rather than of the library or of the world.

To ask the question of what we have learned from formalization since the War is to suggest that the yield has been rather modest.[6] We have learned more in economics from our continuing traditions of political arithmetic and economic philosophy. Human capital, the economics of law and society, historical economics, and the statistics of economic growth have come from economists who trade with someone besides the Math Department.

This is not, I repeat, to set *The Journal Of Economic Theory* below its proper value.

Surely we should have people doing some sort of philosophical job, finding out how much can be wrung from this or that convenient assumption, though we should not assign quite so many people to the job as at present. We are all very thankful to Smith and Marx and Keynes for having inspired those fine theorems by Hahn and Arrow and Samuelson. But we should not be thankful for the reduction of "theory" to a certain brand of mathematics.

In other ways, however, I stand four square with Frank Hahn: "[All] these 'certainties' and all the 'schools' which they spawn are a sure sign of our ignorance ... [I]t is obvious to me that we do not possess much certain knowledge about the economic world and that our best chance of gaining more is to try in all sorts of directions and by all sorts of means. This will not be furthered by strident commitments of faith" [pp. 7-8].

And I stand, too, with our sainted Léon, he of general economic equilibrium a century ago. He attacked then (p. 48) "the idea, so bourgeois in its narrowness, of dividing education into two separate compartments: one turning out calculators with no knowledge whatsoever of sociology, philosophy, history, or [even, McC.] economics; and the other cultivating men of letters devoid of any notion of mathematics. The twentieth century, which is not far off, will feel the need, even in France, of entrusting the social sciences to men of general culture who are accustomed to thinking both inductively and deductively and who are familiar with reason as well as experience." The 21st century hurries near. We may hope by then, after a century of experiments in educational compartments, that Walras' vision of an undivided economics may be fulfilled.

Notes

1. Look for instance at the presidential address of Harry A. Millis to the American Economic Association (delivered December, 1934), especially pp. 4-5 on marginal productivity and the labor problem. Because he did not understand the notion of a function Millis misunderstood Hicks' *Theory of Wages.*

2. Richard Palmer, a physicist from Duke University recalling a conference of physicists and economists, told Robert Pool, "I used to think physicists were the most arrogant people in the world. The economists were, if anything, more arrogant" [1989, 700].

3. I am speaking of neoclassical economics; but anti-neoclassicals should not therefore rejoice. They do the same thing. In Marxian economics, for example, the general statement that commodities are made with commodities cannot be expected to yield specific answers to any question worth asking, either. The various impossibility theorems that make institutional economists happy ("But after all the

economy is obviously not competitive and so all that neoclassical talk is rubbish") are equally vacuous.

4. The recent works of William Milberg at the University of Michigan-Dearborn and of Hans Lind at the University of Stockholm have noted the lack of rigor in the opening and closing paragraphs of theoretical papers. Great rigor in the middle; touchie-feelie on the ends.

5. For that last see Fisher 1989, p. 122.

6. A full catalogue is examined in Henry Woo's book, *What's Wrong with Formalization in Econonmics.*

References

Aldridge, John W. 1990. "The New American Assembly-Line Fiction: An Empty Blue Center." *American Scholar* Winter: 17-38.

Brock, W. A. 1988. "Introduction to Chaos and Other Aspects of Nonlinearity." In W. A. Brock and A. G. Malliaris, eds. *Differential Equations, Stability, and Chaos in Dynamic Economics.* NY: North Holland, (October 30, 1987 draft, Department of Economics, University of Wisconsin).

Brock, William A. 1989. "Chaos and Complexity in Economic and Financial Science". Pp. 421-447 in George M. Furstenberg, ed. *Acting Under Uncertainty: Multidisciplinary Conceptions.* Boston: Kluwer Academic.

Feynman, Richard. 1963. *The Feynman Lectures on Physics.* Reading, Massachusetts: Addison-Wesley. Vol. I.

Fisher, Franklin M. 1989. "Games Economists Play: A Noncooperative View." *RAND Journal of Economics* 20(Spring): 113-124.

Frye, Northrup. 1964. *The Educated Imagination.* Bloomington: Indiana University Press.

Hahn, Frank. 1984. *Equilibrium and Macroeconomics.* Oxford: Basil Blackwell.

Hahn, Frank. 1986. "Review of Collected Works of Kenneth Arrow." *Times Literary Supplement* (August).

Hibbeler, R. C. 1989. *Engineering Mechanics: Statics and Dynamics.* 5thed. New York: Macmillan.

Hodges, Andrew. 1983. *Alan Turing: The Enigma.* New York: Simon and Schuster.

Klamer, Arjo, and David Collander. 1990. *The Making of an Economist* Boulder: Westview Press.

Kline, Morris. 1980. *Mathematics: The Loss of Certainty.* New York: Oxford University Press.

Marshall. Alfred. 1920. *Principles of Economics.* London: Macmillan.

Millis, Harry A. 1935. "The Union in Industry: Some Observations on the Theory of Collective Bargaining." *American Economic Review.* 25 (March): 1-13.

Mirowski. 1989. *More Heat Than Light.* NY: Cambridge University Press.

Pool, Robert. "Strange Bedfellows." *Science* 245 (18 August 1989): 700-703.

Walras, Léon. *Elements of Pure Economics.* Fourth Ed.(1926). trans. William Jaffé. Homewood, Ill.: Irwin, 1954 (Orion reprint, 1984).

Weintraub, Roy. 1991. *Stabilizing Dynamics: Constructing Economic Knowledge.* Cambridge: Cambridge University Press.

Woo, Henry K. H. 1986. *What's Wrong with Formalization in Economics? An Epistemological Critique.* Newark, California:Victoria Press.

In Defense of Formalization in Economics[1]

Donald W Katzner
University of Massachusetts

These days, it seems, a lot of people are dissatisfied with a lot of economic analysis. Numerous articles and books have been written detailing complaints.[1] Numerous sessions at conventions take up the issue. One often sees and hears words such as "malaise," "disarray," and "crisis" applied to describe the current state of affairs. In perhaps the strongest rebuke of received economic theory yet, one of its founding fathers, none other than J.R. Hicks [8, p. 365], repudiated his own work by altering his identity: "Clearly I need to change my name," he wrote in 1975. "Let it be understood that *Value and Capital* (1939) was the work of J. R. Hicks, a 'neoclassical' economist now deceased; *Capital and Time* (1973) - and *A Theory of Economic History* (1969) - are the works of John Hicks, a non-neoclassic who is quite disrespectful toward his 'uncle'." Much of Hicks' subsequently published work appears under the newly-assumed name of its author.

On the list of objectionable facets of economic analysis singled out for special complaint, the formalization of economic reasoning is often at or near the top.[2] Witness, for example, Prest's advice [28, p. 131] to the aspiring graduate student of economics: "The suggested Ph.D. thesis title 'n solutions to n - 1 problems' is a very promising theme for an academic career devoted to High Theory. Nowadays this is the super-highway to eminence and professional acclaim. And you will very quickly discover that your standing and stature will rise in geometrical proportion to the irrelevance and obscurity of what you say and write. Abraham Lincoln was wrong here: "you can fool all of the people all of the time - without much effort, either." I want to argue in this paper, however, that formalization *per se* is not the problem, and that the real difficulty lies in the nature of the questions that economists tend to ask and in the assumption-content of the analyses constructed to provide the answers. Indeed, formalization is, for many of us, a powerful and appropriate means of analytical expression whose avoidance would only weaken our incisiveness and create more problems than its non-use would resolve.[4]

Even the argument of Prest's advice relies on a formalization that relates "standing and stature" proportionally to spoken or written "irrelevance and obscurity."

It should be noted at the outset that although it certainly has contact-points with both areas, what follows is neither an essay on methodology or epistemology. There are a variety of methodologies and epistemologies in economics and most make room for formalization in analysis, using and interpreting their analytical structures in a variety of ways.[5] However, the present discussion accepts the dominant methodology and epistemology in economics today which is based on a separation or dichotomy between reality and thoughts about reality and which, at least epistemologically, results in rationalism or empiricism or some combination thereof. Also accepted are the currently existing standards of scholarly discourse that have emerged from this background. Thus the issues considered here have not so much to do with the general implications of methodology and epistemology for formalization and vice versa, but are concerned, rather, with certain kinds of things that can be said of formalization given the methodology and epistemology employed.

I

Let me begin by defining the concept of formalization and discussing its properties, its purpose, and what it does.

The aim of analysis is to explain or clarify worldly phenomena. Analysis proceeds by organizing and exploring the thoughts one has about those phenomena. The explanations that are achieved may or may not carry with them an ability to predict. In economics there are a number of routes such organizations and explorations may take. To analyze by example requires the examination of highly detailed specific instances or case studies to illustrate the phenomena under consideration. Another form of analysis, storytelling, is the giving of a narrative account of the phenomena in which "... fact, theory, and values are all mixed together in the telling."[6] But the most common method of analysis in economics involves the creation and study of models. A model of something - call the thing T - is a construct having enough in common with the observable facets of T that insight into T can be obtained by studying the model. Albert Einstein and Leopold Infeld [5, p. 33] gave the following illustration for physical models: Imagine you are presented with a watch and asked to explain how it works, but are not allowed to remove its cover. One way to proceed is to obtain appropriate springs, gears, and what not,[7] and build a "model" of the watch whose behavior duplicates the observed behavior of the original. You could then give an explanation of how your model behaves, and say that the original watch works analogously to, or as if it were, your model. Clearly, there are many different models, and hence explanations, that could be built. But all explanations function by identifying something in the model (here, the movement of the model's "hands") with what is observed (the movement of the hands on the original watch). In economics, of course, models are usually not physical things. Rather they are mental constructs based on assumptions, abstract concepts and relations among variables. But they function in much the same way as in the Einstein-Infeld example. Thus, in economics, model-building is different from description and from analysis by example in that it essays to provide an explanation of the thing being scrutinized; it is different from storytelling in that it focuses on relations among variables rather than on narrative. Note, however, that particular economic analyses may combine examples, storytelling, and model-building, as well as other forms of argument in their structures.

With these ideas in mind, formalization in economics may be defined as the development and analysis of relations among variables that constitute part (or all) of an economic model.[8] The relations themselves may be, to a greater or lesser degree, "appropriate" or "relevant," and may or may not identify or be associated with directions of causality thought to be inherent in the phenomena under investigation. Thus the purpose of formalization in economic analysis is to explain - some would add predict - observable economic phenomena.[9] Formalization is neither description nor analysis by example or storytelling in the same way that model-building, as indicated above, is not. The term "formalization" is also used, on occasion, to denote the end result of the process of formalization just described, i.e., to indicate the relations themselves. The name "formalism" is given to the special case of formalization in which the properties of the relations, as well as the implications of these properties, are fully spelled out.

Four observations concerning this notion of formalization should be noted. First, it is implicit in the definition of formalization given above that there should exist, in formalizations that are meaningfully relevant to the economic reality under examination, acceptable accordances between the model of which the formalization is a part and the observed facets of the phenomena being explained.[10] Although I will not attempt here to describe what constitutes "acceptable accordances" between a model and reality, most assuredly each economist has some idea of that which is acceptable to him, if not the acceptability standards of the economics profession at large. Furthermore, these accordances are crucial to the acceptability of both the model proposed as well as the formalizations it contains. Without such accordances, any analysis based on the model or any of its individual formalizations would be regarded as having little significance and relevance for the phenomena under investigation.

Second, formalization does not require that the variables under consideration be capable of measurement.[11] In the absence of measurement, a variable's values can be specified as distinct and discrete verbal descriptions. The variable itself is the thing that can take on as values any description in the appropriate collection of verbal descriptions. Relations among such unmeasured variables can be defined in set-theoretic terms and used in model-building in much the same way (except, of course, that numbers are not available) as relations among measured variables. Thus, without measurement, systems of simultaneous functional relations can be constructed and, under certain conditions, their solutions expressed as functions of parameter values. And in the same context, systems of dynamic, periodic, functional relations can be analyzed for their stability properties. A lack of ability to measure, then, is no barrier to the pursuit of formalization in economics.

Third, all formalizations that make a meaningful attempt to throw explanatory light on economic actuality are constructed through a process of abstraction. Reality is sufficiently complex that it cannot all be included in the specification of a formalization. Things have to be left out. This is so in defining variables, quantitative or not, as well as in characterizing relations.[12] Thus the contents of, or the results derived from, formalization are, at best, approximations of real or observed phenomena that are relevant only under "certain conditions" and cannot have universal applicability.[13] Exceptions necessarily arise. To handle each significant exception requires either a separate formalization addressed specifically to the exception itself, or a generalization of the original formalization that gave birth to the exception. The former leads to "localism" in analysis; the latter to formalizations that assert less and less about the real-world phenomena in question.[14]

Fourth, formalizations, like models, are analogies or metaphors. The distinction between analogy and metaphor is subtle; the following statement, of their divergence will serve for present purposes. When modeling the observed behavior of a firm, for example, to say that the model is an analogy is to think of the firm as behaving "something like" that described in the model. But to take the position that the model is a metaphor means that the firm's behavior is thought of as being described or captured, with a high degree of literalness, by the model's behavior.[15] The difference is that in the first case the model itself (apart from its variables and relations) is an approximate similarity or likeness; in the second it is an "exact" replication.[16] But in either case, the formalizations involved liken observed reality to mental constructions in which the former is conceived of in terms of the latter. In this way those constructions serve as both instruments of thought and as devices for communicating in an intelligible manner.[17] Their force lies in that they focus thoughts in precise ways, in that they provide standards for judging real-world behaviors, and in that they transfer the sense of one person's vision to another.

As an example of formalization in economics, consider the often-criticized general-equilibrium model.[18] This model focuses on the notion of equilibrium and, in the tradition of methodological individualism, is built up by making assumptions about the preferences, technologies, and behaviors of fictitious, individual agents. Its purpose is to explain and clarify the observed, simultaneous, interacting behavior of real agents in an economy. Having accepted the questions this model addresses, and having accepted the equilibrium approach and the assumptions upon which the answers provided by the model are to be based, the economist has no choice but to pursue the relevant formalizations and inquire into the existence, uniqueness and stability of equilibrium in the model.[19] An easy way to see why this must be so is to focus attention on a single, real-world market in isolation. Imagine that one were to observe the market during a particular period of time. In that case, one could see that so much of the commodity was traded at such-and-such a price or, in other words, one would observe a single point in commodity-price space. Subsequent observation in the following period would yield a second point. In building a model to explain how these points came to be seen, the economist could assume (1) that there exist two distinct market demand curves each passing through one, but not the same, observed point, and (2) that there exists only one market supply curve passing through them both.[20] Then, since each observed point is identified as a market equilibrium point in the model,[21] each could be explained as analogous to, or as if it were, the outcome of the interaction of supply and demand. The economist could also assert that the movement from the first point to the second occurred because of a "shift" in demand. Clearly, equilibrium must exist in the model for this explanation to work. If, moreover, the equilibrium in the model were not unique, then the explanation would be incomplete; it would allow the observed point to be identified with many equilibria, each with its own properties, and thus the reason for the movement between the two points would become clouded. Finally, when the observed point changes from the old to the new, the equilibrium in the model would have to adjust accordingly. But if the latter equilibrium were not stable, then whatever dynamics there were in the model could prevent the new equilibrium from being reached and, in that circumstance, the explanation given for the observed movement from the one point to the other would break down. An alternative interpretation of reality would be to locate observed points along time-paths that converge to equilibria in the model rather than to identify them specifically as equilibria. But in either case the questions of existence, uniqueness, and stability have to be explored because that is the only way to be sure that the model can be linked to the real world.

A similar argument applies to the full general-equilibrium model with many goods and many agents. And in spite of the fact that considerable resources and energy have already been devoted to the investigation of the existence, uniqueness, and stability questions in this context, satisfactory answers are available only in the case of existence. The problem is that, although sufficient conditions for uniqueness and stability are known, these conditions, contrary to the tenets of methodological individualism, are expressed as restrictions on aggregated, that is market, excess demand functions. Furthermore, it is not clear if it will ever be possible to give uniqueness and stability conditions that are stated with respect to the preferences or behavior of the individual agents.[22] Therefore, if methodological individualism is to be maintained, even more resources and energy will have to be diverted to the mathematical analyses of general-equilibrium models. And if this quest fails, then without even questioning the realism of their assumptions or the relevance of the conclusions derived from them, general-equilibrium models will have to be discarded because they are unable to provide viable explanations of that which can be observed.

II

Justifications for the use of formalization in general, and mathematics in particular, by economists (and others) go back quite some time. Cournot [3, pp. 2-5] and Jevons [12, pp. xxi-xxv, 3-5] believed that certain forms of reasoning in economics are mathematical in character. Walras [31, pp. 47-48] thought that to be scientific is, in part, to be mathematical. More recently, Suppes [30] provides seven reasons why formalization is desirable: It aids in the clarification of conceptual problems and the building of logical foundations, in the bringing out of explicit meanings of concepts, in standardizing terminology and methods, in permitting the development of a general vision without obstruction by inessential details, in allowing the attainment of a greater degree of objectivity, in setting out the precise conditions required for the analysis to be considered, and in obtaining the minimal assumptions necessary for statement of the analysis. Debreu [4, p.275] cites linguistic convenience and the ability to obtain deeper understanding and analytical extensions that might not

otherwise be possible. Mathematical reasoning, according to Gorman [6, p.273], is important in economics because it helps in determining "... what implies what. It is from the solid basis of such knowledge that one can make imaginative leaps into the unknown." For Solow [29, p.33], mathematical reasoning is preferred because, *ceteris paribus* it is more exposed: "... what you see is what you get." And Weintraub [33, pp. 178-179] argues that, since we comprehend our economic world by creating mental structure, and since doing mathematics is creating mental structure in its "purest form," mathematics is naturally important and relevant in economic analysis.

All of the benefits of formalization contained in and implied by these justifications can be observed in the example of general-equilibrium analysis described in the previous section. Indeed, the general-equilibrium analogy or metaphor created through formalization is powerful, elegant, and appealing, and has led to what are considered by many to be significant results. In addition, formalization in this case can be seen as no less than the means by which the logical implications of the general-equilibrium model are worked out far enough so that its viability and usefulness can eventually be appraised. Because of its immense complexity, such a goal is probably not attainable for the subject-matter of general-equilibrium analysis without formalization.

What, then, is the problem? Why is there so much dissatisfaction? My contention is that the unhappiness arises from two main difficulties with current economic analysis in general. The first has been characterized by Hutchison [10, p. 88] as a "crisis of abstraction" brought about by oversimplification and the consequent irrelevance with respect to reality.[23] Hutchison traces the crisis back to that classical model-builder, David Ricardo. To build a model, as pointed out earlier, Ricardo (like everyone else since) had to abstract from reality and introduce simplifying assumptions. And the most significant of these was his postulate of complete and perfect knowledge. Throughout our history, says Hutchison [10, p. 79], "This postulate has probably been the most important and pervasive single simplification, bearing more logical weight than any other, in the whole range of economic theorizing, analysis, or model-building." It is also the main source of the crisis of abstraction.

"The most criticizable and unrealistic feature of '.... Economic Man,' ...." to use Hutchison's words again [11, pp. 2-3], ".... is not his materialism, or selfishness.... [but rather] his omniscience," and this has nothing to do with the expression of that omniscience in terms of formalizations. Thus the thing that is causing discontent here is the assumption-content of the analysis and not the employment of formalization as a method of explanation.

The second difficulty that causes unease emerges from the kinds of questions that economists tend to ask. There is bound to be dissatisfaction with the application of formalization to answer what are considered to be the wrong questions. But then the problem is not really with the use of formalization. Of course, questions are set by context,[24] and the context most common today is based on the notion of equilibrium. In other words, by postulating an equilibrium framework (this is not necessarily to employ a general-equilibrium model), economists commit themselves to certain kinds of questions, far broader than mere existence, uniqueness, and stability of equilibria. But it is even more significant that when an equilibrium framework is invoked, vast areas of reality are closed off from analysis. Most notable, perhaps, is the exclusion of historical time, the frame of reference for real time, as opposed to the logical or clock time in a mechanistic model. One is reminded of Marshall's comment [22, p. 461] that:

> "The theory of stable equilibrium .... helps indeed to give definiteness to our ideas; and in its elementary stages it does not diverge from the actual facts of life, so far as to prevent its giving a fairly trustworthy picture of the chief methods of action of the strongest and most persistent group of economic forces. But when pushed to its more remote and intricate logical consequences, it slips away from the conditions of real life .... [E]conomic problems are imperfectly presented when they are treated as problems of ..... equilibrium, and not of organic growth ....
> "The Statical theory of equilibrium is only an introduction to economic studies .... Its limitations are so constantly overlooked, especially by those who approach it from an abstract point of view, that there is a danger in throwing it into definite form at all. But, with this caution, the risk may be taken ...."

At any rate, these exorcisms have nothing to do with the presence or absence of formalization as such but they are, it seems to me, the second reason for so much discontent.

The two difficulties or sources of dissatisfaction with economic analysis just described are, in part, transcended by what may be called the "angle of vision" that any scholar brings to his work. Angles of vision emerge from pre-analytical persuasions arising out of backgrounds and experiences, and they influence, in turn, the nature of the questions asked and the assumption-content of the analyses put forward to answer them. In this way, and in a very broad sense, all scholarly enterprise is inescapably contaminated by ideology, politics, culture, and values.[25] Thus, not only are many attacks on formalization more properly understood as attacks on the questions being asked and on the assumptions being made, but also may explicitly or implicitly be raising issues concerning the rightness or wrongness of the angle of vision upon which these elements, as well as the formalizations themselves, are based.

There remains, nevertheless, the issue of whether formalization in economics has gone too far. Have we arrived at the point where economic analysis has become, to use Hick's phrase [9, p. viii], a "good game" in which the pursuit of mathematical "fun" takes priority over the shedding of light on economic phenomena? Were this so, then the fear of Katouzian [14, p.168] that mathematical form and technique might come to determine the substance and content of economic knowledge, would be upon us. However, illustrating his thesis with respect to the development of general-equilibrium stability analysis, Weintraub [34, ch. 4, p. 46] takes the position that this has not yet happened. There exists instead, a symbiotic relation in which both economic conceptualizations select the mathematical tools and the mathematical tools select the economic conceptualizations. Reassuring as this might be, it does not address Morishima's belief [26, p.64] that the marginal productivity of using mathematical argument has declined, ".... not from the increase in the absolute quantity of mathematics at our disposal, but from the ever greater injection of mathematics into a fixed quantity of material."

Nor does it preclude the notion that formalization goes too far when improper uses are made of it. That is, economic analysis becomes a good game when, for example, it engages in arguing out the logical implications of alternative formalized assumptions that can have no analogical or metaphorical relation to the phenomena under investigation. In such a situation the acceptable accordances between the formalizations being manipulated and reality have broken down, and further exploration of these formalizations (which actually cease to be formalizations in the sense defined earlier) is irrelevant to explanation and clarification.

In the end, the issue of whether formalization in economics has gone too far in either of these last two connotations is a judgement call. And if it has, the reason may have more to do with the sociology and psychology of our profession than with formalization itself. For if a scholar chooses to tackle a problem through the use of formalization as opposed to, say, analysis by example or storytelling, it may be all or in part because of the necessities and advantages, described above, that the employment of formalization entails. But in many cases it may also be because, as Prest's advice suggests, that is where the rewards, of publication, recognition, support money, promotion, and tenure are. The scholar's angle of vision notwithstanding, even the selection of the problem to work on is subject to the same reward pressures. And the structure of these rewards tends to be set by the established standards of what constitutes relevant and significant questions, and what makes up the appropriate assumption-content of analyses which purport to provide answers. Clearly the existence of established standards provides a powerful rationalization for the continued use of formalization. I maintain that formalization for the sake of formalization alone has never been, and will never be, knowingly acceptable or confessed to by most economists. But this is not to say that we are immune to being fooled by the questions we ask and misled by our assumptions.

In another sense, formalization in economics cannot go too far. For as I have argued above, as soon as one commits oneself to the pursuit of the questions and assumptions of, say, general equilibrium analysis, then one has no choice but to follow the accompanying formalizations to their logical ends. As the French philosopher Granger said of axiomatization [7, p. 145], which is, of course, a special kind of formalization, "If the axiomatizations proposed by..... the economist are

of any use for the progress of [economic] science, it is not because they appear to ape the constructions of mathematics. It is because they offer to rational thought the sole means of escaping from the attractions of data derived from experience," and one of the few ways of extracting positive structures from the complex and confounding jumble of reality.

Notes

1. The author would like to thank Randall Bausor, Philip Mirowski, Stephen A. Resnick, and Douglas Vickers for their help.
2. For example, Katouzian [14], Klammer and McCloskey [20], McCloskey [23], [24], Ward [32], Woo [36], and the collections of essays edited by Bell and Kristol [1] and Wiles and Routh [35].
3. For a history of how formalization entered economics and became widespread, see Mirowski [25].
4. This is not to say that there are not other means of analytical expression that are equally powerful and appropriate. But given current professional standards and our backgrounds, formalization is often the mode of choice.
5. See, for example, Katzner [16].
6. [32, p. 180]. It is possible to think of storytelling as encompassing both description (including analysis by example) and formalization (including model-building). For example, one might tell a story as description that incorporates "stylized" or hypothetical facts. Alternatively, a story might make use of formalized elements as defined below, or employ both description and formalization in its telling. But in all cases, the distinctive feature of storytelling is narrative. It is in this sense that storytelling is taken here to be distinct from and independent of analysis by example and formalization.
7. Why you might choose specific gears, for example, or even why you might choose gears at all does not matter for present purposes.
8. It is not necessary that these relations be expressed in mathematical form.
9. See Caldwell [2, pp. 179-180].
10. See, for example, Keynes [18, p. 296].
11. Katzner [15].
12. A discussion of the kinds of things that are omitted appears in Katzner [17].
13. Katouzian [14, pp. 157-158].
14. See Woo [36, pp. 29-31, 69-70].
15. In economics, metaphors are sometimes established implicitly through the use of the phrase "as if". Thus, for example, a particular consumer's observed behavior may be explained as if he were a constrained utility maximizer.
16. This is not to exclude the approximateness that comes about in the variables and the relations from the abstraction process described above.
17. McCloskey [23].
18. To provide but one illustration of the criticism it has received, note the following comment of Kaldor's [13, p.13]: "... since Walras first wrote down his system of equations over 100 years ago, progress has definitely been backwards not forwards in the sense that the present set of axioms are far more restrictive than those of the original Walrasian model. The ship is no nearer to the shore, but considerably

farther off, though in a logical, mathematical sense, the present system of derived tautologies is enormously superior to Walras' original effort."

19. There seems to be some misunderstanding in the literature on this point. McCloskey [24, p. 67], for example, incorrectly states, "the problem is that ... [general theorems on existence of equilibrium do] ... not relate to anything an economist would actually want to know." Subsequent discussion addresses the issue.

20. The assumption of a single supply curve is sufficient but not necessary for the construction of the model.

21. Note that demand curves, supply curves, and equilibrium points cannot exist in reality. They can only be present in models. Similarly, to prove that equilibrium exists and is unique and stable in a model can never imply that unique and stable equilibria exist in the real world. The error of thinking that such elements are a part of reality has been referred to by Machlup [21, p, 12] as the "fallacy of misplaced concreteness."

22. See Kirman [19].

23. Note that this irrelevance for reality arises for a different reason than the potential irrelevance, described at the end of the previous section, of the general equilibrium model due to the possible lack of uniqueness and stability of equilibria within it.

24. The epistemological issue of how context is determined is not discussed here.

25. See Myrdal [27, p. vii-viii].

26. A model of the sociology of an academic profession such as economics has been proposed by Katouzian [14, pp. 119-123].

References

1. 1 .Bell, D., and I. Kristol, eds., *The Crisis in Economic Theory* (New York: Basic Books, 198 1).
2. Caldwell, B.J., *Beyond Positivism: Economic* Methodology in the Twentieth Century (London: George Allen & Unwin, 1982).
3. Cournot, A., *Researches into the Mathematical Principles of the Theory of Wealth,* N.T. Bacon, trans. (New York: Kelley, 1960).
4. Debreu, G., "Economic Theory in the Mathematical Mode," *American Economic Review* 74 (1984).
5. Einstein, A., and L. Infeld, *The Evolution of Physics* (New York: Simon & Schuster, 1938)
6. Gorman, T., "Towards a Better Economic Methodology?" *Economics in Disarray,* P. Wiles and G. Routh, eds. (Oxford: Basil Blackwell, 1984), pp. 260-288.
7. Granger, G.G., *Formal Thought and the Sciences of Man* A. Rosenberg, trans. (Dordrech: Reidel, 1983).
8. Hicks, Sir J., "the Revival of Political Economy: The Old and the New," *Economic Record* 51 (1975), pp. 356-367.
9. _____ , *Causality in Economics* (New York: Basic Books, 1979).
10. Hutchison, T.W., *Knowledge and Ignorance in Economics* (Chicago: University of Chicago Press, 1977).
11. _____ , "Our Methodological Crisis," Economics in Disarray, P. Wiles and G. Routh, eds. (Oxford: Basil Blackwell, 1984), pp. 1-21.
12. Jevons, W.S., *The Theory of Political Economy,* 5th ed. (New York: Kelley, 1965)
13. Kaldor, N., *Economics without Equilibrium* (New York:M.E. Sharpe, 1985).
14. Katouzian, H., Ideology and Method in Economics (New York: New York University Press. 1980).
15. Katzner. D.W. *Analysis without Measurement* (Cambridge: Cambridge University Press. 1983).
16. _____ , "Alternatives to Equilibrium Analysis," *Eastern Economic Journal* 11 (1985), pp. 404-421.
17. _____ ,"The Role of Formalism in Economic Thought, with Illustration Drawn from the Analysis of Social Interaction in the Firm", *The Reconstruction of Economic Theory,* P. Mirowski, ed. (Boston: Kluwer Nijhoff, 1986), pp. 137-177.
18. Keynes, J.M., Letter to R.F. Harrod. July 4, 1938, *Collected Writings* v. 14, D. Moggridge ed. (London: Macmillan. 1973), p. 296.
19. Kirman, A., "The Intrinsic Limits of Modem Economic Theory: The Emperor Has No Clothes," *Economic Journal* 99 (Conference, 1989). pp. 126-139.
20. Klammer, A., and D.N. McCloskey, "The Rhetoric of Disagreement," *Rethinking Marxism* v.2, no. 3 (Fall. 1989), pp. 140-16 1.
21. Machlup, F., "Equilibrium and Disequilibrium: Misplaced Concreteness and Disguised Politics," *Economic Journal* 68 (1958). pp. 1-24.
22. Marshall, A., *Principles of Economics.* 8th ed. (NewYork:Macmillan, 1948).
23. McCloskey, D.N., "The Rhetoric of Economics," *Journal of Economic Literature* 21 (1983). pp. 481-517.
24. _____ , "Formalism in Economics. Rhetorically Speaking," *Ricerche Economiche* 43 (1989), pp. 57-75.
25. Mirowski, P., "The When the How and the Why of Mathematical Expression in the History of Economic Analysis." (unpublished manuscript, 1989).
26. Morishima, M., "The Good and Bad Uses of Mathematics," *Economics in Disarray,* P. Wiles and G. Routh, eds. (Oxford: Basil Blackwell, 1984), pp. 51-73
27. Myrdal, G., *The Political Element in the Development of Economic Theory,* P. Streeten, trans. (London: Routeledge & Kegan Paul, 1953).
28. Prest, A. R., "Letter to a Young Economist," *Journal of Economic Affairs* 3 (January, 1983), pp. 130- 134.
29. Solow, R.M., "Comments from Inside Economics," *The Consequences of Economic Rhetoric.* A. Klammer, D.N. McCloskey, and R.M. Solow, eds. (Cambridge: Cambridge University Press. 1988), pp. 31-37.
30. Suppes, P., "The Desirability of Formalization in Science," *Journal of Philosophy* 65 (1968),pp. 651-664.
31. Walras, L., *Elements of Pure Economics,* W. Jaffé, trans. (Homewood: Irwin, 1954).
32. Ward, B., *What's Wrong with Economics* (New York: Basic Books, 1972).
33. Weintraub, E.R., *General Equilibrium Analysis: Studies in Appraisal* (Cambridge: Cambridge University Press, 1985).
34. _____ , *Stabilizing Dynamics: Constructing Economic Knowledge* (Cambridge: Cambridge University Press, forthcoming).
35. Wiles, P. and G. Routh, eds., *Economics in Disarray* (Oxford: Basil Blackwell, 1984).
36. Woo, H.K.H., *What's Wrong with Formalization in Economics?An Epistemological Critique* (Newark: Victoria 1986).

Comment: Has Formalization Gone Too Far?

Edward E. Leamer
Anderson Graduate School of Management, UCLA

I shall concentrate my comments on the paper by Donald Katzner which I greatly enjoyed. Katzner's paper is wide ranging and readable. It is even-handed. It is thoughtful and thought-provoking. It is all this, yet it includes no formal model.

By deciding not to include a formal model, Katzner offers not a defense but an attack on formalism. A persuasive defense would be the presentation of a model that served one of the functions to which Katzner alludes. The model would help us organize our thinking; it would drive out illogical conclusions; it might lead to surprising and unforeseen conclusions; and it would suggest a data analysis. You and I can think of many such models of formalization. A model of industry standards might be interesting. One could assume that there are two alternative but incompatible standards, for example, the beta format and the VHS format for video recorders. The question that would be addressed by such a model is which language would emerge as a standard. To help think about our question ("Has formalization gone too far?") it might be useful to identify the circumstances under which an inferior standard would emerge.

I hope it is clear that what we are discussing is the choice of language. Have we adopted a language that enriches us, or enslaves us? Does it enhance our intellectual growth, or does it impair it? Perhaps you know the intellectual history of the deaf. For centuries, to be deaf was also to be "dumb", meaning stupid. Many of the deaf were herded together into institutions for the mentally retarded. With the invention of the language of Sign in the second half of the eighteenth century there was a great flowering of intellectual life among the deaf. The language of Sign, unfortunately, was a threat to the Victorian ideal of conformity, and in the second half of the nineteenth century the well-meaning Victorians forced Sign from the schools for the deaf on the assumption that the deaf needed to assimilate into "normal" society. The energy needed for the deaf to begin to master oral language was enormous and few could hope to become truly fluent. The result of this Victorian experiment was a great decline in the intellectual achievements of the deaf, a disaster that still lingers today.

Our question today is: Are we, like the Victorians, forcing upon our students a language that few can hope to master? Do our students struggle so hard at this language that there is little room for genuine intellectual growth? Are meetings like this AEA convention, at which hundreds of papers are presented, intellectual marketplaces where we hawk our latest ideas, or are these meetings pathetic theaters where we demonstrate our current state of mastery of our difficult language by repeating over and over phrases that differ in form but rarely in content? Who among our students could compose a literary argument such as Katzner and McCloskey have presented today? And are we not the worse off because the answer is few, very few?

These are not pleasant questions. But they need to be asked. We have witnessed a sequence of several generations of economists, each insisting on more mathematical fluency than the previous one. But there has been little improvement in the mathematical abilities of our students; indeed there may have been some recent deterioration. The Victorian schools for the deaf thus may be an uncomfortably accurate metaphor for our first-year graduate programs.

These thoughts do not substantially conflict with the message of Katzner's "defense". Katzner argues that a model should have acceptable accordances with the world. We should value the content of the message communicated by a model not the mathematical form and technique. The model should not be pushed too far - it is only a metaphor.

Katzner and McCloskey do not disagree on these principles. What they disagree about is whether particular intellectual traditions have reasonably abided by these principles. The example they choose is existence proofs in general equilibrium. According to Katzner #1: "Having accepted the questions this model addresses, and having accepted the equilibrium approach and the assumptions upon which the answers provided by the model are to be based, the economist has no choice but to pursue the relevant formalizations and inquire into the existence, uniqueness and stability of equilibrium in the model." But later Katzner #2 cautions: "economic analysis becomes a good game when, for example, it engages in arguing out the logical implications of alternative formalized assumptions that can have no analogical or metaphorical relation to the phenomena under investigation. In such a situation the acceptable accordances between the formalizations being manipulated and reality have broken down, and further exploration of these formalizations is irrelevant to explanation and clarification." So which is it: #1 or #2? Do we have no choice, or must we always carefully choose how far to pursue the implications of a formal model? I vote for Katzner #2.

Economics as Dentistry

MARTIN BRONFENBRENNER
Duke University
Durham, North Carolina and
Aoyama Gakuin University
Tokyo, Japan

> Thou shalt not sit
> With statisticians, nor commit
> A social science.
> W. H. Auden

> The best lack all conviction, and the worst
> Are filled with passionate intensity.
> W. B. Yeats

I

The title of this sermonette comes from Lord Keynes's pious hope that (in a future of abundance) economists might be as obscurely, as humbly, but presumably not as painfully useful as dentists. But the contents owe more to Professor Richard Easterlin's *Time and Fortune*. I shall argue that, born as I was early in the first World War, I have no reason to regret my choice - my second choice, to be precise - of academic economics as a profession. But any such choice would have been a horrendous mistake for anyone with similar interests born during the second war. The end is not yet, and (on balance) so much the worse for economics as useful, if painful, dentistry.

II

Except for second-generation types like John Stuart Mill and John Maurice Clark, economists are made and not born. And in the process of being made, they come or drift into economics in two different and to some extent hostile streams, one from each of Mr. C. P. Snow's *Two Cultures*. One stream enters from one or more branches of the humanist culture - history and politics in my case - hoping for elements of backbone and determinism in the buzzing, blooming confusions of factsfactsfacts and talktalktalk, with little relation between the talk and the facts. The other stream enters from the scientific culture, including both mathematics and engineering, "Knowing, as well he knows,/That all can be set right with calomel." (For "calomel," read formulas, regressions, laboratory experiments, input-output planning, "human engineering," or "like that.") In addition to "setting things right" for the rest of us, the motivation here is often "second best."

How many a physicist *manqué* have been advised kindly to take his "little potted calculus" across campus as good enough to dazzle the "Babes in Toyland" over here?

Two streams, I was saying. Like the Missouri and the Mississippi coming together a few miles north of St. Louis, where I spent my teen-age years. The two streams can sometimes be distinguished as they pass the city. (The Missouri stream, nearest the city, is usually a bit muddier than the Mississippi one on the Illinois side.) But by the time the river reaches Cape Girardeau, it is pretty well homogenized, despite taking in a few minor additions en route. Would that the same were equally true of the two streams entering our profession!

III

For the two streams of neophyte economists are rarely homogenized significantly. Hopeful historians seldom become masterful mathematicians, or vice versa. Rather the starry-eyed dreamer distrusts the mere technician, and again vice versa. Open conflict is rarer, of course, than reserve or disdain, with compromise at the margin. Nor is all this a peculiarity of the economics profession, although my biased perspective suggests that we suffer it with more-than-average intensity. In the natural sciences, theorists are to some degree ranged against experimentalists. In the humanities, it is the would-be critic, historian, or scholar against the would-be creative genius. In every field I know of, it is the pure teacher, struggling to preserve Grandfather's wisdom from the undecipherability of the vanished culture — "washing bills in Babylonic cuneiform" — against the researcher struggling to open new frontiers at whatever cost in whatever it was Grandfather thought he knew.

Why not simply have more of all these good things? Because, as economists enjoy reminding others more than reminding each other, there is such a thing as scarcity even in a growing economy. Within every branch of higher learning, within every profession, there are only so many loaves, fishes, and tokens of repute to be parcelled out. We can have only so many presidents, cabinet ministers, congressmen, or high court justices at a time, and status differs from mere riches in that the number of prizes proliferate so much more slowly. (Proliferation sometimes mollifies conflict, but not always.) There are only so many Nobel Prizes; if you win this year, I must wait till next year, the year after that, or most likely the Never-Never, for justice to be done to me. And there are only so many prestigious academic chairs; if you are in the Ivy League and I in "academic Siberia," I await your death or retirement, or await expansion of the Ivy League to include Yakutsk and Kamchatka. If there is only so much grant money; the more you and your project get, the less is left for me and mine, at least until next year.

How, if at all, does economics differ from any other discipline in this respect? And with what consequences, for persons considering entry into the profession with somewhat similar interests, and for somewhat the same reasons, as prompted me a half-century ago? Before losing myself in semi-autobiographical details, I had best acknowledge that the circumstances I ascribe to economics also apply, quite possibly in larger measure, in other fields. Biology, philosophy, and physics are three disciplines which comes to this outsider's mind, in which the grizzled veteran of the 1930s is at least equally obsolete, untouchable, and unclean today as he usually is in economics.

IV

In the economics profession of the early and middle 1930s, the loaves and fishes went in unduly large measures - considering their records in anticipating or analysing the Great Depression - to the recruits from the humanities stream. Mathematical and statistical recruits from the natural-science stream were barely tolerated here and there - Columbia was the only university I can recall which had both a mathematical and a statistical economist on its front-line senior staff, both nearing retirement.[1] I think Irving Fisher and Paul Douglas were the only quantitative economists I knew of in America, although I had seen but not read the mathematical appendices in Marshall's *Principles of Economics*. As for statistics, one dealt with them by graphing and "eyeballing;" Douglas was something of a freak who ran regressions and tested theories with them. There were five frontline economic journals,[2] three American and two British; none were precisely *Snappy Stories,* but all were reasonably accessible to inquisitive undergraduates wondering what the professionals said to each other.

I was just such an inquisitive undergraduate, worried primarily about when the Depression might end, and whether I would be employable even after it ended. I was also worried about what the names, dates, and battles of standard political history had to do with the world of Roosevelt, Hitler, and Stalin, and whether the minutiae of institutional political science - the makeup and powers of the Supreme Court of Jugo-Slovenia, the rival theories of papalist Guelphs and imperialist Ghibellines - were any better. I hoped economics had the answers, although my undergraduate instructors did not. Also, I wanted to see whether economists of standing knew about "my" ideas, and if so, what they had to say about them. "My" ideas, four in number and in fact quite unoriginal, were:

1. An economic interpretation of history, more closely akin to a "scandal" theory than to standard Marxism.

2. The inevitability and virtues of centralized central planning along "scientific" lines. The remaining questions were, who was to do the planning and what the "scientific" lines might be.[3]

3. A "maldistribution" theory of the business cycle, of a sort popular in Left New Deal circles and derivable from the theories of John A. Hobson - of whom I had not yet heard.

4. A half-formed notion that there was, for any country at any time, an optimal income distribution, more equal than the American one, which would equate investment and saving at a maximum level of income and employment. (This distribution was attainable by changes in the progressivity of income taxes, and public finance should therefore be my major field of concentration.)

As for preparation, I had a couple of semesters of descriptive statistics - including the summation sign, which terrified some of my classmates. I had had no formal training in mathematics since high school, and disliked the subject. However, I had avoided the horrendous "math allergies" which are the detritus of many demanding mathematics programs. Mathematics, if I needed it, would be bad medicine, but if I had to suffer it, I could. ("What one fool can do, another can.") We had no cook-bookish

---

1. I should classify Henry Ludwell Moore as a mathematical economist and Wesley Clair Mitchell as a statistical economist. Both were embryonic econometricians.
2. Neither *Econometrica, the Journal of the American Statistical Association, the Review of Economic Statistics,* nor the Review of Economic Studies were on this short list.
3. Professor Wassily Leontief's input-output studies might have enraptured me, had I known of their existence!

computer programs in those days, to cover up certain mathematical weaknesses in numerical computation, but standards were low enough in the hinterland for me to be labelled a budding mathematical economist![4]

This background, at that time, sufficed. It sufficed for admission to a good graduate school (Chicago), despite my lack of anything like a formal "major" in economics. After a rocky term or two, devoted largely to remedial study at the undergraduate level, it sufficed for a good graduate career as a first-class citizen among the graduate-student population of my university, although not for a job in economic journalism, which had been my first career choice. Fortunate timing gave me my doctorate just three months before Hitler's invasion of Poland in 1939. Public service, first civil and then military, intervened, but soon after war's end (1947) in the great bull market for academicians - more fortunate timing! - I obtained tenure at another good university (Wisconsin) with a good graduate school of its own. My background has since sufficed for a respectable career, in terms of the profession's loaves and fishes. That is to say, I have made wider ripples, if not precisely a bigger splash, than many of my approximate contemporaries with equal or superior IQs and undergraduate training. And as for those who have made much bigger splashes than myself, all or nearly all have been my intellectual superiors. (I am indeed jealous of their superior endowments, but not of what those endowments have led them to accomplish.)

V

Now let us consider the fate of my hypothetical twin lagged one generation. Born, perhaps, early in the Second World War, as I was born early in the First. He too would have had major interests in history and politics, which might not have been satisfied completely. He too, would have had "original" and unorthodox notions about economic matters, centering perhaps on problems of development and inflation as mine were on problems of depression and unemployment. He too would have shared my considerable distaste for pure mathematics, and for rigor for its own sake. What might my hypothetical twin's career as an economist have been like in, say, the later 50s or the early 60s?

Probably it would have never begun; probably it would have died a-borning. As an undergraduate, he might well have heard "grapevine" rumor about pre-professional economics as a branch of applied mathematics, probably requiring a second major in mathematics and leaving little or no time for history or politics. Had he made bold to open the pages of our leading learned journals, he would have run screaming home to Mother - possibly even to Mother-in-Law! As for his "original" but half-baked ideas, what might have become of them? If his instructor's English were inadequate, or the class a "thundering herd" of several hundred, my twin would neither request or get any answer whatever. If his instructor came from the dominant quantitative stream of economists, he might most likely be told either (a) to restate his ideas in forms amenable to empirical testing, or simply (b) "Get thee to a nunnery, go!" - the "nunnery" being one or another of the "softer options" for emotionalist types. His ideas would be derided as "not economics," or related to it only as natural history relates to biology, or astrology to astronomy. So my twin, born too late, would stand a good chance of never entering economics at all,

---

4. I deduced, in our "Monetary Theory" seminar, that the Fisher equation of exchange, $MV = PT$, implied that P/M and V/T were equal. Therefore, I went on, the strict quantity theory of money required that V and T grew at the same rate, *not* that V was constant, a common "textbook" view.

or of transferring out after the shock of his initial exposure.

Next step: graduate training. After remaining in the field, my twin might end his career by failing to gain admission to graduate school. But more likely, if his record were good and certain of his instructors impressed by his "originality," his would be a low-ranking graduate school somewhere in academic Siberia. If he should by chance receive admission to a ranking graduate department, he would in all likelihood flunk out, drop out, transfer out, or "like a wounded snake, drag his slow length along" the corridors, a second-class citizen among peers more adept in matters mathematical. If he survived all this, plus a dissertation directed either by a "graduate-school Siberian" or by one of a ranking department's "less fortunate appointments," what would await him at the end of the line?

At the end of the line, or at some "consolation-prize M.A." way station, would be - academic Siberia, or its numerous equivalents in various private, public, and semi-public bureaucracies of our society. Nor should we forget the mindless activisms of "the street" or "the movement" for those sufficiently alienated along the way. In any event, my putative contemporary twin's chances of amounting to something or being heard from again (as an economist) are far less than were my own a generation earlier. There, but for the grace of "birth and fortune," goes - myself!

Our profession has turned close to full circle. The quantitative stream from the natural sciences and engineering, now dominates as completely as the literary stream from the humanities did in the old days. And per contra, the literary types are now the more or less tolerated second-class citizens, like the quantitative types of yesteryear.

VI

My obvious belief is that the swing has gone too far, and that it is high time for the pendulum to swing part way - not all the way, mind you! - back to what might be called the inter-war complacency but which (many of us forget) regarded its economics as very much in flux![5] What I have hoped for and even forecast is a succession of damped oscillations around some Aristotelian "golden mean." In a golden-mean regime, both streams of entry into economics are of approximately equal legitimacy, and the best people in each tradition equally likely to achieve recognition without assuming the trappings of the other school or claiming all economic knowledge to be their province.[6] If the new classicism of rational expectations *cum* random walks - an odd couple, that one! - applied internally to the profession as well as externally to the real world, oscillations about the golden mean should be completely damped by now, and nobody should have anything whatever to grumble at - even if the parameters of the golden mean were moving slowly over time. But thus far at least, nothing of the kind is happening, or is a good bet to happen in the short term.

I should also argue, however qualitatively and imprecisely, that without some significant reversion to something like some version of the golden mean, the profession can expect serious difficulties. Economics as dentistry will increasingly lose out to rival tooth-jerkers

---

5. My text here is a well-nigh forgotten volume called *The Trend of Economics,* edited by Rexford Guy Tugwell, perhaps the J. K. Galbraith of his day. The contributors were younger economists, mostly rebels against Marshallian orthodoxy and sympathetic both to the trade-union movement and to egalitarian redistribution. (Tugwell himself later became a prominent leader of the Left Wing of the Roosevelt New Deal.)

6. At a Midwest Economics Association meeting (Omaha, 1955), I hazarded a guess at what the golden mean might be. I said that perhaps three or four of the leading graduate departments of the Midwest might well concentrate on the quantitative side, while at the others course work in mathematical economics and econometrics should be available but not compulsory, with concentration in these fields not encouraged. (Needless to say, I should today yield much more ground to my quantitative colleagues!)

and medicine men. This is decidedly a minority view, which also seems at present decidedly wrong-headed.

For economists are riding high on the hog these days, if I may mix a metaphor. We are high on the professional, especially the academic, income distribution. We have kept ourselves in short supply, and receive more envy than respect. Our high enrollments - enforced by compulsions weak enough to avoid arousing either the American Civil Liberties Union or Amnesty International, but far removed from free competition and *laissez-faire* - set us apart from most of our principal rivals. As for the from-text-to-notebook-without-passing-through-brain aspect of our message to our captive audiences, I know no evidence that other branches of the liberal arts do significantly better at the pre-professional level. (Mathematics and foreign languages may do worse!) So what can be so seriously wrong with such a state of things? Is it not an acceptable rest stop in our progress, even if it falls short of our Utopian destination? Why talk of reversion to the humbler, even if better-paid, status of dentistry?

We cannot yet rule out such questions, or answer them. Let us however point out certain weaknesses in the contemporary position of economics, more obvious outside the profession than inside. These are, I think, five in number, even excluding the "old reliables."[7]

1. Good people from the humanities stream, more literate than numerate, are not only being scared away by economics in its applied-mathematics dress, but are being inoculated with "economics allergy" - meaning, of course, an *anti*-economics allergy. We may be "training" many more enemies than either converts or friends.

2. Important economic problems incompletely amenable to modelling and computer simulation - choices between market and planification systems, for example, or between fixity and fluctuation in the international exchanges - are being "solved" or papered over by lawyers, politicians, and bankers on no apparent bases beyond short-term bargaining. In the dental terms of this paper, all our teeth face extraction by "terrified amateurs" - less terrified than they should be! (Such a fate was restricted by Gilbert and Sullivan to "advertising quacks.")

3. Meanwhile we go our merry ways, debating questions nobody has asked with rigor only a mathematician can appreciate, at the expense of real policy issues. Pirandello writes of characters in search of an author; we offer techniques in search of an application, "all dressed up and nowhere to go." Two popular characterizations of such activities are "rearranging deck chairs on the *Titanic*" and "fiddling while Rome burns," but our ships of state may not be *Titanics* and Rome may not be burning. I personally worry more about comparisons with a medical profession whose costs drive the poor to the faith healers, or a legal profession whose costs drive them to "walking violations of the Sixth Amendment" (quoting Chief Justice Warren Burger), if not to the mobs and the underworld. I also fear the day when amoral colleagues will, if the price is right, program minorities and dissidents to and through the death camps as they now program cattle and hogs to and through feed lots and stockyards. (Compare the last two of the four "old reliable" critiques of Note 7 above.)

---

7. There are perhaps four of these "old reliables: " (1) Our annoying but unavoidable propensity to disagree in pub-lic. (After all, significant issues of policy decision may hinge on what look to outsiders like arcane hair-splitting; (2) Our fondness for expressing ourselves in terms of "what everybody knows, in language nobody understands," although we owe a debt of gratitude to sociologists and psychologists for outdoing us here; (3) Our amoral, sometimes even immoral, willingness to act as "economic attorneys," pleading almost any policy stance when retained by almost anybody, if the price is right; and (4) our propensity to put on the mantle of Newtonian physics and call ourselves more "scientific" than our results justify. (Karl Marx, of course, went further in this direction than his "bourgeois" competitors.)

4. We stand accused, not without reason, of ignoring history, psychology, and other behavioral sciences, of arrogance and condescension toward "literary" practitioners of these subjects, and now of inflating the contributions our quantitative methods can make to them. ("Economic imperialism" in cap and gown.)

5. Finally, most of us care insufficiently about rhetoric and communication - whether or not the world understands what we are doing or saying. "To be great is to be misunderstood," I agree, but the converse is not equally true. The blue pencils of professional journals encourage or even compel us to mystification and incomprehensibility in the guise of saving space. The same blue of pencils also help explain why so many rebels against our cult of unintelligibility are also dissident in their conclusions; the journals are not open to them on equal terms.

VII

If its ranks do not open somewhat more generously, and on something better than second-class-citizen basis, to recruits and potential recruits from the literary side of our culture, our profession may be riding for a fall. This fall may be due to little more than an academic variant of affluence disease. "We are doing quite well, thank you. If we ain't busted, don't fix us!"

In the international arena or rat race, first Britain, then America, and soon probably Japan, have yielded or are yielding just enough to lethargy, ossification, and "the good life" to lose competitiveness to the next in line. Something similar has also happened to academic disciplines. Our prime examples have been the classical and the Romance languages, with "classical" history, literature, and philosophy. What they have lost is not, strictly speaking, competitiveness in any market sense, but rather relevance both to the real world and to the favored countercultural escapes from it.

Ultra-quantitative, ultra-rigorous economics may indeed become the Greek and Sanskrit, or perhaps the "*belles-lettres* and orthoepy" of the 21st century. The burgeoning of "business" or "managerial" economics on our ideological Right, the burgeoning of "political economy" and "economic sociology" on our ideological Left, and the compression of economics to a few snippets in "Social Science" surveys are three straws in the wind. And, if I may cite a sacred text of the New Left, "You don't have to be a Weatherman / To know the way the wind is blowing."

The asymptotic end of all this may be that economists become not humbly useful social dentists but pretentiously useless "music-hall tenors" (from *The Mikado* once more):

> The music-hall tenor whose vocal villainies
> All desire to shirk
> Shall during off hours exhibit his powers
> To Madame Tussaud's waxwork.

If we persist in our present ways, rhetoric, and image, we too may end by exhibiting our powers primarily - not indeed to waxwork but to each other, to our FAX machines, and to the editorial boards of "the journals." And not only the music-hall tenors among us, but the class-room baritones and the instrumental virtuosi of the computer center will lose prestige not only to politicians, lawyers, and bankers as at present but to journalists as well, not to mention the lyricists of pop songs. In one summary sentence: At least half of "economics as dentistry" had better be, at all levels, the economics of its literary stream, while the contemporary cossetting of its quantitative stream is overdue for de-emphasis or even reversal.

Are Economists Accountable?

What do economists economize? Love (Dennis Robertson).

Why Economists Can't Read

*Craig Freedman**
University of New South Wales

"I'd write my Congersman if he could read, if I could write." Walt Kelly

It's not as if we haven't been warned in the past. John Stuart Mill tried to, but his pointed remarks about the strength of cultural inertia have been largely forgotten, buried as they are beneath a welter of Victorian prose.[1] Thorstein Veblen emphatically delineated the power of habits of wont and usage,[2] but economists seemed more intrigued by his sexual forays than his institutional investigations. Of course, both were analysing general economic relations rather than turning the searchlight in upon the economics profession. But cultural inertia leaves just as distinctive an imprint in this area as in those less restricted domains. In all endeavours there is an inevitable resistance to change. Once a convention becomes established, changing it involves significant costs. This can be all to the good, since using such conventions or standard procedures reduce the transaction costs associated with economic activity. But as in those broader economic realms, so it is in the economics profession itself. This tendency to protect the status quo also helps to perpetuate bad habits.

When examined at a distance, the average journal article comes to epitomise such bad habits.[3] As Donald McCloskey has so cheerfully pointed out,[4] the development of economic rhetoric has gone badly astray. The question for those who still nurture a bit of intellectual curiosity is why this should be the case.

McCloskey has done yeoman work in detailing what might be called the supply side determinants of this issue. But in doing so he has not sufficiently emphasised the archetypal story economists like to tell each other, *going to market*. Economists are not an exception to their own rules. In this way, they are no different than butchers, bakers or candlestick makers. Economists carry other goods to market, but also in hope of a sale. Therefore their motley output of tall tales, romances, and epic poems must be constructed with an audience in mind. It takes two to communicate, or if we were dull economists, and in fact we all are, we would say there has to be both a demand for and a supply of information. If we find fault with the aesthetic quality of that output, we cannot at the same time absolve that readership of all blame. In the absence of a regime of imposed central planning, markets are supposed to provide people with what they want, possibly even what they deserve. If the profession is cursed with lame rhetoric, we can only conclude that this is what economists want and what they are capable of digesting. Or, to get more to the heart of the matter, economists can't write because economists have never learned how to read.

This is a particularly dismal conclusion since it minimises the chance for any constructive change. With the market delivering the articles that the profession demands, it is hard to envisage from whence reform of the sort that McCloskey champions can originate.

Here, as in so much of life, we find that standards once formed acquire an inertial endurance. Other alternative formats become more difficult for readers to comprehend and thus less acceptable. Moreover, the constraint of needing to publish in a limited number of dominant economic journals, all of which subscribe to a fairly rigid format, perpetuates a nearly ubiquitous writing style. Strangely enough, the durability of this chosen style is strengthened by its lack of flexibility. By clearly distinguishing those failing to conform, it forms an effective and easily recognisable entry barrier to these key journals. Trends in journals are strengthened and fads perpetuated as hopefuls imitate already published articles. Faced with this flood of uniformity, an editor becomes a virtual prisoner of submitted material.[5] Thus a revolt against these standards is unlikely unless the journals themselves should opt, or be forced, to change. Economists can't read because they have no incentive to learn how to read. While that incentive continues to absent itself, no improvement in the standard of writing can realistically be expected to appear. When the spirit isn't willing, the flesh will necessarily be weak

I. The Tailors of Laputa - Journals and the Canonical Form

> Those to whom the King had entrusted me, observing how ill I was clad, ordered a Taylor to come next morning, and take my Measure for a Suit of Cloths. This Operater did his Office after a different Manner from those of his Trade in Europe. He first took my Altitude by a Quadrant, and then with Rule and Compasses described the Dimensions and Out-Lines of my whole Body; all which he entered upon Paper. And in six Days brought my Cloths very ill made, and quite out of Shape, by happening to mistake a Figure in the Calculations. (Swift, 1958, pp.126-127)

It should come as no surprise that the slow ascent of the journals to a position where they became the makers and breakers of reputation, the arbiters of taste and breeding, began the year after Marshall took up his chair at Cambridge, 1885. Marshall would have as his central goal, if not obsession, the professionalisation of economics as a discipline.[6] This campaign is best represented by his successful struggle "*to establish economics as a science independent of the Cambridge Moral Sciences Tripos*" (Coats, 1991, p.94). Three of the journals that are still essential to an ambitious economist, *The Quarterly Journal of Economics* (1886), *The Economic Journal* (1891), and *The Journal of Political Economy* (1892) followed in quick succession.[7] Hitherto, writers of economics had no officially sanctioned venue in which to publish, one that was universally recognised as such. With their establishment, these journals eventually became the professional bouncers of the trade, defining what was and was not to be considered as a contribution to the field of economics.

> Increasing numbers of researchers, as well as their growing dispersion, encouraged further formalisation and standardisation of the communication system which in turn affected the standardisation of work practices and ways of reporting results. The importance of this system for gaining reputations, and hence rewards, means that its organisation and control are closely linked to the authority structures of different fields, both intellectual and organisational, and it is important to recognise that scientific communication systems are both functional and authoritative. (Whitely, 1991, p.11)

With the advent of the journals, economics took the first step toward standardisation. In the long run, non-professionals would be excluded. The gifted amateur without the proper university credentials would be forced into perpetual obscurity. Recognition of such work would be forever withheld. The desire, welling within self anointed professionals like Marshall, was to reduce future Henry Georges to the rank of mere scribblers.[8] Journal articles, not books, would hold the key to advancement. The journals themselves would be monopolised entirely by the credentialed academic community. In much the same way that the then contemporary medical profession waged war on unlicensed quacks, so did economic orthodoxy root out and destroy unqualified economic theorists.

The process of standardisation has succeeded to an almost mind-numbing degree. Today the journal article has an almost generic feel to it. Given the minute variability in form between offerings, one would be willing to guess that there is at least an implicitly acknowledged format which exists as a core requirement for publication. This format has become a sort of synthetic stretch garment capable of adjusting to any conceivable content.

My interest lies with the way economists choose to convey their analysis. My contention is that this form is not accidental, but the product of meeting the type of demand set by the consumers of these articles. To reiterate, economists are trying to sell their output to the leading journals and thus to the editors and reviewers involved in the publication process. They adopt the structure and writing style which is most pleasing to these potential consumers. In which case, the predominant style of writing need not be solely a reflection of the nature of its content. Instead, it is the end result of an evolutionary process in which the nature of demand has also evolved over the decades.

We can start to understand what sort of commodity is demanded by searching for a structure common to the articles usually published in the leading journals. Instead of presupposing what the ruling standard might be, I chose to examine those articles recently appearing in the two most influential journals. The year selected was chosen at random.[9]

In 1991 *The Journal of Political Economy* (JPE) published forty-two articles (excluding notes and comments) in five volumes. Thirty-six of them had absolutely identical formats. The other six varied in very trivial ways. An article by someone at the Harvard Law School displayed the greatest deviation. We can suppose that he was to some degree ignorant of how strict the standard format has become.

Everyone in the profession is well aware of what this singular structure is, at least at some semi-conscious level. The introduction extends to approximately a page. Most authors feel obliged to formally label the introduction as 'introduction'. A minority is willing to risk the obvious. An author explains exactly what he or she plans to do and how he or she will carry out this plan. The specifics of this exposition make it more than a general run through. Each section of the paper is described in turn. For each section, the reader is made aware of exactly what service these individual sections will perform relative to the whole. The introduction also includes a review of literature which places the article in its proper relation to previous work. This allows the author to describe how his or her article makes a departure, contribution, etc. to this ongoing debate. The individual sections themselves manage to repeat much of this information when they are centre stage. The final section is most often labelled 'Conclusion'[10]. In the way of a farewell, the solicitous author reminds the ever forgetful reader of what the article has just revealed. In short hand the entire process becomes: a) tell the readers what you will do, b) tell the readers what you are doing c) tell the reader what you have done. We've all heard this formula for writing an article satirised. But the reality serves as proof against the power of ridicule.

In 1991, the *American Economic Review* (AER) ran forty-six articles spread out over four volumes (excluding the volume of papers and proceedings). The articles in the AER are more likely to diverge from the strict canonical form. Nineteen show at least some variation.[11] On the whole, articles have greater variation as to the length of introduction, the detailing of sections, and the labelling of the concluding section. One article even starts off with a quote from Garrison Keilor. The formatting straitjacket is relaxed a notch or two, though the end results are immediately recognisable as close cousins to the acknowledged standard. The two articles which demonstrate the greatest departure from this norm are not surprisingly from economists who already have an unassailable reputation, Debreu[12] as well as co-authors Friedman and Schwartz.

These journals serve to grant reputation and thus academic awards to aspiring economists. This internal route is currently the only way for an ambitious economist to achieve success. The journals have increased the need to conform to gain this precious recognition. The unacknowledged but omnipresent fear must be that any deviation from this norm will increase the risk of rejection. Increasing standardisation becomes an effective screening device given the space constraints these journals face.

Even with the best of motives, the young economist must be expedient to be effective. No one will read his or her work if it doesn't get published in a widely read and esteemed journal. The aspiring economist can't publish unless he or she accepts the canonical rhetorical form. Or to be a bit more accurate, publishing becomes increasingly more difficult, especially publishing in one of the more prominent journals. An economist must be able to appeal to the potential reviewers employed by the journal to succeed. Decades of marketing have succeeded admirably. Professional consumers will accept no substitutes.

Thus these articles are demand driven except in the case where the authors reputation precedes him or her. A sufficient reputation creates a Say's Law type of effect. Supply does seem to create its own demand. Once one has a sufficient reputation, it becomes safe to assume that what one writes will be widely read. In a sense, demand for the content is largely guaranteed. One sometimes wonders whether a journal would be equally likely to publish the same submitted article if it bore an unknown name.[13]

Journals grant this license to deviate more readily to those who have already been recognised as masters of the reigning form. Contemplative essays are widely seen as an outlet for well known economists nearing retirement, a sort of indulgence granted to the elders of the profession. Only those economists who are clearly acknowledged masters of the prevailing form are granted such latitude. It's as if Monet would first have had to paint like Ingrés before anyone would deign to take him seriously. Or, as if literary critics had decreed the detective novel to be the one legitimate genre. Only by utilising that format could a writer gain an audience for his or her ideas. Once a reputation was secured, other forms could be ventured. But such alternative approaches could never gain widespread approbation. The established writer's reputation would not be critically impaired. However, only those works cast in the conventional mode would continue to be taken seriously by these critics.

Journal articles weren't always so narrowly defined. I need not remark, as many have before, on the change in the subject matter of the journals and of the techniques displayed there. The surprising discovery to be made lies in the extent to which the actual structure has changed.

There's no need to go back a hundred years to when Veblen was writing on the price of wheat for the JPE to discover this difference. In 1951 the JPE published thirty-seven articles spread over six different issues. Almost none of those papers followed what would become the canonical form for this literature. The only exceptions came in two papers published by a pair of rising young economists, George Stigler and Milton Friedman. It may be indicative that these two economists who would, along with a few others, come to dominate the discipline were already perfecting the future ubiquitous form. We might tentatively posit that the campaign to capture the high ground of economics in the form of control over the leading journals was already underway.[14]

There are also in these issues of the JPE an additional eight articles that resemble to varying degrees what I have labelled the canonical form. But there is altogether more variance in presentation regardless of the content of the piece. This holds true whether the article is largely discursive, empirical, or contains some mathematical formalisation. There seems amongst the authors no awareness or recognition that one form alone should have any innate greater suitability. The same sort of comments could be made if one looks at the twenty-nine articles printed in the 1951 volume of the AER. There was still room in 1951 for Frank Knight to go on for twenty-nine undivided pages without making one single cited reference. In all, the now obligatory review of literature appeared to be optional, instead of serving as a required litany. It was provided only if the author felt it to be necessary. Nor was there an obligation for such a review to be particularly extensive. Overall these articles were written for a mature audience, one that could be depended upon to grasp the obvious.

Change begins with the late fifties and early sixties.[15] By 1963, all the articles in the JPE bear, at least a close resemblance to this standard form while twenty-five percent are identical to it. In the AER the variance in articles has also narrowed with fifty percent of them adopting the now familiar format.

It is also true that the intervening years had seen the increasing mathematical formalisation of economics. But it is far from obvious that such formalisation, whether appropriate or not in all instances, also demanded a standardised form. An alternative explanation is that both are the result of a common agenda successfully accomplished by a core group of economists who were able to rather narrowly define what doing economics involved.

Today, the intelligent lay reader of an economics article might conclude that economists were an unusually inattentive bunch. In reading an article an economist is first prepared for what he or she is about to read. Not only its content but the method of presentation is gone over in some detail as though all economists have dicky hearts incapable of withstanding even the slightest shock. By constantly preparing the reader for what is about to transpire, describing what point is being made as it occurs, and then reminding the feckless reader of what has happened, economists have taken the path blazed by the typical television drama. There, characters alternate in recapping the plot every ten to fifteen minutes. In that way viewers who tune in late or who are given to taking short naps are not placed at a disadvantage. Do economists like TV viewers suffer from ever shortening attention spans? Economists seem incapable of following a sustained argument or grasping the point of an article without having their collective noses rubbed in it several times.

The time has long passed when we could say with any honesty that we are all now Keynesians. But surely we don't want to replace that unanimity by admitting that we are now no more than Sesame Street dropouts. One is loathe to label the average economist with that tag. The question must then become one of finding out why a standard form has been so universally adopted. Surely such ubiquity doesn't flow out of any self evident merit. The best that can be said about the intrinsic value of the form is that it is utilitarian if rather uninspiring. At worst, it is unimaginative and undemanding of any obvious skill on the part of the writer. The pronounced use of stock formulas can gradually destroy the ability of an author to write in a commanding manner.

The mysterious charm of this universal format will remain a puzzle until we come to understand why economists can't read. Accepting that this style is a demand-motivated response, we need to discover why there is no pay-off for displaying an ability to read critically, why no audience exists for papers which demand such skills. It is this inability of economists to read that is reflected in the standard style of an article. We need to turn now to an examination of what is involved in critical reading and why economists regard this skill as largely irrelevant.

II. Ariadne's Thread - Journal Articles As The Source of Reputation

> Now, before Daedalus left Crete, he had given Ariadne a magic ball of thread, and instructed her how to enter and leave the labyrinth. (Graves, 1955, p.339)

To make more explicit what is already apparent in McCloskey, economists write for a particular audience. They must be assumed to be successful at this task unless we want to entertain the possibility that an irremedial distortion in the market process exists. In any case, why economists want the sort of writing that they demand still remains the question. My answer would be that they have never learned to read, but more importantly that they fail to see this as an oversight to be corrected.

Many economists might be tempted to see this increased standardisation of writing as the result of the concurrent increase in mathematical formalisation in economics. Together they would encompass a drive for greater precision in economics, for becoming more scientific in the never ending task of exploring what are very complex problems.[16] In this vision, the current existing form, as well as the predominance of mathematical formalisation, reflects a Darwinian process of evolution. Not only is the dominant form the result of a demand driven process but one that leads to greater clarity and light.

> Survival in the literature is a test of fitness, if an imperfect one. If mathematical techniques continue to produce good economics then, still as a Darwinian, I predict that long before the appendix has disappeared from the human digestive tract most people interested in economic theory will as a matter of course learn some mathematics. (Solow quoted in Caldwell, 1991, pp.27-28)

Solow is not alone among economists who seem to have trouble distinguishing Charles Darwin from Herbert Spencer when they reach for stock evolutionary metaphors. They muddle an idea of natural selection with a specific survival of the fittest scenario.[17] These are far from identical ideas.[18]

Darwinian struggle is removed from the historical rise to predominance of a particular form of economic writing that Solow wants to describe. It is not some impersonal match between environment and species. Economists consciously tried to shape the academic environment in which they operated to reflect their own personal goals. The perpetuation of dubious writing styles is not sustained by chance. The rather visible hand of the profession intervenes to insure a particular result.

Nor, will critical reading[19] eventuate as some fortunate happenstance of an unforeseen process. It takes the sort of deliberate training that is disregarded if not shunned by each generation of entrenched economists. Graduate students who write in veins varying from the expected format soon find the cost of such deviation too heavy to bear. Without a potential audience that reads critically, experimenting with different writing formats is left to those who have already succeeded in the profession and are thus granted greater leeway in their projects. This then is as much a triumph of one set of vested interests over less powerful contenders as it is an intellectual triumph of superior over inferior presentations.

There are more compelling arguments which can explain the increasing standardisation and formalisation of journal articles. Economists tend to deny their own rhetoric, preferring to believe that facts speak for themselves. As a consequence, the deliberate and conscious use of rhetoric must be unscientific. By thinking in this manner, they are sadly in the position of those young Victorian ladies who saw sex as a short but squalid prelude to child rearing. Might it be true, that when economists sit down to write, they close their eyes and think of Science?[20]

This veil of science allows economists to excuse themselves from analysing the advantages that might lie behind one form of writing as opposed to available alternatives. Given only a single orthodoxy, such a problem refuses to intrude. Unfortunately, the prevalence of this rather pedestrian style is more than a simple nostalgia for the absolute. It reflects the defensive style that is now inextricably linked to economic debate. Because so much reading of economic articles is done as a probing action, seeking out points of weakness and possible errors, authors are forced to defend themselves by overstating and reiterating. They cannot assume that their audience will read with care and consideration. Economists grow to resemble the modern medical profession which is notorious for ordering extra and extraneous tests to protect themselves from possible legal action. The pretence of thoroughness is their shield. The result of this in economics is an overemphasis on defining terms to endless lengths and clarifying obvious points. Just as in defensive medicine, this process is costly in terms of the benefits it provides.

The mistake is to take reading for granted as though anyone can do it. Insightful reading is a learned skill not an intuitive one. Without being trained in critical reading, ambiguities become anathemas. Economists suffer from the idea that it is possible for writing to convey only one objective meaning.[21] In that case, interpretation ceases to be an intrinsic part of reading. Economists connect rhetoric with the decorative arts, with the unnecessary construction of needlepoint embroidery, a type of tatting for the timid. Like Sergeant Friday, they profess to want just the facts, the unmediated facts.

Therefore the belief arises that mathematics is more precise, less ambiguous and thus preferable to discursive explanation. Economists like to praise the preciseness of mathematical models. They should give more thought to their appropriateness.[22] Economists in their defence of mathematics seem to muddle the need for precision with the need for appropriate language. Precision implies neither accuracy nor appropriateness. But it does lessen the problem of interpretation. Faced with poor readers, no effort to alleviate confusion is avoided. To justify this position, we have convinced ourselves that we maintain a scientific level of writing, that to violate the canonical form of economic writing is to slip from objective to interpretative prose.

The prevalence of a priori reasoning is similarly demand driven, stemming from a flight from a seemingly ubiquitous and ever threatening ambiguity. A priori formalisation doesn't require specific knowledge. Insights into abstract market processes relieve economists of any such responsibility. They can feel confident in extending their reach unhindered by having to scale any walls of concrete details. Articles that ignore this widespread predilection for a priori constructs, seeking instead to substitute a diet of nuggetty information, will find themselves serving up an uncongenial goulash to the limited palates of their audience.[23]

The standard article is also structured to pander to the potential reader in a roundabout fashion. Economists choose a style that is deliberately reader unfriendly. This tacitly invokes the self importance of its potential audience. The obscurity of the presentation proclaims: 'This is a serious article not open to the casual reader. I, the author, do not pander to the masses.' Simultaneously, the author encourages potential readers to browse through the article based on the provided menu (grazing not reading). The author clearly acknowledges how busy the reader is and that he or she must usually read selectively. The gentle reader is flattered as being technically advanced as well as faced with extreme demands on his or her limited time. Such flattery serves as an effective device with which to ensnare the prospective reader. Part of the charm of a rational expectations model is that it is abstruse enough to require a very concentrated reading. This forces the reader to approach the model seriously since it takes such an expenditure of time to make it comprehensible. A more descriptive style would appear to be too simplistic and self-evident. A conspiracy of convenience ensnares both author and reader.

The specific readers these articles address are the discipline's gatekeepers, an amorphous group of unseen referees who feel obligated to maintain the assumed standards of the profession. At times, it seems as if writers expect no one but these potential reviewers to actually read their articles with any care. Instead they provide quick previews for idle skimmers, like so many trailers for forthcoming movies. The aim is to entice browsers into giving the article a look. It does seem rather a waste of paper to print more than the introduction and conclusions of such articles. The relatively few, dogged readers could apply to the author for additional details or, they could possibly look forward to the establishment of a new publication, *The Journal of Excluded Middles*. The suspicion lingers, that for many articles, only the reviewers ever read the whole piece thoroughly.

Thus there is something not entirely innocent about the rhetoric of the standard journal article. Though previewing the topic is of use given the limited time of most prospective readers, a good abstract accomplishes the same goal. Instead of purely utilitarian, objective prose, there is a subtext of flattery and enticement of the reader. The prickly exterior of non-indulgence, of making the reader struggle to reach the intellectual attainments of the author, has within it a soft core of addressing that same reader's self importance. Anything too simple is considered as pandering to the masses. The reader is seen as someone to be challenged if not defied. Authors use masses of mathematics to cow all but the most determined reader into submission. This strategy of making a reader work unnecessarily hard can prove highly successful. It is unlikely that an economist will entirely dismiss something that has already absorbed so much time and effort, sunk costs notwithstanding. While ostensibly aimed at precision, the standardised and formalised article both protects the writer from attack and indirectly woos the reader with a potent form of flattery.

This idea of an unacknowledged subtext also shows up in the mandatory and standardised way in which a review of literature appears in all introductions. Again there is an impeccable, scholarly justification for its presence, as well as hidden persuaders which lie beneath the surface. Arguments need to be placed within the discourse of any discipline. Given the necessary space limitations of a journal and the limited time of a potential reader, such a practice serves as a shorthand to place an article within the appropriate context. It also allows those not immediately familiar with the literature in that particular context to gain additional information if necessary.

This is the shiny side of the coin. Even here, the more cynical may sometime wonder if, in the case of those papers most frequently cited, the author has actually bothered to read them. This is particularly true when there is a long standing consensus on what such papers say and what they demonstrate. Ostensibly then, this required exercise in name dropping is done to allow serious readers to explore the topic at greater depth as well as to place the argument within the ongoing economic debate. I wouldn't deny these functions. But there is another implicit demand to which the authors cater (the subtext). Readers are unwilling to accept an argument on its own merits alone. Arguments made without such backup authority are disregarded. They are more receptive when convinced that other highly reputable individuals have held similar views or at least have considered the issue to be important, an academic equivalent of the celebrity endorsement, or the wall full of diplomas on a doctor's wall. The reader is reassured of the relevance of the work. Work of this type cannot then be carelessly disregarded.

The logic of this is curious. As Thomas Aquinas (1964) states in his *Summa Theologiae,* "Arguments according to authority are of the weakest sort".[24] Why is an economic model any more legitimate because Milton Friedman believes it or other noted economists have found an issue interesting? Does a breakfast cereal become more palatable simply because some Olympic Gold Medallist endorses it? The review of literature and an incessant citing of sources does serve the purpose of putting the work in context but it also serves as a bit of protective colouration as well. Thus the subtext which explains the format of the article is twofold, a desire to cater to the taste of the consuming public and a need for self protection.

For these reasons, the current rhetoric which is so predominantly deployed in economics is not found wanting by its users. This is hardly surprising since it has been tailored to suit prevailing tastes. Perhaps writers like Bronfenbrenner (1991) are correct. The nature of economic students changed in the post war period. Without any training in critical reading they fell back on rhetorical styles most familiar to them. Unfortunately, once they gained the commanding heights of the profession, they took no prisoners. All other contending rhetorical styles fell like wheat before a thresher. Those occupying the heights of economics refused to read anything not written in the one style they approved.

Educating a budding economist is very much a guild system where the aspirant works his or her way up the ladder from graduate student, to tenure track lecturer, to tenured professor by replicating the techniques of the masters of the trade. Thus there is a conservative status quo to the process. Wagner's *Die Meistersinger* can be consulted as a treatise of the retribution that awaits those that show a rebellious inclination. The end result is that though the founders of the canonical format may have consciously chosen to pursue a set of these specific aims, their followers are likely to be narrower technicians unaware that alternatives exist and disdainful of any variation. These readers will find a non-standard prose style too demanding, too rich for their professional stomachs. For digestion to take place, only the thinnest of rhetorical gruels will serve.[25]

Economists then have become suspicious of polished writing as though it was a piquant sauce covering up some suspicious meat, or a siren's song lulling their critical faculties.[26] But if rhetoric is all pervasive and thus only effective or ineffective, any rhetorical device can be confronted without fear of being duped.

The way economists seem to react either with disdain or fright to any but the blandest of writing styles should reinforce the point just made. After a diet of white bread any pointed remarks or rhetorical flourishes become indigestible. Writing that tries to convince is rejected as biased and unscientific. This misses the object of any article. Why write if not to convince the reader? Spirited writing is not pandering to an audience. Somehow a convention of disdain has grown up among economists. It is up to the poor downtrodden reader to hack through masses of impenetrable prose and mathematical formulation in order to reach the jewel of an idea hidden in that thicket.

Thus Phillip Mirowski's recent book, *More Heat Than Light* (1989), on the mathematical metaphor that nineteenth century economists chose to represent human optimisation, attracted pointed reviews not only for the controversial thesis put forward, but for the rhetorical style he chose to use.

The piece is meant to provoke in the same sense that Keynes put his case strongly, perhaps at times too strongly, in order to stir the pot. The aim is to occasion debate by causing economists to re-examine and defend their positions. Thus even the most extreme stories have their use in combating the stultifying effects of dogmatism. Like the inter-generational battle depicted in Turgenev's (1950) *Fathers and Sons,* conflict can clarify issues by forcing dogmatic beliefs out into the open, paving the way for compromise.

Unfortunately, a pronounced style like Mirowski's serves only as an irritant to the profession at large. Hal Varian (*Journal of Economic Literature*, 1990) not hitherto known for any remarkable dexterity with the English language, can use the description "well written" as the ultimate back handed compliment. The impression conveyed is that good writing is used to cover up weak arguments. Varian stops short of accusing Mirowski of being a foot fetishist but seems as unconvinced by the way he argues as what he argues. In a similar vein, Kevin Hoover (*Methodus*, 1991) seems to have been provoked to the same sort of intemperate fulminations that he finds intolerable in Mirowski. One wonders whether a blander, more standard format would have occasioned such heated ripostes.[27]

This though is not a mere matter of taste. The prevalent inability or deliberate refusal to read in a critical fashion, creates much unnecessary confusion. Communication begins to flow through fewer channels. If only in self-defense, the prevailing rhetoric becomes narrower and more proscribed.

III. The Beat of a Butterfly's Wings The Importance of Critical Reading

> ... this translates into what is only half-jokingly known as the Butterfly Effect - the notion that a butterfly stirring the air today in Peking can transform storm systems next month in New York. (Gleick, 1987, p.8)

A. Friends and Foes

In any act of communication, misunderstanding has such a high probability of developing that only a considerable degree of goodwill allows the process to continue. This was pointed out by Keynes, perhaps filled with some prescient dread of how his own works would be misinterpreted by less than generous readers.

> This means, on the one hand, that an economic writer requires from his reader much goodwill and intelligence and a large measure of cooperation; and, on the other hand, that there are a thousand futile, yet verbally legitimate, objections which an objector can raise. In economics you cannot *convict* your opponent of error; you can only *convince* him of it. And, even if you are right, you cannot convince him, if there is a defect in your own powers of persuasion and exposition or if his head is already so filled with contrary notions that he cannot catch the clues to your thought

which you are trying to throw to him. (Keynes, 1973, p.470)

Economists have largely cribbed their style from what they believe is a standard scientific format. But writers in the natural sciences also unnecessarily ignore their readers, seeming more eager to simply get their data and observations down on paper than worrying if they can be easily understood. This though displays a fundamental misunderstanding of the purpose of writing.

> The fundamental purpose of scientific discourse is not the mere presentation of information and thought but rather the actual communication. It does not matter how pleased an author might be to have converted all the right data into sentences and paragraphs; it matters only whether a large majority of the reading audience accurately perceives what the author had in mind. (Gopen and Swan, 1990, p.550)

As previously stated, communication does not simply take care of itself any more than good teaching is realised by merely picking up a piece of chalk. Reading and writing are two halves of the same Aristophanean egg. Good writing is not an afterthought but rather something that improves the quality of thought. Complex ideas do not demand obscurity of presentation but rather need the preciseness of an appropriate presentation.[28] This is not automatically accomplished by shoving ideas onto the Procrustean bed of formal mathematics.

Critical reading means looking for a comprehensive and consistent explanation of an author's work. We first have to labor to understand what he or she actually intends to say. The author needs to be given the benefit of the doubt. Ideally it is only when we find ourselves unable to rescue a work that we can fairly conclude that it is flawed. At that time we must take upon ourselves the sad task of pointing out the source of the error or the unexplained links in the logic. Readers need to be taught how to do this, but they are also more likely not to take a hostile stance if it is clear that the author has tried to reach out to the reader. Instead of pandering to the presumed reader in the indirect manner already described, an open ended format would allow for a more direct type of appeal.

This flight from words into the supposed precision, the harder currency of mathematical formalisation becomes more understandable if we consider how a failure to read properly has shifted the terms of economic debate in the past and occasioned endless bouts of wrangling.

B. Textual Analysis

> Ancient and rooted prejudices do often pass into principles; and those propositions which once obtain the force and credit of a principle, are not only themselves, but likewise whatever is deductible from them, thought privileged from all examination. (Bishop Berkeley quoted in Kline, 1980, p. 160)

An inability to master textual analysis has produced the sort of aliterate form of writing that predominates in today's leading journals. Given the opportunity, economists have been adept at misinterpreting what they read. For simplicity, let's look at four reasons that can lead down this road.

1. *The Ability to Follow Only Certain Lines of Reasoning*

The narrowly trained mind often operates as if it were an unreconstructed Kantian tied to a priori categories. Faced with any deviation from these few, well-travelled paths, they resolve this potential dissonance by reshaping alien ideas to fit a more familiar outline.

Jensen and Meckling (1976) find themselves unable to assimilate Herbert Simon's assumption of bounded rationality. They are obviously incapable of making sense of a statement outside of the standard economising structure of their analysis. Since they have no intention of being cruel to Simon by casually dismissing his work, and since he is a recognised and reputable economist, they can only make sense of his work by ignoring its stated meaning. That there is no basis for their interpretation seems not to worry them. Either Simon must mean this or he is talking rubbish. Generosity on their part wins out. The naivety of one particular footnote is revealing.

> Simon developed a model of human choice incorporating information (search) and computational costs which also has important implications for the behavior of managers. Unfortunately, Simon's work has often been misinterpreted as a denial of maximizing behavior, and misused, especially in the marketing and behavioral science literature. His later use of the term "satisficing" has undoubtedly contributed to this confusion because it suggests rejection of maximizing behavior rather than maximization subject to costs of information and of decision making. (Jensen and Meckling, 1976, p.306n)

Maximising behavior is however just what Simon has long sought to reject.

> But utility maximization, as I showed, was not essential to the search scheme ... As an alternative, one could postulate that the decision maker had formed some *aspiration* as to how good an alternative he should find. As soon as he discovered an alternative for choice meeting his level of aspiration, he would terminate the search and choose that alternative. I called this mode of selection *satisficing*. It had its roots in the empirically based psychological theories, due to Lewin and others, of aspiration levels. (Simon, 1979, p.503)

Being unable to conceive that reputable economists may take an alternative approach is hardly a problem of recent vintage. Marshall felt that he had to rescue Ricardo from the grasp of those Marxist and Socialists who claimed that Ricardo depended upon a labor theory of value rather than the sort of cost of production theory with which Marshall felt more at home.

> And yet Rodbertus and Karl Marx claim Ricardo's authority for the statement that the natural value of things consists solely of the labor spent on them; and even those German economists who most strenuously combat the conclusions of these writers, are often found to admit that they have interpreted Ricardo rightly, and that their conclusions follow logically from his. (Marshall, 1920, p.672)

The reason for this claim, which Marshall strives mightily to deny is that Ricardo said as much in as straight forward a way as possible.

> We have seen that the price[29] of corn is regulated by the quantity of labor necessary to produce it, with that portion of capital which pays no rent. We have seen, too, that all manufactured commodities rise and fall in price, in proportion as more or less labor becomes necessary to their production. Neither the farmer who cultivates that quantity of land, which regulates price, nor the manufacturer, who manufactures goods, sacrifice any portion of the produce for rent. The whole value of their commodities is divided into two portions only: one constitutes the profits of stock, the other the wages of labor. (Ricardo, 1886, p.60)

Instead, Marshall concentrates on Ricardo's shortcomings as a writer. This becomes a common refrain. It can't be the readers who are at fault, but rather the poor, inadequate writer. The victim of sloppy reading is blamed, the perpetrators spared. The profession, as a result, is quite rightfully distinguished by a fear of prose which can be so capriciously misread.

2. *Reading With Prior Expectations*

How strongly resistant we are to seeing the obvious when it doesn't accord with our own preconceptions and desires. Initially, economic education comes largely from textbooks and lectures. Later on, we may extend our knowledge of earlier work by reading more recent journal articles. Seldom do we make the time consuming attempt to evaluate these interpretations.[30] We seem incapable of recognising them as only interpretations, rather choosing to accept them as summarising indisputable conclusions. Thus those who finally journey back to the source are incapable of approaching a well known work with open eyes. Starting with preconceived ideas, we find in a work what we expect to find. Our prejudices are conveniently confirmed.

An oral tradition allows economists, if they choose, to largely ignore the original work. If everyone already knows what it says, why bother reading it. The force of widely held opinion assures that a mistaken reading can be virtually unassailable.

Generations of economists, both left and right in their political persuasion, have done just this. Such is the power of received habits over men's minds that a tradition that insists on reading Marx as though he were an English classical economist has been sustained over the years. It then ceases to matter how carefully these myths are debunked or even the reputation of the debunker. The oral tradition rolls on impervious to such attacks.

Even careful attempts from the mainstream of the profession will fail. Baumol's (1979) bid to dismiss the idea of subsistence wages (the iron law of wages) from the canon of Marxian folklore fails, just as an earlier attempt by Sowell (1960) at refuting *"the increasing misery of the proletariat"* as a tenet propounded by Marx also accomplished nothing. Vested interests on the right and the left hold on to their cherished myths as they have held onto other common Marxian aphorisms that have no foundation in Marx' work. There is startling little evidence that self styled followers and promoters of various dead economists have ever read these authorities to any advantage. Would their icons feel comfortable at a meeting of their acolytes, or would they be forced to follow Marx in declaring, "Je ne suis pas une Marxiste?"

The myth-making activity of economics is even stronger in the case of Keynes where both the origin of and the force of those myths are evident in every textbook we open. Economists reading Keynes' *General Theory* crave the familiar. They reject the revolutionary content of his book for the more comforting stories of the profession. In doing so, *The General Theory* loses its generality as minor points are elevated to keystone concepts.

One can argue that by focusing on wage rigidity and the liquidity trap, Keynes' system could be domesticated to fit into the standard general equilibrium frameworks then gaining popularity. In journal articles, consumer sovereignty reigns, the consumers being restricted to the class of professional economists.

Thus the more mechanical explanations, those that involved endogenous, equilibrating prices triumphed over those that seemed to rest on exogenous psychological forces. The liquidity trap (not so named by Keynes) is presented as a theoretical possibility only[31] rather than a serious impediment in pushing interest rates low enough to generate additional investment. Rather it is those issues which we might lump together as transaction costs[32] which keep rates measurably above zero.

> There is, finally, the difficulty discussed in section IV of Chapter 11 p. 144, in the way of bringing the effective rate of interest below a certain figure, which may prove important in an era of low interest rates; namely the intermediate costs of bringing the borrower and the ultimate lender together, and the allowance for risk, especially for moral risk, which the lender requires over and above the pure rate of interest. (Keynes, 1936, p.208)

In a similar manner, clinging to the key role played by rigid wages allowed policy debate to be shifted onto more barren ground. Rigid money wages became the institutional friction preventing the perfect spinning of the wheels of the economy. Once this is seen as the crucial analytical assumption, economists can, with good conscience, retreat to telling each other the cosy myths that they find agreeable.

Keynes however wished to make the point that completely flexible wages would not improve the situation but, due to increased price instability would only make matters worse. Not only wouldn't wage cuts lead necessarily to higher employment but they could create even greater uncertainty.[33]

> In the light of these considerations I am now of the opinion that the maintenance of a stable general level of money-wages is, on a balance of considerations, the most advisable policy for a closed system; whilst the same conclusion will hold good for an open system,

provided that equilibrium with the rest of the world can be secured by means of fluctuating exchanges. (Keynes, 1936, p.270)

As readers, economists generally find in an article what they expect to find. They seem incapable of looking at an article with fresh eyes. Perhaps they don't even realise it's a necessary precondition for critical reading. Thus even when economists reject the established myths of the trade, they simply attempt to substitute a new myth for an old one. Keynes is again a fruitful source of this breakdown in reading.

3.   *Deliberate Misreading for Rhetorical Ends*
Is it possible that Homer meant to say all they make him say, and that he lent himself to so many and such different interpretations that the theologians, legislators, captains, philosophers, every sort of people who treat of sciences, however differently and contradictorily, lean on him and refer to him: the general master for all offices, works, and artisan, the general counsellor for all enterprises? Whoever has needed oracles and predictions has found in him enough for his purpose. It is a marvel what wonderful correspondences a learned man, and a friend of mine, draws out of him in support of our religion; and he cannot easily let go of this opinion that this was Homer's purpose (yet he is as well acquainted with this poet as any man of our century). And what he finds in favor of ours, many of old had found in favor of theirs. (Montaigne, 1965, pp.442-43)

The flurry to discover the real Keynes, which would grow into a small cottage industry, began sometime in the sixties with two key publications. Clower (1965) posited a world of producers and consumers not necessarily inconsistent with Keynes' analysis but hardly representative of it. Leijonhufvud (1968) was so insistent in showing that money does play an essential role for Keynes that he practically transforms the idea that money does matter into a monetarist formulation that only money matters.

Each one starts with a quite legitimate critique of the received wisdom concerning Keynes. Each one then substitutes his own personal hobby horse for the discredited notion. They are trying, whether entirely deliberately, or not, to use Keynes to provide an imprimatur for their own ideas. Or to be generous, we might conclude that they simply don't know enough to shed their previous economic baggage before trying to reinterpret an overly interpreted work. It is difficult to know whether they are being dishonest when they quote out of context or use edited quotes to support their cases.

Perhaps they don't even realise the partisan nature of their reading.

Allan Meltzer (1981) follows this route in his attempt to come up with a re-statement of Keynes that is consistent with Keynes' work. The confusion enters when in practice Meltzer equates this as meaning consistent with Meltzer's own work. Meltzer has long focused on rules versus discretion in policy measures as well as on the underlying basis for stable economic systems. Unfortunately, it is hard to credit Keynes with similar inclinations unless we use the terms in a very broad sense. Keynes argues that because investment is inherently unstable, a market economy is unlikely to be able to sustain a full employment level of activity. As Meltzer points out, this led Keynes to call for the socialisation of investment in order to gain this goal and at the same time avoid the worst of the fluctuations such economies are heir to. Sometimes, Meltzer seems to forget the boosting investment part, concentrating instead on the stabilising goal.

Unfortunately it is far from obvious that Keynes has the same sort of stability in mind that Meltzer has. In Chapter 18, which Meltzer quotes from at length, Keynes tries to explain why, despite the inherent instabilities within the capitalist system, the whole structure is unlikely to collapse. The logic of his presentation allows this to be a not inconsiderable possibility. By adding certain psychological propensities and conventions the likelihood of such an occurrence is reduced.

In particular, it is an outstanding characteristic of the economic system in which we live that, whilst it is subject to severe fluctuations in respect of output and employment, it is not violently unstable. Indeed it seems capable of remaining in a chronic condition of sub-normal activity for a considerable period without any marked tendency either towards recovery or towards complete collapse. (Keynes, 1936, p.249)

This is indeed a strange sort of stability. Under such a broad umbrella, any system avoiding the extremes of blood on the streets or full employment would qualify. Meltzer's defence is that the fluctuations are around an intermediate mean. If, though, we accept Meltzer's version of the equilibrium position adapted by Keynes we allow a perfect classical dichotomy between the short run and the long run. This is what Meltzer cannot legitimately squeeze out of Keynes. Conventions, as Keynes points out (1936, p.204) do not themselves rest upon secure knowledge and are liable to change. Is it then not logical to think that those very same fluctuations that Meltzer would like to dismiss could change one or more of the stabilising conditions? In other words the intermediate position around which the economy circles may in fact also be given to change due to short run variations.

Innocence of intentions may inform and partially excuse such re-interpretations. No absolution should be extended when distortions are not the result of errors but rather an indication of malice aforethought. Such instances help to explain the previously discussed trend towards defensive writing in economics.

4.   Reading with the Intent to Destroy

Economists can so dislike the conclusions of an article, or what they perceive to be the conclusions, that they comb through the article with the sole hope of refuting its logic. If these ungentle readers are determined enough, they generally succeed. If need be, they take an intentionally obtuse position, refusing to admit anything that is not pointed out in lavish detail.

When attacking a theory it is perhaps advantageous to present that theory in a somewhat simplified version. At least initially a too nuanced presentation tends to muddle the critique, making it difficult to comprehend. The temptation is to simplify a theory not only for clarification purposes but to further one's own argument against it. When the simplification comes to light, we see a version of the theory constructed to be vulnerable to a specific attack. Equipped with a providentially tailored Achilles heel, critical arrows easily find their mark. A towering theory seems to collapse from its own inherent weakness rather than from the critic's cleverly applied prosthetic device. If presented forcefully enough, future debate focuses on this hot house theoretic version rather than the sturdier and more complex original.[34] With the passage of time too many academics gain stakes in keeping the lame version afoot. Their arguments and counterarguments have been honed to the peculiar requirements of the constructed theory. At the moment when the simplification supplants the original, a tradition, a bit of folklore, becomes firmly implanted in the daily discourse of the discipline and nearly impossible to uproot.

George Stigler, well known for his slash and burn rhetoric, recasts all arguments by thrusting them onto the rack of his own analysis. By assuming that critical reading is a combat sport, he approaches an article like a wrestler facing a deadly foe. Given the set up of his target, it is no great trick to successfully conduct an autopsy into the causes of its death.

Most textbooks have taken Stigler's version (1947) of Sweezy's (1939) kinked demand curve as an accurate representation. Other commentators have gone so far as to reproduce his sardonic humour by using Stigler's ambiguous relabelling of kinky for kinked demand curve.

Sweezy's (1939) article is too short and straightforward to make Stigler's reconstruction of it anything but deliberate. What has entered the textbooks is a model manufactured in order to self destruct in a convincing manner. Stigler does not try to test Sweezy's suppositions but an easily dismissed concoction of his own. What he shoots down is Stigler's version of rigid prices. He does this by drawing conclusions which don't necessarily follow from Sweezy's original model.

Sweezy starts by constructing a model where prices fail to respond automatically to changes in costs. This analysis is done holding demand constant. He not only presents the familiar kinked curve but the less familiar inversely kinked curve which allows for price leadership and secret discounting from listed prices. Once the model is established, he allows for changes in demand, this being his real goal. His purpose is not simply to show that prices are stable, but rather to explore how oligopolies react to changes in demand. His testable hypotheses are clearly listed.

> As far as the cyclical behavior of oligopoly prices is concerned we might expect to find (1) that prices go up easily and openly, in time of upswing; (2) that prices resist downward pressure in times of recession and depression; and (3) that list prices become less trustworthy guides to real prices the longer bad times last. I think this analysis can be developed in such a way as to throw valuable light on the much - debated problem of rigid prices, but to do so would be beyond the scope of this paper. (Sweezy, 1939, p.572)

Stigler ignores what Sweezy wants to do, instead using the model as a device to attack the concept of rigid oligopoly prices. In doing so, Stigler fails to distinguish between price changes due to variations in cost versus variations in demand. Nor does he distinguish the varying market circumstances in the industries he investigates. In other words, his refusal to approach Sweezy's model as anything but an abstract, generalised, equilibrium construct completely runs counter to Sweezy's purposes.

This leads to a famous criticism which appears, sadly enough, in most first year textbooks.

The theory of the kinky demand curve explains why prices that have been stable should continue to be stable despite certain changes in demand or costs. But the theory does not explain why prices that have once changed should settle down, again acquire stability, and gradually produce a new kink. (Stigler, 1951, p.417)

Sweezy is quite clear why he intentionally does not deal with this issue.

No attempt is made to explain how the current price and output situation came about except as it may be explained by reference to a previously existing situation. This is unavoidable since imagined demand curves, unlike the ordinary demand curves of economic analysis, can only be thought of with reference to a given starting-point. That starting-point itself cannot, of course, be explained in terms of the expectations to which it gives rise. Once this is realised, it becomes very doubtful whether the traditional search for "the" equilibrium solution to a problem in oligopoly has very much meaning. Generally speaking, there may be any number of price-output combinations which constitute equilibriums in the sense that, ceteris paribus, there is no tendency for the oligopolist to move away from them. But which of these combinations will be actually established in practice depends upon the previous history of the case. Looking at the problem in this way the theorist should attempt to develop an analysis which will enable him to understand the processes of change which characterize the real world rather than waste his time in chasing the will-o'-the-wisp of equilibrium. (Sweezy, 1939, pp.572-73)

This sort of suggestion is exactly what Stigler seemingly dislikes and which he simply ignores. In Sweezy's case, models are seen as heuristics to aid analysis rather than applicable in some almost mechanical and universal way. The proposed methodological shift is too radical to even prompt Stigler to comment. Instead, Stigler seems more concerned with the paper Sweezy didn't write. It's as though the most salient point to a literary critic about Dashiell Hammett was his glaring failure to write *Look Homeward Angel* rather than his influence on the genre of detective fiction. To reiterate, it seems somewhat peculiar to fault an author for the article he or she didn't write. The issue is how well aims are accomplished and the importance of those aims.

Summary- Given economists as readers, it is no wonder that economists as writers flee from prose whenever possible. The sometimes false precision of mathematical formulation is seen as a safe refuge when compared to the potential ambiguity inherent in discursive presentations. Economists, at times display an almost wilful desire to misinterpret. The result is an innate distrust of any deviation in style from the canonical standard. In this sense, economists follow Plato in seeking to remove poets and other rhetoricians from acceptable economic society. They are regarded as a threat to the rigorous standards of the tribe. If as Freud once remarked, ambiguity is a sign of maturity, then most economists are still in their swaddling clothes.

IV. Hypocrite Lecteur

Hypocrite lecteur, mon sembable, mon frere. (Baudelaire, 1964, p. 16)

If journals have degenerated to a point where they consist of articles by people who can't write, producing articles for people who can't read, what then is to be done to change this depressing situation?

The first step would be an increased tolerance, the sort of tolerance that Donald McCloskey has called for elsewhere. The ubiquitous standard format isn't forcibly discarded. This isn't about substituting one inflexible standard for another, but rather a willingness among readers to view this as just one among many possible alternatives. From there we would hope to progress by demanding higher standards of writing no matter what the format chosen. This means that appropriateness and accuracy of expression is prized more than pure precision. Stylistics then are not to be ignored as some mere matter of form. The content conveyed speaks through the style in which it is conveyed. In fact it is a decisive element of whether the article speaks at all.

Unfortunately, it is praiseworthy but ineffective to call for better writers without first realising that we need better readers in this market driven world. McCloskey urges a self consciousness on the part of the writer.[35] But such a self consciousness would only make the writer aware of why he or she was choosing a particular style. What incentive does this desired self- awareness present which would lead the writer to actually forego a readily accepted rhetorical form?

These articles are written for a particular audience. Would the rhetoric flourish if no one really wanted it? Much in the same way that everyone condemns the proliferation of mindless violence, we all in a similar high minded spirit call for the end of poor and unnecessarily obtuse writing. But deep down we do not want change. Posing costs very little. To actually attempt to change the standards of the economics profession is at best a frustrating endeavour. McCloskey does claim, *If even economics can be shown to be fictional and poetical and historical, its story will become better."* *(1990,p.162)* Why though should this change the stories economists want to read or make them into more critical readers?

Like small children, economists hate having their stories varied. A few plots and ways of telling the story seem to suffice. If then we agree with McCloskey that economists are story tellers, how do these tellers of tales decide which stories to tell and how to tell them? To fall back on the archetypal story of all, they must be giving their readers the narrative the want. For anyone then, but especially for an economist, to complain about the appalling writing appearing in the major journals is in reality to express dissatisfaction with the readership. The writing does have an obvious utilitarian basis. Since writing well takes time, a fill-in-the-blanks style is efficient if no objection is raised by the readership. If there were more discriminating readers, more would be demanded from the writers of journal articles. The limitations of their prose reflect the limitations of their readers. Both proceed in an ungainly, mutually reinforcing tango that removes economists from the responsibility of developing critical reading abilities.

Change is unlikely despite the best efforts of McCloskey and others. If optimists see this as the best of all possible worlds and pessimists are afraid that it is, I suppose I know where to line up in this great division between hope and despair. Change could come only if the reviewers for the acknowledged major journals were to have an inexplicable change of heart. If we are honest, we must admit that the fate of the discipline is largely shaped by what these journals are willing to publish. Publication, more than anything else, holds the key to tenure and recognition in academic life. Economists write in a style they think will meet with acceptance. In other words, they mimic the existing style of those key journals. Reviewers would have to start demanding superior and cleaner presentations. But this smacks of the sort of deus ex machina that Euripides used to mock the pretensions of the human plight. Humans unable to rectify their situation look to miracles as their only hope.

> We know little of how traditions get established, while it seems clear that once established, a tradition does not get changed through calling attention to its absurdity or that of the factual assumptions upon which it rests. Such things happen 'when the time is ripe'. (Knight, 1955, p.272)

* Presented at a AEA-INEM session of the AEA meetings in Anaheim, California, January, 1993.

* I would like to thank but not implicate Peter Kriesler (UNSW), Eric Sowey (UNSW) and Rick Szostak (University of Manitoba) for reading this paper carefully and correcting errors of style as well as substance.

Notes

1. "Political economists generally and English political economists above others, have been accustomed to lay almost exclusive stress upon the first of these agencies, to exaggerate the effect of competition, and to take into little account the other and conflicting principle (custom). They are apt to express themselves as if they thought that competition actually does, in all cases, whatever it can be shown to be the tendency of competition to do. (Mill, 1965, p.242)

2. "... so that the German people have been enabled to take up the technological heritage of the English without having paid for it in the habits of thought, the use and wont induced in the English community by the experience involved in achieving it."(Veblen, 1976, p.364)

3. Throughout the article, I accept Donald McCloskey's concerns about the current state of economic literature. By spurning the value of rhetoric, economists have developed a predilection for unnecessarily turgid prose. The issue I concentrate on is why such writing exists and seems likely to persist. These are the bad habits which far too few in the profession seem eager to shake.

4. McCloskey has been making this point with increasing fervor at least since his 1983 *Journal of Economic Literature* article. This has occasioned some debate but no noticeable results. Those interested should look at such efforts as his book, *The Rhetoric of Economics* (1985) or a latter elucidation, *If You're So Smart* (1990).

5. "Yet even here, an editor is to some extent a captive, a passive recipient of material sent to him unsolicited; and as authors send articles to journals which they hope will publish them any editor tends to get more of the same i.e. having printed material of a certain type or on a specific topic prospective authors will expect him to more or less continue in the same vein. This practice may well restrict the range of his choice." (Coats, 1991, pp.105-6)

6. A fairly comprehensive look at Marshall's role in this process can he gained by reading Mahoney. (1985)

7. Not coincidentally, each of these journals was associated with a leading University, giving these institutions an ever increasing power to exclude. The QJE was an offspring of Harvard, the JPE of Chicago and the EJ, though officially a product of the newly formed British Economic Association, of Cambridge. In particular, Chicago founded the Journal in hopes of enhancing its newly formed Department of Economics. Although Marshall himself was not initially a moving force behind the birth and subsequent status of any of these journals, it is hard to see how his professionalisation process could entirely have succeeded without them.

8. In 1883 Alfred Marshall presented three public lectures in an attempt to refute the claims made by Henry George in *Progress and Poverty* (1958). This book "circulated in Great Britain as no economic work had ever circulated before" (Stigler, 1963, p. 181 n.2). This was an early but singular attempt by Marshall to define a new science of economics. He would later be instrumental in marginalising most of the work produced by J.A. Hobson.

9. According to a recent article (Ellis and Durdeen, 1991) the two most respected economic journals are *The American Economic Review* (AER) and *The Journal of Political Economy* (JPE). I chose the year 1991 by shutting my eyes and selecting a copy of JPE at random from a shelf containing the last six years of the journal. I then used the same year to compare AER. These results cannot be conclusive. But I think they are indicative. Such clear patterns are unlikely to be a pure fluke.

10. Though 'Conclusion' is the most common label this can vary. Sometimes of course it is 'Conclusions' or 'Summary and Conclusion'. Also seen are: Remarks, Concluding Policy Implications, Extensions and Concluding Comments. There are definite differences in these choices. For the most part they are chosen to be appropriate to the material in that concluding statement. But they all share the common characteristic of letting the reader know that the author is about to confess to what has been done throughout the article and why it was done. Though one wonders why readers can't discern for themselves that they are looking at the conclusion to the article.

11. This includes the article with the intriguing title, "Sorority Rush As A Two Sided Matching Mechanism" (Mongell and Roth, 1991). It lacks a review of literature. Since eleven out of the nineteen references cited are by the author or authors, one suspects that this deviation from form was not entirely intentional but driven by necessity.

12. Debreu's article is based on his presidential address at the ASSA convention. As in the case where the Nobel Prize winner's address is reproduced, one can expect some variation from the canonical form. Economists haven't yet reached the point where they speak in the exact same way that they write.

13. Many economic journals, more than half of the top forty, use a single blind reviewing system. Thus the reviewer is aware of the author of the article and the institution where he/she is based. See Rebecca Blank's article (1991) for additional insights into this process.

14. It is important to point out here that I am not automatically identifying this standard form with poor or lacklustre writing. Even the most pedestrian of formats is capable of yielding an outstanding result. Both pieces by Stigler and Friedman are clearly written and lively in style. The focus of this article is on the effect of universalising one particular format.

15. One curious change was the addition of a mandatory list of references at the end of an article. This first became noticeable in the AER during the 57-58 era. By 1959 it was nearly universal. On the other hand, though first appearing in the JPE in 1961, it did not become general practice in that journal until 1967. I have no explanation for the delay in adopting what seems to me to be a very useful practice.

16. "First, the scientific paper in economics has an implied reader it shares with other self-consciously scientific productions of the culture. The implied reader has some features that are unattractive: he is cold-blooded, desiccated, uninvolved. The case of Isaac Newton and his invention, the scientific paper, is the model." (McCloskey, 1990, p. 138).

17. By confusing these two, the defining characteristics of evolution receive a moral uplift which they neither need or desire. Biology provides no obvious or implicit ladder waiting to be scaled over the course of history. Only varying species and changing environments exist. Pre-determined

purposes have a hard time loitering around such premises. Selection, in this context, serves only to confuse since Darwin does not use the term quite so literally. No one selects. A multitude of random variants operate in a time specific environment. Those that make an appropriate match flourish. This is not a matter of superior planning but of chance.

Strictly speaking, there are no edifying lessons to be drawn, no superior claims for one species over another. "Darwins' 'law of the survival of the finest' is often misunderstood; Nature being supposed to secure, through competition, that those shall survive who are fittest to benefit the world. But the law really is that the races are most likely to survive who are best fitted to thrive in their environment: that is to turn to their own account those opportunities which the world offers to them." (Marshall, 1923, p. 175)

18. The traditional misuse of evolutionary metaphors is symptomatic of the failure of economists to actually read critically. Few seem to have read Darwin or other works on evolution. Instead they accept an oral tradition that allows economists to ignore the original work while still citing it as an authority. The consequence of this form of intellectual laziness will be explored further in the following section.

19. The basis for critical reading will be discussed later in the paper. Among other things, it involves looking for a comprehensive and consistent interpretation of an article as well as adopting a generous attitude to an author. This means trying to understand what an author is trying to do before focusing on where he or she has gone wrong. Particularly, the latter objective should not inform the former.

20. "One cause of disagreement is an oversimplified theory of reading. The theory of reading adopted officially by economists and other scientists is that scientific texts are - transparent, a matter of 'mere communication,' 'just style,' simply 'writing up' the 'theoretical results' and 'empirical findings'." (McCloskey, 1990, pp.37-38) "We cannot succeed in making even a single sentence mean one and only one thing; we can only increase the odds that a large majority of readers will tend to interpret our discourse according to our intentions." (Gopen and Swan, 1990, p.557)

21. "Clearly the existence of established standards provides a powerful rationalization for the continued use of formalisation. I maintain that formalisation for the sake of formalisation alone has never been, and will never be knowingly acceptable or confessed to by most economists." (Katzner, 1991, p.23)

At least subconsciously, many economists identify a good paper as synonymous with one which is highly formalised. Wishing to be published, an aspiring economist will not question whether in a particular case formalising is justified. That is simply what the market demands. Though, it would be the height of naivety for anyone, even an economist, to admit that he or she was presenting mathematical formalisation merely for the sake of formalising; that he or she were in effect opening a latch gate with a rocket launcher merely in order to get an article published. Such an innocent, candide like character is hard to imagine. A wise economist knows his or her audience. How many economists when handed the work of a colleague simply respond only partially in jest "Just show me the equations." On such an audience, anything but the most rudimentary rhetorical style would be wasted.

22. Notice the parallel here with management theory of the postwar era. Leading business schools cultivated a dominant belief that one abstract model was capable of encompassing all situations. Lately, given the fiascos of the eighties, more emphasis is being given to the specifics of production.

23. You'll have to trust me on this one. I know it is in there but I'm not prepared to dig through those two huge volumes just to silence the unbelievers.

24. Klamer and Colander (1990) have looked in some detail at the topic of professional education and the type of economists it tends to produce.

25. John Kenneth Galbraith's efforts have long been dismissed as mere journalism, or the work of a novelist. The economics profession has somehow managed to causally link what commonly is termed 'good writing' with superficiality of treatment. Only the most stridently inoffensive, if not turgid, prose is deemed to be serious.

26. Hoover's review is deliberately intemperate, matching Mirowski's confrontational style with spleen.
Yet, reading this book gave me a slowly, rising feeling of outrage. Taken as a whole, it is an outrageous book: neither the history nor the methodology are persuasive; the scholarship is often slapdash; the tone is intemperate; and the style is often obnoxious. Mirowski's hatred of neoclassical economics borders on the pathological: one sometimes wonders if his mother didn't run off with a neoclassical economist, leaving little Phil bereft in the cradle." (Hoover, 1991, 9, 139)
Hoover's review is thus an attempt at demolition rather than a critical review. If indeed he finds the rhetorical style so bereft of redeeming value, it is curious that he should take to imitating it in his review. As such he is guilty of much that he finds objectionable about Mirowski's approach. He should rather explain why the style is inappropriate and then like Varian point out the weaknesses in Mirowski's case. Using ridicule to plead a position is a legitimate choice. It simply does not seem to be an appropriate one for Hoover to use despite his protestations. "Some may believe that my taking such great exception to Mirowski's style is part of an overly refined sense of academic decorum. I do not think so. Some styles of argument are calculated to shut off reasonable discussion. At that I feel bound to protest." (Hoover, 1991, p.145)

27. An appropriate presentation is one that conveys the author's intended meaning in the simplest and most accessible manner possible. This doesn't mean simplified to the lowest possible denominator. Instead, one needs to ask. "How does this presentation convey the intended meaning of the piece more accurately than some feasible alternative? Is this bit of prose, poetry, or mathematical formalisation really necessary to further the aim of this article?"

28. Ricardo is using price here to refer to exchange value as he explains in a note. "The reader is desired to bear in mind, that for the purposes of making the subject more clear, I consider money to be invariable in value, and therefore every variation of price to be referable to an alteration in the value of the commodity." (Ricardo, 1886, p.60n)

29. The lowly status accorded to the history of economic thought reflects the lack of regard the profession has for such work.

This is not regarded as serious research but rather as a hobby capable of amusing economists in their declining years.

30. But whilst this limiting case might become practically important in future, I know of no example of it hitherto. Indeed, owing to the unwillingness of most monetary authorities to deal boldly in debts of long term, there has not been much opportunity for a test. Moreover, if such a situation were to arise, it would mean that the public authority itself could borrow through the banking system on an unlimited scale at a nominal rate of interest. (Keynes, 1936, p.-107)

31. Curiously enough, Coase's (1937) simultaneous foray into the issue of transaction costs would also be largely ignored. Perhaps it just wasn't obvious how to incorporate either insight.

32. Many articles have tried to dislodge this myth from the collective memory of the profession, all to no avail. One good attempt is made by Applebaum, (1979)

33. This is strangely equivalent to literary critics relying on the movie version of James Joyce's work as the basis of their analysis.

34. In a sense, McCloskey imitates the skilful psycho-analyst. Awareness precedes the cure, or to be more exact, the shedding of the old for the new personality. This process of therapy doesn't even start however until there is an initial desire for change. That is why Dr. McCloskey's couch will remain largely unoccupied. The profession is still generally satisfied with itself.

References

Applebaum, E. (1979) "The Labour Market," in Eichner, A.S. ed. *A Guide to Post-Keynesian Economics*, M.E. Sharpe: New York, pp.100-120.

Baudelaire, C. (1964) *Les Fleurs Du Mal*, Eidtions Gallimard: Paris.

Baumol, W.J. (1979) "On The Folklore Of Marxism," *Proceedings of the American Philosophical Society*, CXXIII:2, pp.124-128.

Blank, R.M. (1991)"The Effects of Double-Blind versus Single-Blind Reviewing: Experimental Evidence from *The American Economic Review*," *American Economic Review*, LXXXI:5, pp.1041-1067.

Bronfenbrenner, M. (1990) "Economics as Dentistry," *Southern Economic Journal*, LVII:3, pp.599-605.

Caldwell, B.J. (1991) "Has Formalization Gone Too Far in Economics: A Comment," *Methodus*, III:I, pp.27-29.

Coase, R.M. (1937) "The Nature of the Firm," *Economica*, IV:3 pp.386-405.

Coats, A.W. (1991) "The Learned Journals in the Development of Economics and the Economics Profession: The British Case" *Economic Notes*, XX:1, pp.89-116.

Ellis, E.V. and G.C. Durden (1991) "Why Economists Rank Their Journals the Way They Do," *Journal of Economics and Business*, XLIII:2, pp.265-70.

George, H. (1958) *Progress and Poverty: an inquiry into the cause of industrial depressions and of increase of want with increase of wealth.- the remedy*, Robert Schalkenback Foundation: New York.

Gleick, J. (1987) *Chaos,* Penguin: New York.

Gopen, G.D. and J.A. Swan (1990) "The Science of Scientific Writing," *American Scientific,* LXXVII, pp.550-558.

Graves, R. (1955) *The Greek Myths Volume 1,* Penguin: Middlesex.

Hoover, K.D. (1991) "Mirowski's Screed: A Review of Philip Mirowski's More Heat than Light: Economics as Social Physics, Physics as Nature's Economics," *Methodus,* III:3, pp.139-145.

Katzner, D.W. (1991) "In Defense of Formalization in Economics," *Methodus,* III:3 pp.17-25.

Keynes, J.M. (1973) *The Collected Works of John Maynard Keynes* Vol. IV, MacMillan: London and Basingstoke.

Keynes, J.M. (1936) *The General Theory of Employment, Interest and Money,* MacMillan: London.

Keynes, J. (1973) *The Collected Works of John Maynard Keynes* Vol. XIII, MacMillan: London.

Klamer, A. and D. Colander (1990) *The Making of an Economist,* Westview Press: Boulder.

Kline, M. (1980) *Mathematics and the Loss of Certainty,* Oxford University Press: Oxford.

Knight, F.H. (1955) "Schumpeter's History of Economic Analysis," *Southern Economic Journal.* XXI:3, pp.261-72.

Mahoney, J. (1985) *Marshall, Orthodoxy and The Professionalisation of Economics,* Cambridge University Press: Cambridge.

Marshall, A. (1920) *Principles of Economics,* 8th edition, Porcupine Press: Philadelphia.

Marshall, A. (1923) *Industry and Trade,* MacMillan and Company: London.

McCloskey, D.N. (1985) *The Rhetoric of Economics,* University of Wisconsin Press: Madison.

McCloskey, D.N. (1990) *If You're So Smart,* University of Chicago Press: Chicago.

McCloskey, D.N. (1983) "The Rhetoric of Economics," *The Journal of Economic Literature,* XXI:2, pp.481-517.

Meltzer, A. H. (1981) "Keynes's General Theory: A Different Perspective," *Journal of Economic Literature,* XIX:I, pp.34-64

Mill, J.S. (1965) *Principles of Political Economy,* Augustus M. Kelley: New York.

Mirowski, P. (1 989) *More heat than light: Economics as social physics: Physics as nature's economics;* Cambridge University Press: New York.

Mongell, S. and A. E. Roth (1991) "Sorority Rush As A TwoSided Matching Mechanism," *The American Economic Review,* LXXXI:3, pp.876-891.

Montaigne, M. (1965) "An Apology for Raymond Sebond," *The Complete Essays of Montaigne,* Stanford University Press: Stanford.

Ricardo, D. (1886) *The Works of David Ricardo,* John Murray: London.

Sowell, T. (1960) "Marx's 'Increasing Misery' Doctrine," *The American Economic Journal,* L:1, pp.111-120.

Stigler, G.J. (1951) "The Kinky Oligopoly Demand Curve And Rigid Prices," in Boulding, K.E. and G.J. Stigler eds. *Readings in Price Theory,* Allen and Unwin: London, pp.410-439.

Stigler, G. (1961) "Alfred Marshall's Lectures on Progress and Poverty," *Journal of Law and Economics,* X:I, pp.181-183.

Sweezy, P.M. (1939) "Demand Under Conditions Of Oligopoly," *The Journal of Political Economy,* XLVII:4, pp.568-573.

Thomas, A. (1964) *Summa Theologiae,* Blackfriars McGraw Hill: Cambridge.

Turgenev, I.S. (1950) *Fathers and Sons,* Hamilton: London.

Varian, H. (1991) "More heat than light: A review article" *Journal of Economic Literature,* XXIX:2. pp.595-596.

Veblen, T. (1976) "On the Penalty of Taking the Lead," *The Portable Veblen,* Penguin Books: Middlesex.

Whitely, R. (1991) "The Organisation and Role of Journals in Economics and Other Scientific Fields," *Economic Notes,* XX:I, pp.6-32.

BOOK REVIEW COLUMN

Mirowski's Screed: A Review of Philip Mirowski's *More Heat than Light: Economics as Social Physics, Physics as Nature's Economics*. Cambridge: Cambridge University Press, 1990, Pp. xii + 450. $59.50 IBSN 0-521-35042-5.

Kevin D. Hoover
University of California, Davis

More Heat Than Light! - that sums it up quite accurately. Alas, it will take more than four words to convince the reader of the soundness of such a stark judgement.

Mirowski's book is a sustained attack on the foundations of modern neoclassical economics. He gives a succinct statement of his thesis:

The only way to fully comprehend value theory in economics is to situate it within .... the metaphorical simplex of energy, motion, body and value, and to regard it as part and parcel of the same structures that undergird Western physics. [pp. 141-21]

If true, this thesis has severe consequences for our understanding of the history of economic thought and for the methodology of economics. Beyond economics, Mirowski aims to undermine the nexus between social theory and the natural sciences. A key slogan runs: "Physical metaphors used to describe social processes are spuriously grounded in the natural phenomena" (p. 318).

I hold no special brief for neoclassical economics. Throughout his book, Mirowski scatters many telling criticisms of the details of neoclassicism and of the inappropriate imitation of the physical sciences by economists. He offers some attractive ideas for the development of the discipline. Yet, reading this book gave me a slowly rising feeling of outrage. Taken as a whole, it is an outrageous book: neither the history nor the methodology are persuasive; the scholarship is often slapdash; the tone is intemperate; and the style is often obnoxious. Mirowski's hatred of neoclassical economics borders on the pathological: one sometimes wonders if his mother didn't run off with a neoclassical economist, leaving little Phil bereft in the cradle. Mirowski strikes a flashy, bullying tone throughout the book, patronizing the reader, economists and physicists. He offers consistently uncharitable readings of almost everyone - Veblen, Georgescu-Roegen and a few obscure figures in the history of economic thought excepted.

I

Mirowski's argument is about metaphor and the role of metaphorical exchanges in the development of physics and economics. In the development of energy physics, which is central to this book, accounting notions and notions of economy of action are borrowed from economics. Mirowski cites the suggestive example of Joule, who may have gotten his inspiration for his research into the mechanical equivalent of heat from carefully maintained accounts of his family's brewery: energy was like money - the diligent bookkeeper had to account for every last tuppence. Mirowski maintains that economics readily borrowed from physics as well, and, by the time of the rise of neoclassicism, the exchange was pretty much one way from energy physics to economics.

Mirowski visualizes the metaphorical complex involved in these exchanges as a triangular pyramid, with "energy" at its apex and "motion," "body," and "value" at the vertices of its base. In chapter 2 he reviews the development of energy physics from the late 18th century through the early 20th century as elaborations of one or other of the metaphorical relations of the three faces of this pyramid. Despite its stylistic infelicities, this is the most fascinating part of the book, even for someone who has heard the story before.

Mirowski argues that the notion of energy and its associated conservation law were not simultaneously discovered as standard histories report. First, each of the putative discoverers, Mayer, Joule, Helmholtz and Colding, were elaborating the metaphorical complex rather than finding an "energy" that was out there independent of their own understandings - i.e., energy was not discovered. Second, the "discoverers" were working on different faces of the energy pyramid. This explains why, in Mirowski's view, it did not occur to them that they were all doing the same thing - in fact they were not.

Mirowski then goes on to trace the development of the law of the conservation of energy and thermodynamics. By the end of the 19th century, it appeared that physics was achieving a grand unification with energy as *the* central concept. The energetics movement associated with Ostwald began to view energy as the key to everything. But then, around the turn of the century, it all began to unravel. Planck and others attacked Ostwald as misunderstanding the basis of the existing energy physics; and that physics itself began to disintegrate. Quantum mechanics and the theory of relativity fractured the hard-won unity of physics, and the law of the conservation of energy was transmuted into symmetry principles that were specifically tailored to different physical theories which no longer formed a unified whole. Not only had the conservation of energy lost its overarching status, E $= mc^2$ suggested that energy might not be conserved, but could be converted into matter and vice versa. Further elaborations of relativity theory suggested that the homely thought behind the law of the conservation of energy - nothing comes from nothing - might be wrong: "It now appears possible that the universe is a free lunch" (Mirowski. p. 392, quoting Guth 1983, p. 215).

All economics, at least from the advent of mercantilism, was in Mirowski's view, involved in the elaboration of the same metaphorical complex of energy/motion/body/value. But the two-way street of metaphorical exchange between physics and economics became essentially a one-way street with the marginal revolution of the 1870s, and a divided highway once physics itself lost its unity in the 20th century.

According to Mirowski (p.3) "…. the progenitors of neoclassical economic theory boldly copied the reigning physical theories of the 1870s." He dubs this physics "protoenergetics." It is the energy physics that developed out of rational mechanics before the second law of thermodynamics introduced the notion of the irreversibility of thermodynamic processes. Mirowski's claim is extremely strong: "… those neoclassicals did not imitate physics in a desultory or superficial manner; no, they copied their models mostly term for term and symbol for symbol, and said so" (p.3). Of this claim, more anon.

The central problem for neoclassical economics

is that it failed to see that copying physics leads to absurdity. After the protoenergetics stage, physics developed away from substance accounts of energy toward field accounts. Conservation of energy can be expressed technically as the requirement that energy be represented by an irrotational conservative vector field. The characterization of an economy as the simultaneous maximization of utility functions subject to budget constraints is analogous to the field formalisms of physics. Had economics developed its metaphorical borrowing from physics along the same lines as physics itself developed, it would have been forced to impose the conservation law in the form of an irrotational vector field. But then the analogue of the law of conservation of energy would state that the sum of utility (analogous to potential energy) and expenditure (analogous to kinetic energy) would have to be a conserved quantity. But that is an economic absurdity; utility and expenditure do not have the same dimensions. Mirowski faults neoclassical economics for not exploring the complete implications of the energy metaphor; and, because those implications are unsavory in the extreme, for adopting the energy metaphor at all.

Mirowski notes various physicists and mathematicians who raised questions about the appropriateness of the energy metaphor for economics, and, particularly, about the counterpart to the law of the conservation of energy. These took the form: are utility fields integrable? He maintains that, after the turn of the century, when these questions were not satisfactorily answered, economists - in large measure because of their mathematical incompetence - simply ignored the question of integrability for nearly thirty years. The sores of an inappropriate metaphor continued to fester. In the 1930s, an influx of engineers and mathematicians raised mathematical competence among economists to a new height. Integrability was rediscovered. Now, however, it was seen as an economically insignificant technical point. Mirowski believes that this attitude was part of an elaborate shell game in which the physics of protoenergetics continued to drive the development of neoclassical economic theory, while economists denied the centrality of the physics metaphor for their own discipline. For this charade - for Mirowski repeatedly questions the motives of the economists involved - Paul Samuelson is held chiefly to blame.

II

No one can doubt that economists in the 19th century, as well as before and after, looked to physics as an inspiration for scientific economics, they borrowed its mathematics and found economic analogies for some of its concepts, such as energy. Physics was a resplendent jewel in the crown of the modern intellect. Other disciplines, not just economics, sought to stand in the reflected glory of its scintillating light. Mirowski maintains, however, that physics and economics were bound together more tightly than this suggests: both were elaborations of the single metaphorical complex represented in the energy pyramid. While it is clear in retrospect that the energy pyramid has considerable taxonomic purchase in the history of physics, Mirowski provides no evidence that it had any heuristic power, that it in any way *guided* the development of either physics or economics. Emulation of physics was part of the *Zeitgeist* of the 19th century: it was simply in the air; people talked about energy the way they now talk about quantum mechanics or relativity, usually without rigor and often (as Mirowski himself notes) without understanding or perspicacity. Mirowski denies that the linkage was this loose:

> ..... the research program at each vertex [of his energy pyramid] is *essentially the same metaphor.* Here is the sense in which we are no longer dealing with prosaic notions of intellectual cross-disciplinary influences, *Zeitgeist,* or epistemes. *The research program situated at each vertex derives legitimacy for its radically unjustifiable principles from the homeomorphisms with the structures of explanation at the other vertexes. [p. 1 16]*

Significantly, Mirowski does not provide a single instance of the "word-for-word, symbol-for-symbol" borrowing of physics that he promises. There is much equivocation. Apparently, any time any economist uses the words "energy" or "conservation" Mirowski reports them as buying into the fine details of the protoenergetics program. Similarly, any time a physicist uses a word like "value" or a phrase like "nothing comes from nothing" Mirowski sees an appeal to economics. But all these words have now, and had then, meanings that were not closely rooted in any economic or physical theory. *"Ex nihilo fit nihil fit"* was already known to metaphysics when "economics" referred to housekeeping and was beneath a philosopher's contempt.

The direct and conscious parallels drawn between physics and neoclassical economics that Mirowski cites are invariably surrounded with caveats noting that no analogy with physics will be exact in every detail. Jevons's clearest direct borrowing from physics in his *Theory of Political Economy* is the discussion of the law of the lever. In context, however, it is evident that his point has to do with what sorts of mathematics can be used in certain classes of problems, and not with *precise* analogies between levers and economical systems. Similarly, Fisher is clear that his use of hydrostatic analogies in *The Purchasing Power of Money* (p. 108) and elsewhere are merely suggestive, and not exact. Mirowski reproduces a table from Fisher's doctoral dissertation in which he draws explicit analogies between economics and physics. But Mirowski finds it necessary to construct his own supplement to this table drawing his own further analogies in order to convict Fisher of a complete and precise borrowing of the physics metaphor. Nor is this harmless filling in of obvious lacunae: Mirowski (p. 230) must refer to his own additions to convict Fisher's system of involving absurdities. At the same time, Mirowski is not at all happy that Fisher attempts to insert economic considerations into his table that are not one-for-one with the elements of physics.

It is a good thing that modem physics supports the notion that something may come from nothing, for Mirowski repeatedly draws substantive conclusions from what is not there. His treatment of Fisher's table is a typical example of this rhetorical tactic, which we might name the "evidential free lunch." A few further examples follow.

In Mirowski's view, Fisher's thesis stands convicted of contravening the logic of metaphorical reasoning and failing to perceive the fundamental conflict between the physics of the conservative vector field and neoclassical economics. It happens that J. Willard Gibbs, the imminent thermodynamicist, was one of Fisher's advisers. Unable to produce evidence of Gibbs criticizing Fisher, Mirowski "conjectures" (to use his own word, p. 242) Gibbs's objection:

> Gibbs ..... undoubtedly asked Fisher why Fisher's indifference lines should be able to be integrated into utility surfaces. Far from being a minor technical complaint, Gibbs probably tried to make Fisher aware that the

absence of integrability would necessarily mean that there could exist no such quantity as total utility, and path independence of equilibrium would be compromised. What he apparently never understood was that Gibbs wanted to know why Fisher did not explore integrability as the next logical step towards a dynamic theory of optimization ..... Fisher, uncomprehending, instead went on to say that he did not need integrability for his theory, and indeed, he did not need utility, period. This statement only served to demonstrate that he was out of his depth. We can date the collective neoclassical neurosis with regard to the physics metaphor from this point. [p. 243]

Fisher is convicted for wrongly responding to objections for which there is no tangible evidence that Gibbs made. And this is *the* critical juncture in the history of neoclassical economics! I submit that there is a very good reason to believe that Mirowski's conjectured exchange never took place: Gibbs was Fisher's adviser, and he signed off on his thesis, which he surely would not have done had he imagined it to be fundamentally flawed. Or does Mirowski have further conjectural "evidence" that Gibbs was unusually negligent in fulfilling his academic obligations?

A second example comes from Mirowski's recounting of the inquiries of the mathematician, Hermann Laurent. Laurent, at different times, wrote letters full of searching questions about the mathematics, particularly about integrability, of Walras's and of Pareto's systems. Mirowski presents the economists as, by turns, dunderheaded and evasive. He concludes that they failed to communicate because "Laurent understood the physics, and Pareto [and, by a well-supported inference from Mirowski's explicit comments, Walras] did not" (p. 247). Mirowski then wonders at Laurent's *Petit traite d'economie politique mathématique* for supporting the Lausanne school. "His questions 'about integrability' .... were never adequately answered by the protagonists, and so it appears he just passed them by in his own treatise" (p.247). The fact that Laurent supports the Lausanne school and does not recapitulate his questions suggests to me either that he regarded his questions as having been adequately answered in the end or that he regarded the issue as being of secondary

importance or that he doubted his own standing in the debate. In any case, absent Mirowski's own interpretations of which Laurent was no doubt innocent, the evidence of Laurent against neoclassical economics is weak.

III

A central problem in Mirowski's view of history and method is that metaphors are all important, yet there is no explanation of their mode of influence. Indeed, it is not at all clear what a metaphor is for Mirowski: almost every term in every context is described as metaphorical, so one wonders if Mirowski recognizes words as ever having a primary non-metaphorical usage at all. He may not; for he frequently expresses radical skepticism about the "thereness" of energy, of value, of motion, of body, of just about everything. The mildest forms of "realism" are suspect. He speaks of metaphorical resonances. On the one hand, he accuses economists of detailed copying; on the other hand, he asserts that they (consciously or unconsciously) strive to cover up their tracks. Fisher again provides a good example:

His chosen tactic was to *avoid discussion of the conservation of energy* at all costs, even if it meant some misrepresentation of the model appropriated from physics. [p.230]

Here Mirowski takes Fisher's primary task to be the appropriation and elaboration of the physics metaphor. An alternative and more reasonable interpretation was that Fisher's primary task was to make sense of economic problems. If the physics metaphor implied the absurdity that money and utility were directly commensurable (not that there is any evidence that Fisher understood this implication), then so much worse for the metaphor.

Mirowski subscribes to the *metaphorical imperative:* to use a metaphor is to commit oneself to the complete mapping of that metaphor onto the subject at hand. But surely, if my love is like a summer's breeze, I still have no reason to think that an anemometer would help to gauge the intensity of her devotion.

Mirowski recognizes this but asserts that scientific metaphors are different from poetic metaphors and "have different criteria of efficacy and success" (p.278)

But why? Mirowski's only halfway persuasive reason is that one of the most attractive aspects of analogical reasoning is the prefabricated nature of an interlocked set of explanatory structures and constructs, allowing quickened evaluation of logical coherence" (p.272). But if the choice comes down either to adapting to the requirements of the economic problem or to further prosecuting a metaphor beyond the point at which it is apt, what advantages does such prefabrication provide? Aside from the advantages of prefabrication there simply is no *argument* in favor of the metaphorical imperative. There is only bald assertion. Poetic metaphors, in Mirowski's view, need not be (indeed, should not be) fully prosecuted; but to deny that scientific metaphors must ".... is to deny the possibility of scientific metaphor" (p. 279). This from an avowed enemy of scientism in economics.

Recall that Mirowski is suspicious of all forms of realism, so the imperative of the metaphor replaces the imperative of the economic problem. Explorations of lexicographic preferences are condemned, for example, because they reflect ignorance of the root metaphor of neoclassical economics, no matter how much they may suit the economic behavior of people (p. 366). "Contrary to the ideology of neoclassicism, we are not so indifferently free to choose [the aspects of the physics metaphor we like or dislike]" (p. 272). The metaphorical imperative helps to structure inquiry ".... which might otherwise be even more rife with rampant individualism .... than is already the case" (p. 279). The intellectual connection between nominalistic metaphysics and intolerance and totalitarian impulses could not be more neatly illustrated.

The most frequently employed rhetorical paradigm in Mirowski's accounts of economists is, "When did you stop beating your wife?" Walras, for example, is, on the one hand, savaged for his mathematical incapacities and his inability to complete the analogy between physics and his economics. On the other hand, when Mirowski completes the analogy on his behalf, Walras is convicted of economic absurdity. Interestingly, Mirowski admits that whatever the problems of the first three editions of Walras's *Elements,* the fourth edition is free of taint because it restricts itself to virtual trades (i.e., the auctioneer coordinates everything without allowing false trading) (p. 252). The Arrow-Debreu model is similarly free of taint. What an admission! Walras saw the necessity of altering his model, not because of the energy metaphor (Mirowski assures us that he was too incompetent to pursue that very far) but because of internally generated problems with his earlier account.

Mirowski's view of neoclassical economics is narrow and blinkered: it appears to be coextensive with utility-based general equilibrium price theory. But few self-described neoclassicals worry much about general equilibrium. Marshall, Friedman, and most practitioners of applied microeconomics, including those who invoke general equilibrium most heavily (estimators of demand systems and computable general equilibrium modelers) do not expect a perfect match between neoclassical price theory and the economy. Instead, they find the model suggestive of important aspects of the economy; they are aware of many of the humbler criticisms that Mirowski, along with many others, have made (e.g., absence of an auctioneer, unstable preferences, failure to characterize process); and they are not slaves to the metaphor.

In this, they are hardly different from the physicists. As Mirowski tells it 19th-century physicists dreamed the Laplacian dream of a complete dynamic, deterministic model of everything: a giant Hamiltonian equation in which one need only specify the initial conditions and the future and past of the universe would unfold before one's eyes. But Poincaré demonstrated that Hamiltonian dynamics had severely limited applicability. Nonetheless, Hamiltonian dynamics are still central to many areas of physics. Mirowski observes: "Thus, if the Poincaré theorem was the rude awakening from the Laplacian Dream, most of the dreamers merely rolled over and went back to sleep" (p. 73). Physics has seen no reason to abandon Hamiltonian dynamics or energy or its conservation laws (pp. 90-9 1).

The physicists have very good reasons for maintaining 19th century mechanics in spite of its failure as a model of everything. Similarly, neoclassical economics has its uses as well as its flaws. Marshall saw this clearly. Mirowski, however, is no friend of Marshall: "There was no solution, so Marshall papered the whole thing over with a florid pattern of Victorian common sense" (p. 302). Mirowski is hardly the Poincaré of economics; and economists would do well to stick to Marshallian common sense (florid or plain).

IV

Mirowski's tone is uniformly patronizing. The reader (presumed to be an economist) is patronized: the physics in chapter 2 may be too hard or the reader may not be patient enough or perhaps not civilized enough to have interests beyond economics. The neoclassical economists discussed in the book are patronized: they are all "coy," "disingenuous," "incompetent," and "uncomprehending" with respect to physics and its metaphorical imperatives. Even the physicists are patronized: it is truly amazing that the benighted founders of energy physics advanced their subject at all. And there can be no doubt that Mirowski understands conservation laws better than modern physicists (cf. p. 90). But Mirowski is inconsistent about physics: on the one hand, the scientists do not always get it right; on the other hand, we are repeatedly told that if we, or economists of the past, had only known physics, we or they would have seen through neoclassical economics.

If physicists are sometimes benighted, neoclassical economists are damned; and Lucifer himself is called Paul Samuelson. Or, perhaps, he is only a malevolent wizard: ".... the conjuration of scientific legitimacy by means of vague innuendo abounds in Samuelson's oeuvre" (p. 384). There is more than a little of the pot calling the kettle black here. Samuelson says that his forays into thermodynamics, which he does not think bear a close relation to his economics, are part of a search for a civilizing intellectual breadth; and they are "fun". Mirowski comments: "I think almost everyone would agree this is ingenuous in the extreme: People generally are not given Nobel prizes for 'fun'" (p. 385). (Perhaps Mirowski's own work is a sore burden. Still, if he would consider the biographies of Nobel prize winners in physics (Feynman, for instance) he might find that fun plays a bigger part than this suggests.) He then goes on to accuse Samuelson of promoting mathematical economics as a smokescreen to cloak the true nature of neoclassical economics from those who might expose the incoherence of the physics metaphor with philosophical or other evaluative discussion.

Earlier Mirowski suggests that Pareto, Walras and Fisher wished to browbeat and hoodwink other economists with their mathematics (pp. 249-50). Browbeating with mathematics and physics is something Mirowski knows something about. No

school of thought is spared. For example, of the Cambridge (England) post-Keynesians, he writes (p. 342):

> If they had been acquainted with a little of the history of physics, they would have seen that their mandate was to explore all of the ways in which a substance theory of value was inconsistent with a field theory of value.

In general, if economists are not presented as too stupid to understand the physics, they are presented as sleepwalkers in the thrall of the energy metaphor, not quite understanding how it disfigures their theories.

There is a glaring omission in Mirowski's discussion of the relationship between economics and physics: John von Neumann. Von Neumann has no entry in Mirowski's index. Indeed, he is mentioned only in the process of asserting that his growth model is genuinely neoclassical in comparison with Sraffa's formally similar model. This is a stunning omission; for von Neumann was an economist and a physicist - and worthy of a Nobel prize in both fields. If competence in physics was the central stumbling block, it is queer that von Neumann did not immediately grasp the difficulties of the energy metaphor.

V

Mirowski's intemperate tone is reinforced by his epideictic (I learned this from him) style. Length and repetition replace argument and evidence. Two-bit words abound. One needs a good dictionary to read Mirowski. My *Concise Oxford English Dictionary* was insufficient. Many times I had to refer to the big *OED*, and once I came up short even there. This may have improved my vocabulary, still "quotidian," "tyro," "tergiversations," "ukase" and "farrago" are not words that improve with frequent use. It was also annoying to find a fair number of Cooperisms (so named in honor of Mark Twain's rules in "Fenimore Cooper's Literary Offenses," "12. Say what he is proposing to say, not merely come near it. 13. Use the right word, not its second cousin"): "*frisson* of excitement," "self-reflexive" and "from whence" are redundant; "Hobson's choice" is not a hard choice, but no choice at all; a power series expansion is not a "Taylor expansion"; meteors fall, they do not rise; while there may be some difficulty in homogenizing them, there should be no problem in "pasteurizing chalk and cheese"; many, not few, heard the "siren song," it is just that, since hearing it resulted in their being smashed on the rocks, they did not live to tell of it - we must presume that Joan Robinson, like Odysseus, was tied to the mast.

An author generally only bears a small part of the blame for proofreading; still, there were many typos. It was a great relief the three times I actually found "accommodate" spelled correctly. It is ironic that a book published by Cambridge University Press should have "Cantabrigian" misspelled.

VI

Some may believe that my taking such great exception to Mirowski's style is part of an overly refined sense of academic decorum. I do not think so. Some styles of argument are calculated to shut off reasonable discussion. At that I feel bound to protest. Once we get past the stylistic barriers, we find that Mirowski's historical claims are unbuttressed by persuasive evidence, and that his methodological rule, - the metaphorical imperative, is pure assertion. Standard histories of economics and physics, which Mirowski appears to hold in great contempt, need not be rewritten. Neoclassical economics is open to severe criticisms (Mirowski himself makes a number of telling criticisms in passing), but these are not integrally connected to the energy metaphor. Elaborating the energy metaphor to its fullest extent is of no importance whatsoever.

No doubt Mirowski would believe that I am a mumpsimus. This lovely, rare and ancient word, which Mirowski learned from Joan Robinson, was first used to describe a semi-literate priest who insisted on reading it where the correct Latin called for "sumpsimus." It now means one who persists in an error that has already been exposed. But if those of us who do not find Mirowski's attack on neoclassical economics to be persuasive are mumpsimuses, perhaps we can do no better than to stand defiantly with the poor priest: "I will not change my old mumpsimus for your old sumpsimus."

Note

I am grateful to my colleague, Julie Nelson, for useful comments on the first draft of this essay.

References

Fisher, Irving. (1985) *The Purchasing Power of Money: Its Determination and Relation to Credit Interest and Crises.* Fairfield, NJ: Augustus Kelley.

Jevons, W. Stanley. (1965) *The Theory of Political Economy,* fifth edition. New York: Augustus Kelley.

ECONOMIC NOSTRUMS AND ECONOMIC PRACTICES - ACCOUNTABILITY IN ECONOMIC JOURNALS

Craig Freedman
Macquire University

Your manuscript is both good and original; but the part that is good is not original, and the part that is original is not good (Samuel Johnson quoted in Bernard 1990, p.75).

Graham Green used to divide his work between serious novels and light entertainments. Using this criterion, it would be tempting to categorise any examination of the economics profession as more froth than substance. Few outsiders find economists fascinating. The world seems wisely content in its ignorance. But since for whatever reason or misadventure we all belong to this limited and limiting club, we do find such self-examinations interesting.

If existing knowledge of our own profession is incomplete, it is not for wont of trying. An alarming number of papers have captured every aspect of the job from teaching to research. The results have appeared in top ranking general journals as well as highly specialised publications. One suspects that these papers are among the more widely read articles published[1]. The generous space and attention accorded to them, might be justified if frequent publication led to needed change in the profession.[2] To be openly cynical, the only tangible result of these endeavours has been the development of a strange field in which economists write about publishing and publications in order to be published. Like other hot house specialities, authors cite each other generously and can thus make a case for the importance, or at least the impact, of their journal articles. But either no practical policies are formulated or, if they are, such suggestions are gleefully ignored. Barring any such beneficial impact, these articles can only be categorised as officially sanctioned gossip. Their status as gossip would account for the frequency with which such articles appear in academic journals. The demand for gossip, even when decked out in the camouflage of statistical analysis, is near insatiable. Knowing full well that the chance for serious reform remains slim, it is still important that such attempts be made. Otherwise, the self-satisfaction of a profession that sees no need for internal critics can only hasten its journey to stagnation and irrelevance.

One of the most overworked of these self-referential veins has been the area of academic publications. This is unsurprising. Promotion, reputation, and perhaps professional self-esteem depends on writing articles that appear in refereed journals.[3] The more prestigious the journal, the more value to be gained. Though articles analysing all aspects of the publishing process are numerous, few have pinpointed the key player in this process, the referee[4]. Evaluating the current state of the refereeing process, one is struck not by its faults and problems but by how a system so heavily dependent upon good will and volunteer labour manages to work at all. If individual economists were simple, self-interested agents, this fragile editorial edifice that regulates the future of each and every one of them might easily collapse. It is this anomaly that needs to be explored, namely how a discipline which emphasises self-interested decision making can be dependent on an institutional structure that relies instead on the moral qualities associated with professional obligations.

The motivations of referees, as is equally true of any group of agents, may easily conflict with the stated objectives of a journal (dissemination of high quality research). The submission and publication process will be flawed if such potential conflicts pose real problems. What carrots and sticks ensure that the requisite jobs are performed well, or at all? These are the logical questions an economist would ask when initially evaluating the effectiveness of any institutional structure. In the case of academic journals this means that achieving the goals of a publication depend on how well editors and referees do their jobs. Evaluating the appropriateness of any existing incentives requires a look at the internal organisation of economic journals. Defects in the refereeing process are likely to be the results of poor corporate governance constrained by the relevant input and output markets. Economic journals have largely retained a governance structure which roughly parallels those that characterise non-profit organisations. The subsequent lack, or at least lower level, of accountability which defines such operations is at the heart of the problem confronting all academics who face the twin demands of publishing as well as refereeing articles. Economics is now at a point where on balance the prevailing non-profit structure tends to inhibit, rather than contribute to, the progress of the profession. There seems to be no good reason why an academic journal cannot be based on the type of property rights exemplified by standard rules of corporate governance. Many journals these days are in fact money making propositions. Retaining a non-profit operational structure reflects only historical antecedents which can and should be discarded. If we are to gain some insight into the current limitation of the editorial and refereeing process, then corporate governance is where analysis must begin.

CLUBS AND CULTS - DEFINING THE ACADEMIC JOURNAL

Please accept my resignation. I don't want to belong to a club that will accept me as a member (Groucho Marx quoted in Partington 1992, p.451)

In the last two decades, journals have become the gatekeepers of academic legitimacy[5]. Tenure, promotion and an increasing level of salary[6] depends upon publishing refereed articles. Given the oversupply of academic economists, counting journal publications is a convenient and generally acceptable way to screen job applicants and decide which staff members to retain as well as which to promote. This extends not only to the number of refereed publications, but the quality of the journal in which the articles are published[7] and the number of times each article is cited by other authors. No such parallel standard of quality exists for teaching or other professional functions.

Whether or not citations actually measure the quality of a paper, they do give some rough approximation of the impact a paper has had on the profession (perhaps a more succinct way of discussing quality). A paper that affects the work of other researchers is bound to be frequently cited. It is less accurate to claim that the number of citations is a close proxy for influence. Papers cited need not have been read. Nor is there any need that cited papers will have had the slightest impact on the author's thinking. Citations can be used by an author to signal that he or she knows the relevant literature. Knowing the literature is a way of presenting one's bona fides, a warranty that an article is worth considering[8]. A standard list of citations is to some extent replicated by all authors working in a similar research field. Despite these and possibly other limitations, citations remain the only measurable output we have to judge quality[9]. We often value what we can measure in lieu of being able to measure what we want.

For over a century, academic entrepreneurs have started economic journals to advance their own interests, that of some professional organisation, or to further a well defined ideology[10]. In pre-war days, the limited size of their target audience prevented the sale of sufficient journal copies to make such a venture commercially viable. In addition, the objectivity of the journal itself might seem compromised if its contents were thought to be influenced by financial imperatives. Publishing economic journals in what was a very restricted market clearly remained a non-profit undertaking i.e. a limited public type good, feasible only when supplied with volunteer labour. Governance structures of economic journals were accordingly those of non-profit organisations[11].

Economic journals are today often profit making enterprises owned by commercial publishers. Others remain part of the output of university presses or are still associated with professional associations. (In these cases the subscription to the journal is often part of the membership fee.) One can hazard a guess as to why economic journals are now published by profit making concerns. The explosion of research libraries provided a guaranteed market whose demand, at least for a time, seemed relatively price inelastic[12]. The market depends more on prestige, the value attached to being published in a particular journal, than on price. Subscription rates could be set to capture this institutional rather than individual market[13]. The relatively recent rise in current demand indirectly reflects the rapid increase in academic economists[14] as well as the pressure on these economists to do publishable research.

The ownership of these journals (whether profit or non-profit) seems not to effect its operational control. Only the commercial elements; subscription, printing, and distribution are of any concern to the for-profit publisher. Editorial integrity and independence is signalled by perpetuating the non-profit governance structure which as Hansmann (1980) notes, inspires trust even at the cost of greater efficiency. This also attracts the requisite voluntary labour essential for the commercial viability of these journals. If the governance structure of commercially published academic journals maintains the form developed by the strictly non-profit enterprises, then understanding that particular organisational structure is necessary before commencing any further analysis[15].

A typical academic journal is hard to characterise. Standard corporate governance, reflecting commercial values, is wrapped around a nugget of non-profit structure. This poses a dilemma. Corporations and non-profit organisations serve different constituencies. Corporations have their prime allegiance to their owners. Non-profit organisations have no owners[16]. It is not surprising that in organisations with poorly specified property rights, the contractual responsibilities of agents, especially those supplying voluntary labour should also be poorly delineated.

It follows from these basic notions that the corporate charter serves a rather different function in nonprofit organizations than it does in for-profit organizations. In the case of the business corporation, the charter, and the case law that has grown up around it, protect the interests of the corporations's shareholders from interference by those parties-generally corporate management and other shareholders-who exercise direct control over the organization. In the case of the non-profit corporation, on the other hand, the purpose of the charter is primarily to protect the interests of the organization's *patrons* from those who control the corporation (Hansmann, 1980, p.845).

Patrons can vary depending on the type of nonprofit in question. They may be the supplier or source of cash flow (donors or receivers of the service offered). Or they may be the actual producer of the service. (Non-profit hospitals are sometimes said to cater to its doctors rather than its patients[17]).

We can deal with this patron question by dividing non-profits into four categories. The determining characteristics are the source of funding and type of governance that predominates.

Table 1

NON-PROFIT ORGANISATIONS		
	Mutual[1]	*Entrepreneurial[2]*
Donative[3]	Professional Societies Political Parties	Charities Religious Organisations
Commercial[4]	Social Clubs	Academic Journals Hospitals

Hansmann, 1980, p.842
[1] Mutual refers to those non-profit organisations which have their members choose its executive officers.
[2] Entrepreneurial refers to those non-profit organisations whose management is largely self-perpetuating.
[3] Donative refers to organisations that receive their funding through donations.
[4] Commercial refers to organisation that receives the majority of its funding through user fees, though it may also receive some donations as well

Journals fall into the commercial category. Subscriptions are their main source of funds. There might be some charitable aspect to the decision to subscribe, but for the most part journals are bought for the content they supply or more exactly the use that subscribers believe can be made from that content. More importantly, journals are generally run by a self-elected group who pass on control to their own designated successors. For all practical purposes, effective authority does not rest in any outside body[18]. Outside interests (the broader academic community) could be represented by a journal's editorial board. In practice, they fail to noticeably check, or even appreciably influence editorial decisions[19].

Journals, unlike most non-profit organisations, lack a definitive patron who can check managerial discretion. Readers are a journal's most obvious candidates for this role. Subscription numbers depend upon their direct or indirect decisions. But journals do not exist primarily to meet perceived consumer demand. Journals are more precisely a special type of club. They provide space in which academics can publish and thus gain professional recognition and promotion[20]. Ostensibly, journals do exist to disseminate ideas that extend and advance economic knowledge. This doesn't rule out other, more implicit, motives: (1) journals originate and expand to meet the publication demands of the profession; (2)

entrepreneurial editors can use journals to advance their personal interests whether it consists of promoting their own careers, those of friends and allies or, of pushing a particular line of thought.

Economic journals do not represent standard commercial opportunities, however much their origin may be entrepreneurial by analogy. The impetus for their formation has common cause with the professionalisation of other endeavours. In such cases, whether we are speaking of law or medicine, or in earlier years of the clergy, the idea was to be able to exclude the masses, admitting only a relative few to the club[21]. Although the club existed to promote the careers of its members, the club itself need not and in fact could not pursue profit as its primary goal. Benefits are assumed to be passed to its membership. This would be put in doubt if it was to be run so as to benefit a set of proprietors instead. The key is whether the same rules of exclusion would be in force or if monetary considerations might at least sometime prevail. This is easily understood in the case of professional organisations but also holds for academic journals by analogy[22]. Membership is publication. A membership board either accepts applicants or blackballs them. (This board consists of editors assisted by a select group of referees. The referees are often either known personally to the editors and/or previously published in the journal[23]. Published authors are de facto authorities in the area of their publication).

> A system of exclusive clubs has a natural tendency to become stratified, so that the highest-status individuals gather together in one club, the next-highest stratum of individuals in another club, and so forth. Indeed, such a pattern is fairly easy to discern among the clubs found in many communities. Since most people would prefer to be in the most exclusive clubs, those clubs have a degree of monopoly power. A profit-seeking owner of a highly exclusive club would have every incentive to use this power to exploit his own members, for example, by means of membership dues well in excess of costs. In effect, he would be selling the members their own high status at a monopoly profit (Hansmann, 1980, p.893).

Clubs (like professional organisations) are often unwilling to discipline members unless they act in a manner clearly detrimental to club members. Accountability tends to be lax with agency relationships not sufficiently defined. This inherent weakness is magnified when applied to academic journals. A journal is more of a virtual than actual club. The application procedure forms the basis for the club's existence. As a result, a successful applicant (published author) does not become a permanent member but begins the application procedure again with each new paper submitted. (Though subsequent publication seems easier once the initial acceptance is granted.) Since membership lacks permanence, members fail to have any authority over the membership board, compounding this problem. Unlike most clubs, its membership board and management is one and the same, meaning that a lack of accountability is combined with an absence of any clear incentives to perform effectively. The subservience of its applicants to an often self-perpetuating management/membership board ensures this result. In exclusive clubs, members have the ability to vote out management or membership boards when either one diverts benefits to their personal use or fails to perform satisfactorily. An equivalent control mechanism is conspicuous by its absence in academic journals. Internal incentives for change are weak or possibly nonexistent. Outsiders are coopted with the promise of potential membership. As a result, editors are provided with a wide latitude in what they do and how they do it[24].

WHO'S IN CHARGE? - EDITORS AND OUTPUT

The situation reminds me of a retort Harry Johnson, notorious for his sharp tongue, made to George Borts, back in the 1970s when both were editors, George of the AER, Harry of the Journal of Political Economy. George: "Harry, you must have the same problem at the JPE that we have here at the AER: we get more good articles than we know what to do with!" Harry: "Then why don't you publish a few?" (McCloskey, 1995, p.414).

Neither readers, subscribers, or contributors select editors nor threaten their continued control. For that reason, editors do not directly answer to any of these outside groups. Yet editors ultimately decide what gets published in any journal. Who or what keeps the editors in check?

Editorial positions and editorial boards are somewhat self-perpetuating. The largely voluntary nature of their work, the need to maintain the appearance of editorial independence, causes commercial publishers to be wary of meddling. Without the owners of the enterprise exerting control, non-profit organisational structures prevail. Unfortunately, the absence of any outside patron leaves editors largely to their own devices. In a case where there are no real checks on management, it might be said that the journal as club exists for the sake of those managing. Editors are not explicitly checked from following their own self-interest even when it might conflict with the specified or implicit objectives of a journal[25]. A reasonable supposition is that editors have every reason to shirk their full duties and aim for a minimally acceptable performance. The position, is to a large degree, recognition of an economist's past achievements. For this very reason, time spent in editorial duties must carry a high opportunity cost. Being appointed editor is the honour, the bargaining chip on one's CV. It is doubtful that the specific content of the journal is itself strongly associated with the editor in any lasting fashion. Once appointed, the tendency would be to delegate various duties and to minimise time spent overseeing the work done. As long as disasters are avoided, the editor's reputation escapes largely unscathed.

Nor is it clear that the skills that make for highly esteemed researchers are those required to run a journal, only that they suffer a greater opportunity cost by doing so. Editors match articles with the most appropriate referees; those who will evaluate a manuscript in an unbiased manner, offer constructive criticism, and do their jobs promptly. Whatever leverage editors can exert, comes mainly from the reputation of the journals they represent. There is no particular reason to think that a journeyman economist might not fill such a role in an equally acceptable manner. Unlike most governance systems, there is no clear mechanism by which a less than adequate editor may be removed. "A ... possible cause of problems is editorial malfeasance, as editors change or simply let things slide as they lose interest. Barring palace coups or genuine revolutions, this difficulty is not likely to be removed" (Hamermesh, 1994, p.162). Revolutions, even within the narrow confines of academic journals, are not without precedence. However, we hardly have a check on editorial malfeasance if we need to depend on extraordinary measures to ensure accountability.

Editorial Boards do exist and can conceivably overturn an editor's decision or policy[26]. But again, no obvious incentive motivates the academics who hold these somewhat honorary positions to act[27]. Disgruntled authors might conceivably appeal to such boards. It is not unknown for editorial boards to act on a legitimate complaint. An author though would be risking future publication in that journal as long as the current editor remained, an action more a reflection of a death wish on the part of the author than anything else. Editors can subtly kill an article by sending it to a referee certain to provide a negative report. Even if an article does subsequently get published elsewhere, the potential delay in publication still poses a problem. Unfairness might be suspected, but it would be hard to distinguish such complaints from the usual sour grapes of rejected authors. Appeals of any sort are likely to be rare. Hamermesh (1992), in his primer for young, ambitious economists, advises against any contentious behaviour. "Asking for reconsideration may make you look foolish; you may wish to submit future work to the journal; and there are more fish in the sea of journals" (Hamermesh 1992, p.173). If the wise, self-interested, course of action is always exit, rather than voice, it is difficult to see contributors as providing any check on editors. They are more suppliants than censors.

Readers are also, for the most part, ineffectual since many from this group are exactly those who submit articles. Few would wish to jeopardise their own chance of publication. Response to complaints is relatively slow and uncertain since the viability of many journals depends more on their institutional subscribers. Response to reader dissatisfaction, though not unknown, is still rare[28]. If we eliminate publishers, subscribers and contributors, who is left to effectively circumscribe an editor's action? Non-profits are efficient in achieving their stated objectives to the degree to which a powerful outside patron exists. The clear absence of an effective patron stands out as the weak link in a journal's governance structure.

To a degree, editors and editorial boards act as their own patrons. But what harm is really encouraged by such an arrangement? In one sense the editor is highly constrained and can do little to change the journal he or she inherits. Editors can only choose from manuscripts submitted. These are likely to reflect what has been published in the past. The risk averse economist, especially those who have yet to fully establish themselves, writes not for some larger readership, but primarily to be published. The relevant audience is restricted to the editor and referees. (These may be the only readers who will ever give the work anything approaching a careful scrutiny.)[29]

> When I moved on to *The American Economic Review*, I felt that there, at least, I would be seeing a more representative collection of papers come across the desk. Maybe I did. It's hard to tell whether a collection is representative. But the experience turned out to be shattering. What was remarkable was the absolute dullness, the lack of any kind of new idea, that predominated in the selection of papers I got. Close to a thousand manuscripts a year - and I swear that the profession would be better off if most of them hadn't been written, and certainly if most of them hadn't been published. Most of the published papers could have been left in discussion paper form, with a great benefit to everyone and a great saving of resources (Clower, 1988, p.27).

This unfortunately under plays the impact that editors, especially of the more highly regarded journals, have on the careers and even the understanding of the profession. By acting as gatekeepers, they enforce the conventions of the club and shape what is to be published. Form, for instance, is rigorously pursued, sometimes to the point where journal articles become the last refuge of a prevailing minimalism, the remaining shrine where 'more is less' is taken at face value.

There is a practical reason behind such compression. Editors agree that they compete for only a limited number of available good papers (Laband and Piette 1994a). By intentionally compressing submitted articles, they create room for additional articles. As a result, an increasing percentage of their journals must be filled by more marginal pieces[30]. These articles are not poorly constructed or erroneous, but little would be lost if they failed to see the light of day. After publication they remain unread and uncited. These more marginal pieces reflect the degree of unchecked editorial power. An unrepresentative percentage of such articles tend to be the work of authors with whom the editor has some personal or professional connection (Laband and Piette 1994a). One can argue that patronage is relatively harmless in disseminating economic research[31]. Editors do go after good articles. The remaining slots need to be filled with articles that are unlikely to have much, if any, impact. No harm is done if they are awarded in ways that forward the editor's private interest without injuring the journal's objectives. It is largely a matter of knowing where to draw this line. But such practises obscure a more fundamental question. Why should journals have a number of pre-determined slots that exist to meet an editor's more personal objectives?

> Our findings also have implications regarding editorial favoritism, defined in our terms as publication of papers authored by an editor's "friends" that do not meet the same qualitative standard for publication required of authors having no connection to the editor. It seems possible, if not probable, that part of the implicit compensation offered to journal editors is the opportunity to publish low-quality papers, relatively speaking, written by professional friend (including himself) and allies. Indeed, to the extent that an editor can arrange quid pro quos in the form of invitations to give paid lectures, attend prestigious conferences, join esteemed societies, and the like, this prerogative may, on the margin, be one of the more powerful inducements motivating the supply of editors (Laband and Piette, 1994a, p.202).

Editors, whether corrupt, diligent, honest, or lazy can't operate their journals as a solo venture. Their limited time, and the specialised knowledge needed to cope with an ever burgeoning set of sub-fields which continually threaten to swamp the literature, mean that it is necessary to contract out the job of evaluating submissions. Editors choose the contracted agents (referees) and whether or not to abide by their decisions. They almost uniformly fail to influence the referees' actions in any meaningful way. In the same way that the governance link constraining editorial action seems missing, so does the usual constraints on a contracted agent seem absent[32]. If matching papers to referees is an editor's most crucial task, than any inability to properly monitor and reward referees would seem to undermine the effectiveness of any editor, whatever his or her own efforts and abilities might be. Under such circumstances it remains a mystery how either Type I errors (publishing a paper that should not be published) or the more serious Type II errors (not publishing a paper that should be published) are ever avoided.

MAD, BAD AND DANGEROUS TO KNOW - ACADEMIC REFEREES

> ... the whole editorial process works much less well than we pretend, not only the lags, but the objectivity and quality of the refereeing. Almost everyone complains simultaneously about (1) the stupidity of the papers they referee, and (2) the stupidity of the comments made by the referees of their papers. Since everyone is refereeing each other's papers, there is obviously an inconsistency here (an anonymous author quoted in Laband, 1990, p.341).

Like tax collectors or other bearers of bad news, no one is particularly fond of referees. Horror stories abound concerning referee reports that are either incompetent and/or vicious. Authors may wait for six months, and in some cases years, to receive a report consisting of two vague and dismissive paragraphs. Nor is anyone notably keen to be one. Not because the work itself is particularly disagreeable or because it is intellectually unrewarding, but because of the relevant opportunity costs involved. An academic's time is better rewarded producing original work than refereeing the work of others. In particular, being a referee means hard work performed for an insufficient reward. We all know of colleagues that grumble when asked to referee some hopeless manuscript. Referees are a classic case of a necessary evil. Without them the whole basis for an academic career crumbles. Yet, newly minted Ph.D.s receive no training in how to be one. Much like teaching, the supposition is that the degree automatically grants the ability. Surprisingly, for two of the most vital activities an academic economist undertakes, few guidelines are available[33]. Though journals provide a style sheet for submissions, referees are provided with no guidelines, no hint of what the editor expects besides a deadline for returning the requested report.

Referees can be astonishingly useful to authors when the work is done carefully, done more in the manner of a partner exploring meaning and ideas rather than as someone who reads only to winkle out possible faults. This can be true no matter what the referee thinks about the ideas presented, whether he or she agrees or disagrees. By speaking to the author, the referee conveys vital information to the editor concerning the suitability of the article for publication. There is no real need to address the editor directly. It seems hardly coincidental that reports which are editor- focused, seem more intended to demonstrate the referee's own assumed talents than to assist the author of the submitted manuscript. (Reports which provide little in the way of assistance to the author, which are dismissive or which even sneer, can all safely be classified as editor-focused.) These are attempts to build him or herself up at the expense of the author, sometimes by making contradictory demands. The referee tends to take a negative stance, picking the article apart for errors (relatively easy to do in any submission) instead of attempting the far harder task of trying to stretch one's understanding to encompass the author's effort. To give the benefit of the doubt to the text, knowing how difficult it can be to communicate complex ideas, seems a reasonable rule of thumb.

It is questionable whether the current referee system does improve or add value to the papers submitted, as it should, or simply serves to blackball applicants to a variety of journals/clubs[34]. Laband (1990) has tried to empirically test whether refereeing actually adds value[35], by surveying authors whose work was published in the profession's leading journals. Referees in such cases will tend to be well-cited members of the profession (see Hamermesh 1994).

> The results indicate that reviewers value-added apparently derives from efficient matching of manuscripts and reviewers. While these results do not rule out a screening function for the review process in economics, they clearly demonstrate that screening is not the sole function of the review process (Laband 1990, p.342).

Laband (1990) unfortunately fails to distinguish between what should be and what is. Contrary to what Laband (1990) assumes, referee reports may lead to the production of a worse paper. Referees can be narrow minded, willing only to accept material that fits preconceived ideas of acceptable discourse. Many act more like Victorian matrons faced with social improprieties than open minded and inquisitive academics. Not only the material, but the style and methodology must fit into rather restricted boundaries of what they deem to be professionally correct[36].

Response to a referee's report is largely motivated by a desire for publication. Authors acquiesce to a referee's demands due to publication concerns. An author may try to minimise the damage of such acquiescence but few would be willing to risk that additional line on their CVs by objecting too strenuously to what they conceive to be misguided criticism and objections. Laband's (1990) empirical work fails to clarify this issue. Even if we agree that Laband's proxy for reviewer input is useful, his results merely demonstrate that reviewers' inputs correlate with the quality of a subsequently published article. But this relationship is only significant statistically. If we use Laband's values for the quality of the average input (an author's revision time divided by the length of the referee's comments) we discover that these comments increase the quality of a published paper (measured in citations over a five-year period) by an average of 0.25 citations a year. This is hardly anything to get excited about. From these results we might be tempted to say that referees tend to do almost as much harm as good without fear of contradiction. In other words, attempts to comply with the demands of referees may lower the quality of the published paper nearly as often as it raises it. If we were to picture referee reports as normally distributed and ranging between those that greatly improve a paper and those which do significant harm, we could visualise the mean of this distribution as differing very little from zero, i.e. having little or no positive effect on quality. Laband (1990) chooses to put a more optimistic spin on his results even though this interpretation conflicts with some of the responses from his own survey[37].

Editors have no reliable sticks or carrots available to insure that referees turn in a thoughtful consideration of the submitted article which can potentially improve the end result. It is true that since many referees are in turn authors who submit manuscripts to the same journals, outright refusal is difficult and even unwise unless one's reputation is already well established (see Hamermesh 1994). Pulling in the opposite direction, are strong incentives not to spend too much time on the report. While perhaps dangerous to be an outright cad for fear of alienating a potentially helpful editor, reports that are prompt, well thought out, and useful will only bring additional requests to referee. Given that publications rather than referee services yield more attractive returns, editors have very little leverage to exert over referees.

Since time is an increasingly scarce resource for the modern ambitious academic, referees will take whatever shortcuts possible in completing their task. The limited rewards attached to refereeing mean that the rational academic will attempt to satisfice at some minimum required level. To argue to the contrary would be to ask referees to act irrationally, in other words to expect economists to operate contrary to standard economic assumptions. Empirical evidence indicates that where single instead of double blind refereeing exists, referees are more likely to use the name or affiliation of the author as a signal of quality rather than spend time scrutinising the actual manuscript (see Blank 1991 or Laband and Piette 1994). Given the lack of return from refereeing, the procedure is understandable. Unfortunately, it will not consistently yield the best results. Ideally an article should not be judged on the basis of preconceived quality.

For these reasons, we might be strongly inclined to expect the quality of referee reports to have steadily slipped these past two decades. Given the increased demands on academics today to publish (see Stigler and Friedland (1975) to compare past with present academic research output), a rational academic must logically devote less time to refereeing a given paper. Unless we can mysteriously posit a substantial increase in productivity, we can only assume that there is a strong likelihood that the quality of those reports has dropped. In the market for referees, the quality of the refereeing process adjusts according to the relative strengths of the existing forces of demand and supply. As in any standard market, opportunity cost drives the decisions of the relevant participants. (It is true that the market usually does not any involve explicit payments. Even when it does,[38] this provides for fewer delays in the refereeing process but does not touch the quality of those reports. The *Economic Journal* pays referees according to the judged quality of the report. There is no indication that such a method is effective. The opportunity cost of writing a good or especially an excellent report would tend to be higher than the feasible level of recompense. This practise does point out the inability of editors to bring pressure to bear. The price paid is not meant to cover the opportunity cost of performing the task.) Potential referees (supply-side) will be more abundant and willing to take on the chore if the cost of doing so is low. But such relatively painless refereeing must be of dismally low quality. Given the high opportunity cost attached to painstaking analysis, referees willing to take on the task increase, the lower the quality expected.

Editors (demand-side) on the other hand see the opportunity cost of doing their own job lowered by high quality refereeing. Their demand for such refereeing increases, the higher the quality available. Given the explosion of journals and the increased submissions to each journal, it is reasonable to expect that increases in the demand for referees have managed to outstrip supply[39]. (Journals can not expect the same referee to deal with more than a few articles a year.) During that same period, academic positions haven't increased at an equivalent rate. The probable result should be a drop in the quality of an average report[40] (see Figure 1 next page).

The referee as agent would seem to have little need to consult the wishes of his or her principle (the editor). To test whether editors did apply effective sanctions against referees, in June 1994 I surveyed some thirty-one editors[41]. The list of journals, while not comprehensive, was a fair representation. It ranged from the most prestigious to those which had a narrower focus or whose articles were less likely to be cited. The most prestigious journals coincided with those cited by Stigler, Stigler and Friedland (1995). As noted, the profession generally uses citations as a proxy for the quality or at least the importance of an article and the journal that published them.

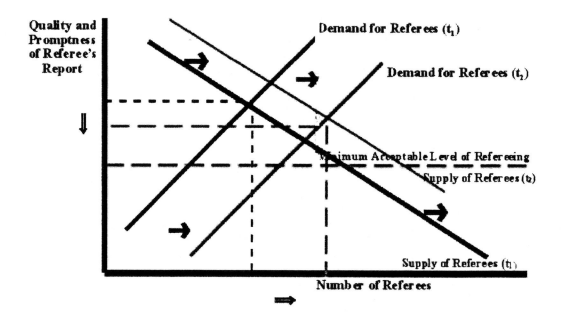

Figure 1 The Market for Referees

Twenty-four of the thirty-one surveys were returned. The percentage of surveys returned did not vary with the type or quality of economic journal. Editors seem a prompt or at least a more punctual bunch than referees. All but three of the returned surveys were received within a month of their initial mailing. The majority arrived within the first two weeks. The survey was designed to promote such a response. It involved only a few minutes of time, perhaps more if one took question number six seriously. Nineteen out of the twenty-four surveys received did take time to write an answer, legible or otherwise, to the last question. These replies, as we will see, were generally compatible with one another, indicating that there is general agreement among editors of what does and does not make for a good referee.

All were promised anonymity. There was no discernable advantage to be other than forthcoming. However, we all are capable of deceiving ourselves. It is impossible to distinguish between the way an editor thinks he or she should act, and the way he or she actually does. But in the case of self-deception, the survey still would convey a consistent picture of desired practise, even if it deviates from actual practise.

The first three questions indicate that referees seldom are given an indication if they are doing a poor job. Without such information, even those with the best of intentions won't improve. Those who are trying to minimise their efforts also won't be shamed into raising their game. The only excuse editors can legitimately plead is the difficultly in obtaining referees who will perform the required task adequately. This may explain the excessive loyalty some editors display in choosing to stick with referees who have a history of poor quality reports.

Table 2

EDITORS' RESPONSES TO POOR QUALITY REPORTS[42]				
	Frequently (91%+)	Usually (50%-90%)	Occasionally (10%-49%)	Infrequently (0%-9%)
Do you inform a referee when his/her report is of poor quality?	8.7%	4.3%	0%	87.0%
Do you cease to use a referee after one or two poor quality reports?	69.6%	26.1%	4.3%	0%
Do you inform a referee that you no longer plan to use him/her?	0%	4.3%	0%	95.7%
If an author of an article convincingly points out the ways in which the referee has failed to do an adequate job does that influence your decision to use the referee again?	22.7%	27.3%	45.5%	4.5%
Do you pass on to the referee critical and/or positive comments by the author of an article concerning the quality of is/her report?	26.1%	21.7%	39.1%	13.1%

Though most editors will drop a non-performing referee, that referee is left to guess the reason why no more requests are forthcoming. More likely the deposed referee is thankful for such a blessing. It is still strange that information doesn't flow more readily. For the last few decades economists have increasingly seen information as one of the key determinatives of any economic system. Yet their own organisations seem excessively sparing with this vital commodity. Editors turn the implicit contractual relations with their chosen referees into something resembling an on-going dating arrangement. When editors tire of a referee, the calls simply stop with no further explanation.

As might be expected, the same lone editor in the survey that had the courtesy or the courage to inform referees when they were to be discontinued also informed referees when an inadequate report was submitted. If one editor can operate by assisting the flow of information to referees, it is a wonder why others can't operate the same way as well. This may depend upon the number of submissions made to the journal and its subsequent demand for referees[43], but the one maverick editor in the survey could claim no special advantage or circumstances.

One editor surveyed commented that, "Referees are volunteers who are underpaid. Editors have very little leverage over them. If a ref is really slow or if he fails to respond at all we "black ball" him. We do not respond to referee failings however". This is a very honest admission but one that doesn't inspire faith in the refereeing process.

Editors, with rare exceptions, see little use in attempting to discipline referees or even in reacting to information throwing doubt on their performance. The response to question four of the survey may indicate that editors to a large degree think it is not in their power to improve the standard of refereeing, though it is in their interest. (Editors benefit from prompt and high quality reports. It makes their job easier.)

An editor cannot always be aware if a referee has failed to do an adequate job of evaluating a paper unless the editor does a careful reading of each and every paper submitted. Time constraints will simply not allow this. The author knows the paper intimately. He or she is more likely to detect a biased, shallow or otherwise badly done refereeing job. If the editor is convinced by the author's argument, this should put a referee's future (and past) work in doubt. It may not dissuade against use of the referee immediately, but should make an editor more cautious. Of course, as one editor remarked, it does depend on the referee's past performance. But suspicions should be aroused that perhaps this wasn't a once off failure. Some of the previous reports might have been similarly tainted, but could have gone unnoticed.

The refusal of many editors to pass on information to reviewers from those reviewed is especially unhelpful. One would expect editors not to pass along gratuitous insults. Although passing on a remark in no way endorses it, there is still a reluctance to transmit out and out rudeness. This seems common courtesy. Passing on positive comments is also a matter of courtesy, whatever one's time constraints. Not doing so would indicate a touch of laziness. However, it is reasonable to assume that the majority of comments by authors would be negative. People are more easily roused to complain than to praise. In which case, the infrequency with which such remarks are passed on indicates the unwillingness of the editor to risk offending a referee, even if the editor doesn't endorse the criticism. This unwillingness would seem to explain the spread of survey responses to question five. Half are inclined to pass on bad news, the other half aren't. Ideally such remarks should be passed on (other than insults) since this can only improve a referee's future performance. Similar censorship of referee reports would be considered unprofessional. These are passed on verbatim, including any and all insults. Even though this survey is mostly impressionistic, given the limited number of those surveyed, still the evidence does strongly indicate that editors feel unable or unwilling to provide and exert any guidance in terms of their referees. This can only strengthen the already strong incentive not to put in the time necessary to produce a quality report.

Editors are generally clear as to what a bad report is. The consensus here is once again strongly held. Many of the remarks concerning the characteristics of a bad referee seem to reduce to descriptions of people refusing to take on their full responsibilities and cutting corners instead. These referees fail to assist either the editor or the author. Unsatisfactory reports tend to be characterised by: narrowness[44], bias, gratuitously offensive remarks, nit-picking, and suggestions for additional work yielding more costs than benefits[45]. They can be poor in diverse ways. Some are perfunctory and either fail to connect with the substance of the paper or judge it on some peremptory basis. Others fail to sort out large from small issues and bog down in nit-picking. Occasionally a referee simply makes a substantial analytical mistake. Sometimes a referee suggests additional work without giving thought to the benefits and costs involved or the feasibility of the suggested extensions..

Economic journals are run like non-profit organisations which have no owners to please. Their members are closer to suppliants, authors desiring more to publish their output than to control the editorial process. These non-profit clubs seem to be run for the benefit of insiders who see no reason to discipline the agents they employ. Yet for the most part, the editors surveyed intimated that bad referees were more the exception than the rule. Most are even relatively prompt with their reports (Hamermesh 1994). If the standard devices common to corporate governance and principle/agent contracts are not in force, we need to ask ourselves why journals run as well as they do, given all these inherent handicaps.

PROFESSIONAL CODES

A woman's preaching is like a dog's walking on his hinder legs. It is not done well; but you are surprised to find it done at all (Samuel Johnson quoted in Partington 1992, p.372).

Many economists may want to do a good job as a referee in the hopes that it will improve the chances of future submissions being published. This is typically risk averse behaviour. While not believing that editors publish bad papers in return for services rendered, there are still many small decisions that an editor can make which may tip a marginal paper into the acceptance bin. Still, something stronger must be at work because an economist when approached as a potential referee faces a classic free rider dilemma. Refereeing must be done but it would best be done by someone else.

We need to look further afield for an explanation of the prevailing behaviour that eases the lethal nature of this free riding problem. Altruism would be a likely suspect, but economists are not particularly known for their generosity[46]. They may proffer advice with a free hand, but charitable acts seem not to be their style[47]. A few economists have examined altruism as a choice system. Most however continue to behave as though they were striving to emulate the actions of their own creation, *homo economicus*[48].

Conventional behaviour is also inadequate if "by a *convention*, we mean a pattern of behavior that is customary, expected and self-enforcing" (Young, 1996, p.105). Refereeing papers, or for that matter commenting on a colleague's work, is not unlike conventional behaviour. But refusing to follow conventions usually has a direct disadvantage to those that flout such behaviour. Driving on the wrong side of the road is a simple, graphic example. Few adverse consequences arise from refusing to cooperate fully with a refereeing request. Even the knowledge of such a refusal may go no farther than the editor of a specific journal.

It is more than simple conventional behaviour. There are strong group pressures, norms of the profession that work to relieve many of these free riding tendencies. Part of becoming an economist is a socialisation process. Graduate students are indoctrinated step by step, weeding out the potential doubters and trouble makers in much the same way as cults define their membership (see Akerlof 1991 for an analysis). Indoctrination depends on the perceived rationality of each step, even though the end result may seem undesirable if viewed from an initial, pre-indoctrination standpoint.

We feel guilty if we fail to do our duty.[49] Duty rather than any narrow self-interest must need be the dominant motivation. A good referee is necessarily implied to be a dutiful one. Certainly the slim chance of winning a spot on the editorial board is not sufficient motivation despite its doubling in size during Ashenfelter's decade as editor. In 1995, 1060 outside referees were employed. The editorial board consisted of thirty-six members. "We resolve never to be guilty of the like, nor ever, upon any account, to render ourselves in this manner the objects of universal disapprobation" (Smith, 1966, p.224). Perhaps among economists there are those who can entirely disregard the opinions of others, caring only for their work and their own self regard[50]. But even economists are social creatures[51].

Nature when she formed man for society, endowed him with an original desire to please, and an original aversion to offend his brethren. She taught him to feel pleasure in their favourable and pain in their unfavourable regard. She rendered their approbation most flattering and most agreeable to him for its own sake; and their disapprobation most mortifying and most offensive (Smith, 1976, p.116).

SOLUTIONS

Difficult do you call it sir? I wish it were impossible (Samuel Johnson quoted in Partington 1992, p.374).

Mention solutions to most economists and they will outline the need to strengthen market incentives. This will at least be where they start. What should be clear by now is that the current system of refereed journals depends on implicit and poorly articulated rewards. The glue in the system is a sense of professional responsibility which may be less developed among economists than among similar occupations. Surely it would be better not to depend only on such ineffective constraints. Economists, more than most, need clearly defined incentives where their self interest is undeniably at stake, they crave the blessings of market incentives.

The right incentives could improve the quality of the refereeing process[52] while bolstering a reputation for fairness.[53] The solution is a rather simple one. I will only develop a mere sketch of what could be a effective and workable structure. As a natural pessimist, I will take my hint from Stigler (1971). Based on the current vested interests within the profession, I see it as unlikely that change will come from insiders. As in the past, any successful movement to reform the fundamental institutions of the profession will be more likely the result of some outside shock. The solution itself is suggested by Aoki's (1990) description of the separate job ladders found in Japanese firms. In such firms, engineers, for example, don't have to become managers in order to gain promotions and salary increases. A separate job ladder allows those whose comparative advantage lies in engineering to remain and contribute as engineers instead of as second rate managers.

The economics profession needs similar separate job ladders where one can make one's mark not only as a researcher but as a teacher, a referee, an editor or even an administrator. There is no reason to assume that the best researchers make the best referees or even the best editors. Nor are these activities necessarily the best use of their time. The supply of referees would increase if rewards were clearly in keeping with the importance of the task. Few would argue that high quality, prompt reports would not improve the papers published. With the requisite recognition rewarded for such service, economists would compete to referee for the best journals. Editors could then readily discard those referees who failed to perform. They would also be less reluctant to tell referees what was expected of them and to let them know in what ways they had failed. Referees would demand such information if only to gain future contracts.

A large pool of responsive referees would eliminate any sound reason for prohibiting multiple submissions. Authors would no longer need to calculate the probability of acceptance in order to construct a hierarchy of submission. As it stands now, with a rejection taking some five months or more, years may pass before a paper is actually published. Such long turn-arounds can serve no one's purpose.

Law article are reviewed by law students, where there are fewer papers than willing referees. Economics articles are reviewed by reluctant referees where duplication of effort is costly (Lazear, 1993, p.44).

There are many law journal referees not because law students are used but because there is a tangible reward attached. To be part of a law review is a recognised honour which enhances future job prospects. For an economist, refereeing is often an unwelcome obligation. In a typically overextended professional schedule, compared to other activities, refereeing provides relatively low yields in terms of professional advancement. Yet it would be hard to demonstrate that law journals are clearly inferior to their economic counterparts. Graduate students are not the only alternative. The number of economists, now turning out second rate research, could adequately handle what would necessarily be a reduced volume of submissions. Journals would simultaneously compete for the best articles. Part of winning such a competition would depend upon the quality of editing and refereeing offered.

Editors, if recognised for their service, might also be persuaded to be more conscientious in the performance of their duties without the need for a journal to turn a blind eye to self-dealing. The strictly limited number of editorships would necessarily be hotly contested thereby gaining in prestige. Editors could be tied to explicit contracts with regular performance evaluations including the downside risk of termination. In a similar manner, editorial boards would see it in their own interest to monitor the progress of a journal more carefully. This need not extend to actual interference in a journal's day to day operation, but could provide additional pressure on the editor to perform. An editor would be more willing to devote the time necessary to improve the quality of a journal if his or her own self interest was tied intrinsically to achieving some specific set of objectives. This at least is what we all believe as practising economists. Creating increased accountability therefore, poses no insurmountable difficulties.

Solutions are simple to devise, so simple that a further elaboration is basically unnecessary. The problem lies in implementing any one of them. The profession itself seems largely self-satisfied. Complaints come from those discouraged by failure or from the chronically disgruntled. The impetus for change is more likely to originate outside the profession. Such pressures are becoming evident. University libraries, faced with limited budgets, are trimming back their serial collections. Journals are opting to go electronic. The uncertainty caused by a changing environment places traditional methods in doubt. Commercial publishing houses, finding it no longer profitable to keep large stables of journals, may exert pressure on the management of each journal to respond more to its readership.

It is ironic that economists have constructed a governance system which critically depends on duty. That the profession has unconsciously emphasised the values analysed in *The Moral Sentiments* rather than *The Wealth of Nations* makes for a rather good joke. From an economic point of view, such a solution is less than ideal. Change is almost certain, though not as a result of this article or others like it. Then again such anticipations may prove to be "the triumph of hope over experience" (Samuel Johnson quoted in Partington 1992, p.373).

REFERENCES

Akerlof, George A. (1991) "Procrastination and Obedience," *The American Economic Review*. 81(2): 1-19.

Ashenfelter, Orley (1996) "Report of the Editor," *The American Economic Review*. 86(2): 481-490.

Aoki, Masahiko (1990) "Toward an Economic Model of the Japanese Firm," *Journal of Economic Literature*. 28(1): 1-27.

Bernard, André (ed.) (1990) *Rotten Rejections*. Wainscott, NY: Pushcart Press.

Bell, Carolyn Shaw (1994) Data and the Economists," *The Eastern Economic Journal*. 20(3): 349-353.

Blank, Rebecca M. (1991) "The Effects of Double-Blind versus Single-Blind Reviewing: Experimental Evidence from *The American Economic Review*," *The American Economic Review*. 81 (5): 1041-1067.

Buchanan, James (1965) An Economic Theory of Clubs," *Economica*. 32(1): 1-14.

Carroll, Lewis (1962) *The Annotated Snark*. New York: Penguin Books.

Carter, John and Michael Iron (1991) "Are Economists Different, and If so, Why?" *The Journal of Economic Perspectives*. 5(2): 171-177.

Clower, Robert W. (1985) "Report of the Editor," *The American Economic Review*. 75(2): 432-437.

Clower, Robert W. (1988) "The state of economics: hopeless but not serious?" in Colander, David C. And A.W. Coats (eds) *The spread of economic ideas*. Cambridge: Cambridge University Press pp.18-31.

Coats, A.W. (1991) The Learned Journals in the Development of Economics and the Economics Profession: The British Case," *Economic Notes*. 20(1): 89-116.

Colander, David (1989) "Research on the Economics Profession," *The Journal of Economic Perspectives*. 3(4): 137-148.

Cole, Jonathan R. and Stephen Cole (1973) *Social Stratification in Science*. Chicago: The University of Chicago Press.

Davis, P. And G. Papanek (1984) "Faculty Rankings of Major Economics Departments by Citations," *American Economic Review*. 74(1): 225-230.

Day, Colin (1988) "Journals, university presses, and the spread of ideas," Colander, David C. And A.W. Coats (eds) *The spread of economic ideas*. Cambridge: Cambridge University Press pp.61-78.

Feige, Edgar L. (1975) "The Consequences of Journal Editorial Policies and a Suggestion for Revision," *The Journal of Political Economy*. 83(6): 1291-1296.

Frank, Robert H., Thomas Gilovich, and Dennis T. Regan (1993) "Does Studying Economics Inhibit Cooperation?" *The Journal of Economic Perspectives*. 7(2): 159-171.

Freedman, Craig F. (1993) "Why Economists Can't Read," *Methodus*. 5(1): 6-23.

Friedman, David D. (1990) *Price Theory - An Intermediate Text*. Cincinnati: South-Western.

Gans, Joshua S. and George B. Shepherd (1994) "How Are the Mighty Fallen: Rejected Classic Articles by Leading Economists," *The Journal of Economic Perspectives*. 8(1): 165-179.

Gerrity, D.M. and R.B. McKenzie (1978) "The Ranking of Southern Economics Departments: New Criterion and further Evidence," *Southern Economic Journal*, 45(2): 608-614.

Haley, Bernard (1956) "Report of the Editor," *The American Economic Review*. 46(2): 613-617.

Hamermesh, Daniel (1992) "The Young Economist's Guide to Professional Etiquette," *The Journal of Economic Perspectives*. 6(1): 169-179.

Hamermesh, Daniel S. (1993) "Professional Etiquette," *The American Economic Review*. 83(2): 34-38.

Hamermesh, Daniel S. (1994) "Facts and Myths about Refereeing," *the Journal of Economic Perspectives*. 8(1): 153-163.

Hamermesh, Daniel S., George E. Johnson, and Burton A. Weisbrod (1982) "Scholarship, Citations and Salaries: Economic Rewards in Economics," *The Southern Economic Journal*. 49 (2): 472-481.

Hansmann, Henry B. (1980) "The Role of Nonprofit Enterprise," *The Yale Law Journal*. 89(5): 835-901.

Keynes, John Maynard (1973) "Fragment of a Proposed Preface to *The General Theory*," In *The Collected Writing of John Maynard Keynes Volume 14 The General Theory and After Part II Defence and Development*. Moggeridge, Donald (ed.) London: MacMillan, pp.469-471.

Laband, David N. (1986) "Article Popularity," *Economic Inquiry*. 24 (1): 173-180.

Laband, David N. (1990) "Is There Value-Added From The Review Process In Economics?: Preliminary Evidence From Authors," *Quarterly Journal of Economics*. 105(2): 341-353.

Laband, David N. (1994) "Favoritism versus Search for Good Papers: Empirical Evidence Regarding the Behavior of Journal Editors," *Journal of Political Economy*. 102(1): 194-203.

Laband, David N. and Michael J. Piette (1994a) "Does the "Blindness" of Peer Review Influence Manuscript Selection Efficiency?" *Southern Economic Journal*.60(4): 896-906.

Laband, David N. and Michael J. Piette (1994b) "The Relative Impacts of Economic Journals: 1970-1990," *The Journal of Economic Literature*. 32(2): 640-666.

LaFollete, Marcel C. (1992) *Stealing into print: Fraud, plagiarism, and misconduct in scientific publishing*. Berkeley: University of California Press.

Lattimore, Ralph (1992) "Are Economists Different?" *The Journal of Economic Perspectives*. 6(2): 199-201.

Lazear, Edward P. (1993) "Discussion: The Economics of Professional Etiquette," *The American Economic Review*. 83(2): 44.

Lovell, M.C. (1973) "The Production of Economic Literature: An Interpretation," *Journal of Economic Literature*. 11(1): 27-55.

Mackie, Christopher D. (1998) *Canonizing Economic Theory*. Armonk, New York: M.E. Sharpe Inc.

Mahoney, John (1985) *Marshall, Orthodoxy and The Professionalisation of Economics*. Cambridge: Cambridge University Press.

Marwell, Gerald and Ruth Ames (1981) "Economists Free Ride, Does Anyone Else?: Experiments on the Provision of Public Goods, IV," *Journal of Public Economics*. 15(3): 295-310.

McCloskey, Donald (1995) "Kelly Green Golf Shoes and the Intellectual Range from M to N," *Eastern Economic Journal.* 21 (3): 411-414.

Newhouse, John (1970) "Toward a theory of non-profit institutions: an economic model of a hospital," *The American Economic Review.* 60(1): 64-81.

Niskanen, William (1971) *Bureaucracy and Representative Government.* Chicago: Aldine.

Partington, Angela (ed.) (1992) *The Oxford Dictionary of Quotations - 4th Edition.* Oxford: Oxford University Press.

Rose-Ackerman, Susan (1996) "Altruism, Nonprofits, and Economic Theory," *Journal of Economic Literature.* 34(2): 701-728.

Simon, Herbert A. (1993) "Altruism and Economics," *The American Economic Review.* 83(2): 156-161.

Shepherd, George B. (1995) *Rejected - Leading Economists Ponder the Publication Process.* Sun Lakes Arizona: Thomas Horton and Daughters.

Smith, Adam (1966) *The Theory of Moral Sentiments.* New York: Augustus Kelley.

Smith, Adam (1976) *The Theory of Moral Sentiments.* Oxford: Clarendon Press.

Stigler, George J. (1961) "Alfred Marshall's Lectures on Poverty," *Journal of Law and Economics.* 10(1): 181-183.

Stigler, George J. (1963) "On Scientific Writing," *The Intellectual and the Marketplace, and Other Essays.* New York: Free Press, pp. 45-56.

Stigler, George J. (1971) "The Theory of Economic Regulation," *Bell Journal of Economics and Management Science* 2(Spring): 3-21.

Stigler, George J. (1982a) "Does Economics Have a Useful Past?" In *The Economist as Preacher.* Oxford: Basil Blackwell.

Stigler, George J. (1982b) "Do Economists Matter?" *The Economist as Preacher.* Chicago: University of Chicago Press, pp.57-68.

Stigler, George J. (1988) *Memoirs of an Unregulated Economist.* New York: Basic Books.

Stigler, George J. and Claire Friedland (1975) "The Citation Practices of Economists," *Journal of Political Economy.* 83(3): 477-507.

Stigler, George J. and Claire Friedland (1982) "The Citation Practices of Doctorates in Economics," in *The Economist as Preacher.* Chicago: University of Chicago Press.

Stigler, George J., Stephen M. Stigler, and Claire Friedland (1995) "The Journals of Economics," *The Journal of Political Economy.* 103(2): 331-359.

Stigler, George J. and James K. Kindahl (1973) "Industrial Prices, as Administered by Dr. Means," *The American Economic Review.* 63(4): 717-721.

Whitely, Richard (1991) "The Organisation and Role of Journals in Economics and Other Scientific Fields," *Economic Notes.* 20(1): 6-32.

Yezer, Anthony M., Robert S. Goldfarb, and Paul J. Poppen (1996) "Does Studying Economics Discourage Cooperation? What We Do, Not What We Say or How We Play," *The Journal of Economic Perspectives.* 10(1): 177-186.

Young, H. Peyton (1996) "The Economics of Convention," *The Journal of Economic Perspectives.* 10(2): 105-122.

NOTES

[1] It would be interesting to discover whether articles purporting to research some aspect of our own profession are more likely to be accepted for publication than comparable articles on another subject.

[2] Others have attempted to justify this on-going display of professional narcissism.

The economics profession is interesting to economists for a number of interrelated reasons:

(1)   For prurient and professional interest: It is fun to know about oneself and one's profession.

(2)   As a case study: If economic theory is correct, it should apply to the economics profession. Since economists have firsthand knowledge of the economics profession and relatively easy access to data, it makes an excellent case study.

(3)   Because one has an interest in the sociology of knowledge: Recent developments in methodology and philosophy of science have made a knowledge of the scientists an important aspect of a knowledge of science; they are the lens through which science is interpreted. Understanding the tendency of scientists to aim that lens in particular directions and to distort the reality they are studying is necessary if one is to interpret their analysis correctly (Colander, 1989, pp.137-148).

By narcissism, I intend not to entirely dismiss the legitimacy of this work. The relative number of such publications still seems to be out of all proportions to their professional contribution. If economists were dispassionately looking for case studies, a trade, skill or profession with greater impact than that contributed by economists would surely be preferred. Equally, the number of practising economists who read these articles due to their keen interest in the sociology of knowledge would surely be only a scattering unless the vast majority of the profession is cooly disguising where their true interests lie. On the other hand, as every tabloid knows, gossip sells.

[3] For those interested in an attempt to estimate the monetary reward for publication see Hamermesh, Johnson and Weisbrod (1982).

[4] Laband (1990) questions the value referees add to the process. Hamermesh (1994) investigates their role in delaying the review process. Neither one looks deeply into the motivations of referees. A better place to start is with Shepherd (1995) and Mackie (1998) who focus more directly on the refereeing process itself.

[5] Increasing numbers of researchers, as well as their growing dispersion, encourage further formalisation and standardisation of the communication system which in turn affected the standardisation of work practices and ways of reporting results. The importance of this system for gaining reputations, and hence rewards, means that its organisation and control are closely linked to the authority structures of different fields, both intellectual and organisational, and it is important to recognise that scientific communication systems are both functional and authoritative (Whitely, 1991, p.11).

[6] Stigler and Friedland (1982) looked at the publications of those receiving doctorates in 1950 from Berkeley, Chicago, Columbia, Harvard, M.I.T. and Wisconsin. During the eighteen years following the granting of their degree, 242 out of 700 graduates had not published a single article. Only 19 had published more than 21. For most academic economists these days, even those working in relatively obscure institutions, a record of one publication a year would not be unusual.

[7] By circular reasoning one could claim that quality journals were those which published quality papers. But it is true that those journals with the greatest prestige are those which receive the best articles. The reason is obvious. These journals are the ones most widely read, or at least seen, and those which provide the greatest returns to their authors in terms of promotion and salary increases. For a discussion of journal quality, Laband and Piette (1994b) is one place to start.

[8] But there is another implicit demand to which the authors cater (the subtext). Readers are unwilling to accept an argument on its own merits alone. Arguments made without such backup authority are disregarded. They are more receptive when convinced that other highly reputable individuals have held similar views or at least have considered the issue to be important, an

academic equivalent of the celebrity endorsement, or the wall full of diplomas on a doctor's wall. The reader is reassured of the relevance of the work. Work of this type cannot then be carelessly disregarded (Freedman, 1993, p.12).

[9] The practice of using citations as a convenient stand in for quality is a long-standing convention of the profession as any practitioner may discover during salary negotiations. For those interested in discussions centred on the legitimacy of such a proxy, the reader is advised to examine Cole and Cole (1973), Lovell (1973), Stigler and Friedland (1975) Gerrity and McKenzie (1978), Davis and Papanek (1984), and Laband (1990). Readers should also be struck by the eminence of the journals in which many of these discussions appear.

[10] Not coincidentally, each of these journals was associated with a leading university, giving these institutions an ever increasing power to exclude. The *QJE* was an offspring of Harvard, the *JPE* of Chicago, and the *EJ*, though officially a product of the newly formed British Economic Association, was closely tied to Cambridge. Chicago, in particular, founded its journal in the hopes of enhancing the reputation of its newly established Department of Economics.

[11] Historically, non-profits have provided public or quasi-public goods which governments have not deemed feasible to supply and which private firms have regarded as offering no commercial advantage. (It is of course possible to imagine a government subsidy financing a journal, but a century ago, such functions were not commonly performed by government. Even if conceivable, concern over government interference in the editorial process would make such funding suspect.)

Stigler (1988) relates the pressure bought to bear on an economist at Iowa State who had either the courage or naivety to publish a war-time pamphlet suggesting the public switch from butter to margarine. This naturally outraged the local dairy industry and its allied state legislators who demanded a retraction.

> A weak college president forced the withdrawal of the pamphlet and a year later a revised edition appeared ...
> Professor T.W. Schultz, head of the Department of Economics and Sociology when the pamphlet was recalled,
> resigned and went to the University of Chicago (Stigler, 1988, p.172).

[12] Commercial publishing houses are estimated to make a profit of 40% or more on academic journals (*Economist* January 24th 1998:81). This would indicate a rather inelastic demand. Institutions buy journals so that its users may have access to them. In this sense they are a form of quasi-public good. (Marginal cost of another user is near zero involving only minor congestion expenses. Since such serials are not generally for loan, exclusion is not attempted). Because they do not directly pay for the serials, academics will request serials based on potential usefulness to their research rather than on price. The demand for increased research output will in turn put pressure on research libraries to maintain an extensive serial collection. Only increasing budget constraints can affect institutional demand. In which case journals will be lopped according to some determination of use rather than on any strictly cost basis.

Individual users find it much more cost efficient to simply photo-copy the few articles of interest rather than subscribing to the journal as individuals. The higher institutional subscription rate reflects in part the opportunity cost of losing individual subscribers by making the journal available to research libraries and institutions.

[13] The yearly rates, even though lower for individual subscribers, are now largely beyond the means of most economists with the exception of those journals that are included in the membership dues of professional organisations. Most individuals limit personal subscriptions to a handful associated with professional organisations and perhaps a specialist journal. Additional volumes would go mostly unread given a typical academic's limited time. It is doubtful that price competition or price discrimination would be effective. This seems to explain why commercial publishers have not chased market-share in this more traditional manner. Instead they have been able to price at relatively high rates without greatly affecting institutional or even individual demand for the journal.

[14] The National Science Foundation identified a population of 12,000 professional economists in 1964. By 1986 there were 164,000 (Quoted in Bell 1994:355).

[15] In some cases, journals are first initiated by entrepreneurial academics and, if successful, picked up by a commercial publishing house. This is obviously of mutual benefit since the publisher buys an on-going journal with a list of active subscribers while the academic entrepreneurs are relieved of administrative and other business functions for which they are often ill-suited. (Though many of these same skills are now provided by non-profit university presses.)

[16] Corporations owe obligations to a number of constituencies. The contestability of ownership, in a publicly traded company, or the identity of ownership and control in a private one, places owners in a unique relationship to the other constituents.

[17] See Newhouse (1970).

[18] There are two possible objections to this: (1) Professional organisations do elect officers who oversee, however tenuously, the running of the house journal. But it can be argued that these elections are more closely equivalent to those of the old Soviet Union. More importantly, whatever the mechanism of their election these officials would be loathe to interfere in the running of the journals. (2) Journals do have editorial boards to provide a check on the activity of managing editors. But once again, these boards are largely self-perpetuating.

[19] Editorial boards are sometimes elected, but elections would either be pro-forma, with a management ticket being rubber stamped (much like AEA officers) or general apathy would be manipulated by a small group for personal gain. Appointed boards are even less likely to noticeably check, or even influence, editorial objectives.

[20] It is also possible to think of the club as consisting of the editors and boards who together dispense rewards to worthy applicants much as grants are awarded to those successful at petitioning foundation boards or as other governmental or professional groups award honours. No matter how you describe the nature of the club, the key is that a number of outsiders seek recognition of some sort. Whether the prize or honour associated with recognition is granted depends largely on a group of self-perpetuating gatekeepers.

[21] The economic function of clubs and the use of clubs as an attempt by analogy to interpret certain types of goods has an extensive literature attached to it. Buchanan (1965) is the place to start.

[22] The analogy with clubs is striking. Clubs are run for the benefit of their members. Journals also exist for the same reason (at least in part). Their members however are not their subscribers (anyone with the willingness to pay can become a subscriber). Only publication can guarantee that you are a member of a restricted and, in some ways, an elite group.

> The answer seems to derive in large part from the social exclusivity that characterizes most country clubs. Typically, membership in a club is not open to everyone who is willing to pay the dues. Rather, to become a member an applicant usually must also be socially acceptable to the other members. Such exclusivity assures that the club's members will exhibit at least a minimal set of those personal qualities considered attractive by the other members. In fact the opportunity to associate with people who exhibit these qualities is one of the principal attractions of joining a club-sometimes much more important than the actual services that the club provides (Hansmann, 1980, p.892).

[23] See Laband (1994).

[24] Economists want to join the most exclusive clubs. These are the ones with the widest readership and whose articles are more likely to have a larger impact. They provide the sort of recognition which stokes the academic ego and provides the hard nosed financial rewards which fills the academic pocket. Academics, even those previously published, go more as suppliants to these journals than as patrons. Unlike social club members, they are loathe to offend management.

[25] Laband and Piette (1994, p.899) point out the lack of any generally agreed upon and well specified objective function for editors. It is difficult to judge the performance of any one editor lacking such a benchmark. Most economists would find it hard to disagree that journals should seek to disseminate high quality research. Or, that editors "act as agents of their respective communities of scholars and these scholars want editors to function as "gatekeepers" of knowledge," (Laband and Piette, 1994, p.899).

[26] When George Borts, editor of the *American Economic Review* in 1973, refused to print Gardiner Means' reply to an article by Stigler and Kindahl (1973), Means unsuccessfully appealed to the

board of that journal. The author of this article has personally, if not wisely, been successful in appealing a decision of an editor to that journal's board.

27 Board members may contribute time, ideas and effort to the running of a journal. They do not usually oversee or check a journal's editor in any significant pro-active way.

28 *The Journal of Economic Perspectives* was clearly such a case. It was to be a more popular, less technical, journal which would feature articles of general interest to the profession as a whole. Cynics might say that it merely let the *AER* off the hook.

> I believed it would let the *American Economic Review* off the hook in the matters of intelligibility and general interest (it has). As a matter of fact in some circles the *JEP* was viewed at its founding precisely as a protective belt for the *AER*. This theory persists. As it was expressed to me by an eminent senior member of our profession, *"The Journal of Economic Perspectives* is a stupid journal for stupid people" (I quote exactly), and in his view it was intended to be so (McCloskey, 1995, p.414).

29 Indeed he probably is thinking only of the referees and editors as he writes the article. He has just that handful of readers in mind. Acceptance for publication is such a formidable obstacle that in the vast majority of cases the individual author has to allow the journal editor to make the critical decisions about the needs of the target audience (Day, 1988, p.63).

30 The number of long articles per year in the *American Economic Review*, rose from 21 in 1955 to 52 in 1984. Shorter articles, replies and communications rose from 14 to 86 (more recently down to 33) (Haley 1956; Clower 1985; Ashenfelter 1996). Brief articles are also more likely to reviewed promptly (see Hamermesh 1994).

31 This is very reminiscent of Niskanen's work on bureaucracy (1971). Bureaucrats (journal editors) seek to expand their empires by increasing their power of patronage.

32 > In response to my survey, one long-running editor writes: "... I regard the choice of referees as perhaps the most important decision that editors make." The fact that certain editors normally do not comment substantively on authors' manuscripts should not reflect negatively on their abilities. Editors undoubtedly differ with respect to their ability to efficiently match authors and referees as well as with respect to their constrained ability to offer comments on manuscripts (Laband, 1990, p. 349n.11).

If matching papers to referees is an editor's most crucial task, than any inability to properly monitor and reward referees would seem to undermine the effectiveness of any editor, whatever his or her own efforts and abilities might be.

33 Under pressure to retain a shrinking student population, some departments now insist that poor performers in the classroom seek assistance. In fact, the rational career minded academic would care to achieve only a minimal competency. Good teaching takes time. Lessons and effective presentations need to be thought out. Considering the rewards to teaching, the opportunity cost of pursuing any degree of excellence in this area is simply too high.

34 Blackballing does prevent would-be authors from publishing in more prestigious journals. A group of a dozen or fewer journals widely gain the nod as being elite publication venues. This assessment is based on the frequency with which their articles are cited in the literature. Stigler, Stigler and Friedland (1995) list what they term nine core journals. Interested readers will be referred there to earlier articles featuring similar lists. The bulk of these journals are the long established, general journals such as the *AER* or the *JPE*. A first mover principle seems operative here. Additions to this list like the *Review of Economic Studies* or the *Journal of Finance* generally grabbed market niches ignored or disdained by the then existing exclusive clubs. Thus the refusal of the *Economic Journal* under Keynes to print technical pieces led to a new club for younger members of the profession, the *Review of Economic Studies,* gaining a rapid reputation in the thirties.

But the determined author can almost always find an outlet for anything he or she writes by simply working down the hierarchy of existing journals. Supply has simply expanded to meet the rapidly rising demand to publish. Barriers to entry appear to be very slight as shown by the proliferation of specialist journals.

> The second characteristic is the relative freedom of entry into journal publication, amply illustrated by the 300-odd journals at the present time. Entries such as the *Review of Radical Political Economy* (more than 20 years old) and *Games and Economic Behavior* (new) reveal the market's ready response to relatively few readers (Stigler, Stigler and Friedland, 1995, p.344).

[35] This is equivalent to asking whether referees do their jobs. Screening by itself seems insufficient to justify the refereeing procedure in its present form.

[36] Mistaking lugubriousness with seriousness, many referees are quick to squelch any sign of humour or lightheartedness. Akerlof relates how early referees of his *Lemons* paper objected to a rather informal style of presentation (see Gans and Shepherd 1994). I can remember one referee noting that he himself had much enjoyed my style but that others would be offended.

> The third is its slowness in taking a jest.
> Should you happen to venture on one,
> It will sigh like a thing that is deeply distressed:
> And it always looks grave at a pun (Carroll, 1962, p.59).

[37] This is naturally not the only way to read the results, but one that is not inconsistent with those same results. Given anecdotal evidence from economists of varying levels of renown (see Shepherd 1995), this explanation is not without some appeal.

[38] Paying referees for promptness, as a few journals, such as the *JPE* does, seems to work. This is because those who intend to write a report sometime in the future will find that the opportunity cost of procrastination is now too high. Experience shows that it doesn't take all that much of an incentive to tilt the scales away from procrastination (see Akerlof 1991 or Hamermesh 1994).

[39] In 1955 the *American Economic Review* needed one editor, one managing editor, seven members of an editorial board and forty-three outside referees to publish the journal (Haley 1956). In 1995 the numbers were now one editor, three co-editors, two managing editors, thirty-six members of the editorial board and 1060 outside referees (Ashenfelter 1996). Submissions were up from 245 to 958 (Haley 1956; Ashenfelter 1996).

[40] There does seem to be a general agreement amongst editors on what distinguishes acceptable from unacceptable refereeing, a minimum standard of competency. (See the survey results below).

[41] SURVEY

EDITOR'S RESPONSE TO POOR QUALITY REPORTS

1. Do you inform a referee when his/her report is of poor quality?
Frequently (91%[+]) ___ Usually (50%-90%) ___ Occasionally (10%-49%) ___
Infrequently (0%-9%) ___

2. Do you cease to use a referee after one or two poor quality reports?
Frequently (91%[+]) ___ Usually (50%-90%) ___ Occasionally (10%-49%) ___
Infrequently (0%-9%) ___

3. Do you inform a referee that you no longer plan to use him/her?
Frequently (91%[+]) ___ Usually (50%-90%) ___ Occasionally (10%-49%) ___
Infrequently (0%-9%) ___

4. If an author of an article convincingly points out the ways in which the referee has failed to do an adequate job does that influence your decision to use that referee again?
Frequently (91%[+]) ___ Usually (50%-90%) ___ Occasionally (10%-49%) ___
Infrequently (0%-9%) ___

5. Do you pass on to the referee critical and/or positive comments by the author of an article concerning the quality of his/her report?
Frequently (91%[+]) ___ Usually (50%-90%) ___ Occasionally (10%-49%) ___
Infrequently (0%-9%) ___

6. What in your opinion characterises a bad referee's report?

[42] Percentages are based on twenty-three returned surveys. One editor claimed never to have seen a bad refereeing report. This runs counter to any reasonable estimate of probabilities, but the editor must be accepted at face value. On question number four, only twenty-two of the returned surveys responded.

[43] In another survey, Laband (1990) also discovered a journal where a tough line was taken and referees kept informed. Again, this did not seem to leave the journal in want of adequate referees.

> The editors of the *Journal of Finance* make no bones about their concern for timely, high-quality reviewing and have explicitly made referees partial residual claimants to the quality of their review services: "We keep detailed records of ad hoc reviewers. We record both the time the reviewer took and the quality of the review. The quality of the author as a reviewer is a strong influence on our decision to whom we will send a manuscript. Once again, the best way to ensure a good review is to be a good reviewer when called upon (Laband, 1990, p.335).

[44] Referees appear to be extremely risk averse. They have a tendency to reject anything that doesn't fit a pre-existing mould. They prefer manuscripts that look like what they have seen before, especially in the relevant journals. Papers which are incremental extensions of existing work are more likely to be published (such papers are more quickly read and disposed of) than papers presenting truly novel approaches or ideas (these can be extremely time consuming if taken seriously). See the discussion in Shepherd (1995) or Mackie (1998).

[45] Comments from editors (What characterises a bad referee's report.)

1. Shallowness, Terseness, Bias, Lack of Empathy
2. Delivery well beyond date given; failing to deliver clear advice on article's quality;
Failing to produce clear statement of points of difficulty (ideally helpful suggestions about alternative approach; work is plainly sloppy, generalised and lacking constructive detail).
3. Summary judgement without evidence; evaluation based on a prejudiced view about a whole category of work, rather than a thoughtful reading of the paper; Nasty or preemptory comments; Evidence of carelessness in reading the work.
4. Careless, sloppy, inadequate, unmotivated, uninformed, etc. work.
5. One which shows little evidence of having read the article carefully.
6. Poor judgement, unsatisfactory technical understanding
7. An unhelpful (i.e. not constructive) critique.
8. Referees are volunteers who are underpaid. Eds have very little leverage over them. If a ref is really slow or if he fails to respond at all we "black ball" him. We do not respond to referee failings however.
9. This may sound hard to swallow, but I've been highly impressed with the quality and thoroughness of referee reports supplied to the ... Journal. The reports are typically several pages long and substantive - not brief, arrogant, and catty. I haven't seen a bad report, though if I did I would seek another report before corresponding with the authors and would not use the referee again.
10. Too brief; points made vague or unspecific; insufficiently critical in the sense of making reasonable evaluative comments.
11. Failure to demonstrate that the referee understands the paper deeply, or understands the paper's contribution to the literature. Most often, a poor referee is one who is too easily impressed with a paper's merits; Less often (but still a significant problem), a poor referee is one who criticizes a paper because it doesn't follow the referee's own narrow preferences in methodology and results: most of our referees fall into neither category b or c.
12 Failure to understand and deal fairly with the content of a manuscript.
13. Glib remarks about an entire literature; errors in reading a paper; I do not consider detailed comments or length a virtue per se; I do value insight and thoughtful judgement.
14. Usually they are simply uninformative. The referee has failed to work hard on the paper. Less often, mistaken assertions.
15. Careless reading or analytical error

16. Superficiality: not sufficiently (trying to) understand what the author wants to say. Narrowness: looking at any paper exclusively from the point of view of accepted knowledge and thus diminishing new thinking. Impossible demand: in particular, when empirical evidence is demanded where it cannot (yet) be produced.

17. Rejection without providing specific reasons; demanding that the author write a quite different paper; failure to spot technical errors or lack of originality; gratuitously offensive remarks

18. Non-neutral tone; obvious bias; unconstructive comments

19. They can be poor in diverse ways. Some are perfunctory and either fail to connect with the substance of the paper or judge it on some peremptory basis. Others fail to sort out large from small issues and bog down in nit-picking. Occasionally a referee simply makes a substantial analytical mistake. Sometimes a referee suggests additional work without giving thought to the benefits and costs involved or the feasibility of the suggested extensions.

[46] Altruism seems to involve a complex of motivations, including a sincere commitment to assist others. Charity work often involves altruistic rather than narrowly, defined self-interested actions. See Simon (1993) for an introduction to the topic.

> Some giving is the result of feelings of commitment; some results from sympathy; some arises from belief in the moral value of reciprocity; some is motivated by private benefits to the donor such as prestige, pride, and attendance at elite parties. Motivations for giving are inextricably linked. One can obtain prestige from making a gift only if others view one's action as worthy. If the narrow private benefits of gift giving are too obvious and large, gift givers will not be praised for their self-sacrifice (Rose-Ackerman 1996, p.714).

[47] Recent empirical work seems to indicate that economists are less likely to be altruistic than others with a similar education and background. See Carter, John and Michael Iron (1991); Frank, Robert H., Thomas Gilovich, and Dennis T. Regan (1993); Lattimore, Ralph (1992); Marwell, Gerald and Ruth Ames (1981); Yezer, Anthony M., Robert S. Goldfarb, and Paul J. Poppen (1996) for descriptions and debates on this topic.

[48] Those economists closely aligned with the Chicago School seem more likely to put their theory into practise. This is not surprising in a place where economics is closer to a cult than a mere academic discipline, a place where economics isn't merely discussed but lived. Milton Friedman's son, David (1990), proudly relates a story of being taught the importance of opportunity cost and choice at a rather tender age. Fortunately for the family, he became a convert rather than reacting like B.F. Skinner's daughter who in later life sued her illustrious father for using her as an experimental subject.

[49] Since Orley Ashenfelter took over as editor of *The American Economic Review* in 1985, the rewards for dutiful performance as a referee have been carefully spelled out. The exact same statement has been made by Ashenfelter for the last ten years.

> [Editorial] Board members are also selected because of their conscientiousness, good judgement, and professional reliability. When possible, we like to select Board members from those economists who have been especially helpful in the outside refereeing process (Ashenfelter 1996:483-484).

[50] Economists are keen to gain the applause of their profession even if they are among those rare individuals who care nothing about the opinions of others. Recognition within one's own set can translate into earnings.

> ... to a scientist educated hands make more melodious applause than ignorant hands, but too often the educated hands seem to be sat upon by educated asses (Stigler, 1982b, p.67).

[51] Mackie's (1998) survey of referees does lend support to the idea of professional obligation as a prime motivating factor.

[52] If referees consistently did their jobs, papers would consistently improve.

[53] It is unlikely to do much for the narrow range of what journals find to be acceptable. This would depend on a new breed of editor. Unfortunately such a new breed would reflect a basic change in the profession itself. It is doubtful that such a change is likely to take place. The incentives discussed would only improve the quality of the prevailing product.

ECONOMIC TEXTBOOKS: MISSING AND MISPLACED INCENTIVES

Craig Freedman
Macquire University

'We called him Tortoise because he taught us,' said the Mock Turtle angrily: 'really you are very dull!' (Carroll 1974:92)

In 1962, Gary Becker, never contented with meekly accepting the prevailing wisdom of the profession, stood Marx on his head by using a striking metaphor to capture the way in which labour was not unlike capital. Human capital theory saw individuals as choosing to invest in education and training. By building up their mental assets, they could boost the value of their subsequent labour. Like any production process, optimum results inevitably depend, in part, on the inputs chosen. We can easily extend this analogy to the way in which economics is taught. Assuming that undergoing instruction in the mysteries of economics adds to the stock of human capital, inputs into this process deserve more than just a passing glance.

The standard inputs are instructor, textbook, and all the rest of the auxiliary paraphernalia which can vary widely[1]. To be exact, the form in which the instruction takes place or what strictly speaking constitutes a text are themselves likely to appear in many guises. Whatever those appearances may be, most academic economists consigned to exploring the mixed pleasures offered by teaching an introductory course, seem to think that the textbook chosen does in fact matter. This would be the only way to explain the occasionally pitched battles that break out over the selection of a text in economic departments throughout the world. This again is nothing new.[2]

Yet despite this unshaken conviction that textbooks matter, little solid evidence exists to substantiate this claim. The few attempts to test this proposition have been largely inconclusive. Meinkoth's (1971) study indicates a statistically noticeable but practically limited change in student performance due to changing textbooks. Any change could probably be attributed to allowing the instructor to choose his or her own text rather than having one assigned [the Jevons state of despair]. Increased enthusiasm alone, conveyed adequately to students, may be sufficient to generate any limited improvement[3].

Given that the search for the best possible first year text takes on something of a search for the holy grail (though perhaps in the Monty Python version)[4], I want to ask three fundamental questions:

- Why do we have textbooks?
- Why do instructors think that the text they choose matters?
- Does the selection process yield anything like satisfactory results from the standpoint of any of the participants in this annual collegiate minuet?

Exploring these issues should provide us with some understanding of why textbooks are inevitably unsatisfactory (except perhaps to their authors and publishers).

FREE TO CHOOSE

Tweedledum and Tweedledee
agreed to have a battle;
For Tweedledum said Tweedledee
Had spoiled his nice new rattle.
(Carroll 1974:162)

Let's for a moment extend Becker's (1962) industrial metaphor. The task of selecting inputs for a production process is not assigned randomly in the world of private enterprise. Given a sufficiently large business to allow for some specialisation, purchasing devolves upon a differentiated department. These employees act as agents of the owner of the enterprise with all the standard adverse selection and moral hazard problems inherent in any agency relationship. Even consumers may employ expert advice when dealing with a complex purchase. Financial advisors, mutual funds, in fact the whole array of available financial services all aim to entice increased investment by reducing informational barriers. In much the same way, students rely on instructors to select the most suitable texts. One could argue that if students were themselves capable of selecting the best texts they probably wouldn't need to take a first year economics course. The assumption is that only years of training allow someone to prescribe a text much as only a similar number of years afford medical doctors the ability to safely prescribe the right medication.

> I am always bothered about how textbooks are selected, because we so blithely ignore consumer choice. We are like physicians, with the students as our patients: they all receive prescriptions (in our case the name of the textbook); they buy and pay for the treatment; they use it and hope for the best. We, like physicians, check up on progress with a series of tests at intervals. The instructor/physician chooses the treatment; the student/patient pays for it (Bell 1988:135).

The similarities, despite Bell's doubts, are more than entirely superficial. As in any agency relationship, either the doctor's or instructor's own objectives can conflict with the aim of providing his or her principal (patient or student) with the best value for money[5]. The problem is aggravated in the case of a student. For pedagogical reasons one text must be prescribed to possibly more than a thousand students. Just as one size won't fit all when it comes to pills, the same applies to students. But while it is quite possible and even standard practise to customise prescriptions (to do otherwise would be to court a malpractice suit), it would be chaotic to try to coordinate a course where students are pursuing their studies via a variety of texts, much like conducting a chorus where each singer is permitted to select the key with which he or she is most comfortable. An unique outcome is unlikely to occur unless the choice of textbook is delegated to a de facto central purchasing agent. While instructors can urge students who are struggling with the favoured text to look to alternatives, only one text can dominate. Nor are students allowed a second opinion. Patients can opt to see another physician. They don't simply have to swallow the medication provided blindly. Students who are unhappy with the text chosen may find that they have nowhere else to go. Often departments will use a uniform text even when there are different lectures given by different instructors. The rationale is that students must receive the same basic instruction to prepare them for further courses. This has always been a curious argument usually made by departmental members dedicated to fighting against failing standards and what they see as a general lack of rigour displayed by many of their colleagues[6]. From a practical standpoint, some sort of common examination should be sufficient to ensure that all first year courses make similar demands on their students. To be completely realistic, even when students are allowed a choice between instructors, or are able to vote with their feet, it is doubtful that the text used casts any deciding influence on their decision. Scheduling constraints seem to dominate with perhaps reputation of and reaction to the instructor having a secondary impact.

Textbooks then are primarily aimed at those who should have little need for them, namely the instructor[7]. The student is forced to delegate the task of choosing a textbook based on the convincing justification that students are insufficiently informed to make a reasonable choice. Given the choice, students would ideally want to minimise the cost of passing their economics course. Unfortunately, they would have little idea as to which text would best accomplish such an objective. Price alone would not necessarily be a reasonable indicator[8]. Books then will be structured to find favour with lecturers in the same way that baby food manufacturers target the tastes of parents. It is true that babies and students are the ultimate arbiters. Food that babies resist swallowing, or textbooks that generate too many negative comments and poor course results, will not last. The user cost of these products simply becomes too high for parents or instructors, more time has to be spent spoon feeding either the bawling baby or the somnambulant student.

Since publishers market primarily to lecturers (the agents rather than the users), publishers commission texts they think will sell to this target audience. This means that publishers prefer that their chosen authors pitch their books directly to the lecturers who will make the decisive choice. In fact, little if any pressure is necessary. Most textbook writers don't know how to write to their supposed target audience, first year students. If in fact they do, it remains a well kept secret. Trained economists, sitting down to write an introductory text, are incapable of putting themselves at that stage where economics is still an alien way of thinking. It's like asking a native Japanese speaker to imagine what it would be like not to know how to speak Japanese, to imagine the questions and issues that would run through the mind of a novice. Textbook authors write for those who already understand economics. A professional might scoff at a book that asked 'dumb' questions or made 'obvious' statements. The fact is that many authors seem incapable of putting themselves in the place of the typical student with no knowledge of economics. Even if they are capable in a Proustian moment, perhaps triggered by the smell of burnt coffee in their study, of recapturing their experience as a novice student of economics, odds are that they did not then represent that average student the textbook aims to enlighten. The average student is unlikely to pursue a career as an academic economist. Textbooks inevitably are written for those who do not need them, the already initiated. Attempting to do otherwise, given the economics of the publishing business, would be counterproductive. Such a text is highly likely to be dismissed out of hand as too simple. Radical departures from the norm of first year texts do not generally fare well.

Instructors are naturally inclined to the familiar. They are most comfortable with a text that resembles those on which they were themselves raised. The tyro instructor, unsure of what he or she should do, opts for the low risk route. They want a text that offers no surprises and which contains nothing they do not already know. Absorbing new information or techniques is simply too time consuming given the constraints faced by a newly hired member of staff. Established staff members are loathe to restructure their lecture notes and even more so the course itself[9]. Simply flipping through most sample first year texts is enormously reassuring. What we find is predictable and is compared easily with other texts which are on the market. Unfamiliar texts take more time and effort to judge, raising the user cost of adopting a non-standard text.

A casual examination allows some rather ineffective texts to slip through in much the same way that substituting other forms of signalling for a careful examination may also go sadly awry. A well-known author or widespread use does not automatically guarantee quality though judging from the accompanying advertising, one would assume that it does[10]. This stems from the way in which the user cost attached to a text so heavily influences an instructor's choice. Thus, texts are packaged with an array of teaching aides all with the purpose of lowering the user cost of adopting any particular text. Test banks, overhead slides, or even computer-generated graphics leave an instructor with less to do. The rise of the World Wide Web means that sites for texts provide students and instructors with continual updates as well as assistance in using the textbook. Imitation is the chief driving force that shapes economic teaching and thus economic texts. Lecturers produce a version of the course they themselves took. This represents an enormous savings in time. To be original is a labour intensive procedure defined by the uncertainty of the outcome. Moreover, few novice instructors would have themselves been trained to teach in any way, shape or form. Most graduate departments would consider such activity to be too obvious to need expounding. The necessary knowledge is somehow produced by the simple act of standing up in front of a class holding a piece of chalk (or these days a felt tipped marking pen).

The difficulties, as with any agency problem, lie in the underlying conflicting objectives of the agent (instructor) and the ostensible principal (student). Instructors interested in advancing their careers want to produce a satisfactory level of teaching output at minimum cost to themselves. The opportunity cost of pursuing teaching excellence is simply too high for most academic economists. Despite all the administrative comments to the contrary, teaching is not what boosts one's career or earns the attention let alone the respect of one's professional colleagues. Applause and subsequent financial remuneration flow from research. Teaching leaves all too little time left for more lucrative options. Excellent teaching leaves even less, condemning those who pursue this virtuous option to the bottom half of the career ladder.

For the struggling student, the textbook acts as both a complement and substitute to the lectures themselves. Those students, who find grasping ideas and information in lectures difficult, use textbooks as a security blanket. At a self regulated pace, they can possibly puzzle out the relevant issues. Lectures for such students may be largely irrelevant. Providing this sort of fall back position reduces the risk of failure attached to the course in question. In any case, such students prefer that lectures closely follow the text, serving to both condense and explicate what appears there. Other students will use the text as a way of preparing for lectures and as a handy reference to clear up points which the student is unsure about or as a source of additional information. For many students the text provides a vehicle which helps them to study for exams. One should not forget that passing exams form the major objective of perhaps a sizeable majority of students. Books of these students are soon transformed by a rainbow application of hi-lighter pens.

Textbooks may be the rather flimsy lifeline thrown to struggling first year students, but as stated, they are written and marketed to instructors. As economists, we probably do get the textbooks we deserve[11]. The question is whether this selection process, employing the instructor as purchasing agent, responds well to what a student needs in order to get a basic understanding of the subject. Here I think it is harder to answer in the affirmative. Textbooks are seemingly written without first thinking about objectives[12]. Besides maximising the number of books sold, there seems very little else driving the production of most textbooks. What in fact do the authors of these very weighty tomes want their readers to end up understanding? What is the limited number of interconnected themes that make sense of all the detail crammed into these ever expanding texts? Without such linkages, the authors are writing the economic equivalent of a cookbook loaded with lots of useful how-to-do instructions and appetising graphs and figures. In fact, new editions of texts seem much more concerned with lowering the user cost attached to the text through the use of new technology rather than increasing the service flows derived from reading it. The packaging improves and the learning aids expand, but what remains is still the same old collection of topics which students attack as isolated chunks of information to be swallowed whole.

> The teaching in general is pretty poor because we have not defined our aims. Too frequently we undertake to give a course in economics by choosing a textbook, and perhaps a book of selected readings, and then simply attempting to cover the book and the readings, with no aim beyond that (Burbank[1920] quoted in Brandis 1985:278).

The problem that remains to be resolved is why instructors, despite their requisite grumbles, appear perfectly happy with the first year texts available. This acquiescence which occurs over rides an imperfectly acknowledged feeling that these books don't really seem geared to their actual consumers. If textbook publishers are simply responding to their target audience (economics instructors) and if, as does seem the case, this market is operating in a reasonable manner, it is necessary to fully understand the incentives motivating these instructors. Unless such incentives are changed, economists driven to believe in the rationality of their own choice will largely maintain the status quo. Given these existing constraints, it is possible to improve upon the current prevailing standard, to perhaps continue to lower the user cost of the texts, but innovations are unlikely to wander any distance from the generally accepted standard. As a result, too much of the change in textbooks has been mere style or gimmickry, meaning that given the obvious advances in technology, textbooks are glossier and associated teaching packages have become ever more comprehensive. This doesn't mean that they are any more effective as a teaching tool when compared to their more simple ancestors. Given the increasing risk averseness of publishing houses, as they merge into ever bigger enterprises, the support for a revolutionary text, like the first Samuelson text in the post war period, is unlikely to occur. The real possibility for a break through may come with the increasing ease of self publishing.

TEXTUAL READINGS

'Let's hear it,'said Humpty Dumpty. 'I can explain all the poems that ever were invented - and a good many that haven't been invented just yet.' (Carroll 1974:194).

Textbooks are the ultimate crutch tyro instructors lean on to get through their traumatic first brave attempts to bring the sweet reasoning of economic thought to the great masses of first year students[13]. Any good economist is bound to learn more than their students when working his or her way through an assigned text. Ideally though, each instructor should be required to write his or her own text. It seems reasonable to suspect that writing a course text could only improve each lecturer's teaching by forcing him or her to figure out how best to communicate with his or her students. This may fly in the face of the basic economic principle of specialisation through division of labour, but it would allow any instructor to customise the course and more particularly to force each instructor to think through essential economic principles instead of letting a textbook do the thinking. Given standard teaching loads, the demand to publish, as well as the insistence that staff undertake dubious administrative chores, all but the most self destructive instructor uses an off the shelf textbook to reduce time. It then makes perfect sense to contract this chore out to publishing firms. The weak point of such analysis is the basic inability of economists to turn out student-friendly books. The publisher seems to think the problem lies in the packaging rather than the content of the package. There is much investment in computer packages, work books, multi-coloured printing and even web sites. This is why so much of what is new in textbook technology is related to reducing the preparation time for the instructor; directly, by offering prepared questions, overhead slides, computer test banks and indirectly, by including self-testing devices for students as well as computer tutorials. The more students can help themselves, the less assistance instructors need offer outside of lectures, freeing up time for more financially and intellectually rewarding projects. Thus a text which students find difficult to comprehend will ultimately be judged as inadequate by an instructor if it increases demands on the instructor's time.

This bias toward user cost reduction is noticeable in the way in which publishers market texts to their target audience. Thus a 1983 advertisement for the third edition of the Gwartney & Stroup text[14] promises the "most current treatment of modern economic thought in any principles text". It also promises to "bridge the gap between the ideal, theoretical 'solutions' of economists, and the events of the real world". This appeals to recently minted PhDs who would cringe at the idea of teaching passé Keynesian models as well as more experienced instructors who tire of trying to explain how what they teach relates to the real world. There is also a long list of auxiliary devices[15], all created to assist the time constrained instructor. (It is still questionable whether all these innovations now packaged with the text actually ends up leaving students with anymore understanding than their less chrome plated predecessors.) The blurb for the Ruffin & Gregory (1983) text offers much of the same. 'The most important new principles text of the '80s'; 'Unquestionably, the best and most modern coverage'; 'the strongest text pedagogy'; 'most complete pedagogical package available'; 'the most analytical **Study Guide** available, testing reasoning rather than memory'.

The same approach is still in evidence in the nineties. Mankiw's Macroeconomic text[16], though meant for second year students gets a similar sell by its publisher[17]. The advertisement attempts greater versimiltude (a word I thought I'd never get to use) by employing quotes from actual instructors. It does seem to work with washing detergents whose manufacturers are fond of quoting testimonials from users as well. As before, the quotes stress the response of students: "Students have repeatedly commented that Mankiw is the best economics text they have ever used, and not a few have said Mankiw is the best college textbook they have ever read" (surely not strong competition here). They emphasise the assistance provided to instructor: "This **Instructor's Resources** by Andrew John is an amazing piece of work. It is in a class by itself." Of course there are the auxiliary aides for the student: "I find this software package (**MacrobytesII**) excellent on all counts, and would highly recommend it to one who is thinking of adopting the Mankiw textbook." To repeat, textbooks are marketed to instructors who furthermore want to limit the time they devote to actually choosing a text. The last thing they want is to labouriously work through the whole text, let alone all the auxiliary bells and whistles. Most texts are chosen by glancing through them and comparing what they see with a mental checklist which will vary from individual to individual but is likely to be surprisingly consistent throughout the profession.

In choosing a text there is a heavily paternalistic element necessarily present. It's not a simple issue of whether students have or might like the text. Students want one that has attached to it the lowest user cost to themselves which will at the same time allow them to squeak through the course. The issue for the instructor should be whether or not the text[18] efficiently assists students toward the stated objective of the course. The problem is that the objective of the course is not always clear in the mind of the instructor. Most succinctly put, an objective should state the minimum level of learning a student should have grasped by the end of the course.

Like the courses themselves, the texts also seemingly lack any justification for their existence. The problem is that most texts do seem to be a collection of topics and courses are taught accordingly. Students learn to strategically memorise a few of those touched upon in the course and in this manner pass a final exam, usually one replete with choices. Only very good lecturers can successfully try to integrate what are in essence disparate pieces into a logical argument.

This is of course the way most instructors were taught. Replication is less time consuming than innovation. The mind set of most economists in regard to this approach becomes clear when there is any attempt to reduce the number of topics covered in any first year course. There are always faculty members who refuse to see how a department can put on a first year course without covering topic x or topic y. What is apparent is that trying to rate topics is a hopeless muddle, a wrong way to think about first year courses. The problem is in the initial assumption that a first year course needs to cover a set of topics rather than accomplish a simple set of objectives. There's more than a bit of rationalisation that goes on in justifying the approach one finds most convenient to teach. In this case a strong defence is concocted for utilising a formal rather than problem solving methodology. We explain our choice by claiming that tools must first be developed before problems can be resolved. But it is in fact the problems and issues that bring forth the tools. Courses could with some effort be taught that way. The key word here is effort. Given the demands on an average instructor's time, the extra effort to depart from the standard course and textbook structure comes at a high cost. It is also a high risk strategy. No one is punished for following standard procedure. Departures from the norm attract attention and thus have greater consequences. To be blunt, since teaching is not highly rewarded, an ambitious young academic would be foolish to invest a substantial amount of his or her scarce time involved in high risk strategies to improve first year teaching. Furthermore, it is simply easier to teach a succession of models than to try to explain how to apply economic thinking. As a consequence students do tend to complain that second year economics simply repeats first year. We respond by loftily dismissing such arguments. After all, we do go into these topics at much greater depth. In fact, the complaint reflects the profession's basic inability to teach economics at the first year level. The allure of teaching topics however undermines any attempt to actually teach economic thinking and concepts, to demonstrate how to apply economic reasoning. What we forget is that a very slim percentage of any first year class will ever go on to become economists of any type, let alone academics. We however insist on training students as if they were all headed for professional economic careers. It might even be time to rethink the training of professionals and ask whether even they leave our care with any basic economic intuition.

As pointed out, textbooks reflect the incentive system motivating the instructors. Publishers aim at a mass rather than a niche market. Most are clones of Samuelson's original text[19]. We have in fact a typical Hotelling (1929) location problem. Almost all texts try to stake out the middle ground. They all look alike and try to cover as many topics as possible. It seems wiser to aim for at least a small percentage of the mass market rather than gambling on grabbing a large percentage of a much smaller fringe market[20].

Texts which are uncontroversial and unobjectionable will tend to do the best. It is ideal to be everyone's second choice when the textbook must be decided by departmental consensus. Even when the text is ostensibly delegated to one individual, there is an implicit veto exerted in that a controversial choice will rub some colleague the wrong way. Since it is impossible to be everyone's first choice, being the perfect fall back position is optimal. Departments do change texts periodically. Sometimes it is simply to accommodate someone new taking charge of the first year course and trying to leave his or her mark on the course the easiest way possible, namely by changing the prescribed text. There is little available that doesn't closely resemble what has already been tried in the past[21]. Perhaps the slant will vary but not the basic structure or rhetorical approach. As pointed out previously, it is all based upon what an instructor thinks an economics textbook should look like, not what would perhaps be most effective. New textbooks on the market simply try to convince instructors that they do the standard formula better than the competition, have included all the latest professional fads (or at least those of a few years past) and contain all the paraphernalia which will lessen the burden of actually teaching the course. This is a classic product differentiation strategy characteristic of a monopolistically competitive market[22].

Of course, given this marketing approach, textbooks in reaction have become increasingly fatter as more topics have to be included to appeal to as many potential instructors as possible. To leave out someone's pet topic risks not being adopted by a particular instructor and makes it even more difficult to get past a committee composed of the usual group of academic prima donnas[23]. Like most word processing programs, first year text books are crammed with material of which any student will find only a limited portion useful.

All of these criticisms have been voiced for a number of years. They are not dealt with for two major reasons. Despite their protestations, most economists don't want a different type of text. The opportunity cost of adjustment would be too high. In defence of the current state of textbooks, Edwin G. Dolan (1988), a veteran textbook writer, makes some telling points about existing constraints. Quite frankly what instructors say they want is not reflected in what they do. Despite the inevitable and repeated claim by instructors that they want to spend more time teaching the basics, most instructors feel quite safe in the belief that their faith will never be put to the test. Devoting more time to the basics has a high opportunity cost. It is difficult to do properly, especially in any compelling way. It is far easier, entailing less preparatory time, to get on with the graphical displays which can be demonstrated in a state of near unconsciousness[24].

Lastly, it is difficult to actually write a text that is a real departure. Samuelson's original took three years to complete much to his own surprise. It should come as no shock that even very talented and incisive economists fail when they attempt such a daunting task. Joseph Stiglitz accurately pinpoints the problem with first year texts.

> The textbooks that are available affect the nature of the principles course. But the textbooks that are available are also a reflection of the nature of the principles course and of how decisions about principles textbooks are made. And these courses are, to a large extent, a reflection of the nature of the academic economics profession in the United States today (Stiglitz 1988:177).

In his own principles text, Stiglitz (1993) does try to overcome many of the problems he points out, to highlight the importance of information in economic analysis and to make his ideas comprehensible to a first year student. He tries to ground his approach in the solution of practical problems. Yet his text remains something of a Monet - a book that doesn't stand up well to close examination. It remains unclear on some very basic principles, like sunk cost or even opportunity cost. It lacks the overall coherency and clarity that would and should make teaching from it a joy. There is yet a final difficulty in employing a text that departs from the norm. Despite the text, the course outline as demanded by departmental consensus still remains a collection of favourite topics that must be covered if students are to pass a standardised exam. Thus, a nonstandard text becomes doubly inappropriate.

WE ARE ALL SATISFICERS NOW

> 'Reeling and Writhing, of course, to begin with,'the Mock Turtle replied; 'and then the different branches of Arithmetic - Ambition, Distraction, Uglification, and Derision'(Carroll 1974:94))

It should be clear that the incentives of the instructor as agent don't lead to the best result for the consumer[25]. The instructor has more demands on his or her time than simply teaching. It is perhaps a tribute to the professional standards of the economic profession that first year teaching and textbooks are not quite as bad as the incentive system would indicate. But the fact of the matter is that teaching is just another demand to be balanced against all others and one without as large a payoff as research, consulting or even administration. The instructor becomes an example of Simon's classic satisficer. Instruction has to be good enough to reduce complaints to an acceptable level. Anything beyond that is a rather noble gesture. Textbooks reflect these objectives and relative opportunity costs. There is room to do what everyone else has done better in the way that Mankiw (1997) apparently is attempting. As every publisher knows, there is always room to lower the user cost to the instructor either directly by more or less offering a ready to use course and course package, or indirectly by providing additional auxiliary aides to students. In this direction, new technology will make advances possible. Web sites will update text frequently, including corrections, additions and updates on macro data. Perhaps there might even be a changing array of relevant case studies.

It is also now quite feasible and cost efficient, for publishers to customise a text for each instructor provided there are a sufficient number of students involved. In other words there would be no need to force students to buy door-stoppers of which they might use only half at most. Even more to the point, desk top publishing makes it possible for each instructor, or certainly each department to issue their own text containing exactly what they think a first year student needs to master. This would easily be updated yearly. The problem is that even were more departments to head in this direction, the results would look surprisingly like the volumes already on the market. Perhaps economists are at heart dull and plodding and textbooks merely reflect this rather sad reality. Whatever the truth of the matter, if economists are the rational agents they profess to be, textbooks will always remain with us and these self-same textbooks are unlikely to change.

REFERENCES

Becker, Gary (1962) "Investment in Human Capital: A Theoretical Analysis," *Journal of Political Economy, Supplement*. 70 (2): 9-44.

Bell, Carolyn Shaw (1988) "The Principles of Economics from Now until Then," *Journal of Economic Education*. 19(2): 133-147.

Brandis, Royall (1985) "The Principles of Economics Course: A Historical Perspective," *Journal of Economic Education*. 15(4): 277-280.

Carroll, Lewis (1974) *The Philospher's Alice*. New York: St. Martin's Press

Dolan, Edwin G. (1988) "Observations on the Use of Textbooks in the Teaching of Principles of Economic: A Comment," *Journal of Economic Education*. 19(2): 169-171.

Hotelling, Harold (1929) "Stability in Competition," *The Economic Journal*. 39(1): 41-57.

Mankiw, N. Gergory (1997) *Principles of Economics*. New York: The Dryden Press.

Mankiw, N. Gregory (1994) *Macroeconomics Second Edition*. New York: Worth Publishers

Gwartney, James D. And Richard Stroup (1983) *Economics Third Edition*. New York: Academic Press.

Meinkoth, Marian R. (1971) "Textbooks and the Teaching of Economic Principles," *Journal of Economic Education*. 2(2): 127-130.

Ruffin, Roy J. and Paul R. Gregory (1983) *Principles of Economics*. Glenview, Illinois: Scott, Foresman.

Samuelson, Paul A. (1997) "Credo of a Lucky Textbook Author," *Journal of Economic Perspectives*. 11(2): 153-160.

Sichel, Werner (1988) "Principles of Economics Textbooks: Innovation and Product Differentiation - A Response," *Journal of Economic Education*. 19(2): 178-183.

Stigler, George J. (1982) "The Literature of Economics," in *The Economist as Preacher*. Chicago: University of Chicago Press, 223-244.

Stiglitz, Joseph E. (1988) " On the Market for Principles of Economics Textbooks: Innovation and Product Differentiation, *Journal of Economic Education*. 19(2): 171-178.

Stiglitz, Joseph E. (1993) *Economics*. New York: W.W. Norton..

NOTES

[1] The use of textbooks to convey economic wisdom goes back to the early days of the profession and is by no means a recent innovation. J. Lawrence Laughlin as a youth at Harvard in 1878 (if one can entertain that possibility) endured an introduction to the subject by Charles F. Dunbar who might be said to have inaugurated the teaching of economics in the US. Dunbar used a textbook.

In a 1897 survey of colleges and universities teaching economics conducted by one Frederick R. Clow, "thirty of the thirty-nine respondents used a textbook as the basis of the course," (reported in Brandis 1985: 278).

If we look at the English tradition we find W. Stanley Jevons despairing of having to teach economics to undergraduates by using John Stuart Mill's *Principles* . This perhaps established the long running tradition of economic instructors who despair when compelled to teach from a text foisted upon them.

[2] Debates of this sort seem driven by ideology or other often theoretical issues that matter to economists as professionals. Thus the new wave of post-war Keynesian textbooks met resistance from the old guard as well as politicians and businessmen sniffing out anti-free-market (communist) influences.

> I [Carolyn Bell] occasionally met a student who asked if it was true that the book [Samuelson] was communistic and if she would be required to read that radical, Keynes. Like the parents who prompted these questions, many economics faculty condemned the new approach, sometimes in a destructive power struggle. One highly thought of institution was still having difficulty in recruiting in the early sixties because its senior members had for so long adamantly refused to consider appointing anyone using Keynesian analysis (Bell 1988:147).

Later, similar strife would appear in the seventies when left wing economists squabbled with the existing old guard over mainstream texts or again in the eighties when newly minted PhDs steeped in the rational expectations literature scoffed at the old style Keynesianism of senior departmental members. It is doubtful whether any such pitched battle has been fought from the standpoint of the ultimate consumers, the poor students condemned to work their way through often turgid prose.

[3] Economics instructors for the most part would find such evidence counter-intuitive. All can cite cases where a text made a significant difference to a student. There are however two problems which help to differentiate any statistical evidence from our own intuition as teachers. A text may make a significant difference to a small subset of students, though too small to show up in any statistical analysis. Or perhaps even more subtly, the affect of a textbook can only be demonstrated in non-quantitative ways. Most tests rely on a student's memorisation skills and desire to achieve a passing grade in the course. A poor text may call for more effort from the student but won't show up in the final exam results. Understanding is more elusive as is the degree of affection students tend to develop for the subject. The Meinkoth (1971) study does indicate that the textbook used did not seem to influence the decision to take additional economics courses or to follow economic issues in the news.

[4] Certainly the choice of a text is not a trivial matter to textbook publishers who seem quite willing to advance a million dollars to enterprising economists like Mankiw in hopes that the result will be the next 'Samuelson'. I limit the discussion to first year texts because the problem is most clearly defined at this level in part due to the number of students and hence the potential market for textbooks.

[5] Unfortunately, I think physicians know more about the effectiveness of new drugs than economists know about the usefulness of new textbooks. We "examine" a textbook - and we all have our favorite ways of checking a new publication - but nobody does careful research on the outcome of textbook use. Nor do we have the equivalent of the Food and Drug Administration standing watch over publishers' claims (Bell 1988: 135).

[6] The underlying issues usually have more to do with departmental politics, ideology, or in fact most anything but teaching effectiveness.

[7] This they share with the pharmaceutical market. Company representatives provide doctors with information about their current products as well as free samples. Doctors, like economic lecturers, rarely are well informed about the alternative medicines in the market or their possible efficacy. Though quite recently there has been some attempts to market directly to the consumer, most of the marketing budget in the drug industry still is aimed at the dispenser rather than the user of their products.

[8] Predictably where choice is not left to the actual consumer, textbooks do not largely compete on price. Since publishers are appealing to lecturers rather than students, the issue of price will not be decisive. Other aspects, those that meet the objectives of the lecturer, will be those more likely to be stressed. Despite this, most lecturers will give some consideration to cost, shying away from any text that deviates significantly above the average. For this reason, most first year texts will cost roughly the same, thus removing the price decision from the lecturers' considerations (though there are a sizeable number of lecturers who would be hard put to tell you the cost of their prescribed text).

[9] Textbooks are somewhat slow to pick up departures in economic thinking as it would cause the necessity for established instructors to discard some of their lecture notes, or even to drastically revise them. We then can continue teaching what we may no longer believe simply because it has been taught in the past, is easy to teach, and easily examinable. The money multiplier may have outlived its usefulness in any practical sense save its ability to use up a reasonable block of lecture time.

> A second hypothesis is that the textbooks of a discipline play a powerfully conservative role in the transmission of doctrine ... The writing of textbooks is apparently not a thought-intensive activity: the modal number of changes of any sort between editions of a textbook in its discussion of the kinked demand curve is zero (Stigler 1982:238).

[10] Popularity alone cannot be an ultimate criteria or we would all be convinced that 'Barney' videos represented musical excellence.

[11] An argument can be posed that if there was true dissatisfaction amongst instructors some entrepreneurial publisher would commission a likely author to write a text that would respond to the unmet needs of the marketplace. This is supposedly what was done in the case of Mankiw's now almost fabled advance. Certainly there is no lack of texts to choose from. Though it is also true that a limited number grab the lion's share of the market. One would suspect that many of the fringe entries are mostly dependent on healthy sales in the author's own university.

> Although there are many beginning economics textbooks in print - perhaps as many as two hundred - most have very little market share and are, at best, fringe competitors. Also, several of the major publishing firms in this market offer two or more principles of economics textbooks. I have not carefully investigated this industry, but casual empiricism leads me to conclude that perhaps 90 percent of the sales are accounted for by ten or so firms (Sichel 1988:179).

[12] Saying this I court the opprobrium of all living textbook writers (and possibly those who are dead as well). I would still contend that they all very much resemble a cast of characters in search of a plot.

[13] Interviewed for a job the author was once asked if he could teach international economics. The author in perhaps a self-destructive bout of honesty replied that he had very little familiarity with the subject. 'Not to worry,' was the reply. 'You can read the text while our students are either incapable of doing so or just can't be bothered.' Teaching what one doesn't know has a long honourable tradition.

> [It was] quite natural that the teaching of economics at that time should have depended so much on the textbooks. That, it seems, must be attributed in the main to the lack of training and preparation of the instructors (Laughlin quoted in Brandis 1985:279).

[14] This appears in the Winter 1983 edition of *The Journal of Economic Education* as does the advertisement for the Ruffin & Gregory (1983) text.

[15] More than just a study guide the Coursebook contains true-false and multiple choice questions in addition to questions for discussion; almost every chapter offers an article intended to supplement the classroom teaching of important economic concepts presented in the text. Contrasting positions are presented that challenge students to demonstrate their understanding of the material. As in the textbook, the emphasis is on helping the

student develop the economic way of thinking. An *Instructor's Manual* containing teaching tips, sources for supplementary materials, and detailed outlines of each chapter in lecture-note form is available. Also, an *Instructor's Test Bank* with over 2,000 multiple choice test questions is available on computer tape and in paperback (*The Journal of Economic Education* 1983:3).

[16] Mankiw's (1997) attempt at writing a 'Samuelson' is handled somewhat more coyly in *The American Economic Review*(1998):88(1). There is only a quote from Heilbroner "Mankiw's style is engaging and unpretentious ... Clarity is everywhere." This teaser is supplemented by a web site address. A visit by the author was quite disappointing in part because a password was needed to get into the inner sanctum reserved for instructors. It did though include a non functioning glossary plus updates on economic data for the macro section of the text. However browsing through the table of contents, which is what most would be adopters are wont to do initially, finds very little that is new. The microeconomics section, after a few brave attempts, falls back into the comfortable world of topics. The macro section looks surprisingly like a first year version of Mankiw's intermediate text. The preface to the student has a distinct deja vu feel about it. Whether Mankiw has done more than write yet another 'Samuelson' would require a term spent teaching from it, an honour that has so far eluded this author.

[17] This particular advertisement appeared in *The American Economic Review* (1994) 84(5).

[18] An auxiliary qualification might also be the extent it allows more self-motivated students to advance their knowledge of the subject. But given that this subset of students may be increasingly in the minority, it would be foolish to weight this characteristic otherwise than lightly.

[19] Given that Samuelson's text has been around for five decades, meaning that students first taught their economics from that text are now in retirement, we tend to forget that it was considered revolutionary at the time. This was not only due to its incorporation of Keynesian macroeconomics but also as a result of its format and instructional methodology. It triumphed because with a few exceptions it competed against texts which were conceived decades before and were considered outdated. Samuelson's text floated in on the swelling waves of analytical economics. The young Turks, newly minted instructors and professors, of the post-war period championed this cause. As first mover, Samuelson gained a stranglehold in the market which was only gradually whittled away by clones. It is unlikely that we will ever see another 'Samuelson' come on to the market. Any success would be more quickly imitated, undercutting the first mover advantage. See Samuelson's (1997) own entertaining account of the birth of his now famous textbook.

[20] We could describe this as opting for the IBM clone strategy instead of the far riskier Apple Macintosh approach.

[21] Publishers most likely factor in such ebb and flows. The leading texts can expect to lose a percentage of the disgruntled or of would be innovators amongst instructors, but pick up approximately the same number fleeing the other major volumes. In the sixties the big three car companies in the US seldom responded to dissatisfied customers since car buyers had no where else to go. While some purchasers might switch from General Motors to Ford and others from Ford to Chrysler, still others would be moving from Chrysler to General Motors. As a result, market share would not vary noticeably from year to year.

[22] See Stiglitz (1988) for an interesting analysis of the text market as being characterised by monopolistic competition.

[23] This demand by publishers that authors need to cover all possible bases has made it difficult to write texts for more specialised economic subjects. A veteran teacher of Industrial Organisation sagely commented to the author that trying to write a general text for the subject was a fool's project since instructors of the subject were so idiosyncratic that no text would possibly be satisfactory to a large number of them.

[24]
    ... if one looks at instructors' actual course outlines, one sees much time devoted to topics that are of conceivable use only to future economics majors - indifference curves, *IS-LM* analysis, and so on. Any rational royalty maximizer worth his salt knows that one of the biggest mistakes that can be made in this market is to offer the customers what they say they want (more basics, more

applications) rather than what they actually want (more graphs and more models) (Dolan 1988:169-
170).

[25] It is obviously not as bad as the incentives which allow a Japanese physician to receive a percentage of the price of each drug he prescribes. Perhaps instructors are more like American doctors who fall back on familiar, name brand drugs pushed by the pharmaceutical companies (those with the highest profit margins) rather than expend the time evaluating generic equivalents or other alternative drugs that may be equally effective at lower prices.

Is Economics a Useful Science?

The author is a positivist, i.e., one of those who always thinks of "science" with a capital S (if they do not always write it that way) and uses it in a context which conveys instructions pronounced in the awe-inspired tone chiefly familiar in public prayer. This emotional pronouncement of value judgements condemning emotion and value judgements seems to the reviewer a symptom of a defective sense of humor (Frank Knight).

THE WHIMSICAL SCIENCE

Richard A. Levins

Three interviews, fictitious in varying degrees, are used to explore some fundamental questions of economic methodology. The role of mathematics in economic reasoning, the question of truth in assumptions, and whether rigorous arguments will necessarily lead to important results are examined. The use of models in science is usually justified on grounds of prediction or explanation. The general theme of this paper is that many mathematical models in economics fail on both criteria.

Introduction

Last year I began to feel I had been spending too much time in the field teaching farmers and not enough time reading journals and keeping up with new research results. Resolving to do better, I took a brief study leave, dusted off a few copies of *the American Journal of Agricultural Economics,* and got to work.

Now mind you, I wasn't looking forward to this task. I'd never been one to question Carlyle's judgment that economics is the "dismal science." And even though the *AJAE* is widely regarded as the top journal in my field, the president of the American Agricultural Economics Association, when faced with a membership that couldn't read its own journal, chose a "let them eat cake" defense - the journal was "of more importance to writers than readers" anyway (Padberg).

So imagine my surprise when reading the *AJAE* turned out to be thoroughly enjoyable.

Richard A Levins is Extension Farm Management Specialist and Associate Professor, Department Of Agricultural and Applied Economics, University of Minnesota, St. Paul, Minnesota 55108.

Acknowledgement. For any arguments presented here which appear substantial or convincing, I thank Michael Root, Dona Warren, and Winston Rego. For anything resembling good writing style, I thank Jane E. Dickerson. For the encouragement to finish this article, I thank many friends, especially Tim Hewitt. For the time to write, I thank the University of Minnesota for granting a study leave. I accept full responsibility for whatever remains.

Rather than worry us with predictions of gloom and doom, the economists I read seemed content to spend their time imagining worlds which, if nothing else, were thoroughly amusing. "Why this is no dismal science at all!" I remember thinking. "This is a whimsical science."

The first article I read promised to analyze "the implications of income, profit, and consumption taxes on the economic decisions of farmers." I was barely into the second page of the article when I read:

Farm households, therefore, solve

$$\max_{c, L_1, L_2} \int_0^\infty u\big(c(t), H - L_1(t) - L_2(t)\big)e^{-\delta t}dt$$

subject to

(i) $\dot{E} = \rho\big(E(t), L_1(t), v\big) + wL_2(t) + y(T) - c(t)$

(ii) $E(0) = \overline{E}$

All of a sudden, images of the farmers I had been working with came to me. I saw them finishing up a hard day in the fields with a bout of equation solving. You know, "Gol' darn, it, Martha. First the truck breaks down, then a sick cow, and now we've got to stay up all night solving this blasted equation." I couldn't stop laughing for the longest time.

The more I looked into it, the more often I came upon economists who claimed that farmers routinely tackled even the most intractable of equations. For example, the 1988 AAEA Outstanding Journal Article award went to the developer of an econometric model which required data "assumed to be generated by farmers solving a single-period maximization problem." The particular farmers in question were not, by the way, on sabbatical in the Harvard Mathematics Department; they were peasant rice farmers in a village in India.

Some more recent examples show that using irrigation requires solving not one, but two, equations bristling with Greek letters and arcane symbols. And as for the mathematics of deciding when to apply nitrogen, well, let's just say it's not a pretty sight - five full journal pages that at first blush look like a flight plan to Jupiter.

An article on how cheating (moral hazard, if you prefer the parlor term) must be considered in designing all-risk agricultural insurance policies gives both farmers and insurers the usual complement of equations to occupy their idle hours. But it doesn't stop there. All of reality seems up for grabs. Here are a few highlights:

* *All farmers are identical.* This, coupled with the consistent reference to farmers as "she," could lead to some serious barroom brawls with the macho heroes of herbicide ads.

* *Farm profits do not depend on government programs.* This should go over big with farm-state legislators struggling to justify billion-dollar subsidies.

* *Farmers are indifferent between income from honest farming and that gained by cheating insurance companies.* We have apparently come a long way from the days of agrarian fundamentalism and the view that farmers were somehow good folks.

* *Insurers have no preexisting wealth with which to finance claims.* Perhaps a fantasy, perhaps a premonition of the S&L crisis - I'm not sure here.

These are but a few of the many surprising observations to be found in the article. Most are merely whimsical and, one supposes, harmless enough if not taken too seriously. A few, though, like that of farmers' indifference to cheating might best have been examined carefully before publication to avoid libel suits from farm groups.

I am also indebted to this particular article for introducing me to "stylized" facts. Its author briefly speculates that, "the gains from risk sharing in agriculture are smaller than the gains from risk sharing in other industries . . . especially given the presence of large government programs and active futures markets." As reasonable as this might seem, it "does not fit with the stylized facts of agriculture as usually perceived by agricultural economists" and

is summarily dismissed from further consideration. Now, I'm not going to try and convince you that economists in general, much less agricultural economists, don't have style. A visit to any annual association meeting clearly shows they do. But "stylized facts?" Perhaps a new journal, modelled after *Gentleman's Quarterly* or *Cosmopolitan,* is in order that can give these stylish facts the treatment they deserve.

Whims sometimes collide as journal articles pass in the night, but no one seems to care. For example, a recent *AJAE* article claims that only the amount of water a plant takes up determines yields. Forget the bugs, hail, and equipment breakdowns. In the same issue of this journal, another article claims that crop yields are a function of not one, but two things, water and nitrogen. The author of the first article pointed out that the case of water and fertilizer was tried, but "little insight was gained" and "the costs in terms of analytical complexity were substantial."

I'm the first to admit that a little disagreement never hurt anyone, and I'm the last to argue for consistency at all costs. I draw the line, however, at fairness. It hardly seems right that some farmers get by having to solve relatively simple single-period equations, while others must solve nasty-looking monsters that cover several lines and require knowledge of everything from now until infinity. This is, after all, a country in which all are created equal, and I think that should be respected.

From time to time, I've been tempted to show some of the farmers I've worked with the equations from our journals and ask if they really solve them. To be honest, I just don't have the guts to do it. No telling what might happen. Then, out of the blue, the *AJAE* announced that students, too, solve equations in order to allocate study time. I seized my chance.

The particular equation students solve is this:

$$\max \Omega = \Phi(L, M) \; h(z_1, z_2, w_1, w_2)$$
$$-[z_1 + z_2] \, v(z_1 + z_2)$$

Meanwhile, their instructors are struggling with this one:

$$\max \; \Phi = \rho\left(L, 1\right) * h\left(z_1, z_2, w_1, w_2\right)$$
$$-\left[x_1 + x_2\right]\omega\left(x_1 + x_2\right)$$

As you might expect, the instructor's equation is more complicated than that used by students; it also has four mathematical constraints that are not shown here.

I prepared a questionnaire for the students in a graduate course I was attending on the philosophy of social science. All 16 students present that day, as well as the professor, agreed to provide data.

First, I showed them the equation they were supposed to have solved. My initial questions revealed not only had none of the students ever solved it; none had ever seen it before. Inquiring further, I learned that only two of the students thought they had the mathematical ability to solve the equation, but neither could recall having solved any equation whatsoever in allocating their study time. The instructor was no better. He had never seen his equation nor anything like it, and said he couldn't solve it anyway.

I also wanted to check if the students had a well-behaved "learning production function" of the type suggested in the article. First, I asked the question, "If you study one extra second, do you always learn more?" One said "yes," 15 said "no." I also asked which best described the units in which they allocated their study time: nanoseconds, seconds, minutes, hours, or days. One chose minutes, one said hours sometimes, days others, and the remaining 14 said hours. To have functions of the type used in the article, you need what mathematicians call "continuity." The results I obtained don't support the assumption of continuity at all.

One assumption buried among the equations and symbols seemed especially cynical - learning has diminishing utility. Hamburgers have diminishing utility, I suppose. The first one tastes great, the second is a bit less enjoyable, and the tenth one is just about more than you can handle. But learning? I have always hoped that those I taught felt as I do -

the more you know, the more you value learning. So I asked the students directly, "The more I learn, the less I value learning - true or false?" One said true, 15 said false.

Surely, not all of economics could be as whimsical as this, I thought. I headed back to the library to get some copies of the even more prestigious *American Economic Review*. But on the way, I remembered that some well-known general economists, (Leontief and McCloskey came to mind), have from time to time come before our association. Their message, incredible as it now seemed, was that in comparison to *AER* and similar journals, agricultural economists had done a commendable job of preserving their connection to the real world.

What was going on? I was tired of reading and decided to ask some experts.

Dona W. Hardy

According to one of the papers presented at the 1987 meetings of the American Agricultural Economics Association, many people think professional journals are "filled with mathematical erotica" (Johnson). What constitutes the erotic is obviously a personal judgment, for search as I might, I find nothing remotely titillating in the back issues of my journals.

What I do find, however, is enough mathematics to make my old calculus books seem readable by comparison. In fact, a few years ago when physicists met economists at a showdown over who had the fanciest mathematical models at the Santa Fe Institute (Pool), the underdog economists put up a surprisingly good fight. The economists were properly shocked when a leading physicist admitted (with apologies, one hopes) that he had stooped to experimentation rather than using proofs in trying to figure out how the world works.

Every article in my latest *AJAE* had enough symbols and such to keep hieroglyphically-impaired academic riff-raff such as myself safely at bay. Could all this math be disguising more whims, or, better yet, erotica? I would clearly need a translator to find out. The name Dona W. Hardy came to mind. I had attended a seminar she gave in Washington, D.C. on the relationship between mathematics and logic a few years back. I could hardly understand a word she said, but couldn't help thinking Dr. Hardy was an impressive mathematician by any standard.

I'm not sure which was more difficult, getting Dr. Hardy to agree to speak with an agricultural economist about mathematics, or getting my department head to fund a trip to England when our budget was facing its annual pruning by the legislature. Miraculously, both were accomplished and I was on my way to meet her.

I don't know what I expected, but nothing can fully describe the sense of academic tradition permeating Assumption College. The mathematics department was in a centuries-old stone building covered, as you might expect, with ivy. Dr. Hardy's office was on the sixth floor of a building that appeared to have only five. A spiral staircase led to a room in a turret; floor-to-ceiling bookcases surrounded both her desk and the single overstuffed chair across from it. A photograph of an elegant-looking cat sat on her desk. A portrait of an even more elegant looking gentleman, G.H. Hardy, dominated the only wall space not covered with books.

Dona W. Hardy, tall and thin, shockingly red-haired, rose from her desk to greet me. "My great uncle," she said. "We Hardys are a long line of mathematicians. Of course, he's the most famous, but both of my parents are mathematicians as well."

I asked if she had found time to look over the single issue of *AJAE* I had sent earlier. Not only had she read it; she seemed genuinely interested.

"I was absolutely amazed at what you economists are doing with mathematics," she declared. "I had no idea."

"Most of us in my profession have a lot of trouble reading the math in these articles," I said. "I don't suppose that was a problem for you."

"Actually, you're wrong about that. I had a beastly time reading most of it. There is so much mathematics to digest, and the text is a constant distraction. Just as soon as I would get one side of my brain engaged for mathematics, I'd have to stop and change gears for some digression on fertilizer."

"That wasn't the worst of it, though. When I finally got to the end of an article, I kept looking for what of significance had been said. I didn't find much."

"What do you mean?" I asked.

"I admit to knowing very little about agriculture, but I have studied education rather extensively. The article in your journal about teaching innovations was, in all honesty, the most bizarre article I've ever read on the subject. On the one hand, you have to struggle through clock-wise rotations of curves, and on the other, you have conclusions that are completely obvious. Why do you publish such articles, anyway?"

I allowed that such decisions weren't up to me, but I was sure there must be some good reasons. Trying to dodge further implications of responsibility on my part, I asked, "What do you think about the level of mathematics used in the journal?"

"I found it completely uninteresting. That's understandable, though. I'm only interested in mathematical results, not applications of hundred-year-old techniques. Applications in general are not highly regarded around here. I once fell in love with a physicist and my parents almost disowned me. To this day, I hope my father's heart attack wasn't a direct result of my bringing Abraham home for his approval. Well, you didn't come all the way to England to hear about me."

"What is your area of specialization?"

"Abstract algebra, group theory, that sort of thing. As best I can tell, it has no application, but you can never be too careful these days. Everybody wants to apply mathematics. It's ruining a perfectly beautiful subject."

"I see. What else struck you about the journal I sent?"

She thought for a minute, then said, "Well, there is one other thing. Remember, now, I'm no expert on agriculture, but the way everything from continuity to convexity to differentiability was assumed at the drop of a hat bothered me a bit. These are all very technical concepts, and I would be surprised if they very accurately described much in agriculture. I had the feeling that a lot of the assumptions were being made solely so that mathematics could be applied. "That may be," I admitted. "But as long as mathematics is used, at least we can be assured of accurate results. That no doubt motivates much of the work I have shown you."

Dr. Hardy surprised me by responding, 'There's no reason to expect accuracy from this sort of thing. Let me give you an example from this short paper on poultry production that was stuck in the journal you sent."

So that's where that paper was! It must have slipped in there by accident. "Drumstick Production in a Mississippi Chicken Processing Plant: A Mathematical Approach" by Dr. L.S. Legus may seem simple now, but 15 years ago it created quite a sensation. While some jokingly refer to L.S. Legus as the ChD, the "Doctor of Chickens," most credit him with fathering the revolution in methodology that changed Poultry Husbandry into Poultry Science.

In his seminal paper, Legus recognized what everyone knew, that each chicken processed would yield two drumsticks. To use his notation,

$$D = 2 \times C$$

Of course, the problem facing the processing plant was not one of seeing how many drumsticks they would have if a certain number of chickens were processed. Rather, they needed to know how many chickens to process to get a certain number of drumsticks. The paper was the first to use mathematical methods to derive the now-famous Legus Equation:

$$C = \frac{1}{2} \times D$$

What had originally been a tedious trial-and-error method of trying to guess how many chickens it would take to get a certain number of drumsticks became a matter of applying a single formula.

"This approach, while in some sense mathematically correct, can easily lead to wrong answers," she continued.

'That's a very famous result,' I said. "How could it give wrong answers?"

"Simple. To get 25 drumsticks I'd have to process 12.5 chickens. Chickens don't come in halves. The answer is wrong."

"Maybe in some technical sense, but not practically," I objected. "All you need to do is round to the nearest whole chicken."

"Perhaps," she said thoughtfully. "You see, we seldom face those problems in pure mathematics. We use real numbers that don't need rounding. In pure mathematics, at least, I'd be very careful about rounding anything off. Strange things can result. How would you round off 12.5?"

"To 13, of course," I responded.

"Why not 12?" she asked. "It's as close to 12.5 as 13."

"Obviously," I responded, "because you wouldn't have enough drumsticks. Everyone knows that."

"Maybe everyone. But not mathematics. Mathematics knows nothing about chickens, and that's why you can't trust it to give you a right answer outside of the world of pure mathematics."

I was starting to get worried for Dr. Legus. He had recently received a large grant from the Highway Department to study road-killed poultry. The project was considered a stroke of genius. Legus turned road-kill study on its head by proposing to study causes, not effects. While everyone else looked into ways to dispose of dead birds, Legus proposed to use mathematical models of poultry behavior to determine why chickens crossed the road in the first place. But if mathematics had nothing to say about chickens, what would happen?

I tried to change the subject once again. "I heard your seminar on mathematics and logic a few years ago. It seems we might be more careful about accuracy when doing computations, but most of our work with mathematics is of a different nature. In most of our work, mathematics is a logical tool which guides our reasoning about economic matters."

"I object to the way you are using the term 'reasoning'," she said. "'Rationalizing' is more accurate. You see, since mathematics has nothing to say about any of the topics you apply it to in your journals, it can't lead to any conclusion that is not first arrived at by other methods. You first state a problem, then determine a conclusion, then fill in the middle with mathematics. But if you didn't already have the conclusion, you would have no idea where to take the mathematics. That's why I call it 'rationalizing'. And mathematics is so abstract, that virtually anything can be rationalized in this way. I wouldn't call any of it reasonable, though."

"As I was reading the articles, I couldn't help but think that this might explain why they came to such trivial conclusions," she continued. "The mathematics is not only offering no help in finding surprising results, it positively gets in the way of rationalizing even simple ones. As obvious as some of the conclusions are in the articles you showed me, it was clear that someone had gone to a lot of work to get even that far with mathematics."

"What would you have us do?" I asked.

"Trust your own profession more and mathematics less. After all, I'm not coming to you in search of ways economics or poultry science might tell me more about mathematics. Why should you be coming to me thinking I can be of more help to you? I'm sure you can think of better ways than mathematics to describe and reason within your profession. Save the mathematics for the simpler tasks, like counting chickens."

Simple things, indeed. Wasn't she aware of Dr. Legus's article, "Counting Chickens Before They Are Hatched: A Probabilistic Approach?" Probably not, I surmised.

The plane ride home was a long one, and I couldn't get Dr. Hardy's claim that articles in the journal led to trivial conclusions off my mind. She didn't seem the type to recognize an important finding in agriculture anyway, I thought.

I had time on my hands and browsing through the *AJAE* she had returned seemed no worse than reading airline in-flight magazines. Granted, the teaching article's conclusion that innovations may save time in addition to enhancing learning didn't seem all that startling. Nor did the assertion that questionnaires that evaluate innovations should "center explicitly on the innovation rather than the entire course."

I turned to the next article, and there in the abstract I read, "Thus, conservation may be a key to solving resource scarcity problems." Two articles later, I learned that, "the evidence indicates that agricultural banks that failed in the 1980's took relatively high risks and suffered the consequences in an agricultural downturn." Later, "multinominal logit techniques," whatever they are, revealed "older farmers are less likely to use computers and educated farmers are more likely to use them."

As I read still more seemingly obvious conclusions, the *AJAE* was working its dependable cure for insomnia. Drifting off to sleep, I remembered something that happened to me way back in the dark ages when I was just starting out as an extension farm management specialist. I was making a presentation to a bunch of rough-looking farmers in Florida and apparently said something that was obvious to all but me. Worse yet, I said it as if it should have been news to everyone. One crusty old cowboy up front, his eyes squinting under his cap, looked up and, in a loud voice, said, "The hell you say." It left a lasting impression on me.

Michael D. Root

What makes practitioners of the whimsical science choose one whim over another? Certainly not considerations of what is true, because their imaginations are freed from such concerns. And how can "rigorous arguments," the style of choice among fashionable journal articles, lead to meaningful conclusions if they start with whims? In hopes he might help me with these questions, I visited my friend Michael Root.

Dr. Root is the Director of Graduate Studies at the University of Minnesota's Philosophy Department. His long-standing interest in economic theory has given us a chance to co-direct a few graduate students. I've also sat in on the Philosophy and Social Science course he teaches and have reviewed his excellent manuscript, *The Liberal Sciences: Seeking the Facts and Hiding the Values.*

We met for lunch in the University of Minnesota's faculty club. As we reached the end of the serving line, he politely asked the cashier to put both meals on his bill. One of my longest held beliefs from economics - there is no such thing as a free lunch - had been seriously challenged, and we hadn't even started our interview.

Dr. Root began by thanking me for letting him borrow my most recent copy of the *American Journal of Agricultural Economics* and suggested we discuss an article that developed a general mathematical model for studying technologies that conserve inputs. When applied to irrigation of crops, the model showed that introducing a pollution tax is likely to reduce both water use and pollution. The conclusion may not have been too surprising, but there was more than enough mathematics in the article to qualify it as rigorous in my book.

"One thing puzzles me," he began. "Barely three sentences into the description of the model, the authors choose to look at only two irrigation technologies. I don't know that much about agriculture, but aren't there more ways to water crops?"

"Yes," I admitted. "Even in the example used later in the paper, four types of irrigation are considered. But as the authors clearly say, they're only trying to simplify the problem they have at hand."

"I see." Root now directed my attention to the next paragraph of the article in which it was assumed there was only one crop, that returns to scale were constant, and that there was only one input used in growing the crop. "Do farmers usually have only one crop they can possibly grow?" he asked.

"Actually, this study was done in California where there is tremendous variety in crop production," I answered.

"Do you think the authors were aware of that fact?" he innocently asked.

"No doubt. I'm sure that this assumption, too, was for simplicity."

"Ah," he said. "I'm just guessing now, but isn't it generally the case that farmers can affect water use and pollution by changing crops?"

"Of course," I answered.

"Can I then gather that a whole range of solutions to the pollution problem have been eliminated for simplicity?"

"It would seem that way," I had to admit.

"And don't constant returns to scale rule out any argument a person might make that small farmers use techniques that pollute less than those used by larger farmers?" he continued.

"Yes, it does," I said, "but the authors say right here in the footnote that it doesn't matter because all of the farms in the area were large anyway."

"Isn't it conceivable that this could be changed?" he asked.

"I suppose. Are you suggesting that not considering farm size was also a matter of simplicity?"

"Now you're getting the picture," he said with satisfaction. "Can you see how this would also be the case with the assumption that there is only one input, water?"

This was a good point. Here in Minnesota, at least, much of the research on controlling pollution from agriculture involves sustainable systems which vary practices on a system-wide basis. Changing only one input is considered a fine way of missing the whole point of environmentally benign farming. When I explained this to him, he pointed out that once again a whole class of options for dealing with the pollution problem had been eliminated.

"So, what the article says "for ease of exposition", that only water matters in crop production, carries a high price tag both in terms of contradicting facts and in the way it limits how to look at the problem. In my field of philosophy, ease of exposition has never carried much weight as a value."

No argument there. One of the few things I remembered from the philosophy classes I took in college was that the more difficult someone's writing was to understand, the more highly regarded it seemed to be.

At least we had gotten through page two of the article. But, alas, we were a long way from being in the clear. For at the top of the next page, the assumption was made that the farmer was a pure profit maximizer.

"Why do you think this assumption was made?" he asked. "Do the authors think farmers should be completely greedy and act with complete disregard for the well-being of their neighbors? I suspect that at least some agricultural economists, farmers too, for that matter, go to churches that teach otherwise."

"The authors don't come right out and say why they chose this way of looking at farmers, but it seems likely to me that it was done, to simplify the analysis. I doubt the authors think farmers really act this way, but treating them like they do makes life a bit easier for the researchers," I surmised.

"I see," he said. "And how about the mathematics they use to find the maximum profits. Does it have any assumptions built into it for simplicity?"

"Yes," I explained. "The assumptions are so common they are not always spelled out. But without them, analysis of this type would be difficult, if not impossible. The assumptions, of course, are not strictly true."

"What do you make of the way selecting an irrigation system is predicated upon the farm being able to cover land rent?" he asked.

"It's a standard and obvious assumption," I said.

"Does the article offer any general way of saying whether such costs will be covered, or is the issue of farm survival also tossed out the window of simplicity?"

It seemed to be, I granted. As we continued our journey through the article, he stopped me every paragraph or so to ask questions. At last, we made it through to the conclusion that "in sum, introduction of a pollution tax is likely to reduce water use and pollution."

"Now this is interesting," he announced. "We made it all the way to a conclusion such as this in a supposedly scientific article and, unless I have missed it, have never once made reference to anything factual. In fact, several things that are readily admitted as false figure heavily into the chain of reasoning that led to the conclusion."

"What does that matter?" I asked.

"At the very least, the conclusion should read "*If* there are only two irrigation systems, and *if* there is only one crop, and *if* farm size doesn't matter, and *if* only water use affects crop production, and *if* farmers act only out of greed, and *if* the calculus invented for use in physics also applies to farmer behavior, and *if* the tax doesn't cause the farmer to

go out of business, *then* introduction of a pollution tax is likely to cause one farmer to choose the one (of two) irrigation system that reduces water use and pollution'."

"And there's more," he went on. "The authors don't mention it until the conclusion, but we must also add three more ifs to the list: *if* land quality does not vary in a field, *if* there is no problem that all farmers taken together will act just like any one farmer does, and *if* nothing important changes over time."

"That's quite a mouthful," I said. "Maybe they chose to say things as they did for simplicity."

"If so, I object," said Dr. Root. "The reason is that the matter being discussed is one of consequence. Someone might actually take the study seriously and add to the tax burden of California farmers. I suspect the farmers would find this rather distasteful."

"Yes, but at least pollution would be reduced," I reminded him.

"You miss the point. There is no way to know from this study if pollution would be reduced or not by adding to farmers' tax bills. What if farmers had been characterized differently? What if they were assumed to be concerned about pollution resulting from their operations and were doing everything they possibly could to prevent it while still staying in business? In this view, taxing their irrigation water would leave them with less money to carry out their desire to minimize the pollution resulting from their operations. And the study gives us no evidence whatsoever to support one view of farmer behavior over the other. All we know is that one is simpler."

"How should we regard the conclusion that raising taxes will reduce pollution, then?" I asked.

"Not as having been shown to be true, because it follows from several premises admitted to be false. I suppose many economists may find the tax-effect to be somehow self-evident, a matter of faith, so to speak. But anyone who needed convincing will find no facts to back up the claim, only a long list of curiously simplifying assumptions. In no sense, however, should the relationship between taxes and pollution be characterized as having been supported by objective study."

Even though Dr. Root was convincing on this article, I thought he might be overlooking one of the mainstays of research in agricultural economics, empirical work that rests solely on data, not whims. While it is common to have a whimsical introduction in an article, many sooner or later get down to objective analysis of data.

"Do you remember the teaching article I used in the survey of your students?" I asked him.

"Yes," he replied. "Your results did little to support the assumptions used in the article."

"But there was a second part of the article in which data were used to support the conclusions. Did you have a chance to read that?"

"Yes, I did. It, too, was interesting. As I recall, the mathematical model was based on variables for which no data existed. Rather than stop there, the article resorted to "proxies and subjective data". These data were collected for only one class, and then only at the end of the class, even though changes in learning were the main focus of the paper. Are practices such as these common?"

"Compromise is the price you pay when working in the real world," I said.

"So, thanks to compromise, there are data on cumulative grade point average, test results, and ethnic background of students. By the way, why were these data converted to logarithms?"

"The authors don't say," I answered, "but it is common to try various functional forms in a regression to get a better fit with the data."

"Does the R^2 of .387 reported in the article mean a good fit was obtained?"

"No, the author admits it was not especially high." Actually, I thought it was shockingly low. The tests of variable significance weren't very encouraging, either.

"But still he pressed on?" he asked.

Pressed on, indeed Dr. Root and I reviewed the regression results together. Some variables behaved themselves the way good statistics should; others didn't and were unceremoniously expelled from further consideration. A negative correlation turned up between learning and minority status, both U.S. and foreign. Dr. Root perked up.

"A significant result at last! Teaching in the classroom is clearly biased against minorities! "His excitement faded as I explained this was hardly the point of the paper. Instead, we went on to the hypothesis concerning how students allocate their study time to innovations. There was not much in the way of data here, either. Where continuous variables of infinite range were employed in the theoretical model, the students surveyed had only four choices: Disagree Strongly, Disagree, Agree, and Agree Strongly. We turned our discussion to the statistical analysis of these data.

There were four variables the theoretical model claimed would be important. Of these, the first two were not significantly different from zero. No matter, though, because they were otherwise "consistent with theoretical expectations." The article assured us that the statistical problem arose from weaknesses in the data set, not the theoretical model. The third variable was "consistent with theoretical expectations and is significant at the 10 percent level."

"Couldn't there be data problems with the third variable, too?" asked Root.

"I suppose," I said, "but that was the only one of the four variables that acted as expected. The fourth variable was worst of all - it was statistically significant *and* of the wrong sign."

In light of the unrealistic assumptions of the theoretical model, the statistical problems encountered, and the author's own concerns about the one-and-only data set applied, both Michael and I expected a somewhat tentative conclusion at best. Not so - "The empirical results support the notion that economics plays a role in learner time allocation."

"Well, I've got a class to teach, so I'd better run. There's one last question, though. What would it have taken for the empirical results to reject the hypotheses of the article?"

He had me on that one.

Thomas J. Jackson

Although I never knew him well, Tom

Jackson has always intrigued me. I took a philosophy course from him as part of my undergraduate program at the University of Florida in the late 1960's. Some 15 years later, I returned to the University of Florida on the Food and Resource Economics faculty. I was surprised to hear he was working with the Economics Department to establish a Center for Study of Economic Methodology. As things turned out, I moved to Maryland before the project really got off the ground, and never heard much about the center.

Professor Jackson seemed an ideal candidate to discuss some of the philosophical questions left hanging by the whimsical science, so I decided to look him up. After some effort, I located him at his modest house in the Cross Creek area of Florida, just south of Gainesville. He was tying his Ranger Bass Boat to the dock in front of his house as I greeted him. Tom was much the way I remembered him - a little grayer in the beard, a little more tan, and a little broader at the belt line - with one major exception. Where his left hand used to be, there was an awkward-looking mechanical contrivance.

"Gator," he said. "A great white one, at least 16 feet. Got me late last year in the dark of night while I was reaching down to land the biggest bass I've ever seen, much less caught. Twenty pounds, maybe more. Damn gator took my hand, the fish, everything, and was gone as fast as he came up. Thank God I had a buddy with me and the Ranger here is a fast boat. Otherwise I'd have bled to death."

"Not that it's any of my business, but aren't you a little worried to be out fishing, knowing that gator's still out there?"

His eyes directed mine to the 12-gauge up under the front seat of the boat. "I've changed my equipment since then," he said wryly. "Come on up and have a beer with me. It's hot today."

We settled down on the screened porch and began our discussion. I showed him two predictions I'd brought along. The first was from Countess Sophia Sabak's column in the *Weekly World News*. She advised "Lovelorn Guy in Syracuse" that "You'll meet the woman of your dreams on February 14. Her initials are J.G." The second was from a flyer for "noted New Age researcher" Brad Steiger's book *Overlords of Atlantis and the Great*

Pyramid. In the book, Mr. Steiger predicts that Atlantis will rise during this decade.

"Predictions play a big role in discussions about modem economics. What is the difference between predictions like these and those which economists so often use to justify their methods?" I asked.

"I'll tell you what the difference is," he answered. "These predictions are a lot better than anything you're going to get out of your typical academic economist. At least you can tell if these predictions are true or not. Just wait until February 14 or the end of the decade and see what happens. It's that simple."

"Not so with economists. If one of their predictions turns out to be true, they go running around with a smug "I told you so" written all over them. But if things don't fall as planned, they give you dozens of reasons why the real world didn't behave itself, or their "everything else being equal" didn't hold water - anything but their models failed, and failed miserably. During my two years at the economics department, not once did I hear anyone say something like "We cooked up this ridiculous theory, but nothing we got out of it made any sense, so we dropped it". Not once."

I must admit, I expected a slightly different response from a man who devoted so much time to setting up a Center for Study of Economic Methodology. "How did your efforts with the center turn out?" I asked.

"What center? After two years of working with the only people in the world who think all issues of scientific methodology are either resolved or uninteresting, I took an early retirement rather than continue. It cost me, not getting in those last few years, but it was more than worth it. And besides, if I'd landed that big bass, I could have made more money endorsing crankbaits and coolers in a month than a philosophy professor makes in ten years."

"You mean your decision to retire here was basically an economic one? You weighed the costs and benefits of continuing, discounted the risk factors associated with catching big bass, and maximized your utility accordingly?"

"Listen here. One more crack like that, and this interview is over. You understand? It was just that kind of nonsense that I could never stand. I fish because I like to fish. That's it, pure and simple. And the last thing I want is some economist coming along and telling me otherwise."

Now he really had me worried. "Please forgive me, but such notions could predict your presence here today, couldn't they?"

'The Countess could have predicted my presence here today, too, I suppose. So what? The idea that predictions are all there is to science went out with the nineteenth century. At least for everyone but economists. They still seem to think Milton Friedman said all there was to say."

"If not predictions, then what is it we should be after in science?" I continued.

"Explanations. Why things happen. What causes things to happen. Understanding. In short, all the things that go out the window when you focus exclusively on one-upping the Countess."

"Can't you both explain and predict?"

"Only if you haven't given yourself a license to fictionalize the world. Now all sciences do some of this, granted. It's called using 'ideal types'. We studied that way back when you were a student. You remember, using frictionless surfaces in physics, that sort of thing."

"But these idealizations," he continued, "while not completely accurate, show respect for reality. What your man Friedman did was take things overboard. For him, since no statement was going to be completely accurate, why worry? Just assume anything you want."

"What's the problem with that?"

"For one thing, you lose your ability to explain anything. Imagine going before some Congressional Agricultural Committee with this story: 'Well, it's like this. We have more wheat this year because the first order conditions of the multiperiod maximization problem, given limited inputs and convex risk surfaces, indicate that, all other things being equal, there should be a rise in output'. Where there should be an explanation, we only have gibberish."

"What economics has set itself to doing is the lowest of all scientific pursuits, that of building a barometer. A barometer will tell you when a storm is coming, but tells you nothing about why the storm is coming and does nothing to increase your understanding of storms. The big difference is that at least barometers are reliable, which is more than I can say for economic predictions. Even the big corporate economics shops are closing because no one can predict any better than the Countess. Meanwhile, economists go on justifying all manner of methodological outrages based on their predictive power."

I somehow thought a fisherman like Tom would show more enthusiasm for barometers. "Can't barometers also be used to predict when fish will be feeding?" I asked.

"Some people think so, and they'll get no quarrel from me. But you don't seriously think whoever invented the barometer had so much as seen a trophy bass, do you? The relationship between barometric pressure and fish feeding was learned by crafty bassers, not deduced from some high theory."

"Of course, there's probably some economist out there right now devising a theory of how bass maximize the utility of feeding subject to the risk of getting caught. Once we figure out what equation it is and get as good at math as a common bass, wham!, you know what a fish should be doing to meet her goals, and then she's as good as in the boat."

"Sounds crazy, you say? Do you know what an economist who should have known better told me back in my center days?"

I admitted I did not.

"That birds know physics, otherwise they couldn't fly. And here we have whole departments trying to teach college students what birds already know. Yessir, everybody's pretty well hard-wired in the world of economics. The same method applies to choosing fertilizer as to choosing college courses, to boardrooms as to bedrooms. Nothing is sacred. It's a damn insult, that's what it is. An insult to Creation and Creator alike."

"I've never heard an argument against economic methods quite like yours."

"Yes you have," he told me, "if you would only listen. It all goes back to Thomas Carlyle and the dismal science. All you economists seem to think Carlyle nailed you because of someone or another's dismal predictions. That's not how I see it at all."

"You see, the Industrial Revolution in England was Carlyle's worst nightmare. He saw society becoming increasingly inhuman, measuring every obligation by money and profitability. When he put his thoughts in writing as the *Latter-Day Pamphlets,* he managed to offend nearly everyone. Even his friends thought he had taken to whisky."

"In the first of the *Pamphlets,* an essay on slavery with the unfortunate title the 'The Nigger Question', he argued with the dismal economists who thought how much work people did was no more than a matter of supply and demand. Carlyle's religious background held that people had a moral right to work regardless of what economics might say. For him, people had a calling higher than the laws of supply and demand, and governments should strive to more than letting people alone."

"No, I don't think Carlyle found the economists' predictions dismal. It was the attempt to discover laws like those of physics that governed the behavior of the individual that was so dismal. And, if he could see the farmers, students, and everyone else who solve equations, thereby revealing their behavior to the skilled economist, he would no doubt say economics is more dismal than ever."

It was getting late, and I knew our interview would soon be over.

"Darkness coming," he said. "That's where you'll find the big ones. I'm going fishing. Besides, you probably won't be able to use any of my rantings anyway."

"Oh, I don't know about that." He was already walking toward the boat when I called out, "Good luck, and watch out for that gator. No telling what equation it's going to be solving tonight."

Conclusion

I still look back fondly to my boyhood in rural Florida. My friends and I sat around the radio for hours, listening for our favorite song -"My Heros Have Always Been Ag Economists":

"I grew up dreaming of being an ag economist
And working on computers all day,
Solving them problems that no one cares about.
And assuming the others away."

How could police officers and fire fighters compete with heros such as these? we asked ourselves as we dressed in discarded ties and made complex-looking calculating devices from old cardboard boxes.

When Willie Nelson revised the song to one about cowboys, I suppose I should have known something was amiss, but boyhood dreams can be amazingly persistent. As for my graduate student days, there was so little time for music that "Mamas Don't Let Your Babies Grow Up to Be Ag Economists" went by completely unnoticed. How my life might have been different had I heard even the first verse!

"Mamas don't let your babies grow up to be ag economists.
Don't let them make assumptions and drive them state cars,
Make them be cowboys and tenders of bars."

Throughout my readings and interviews, two questions about the whimsical science bothered me the most. One was "So what?" and the other was "Why?"

"So what?" seems seldom addressed by whimsical scientists. They are much more likely to discuss the rigor of their arguments. But I see little value in rigorous arguments, mathematical or otherwise, that can't reach beyond trivial conclusions. That other conversational standby, predictive power, also seems to run aground on the reefs of triviality. So what if something can be predicted, if it is not important? And how, I ask myself, are arguments based on whims ever to be persuasive? Even if the argument somehow comes to something true, can the suspicions that surround dowsers and astrologers ever be completely put aside?

As for "Why?" my sad conclusion is this: The entire method of whims is geared toward the publishing of articles. No wonder academics, pressured as they are to "publish or perish," are so eager to jump on the whimsical honey wagon. The world is viewed as being completely determined by mathematical laws; messy observations and data collection become unnecessary; and the vast part of an article can be devoted to whims and rigorous manipulations of them. The subjects of the research, farmers or otherwise, are confined to acting "as if" they were cynical cartoon figures. "Simplicity" is a virtue of the highest order. And, lest we forget, the most obvious of conclusions are fair game if they are presented in a sufficiently pious way.

While this may be an ideal environment in which to write articles, it does little for those who try to read them. Commenting on the *AJAE,* a recent president of the American Agricultural Economics Association noted that "many (most?) members can't or don't read it becomes less of a bother." On this point, I disagree - it is a bother.

What's to worry about is best illustrated by a letter a non-academic member of the American Agricultural Economics Association wrote to the president in 1990. The writer was putting the association on notice that this would be the last year in which he would pay dues. He sent a copy to me, and, with his permission, here is an excerpt:

> "I would be more inclined to pay the $60 (dues) with a smile, however, were the *AJAE* a little more relevant to those of us out here in the real world, instead of being dominated by a cast of misplaced mathematical economists and statistical theoreticians for whom agricultural problems are just convenient examples for use in their various unintelligible, irrelevant, almost universally unrealistic models. They may need to publish this nonsense to advance in the academic circles where this sort of thing is thought to be important; that's too bad for them. But it is no justification for diverting the bulk of the space in our perfectly good journal to these sterile and recondite exercises in methodological obscurantism, making the rest of us into victims of their 'writing'. It is a failure of leadership to allow this to continue."

Must we bid farewell to whims? I raise this question with some sadness, for the cost of a whimless economics will be frightening if measured in terms of foregone professional amusement. Arguments will have to go back to the old-fashioned ways of Logic 101 and begin with true premises. Common sense, long held in contempt by modern methods, must be restored to respectability. And mathematical modelling, with its seemingly insatiable appetite for whims of the "simplifying assumption" variety, will have to play a much smaller role in the methods chosen by economists. Without whims, economics would require simple methods for dealing with complex reality, not complex methods for dealing with simple reality.

Voltaire's story of *Candide* is one of my favorites. After a long and tormenting journey, Candide and his companions settled down to farming. In this setting, Martin says, "Let us work without theorizing, 'tis the only way to make life endurable." There follows one last flourish of philosophizing by the good Dr. Pangloss, to which Candide replies, "'Tis well said, but we must cultivate our gardens."

And so we must. But that, I'm afraid, requires experience and common sense, not the rigorous application of whims to imaginary problems.

References

de Voltaire, J.F.M.A. *Candide.* New York: The Literary Guild, 1929.

Johnson, M.A. "Promotion, Tenure and the Extension/Research Interface." Department of Agricultural Economics, Staff Paper 88-3, Kansas State University, 1987.

Padberg, D. "President's Column - AAEA Publications. *AAFA Newsletter* 10(1988): 1.

Pool, R. "Strange Bedfellows." *Science* 245(1989):700-3

WHY I AM NO LONGER A POSITIVIST*

By DONALD N. MCCLOSKEY**

University of Iowa

In 1964 all the good people were positivists, or so a first-year graduate student in economics was likely to think.

True, among philosophers the doctrines of strict positivism were mostly dead. Philosophical positivism had long since had its day, a glorious one, in the 1920s. One of the headings of Karl Popper's splendid intellectual autobiography, *Unended Quest* [1976 (1974), p. 87f] asks "Who Killed Logical Positivism?" He answers, "I fear that I must admit responsibility." His book of 1934, written when he was about 30 and translated into English 25 years later as *The Logic of Scientific Discovery,* was the death knell. He quotes the Australian philosopher John Passmore as writing in 1967 that "Logical positivism, then, is dead, or as dead as a philosophical movement ever becomes." [Passmore, p. 56] Even the broader doctrines of empiricism under which logical positivism sheltered had been under attack for a long time. W. V. Quine's "Two Dogma's of Empiricism" had in 1951 dynamited the distinction inherited from Kant between analytic and synthetic statements. Over in the philosophy department, then, no one earned prestige by declaring himself to be a positivist. Not in 1964.

Over in the economics department, however, there was still prestige to be earned by sneering at the soft little qualitative people. No one in economics at Harvard had heard that positivism was dead, or if they had heard they weren't telling. The division of "soft" and "hard" was irresistible to a 22-year old. A beginning graduate student wanted to be hard as nails, of course: that was why one studied economics rather than history or, perish the thought, English. The

*0034-6764/89/0901-225/$1.50/0.

**Originally delivered to the conference on Economics, Truth and Logic: The Impact of Logical Positivism on Economics, University of Wisconsin, March 4, 1989. I thank the participants for their comments.

economists, like many other academics around 1964, espoused a positivism cruder than the philosophical kind.

Now, a quarter of a century later, the crude version persists. An economist who uses "philosophical" as a cuss word ("That's rather philosophical, don't you think?") and does not regard philosophical argument as relevant to his business will of course not reexamine the philosophy he lives by, regardless of what is going on in the philosophy department. Even grown-up economists, therefore, do not have an occasion to rethink their youthful positivism. Economists young and old still use the positivist way of arguing. They talk a lot about verifiability, observable implications, meaningful statements, science *vs.* pseudo-science, the love of physics, the unity of sciences, the fact/value split, prediction and control, hypothetico-deductive systems, and the formalization of languages. Logical positivism of the crude sort had charmed the young men of the 1920s and 1930s. It charmed the young men of the 1960s. It still charms the young men of the 1980s (the young women find it less attractive). Milton Friedman's famous article of 1953, usually interpreted as straightforward positivism [contrast de Marchi and Hersh, forthcoming] and confusingly named "positive economics" by Milton himself, is all that most economists think about what they do. Sentences from Milton's pen still provide the philosophical stage directions for the field. Until something changes, as it has shown recently a few signs of doing, the history and appeal of positivism will continue to be news in economics.

So the data about the graduate student of 1964 may help us think about the story of positivism in economics. I do not want to laugh too harshly at the young man I once was. Professors forget that from Olympus they are all pretty funny looking. And I want to emphasize at the outset that I do not regard positivism as a useless or silly movement. In its time it did a great deal of good. In 1938 Terence Hutchison argued effectively against the a priorism of the 1920s and 1930s; in 1953 Friedman argued effectively against the refusal to examine facts of the 1940s and 1950s. But its time has passed; its values require scrutiny; it has become an oppressive rather than a liberating force in field after field, in economics, in sociology, in political science. We must grow beyond a fanatical adolescence, which is not to say that the adolescence was worthless or unnecessary.

Why then was our young man a positivist?

A young non-philosopher who declares himself to be a positivist in 1964 must be seen as declaring an allegiance vaguely understood. The young are good at vague allegiances (something we should bear in mind when teaching them) but not so good at doctrine. The same young man was beginning to stop thinking of himself as a socialist, yet even during his socialist phase had not read much of *Capital* or much else of the doctrine. On the positivist front he seems to have owned a copy of A. J. Ayer, ed. *Logical Positivism* [1959], but internal evidence suggests that he did not read it until later, and never more than a couple of essays. (At the head of the essay by Otto Neurath he wrote in pencil "This paper reeks of metaphysics," which is either a complaint from a positivist against backsliding or a sophisticated anti-positivist observation that logical positivism requires metaphysics to live; probably the former.) A year or so into graduate school, following the economist John R. Meyer, his mentor, he read the first half of R. B. Braithwaite's book [1953] and fancied himself to be daringly advanced about hypothetico-deductive systems in science. At about the same time, having decided to study economic history, he read Carl Hempel's "The Function of General Laws in History" [1942] and decided that storytelling could be reduced to model testing. He therefore believed that hypothetico-deductive testing of models covered what was of value in human thought, and he tried to force his work on British economic history into the plan. He had been taken by Friedman's article, especially the part about leaves on trees not having to know that they "want" to face towards the sun, and remembered Hendrick Houthakker's diffident lecture on the matter to the first-year students of price theory.

His grasp of the doctrines of the new religion, then, was weak in book learning. Yet one did not need book learning in 1964 to be a thoroughgoing positivist. The intellectual world then was positivist. A sense in which it was positivist was soon to be demonstrated in the Vietnam War: here were social engineers, committed to the observable and the verifiable, armed with falsifiable hypotheses deduced from higher order propositions, unencumbered by the value half of the fact/value split, seeking passionately for dispassionate data and body counts from the river patrols. Positivistic thinking, if not philosophical positivism, pervaded intellectual life [for painting and economics see Klamer 1988].

Amateur positivism fitted with the trend of Western philosophy, or at any rate the trend as discerned by the logical positivists themselves, the best of the philosophical crop 1920-1950 and the writers of the books that young men bought and admired. Our young man of 1964 had browsed on the nontechnical works of Bertrand Russell in the local Carnegie library when in high school. He had at least picked up Russell's scornful attitude towards the past. Logical positivism could be seen as a culmination. Glorious if muddled Greek beginnings; Christian fall back; then the ascent to Descartes, Hume, Kant, and Russell.

Positivism, therefore, appealed to a young man's desire to be up-to-date. And it was clearly scientific. A touching faith in what science could do seemed justified - scientism. Science seemed then, as it still seems to people who have not examined the history, to have been the main engine of economic progress since 1700. And the history of science had not yet established that the rational reconstructions of which philosophers talked had nothing to do with how science worked. The sociology of science that looked closely at laboratory life was still a decade away. Even in 1964 the doubts may have occurred to scholars working in the history of science, but they had not occurred to outsiders. Someone trying to become an economic scientist was going to latch on to a theory of how to be scientific. How do I know what Scientific Economics is? Positivism tells me what, right here in this book.

Being Scientific means in English being different from the common herd. Demarcating Science from other thought was the main project of the positivist movement. Perhaps the mixing of the English definition ("science" in other languages means merely "inquiry") with the positivistic program of demarcation explains why positivism of a sort has stuck so firmly to the English-speaking world. English-speaking people even now worry a good deal about whether they are scientific or not. Witness the sneers that journalists in America and Britain adopt against social "science." In Italian by contrast *un-scienziato* is merely "a learned one," and mothers use it to brag about their studious little boys. A graduate student in 1964 had less desire to be "learned" than to be "scientific," in the English, honorific, lab-coated, hard-nosed, and masculine sense of the world [the desire of students has not changed: see Colander and Klamer 1987].

Importantly in 1964, as I have said, the exemplary scientists were positivists. I mentioned John Meyer, whose work with Alfred Conrad on the economics of slavery and on quantitative economic history had come out as papers a few years before. The graduate student in question had been a research assistant for Meyer, helping him put the papers into *The Economics of Slavery and Other Studies in Econometric History* [1964]. Bliss was it in that dawn to be alive/But to be young [and positive] was very heaven!

The student was soon to meet his next model, the economic historian Alexander Gerschenkron, and to get another dose of an admired scholar talking positivism (while doing something else, but the point here is the official doctrine, not the behavior). Near the beginning of Gerschenkron's famous essay "Economic Backwardness in Historical Perspective," he declared that "historical research consists essentially in application to *empirical material* of various *sets of empirically derived hypothetical generalizations* and in *testing the closeness of the resulting fit,* in the hope that in this way certain uniformities, certain typical situations, and certain typical *relationships among individual factors* in these situations can be ascertained." [1952, *aet.* 48 (reprinted 1962, p. 6), italics added] The sentence has a whiff of Bacon in it but could pass for the usual positivism of the chair. And elsewhere he said repeatedly that the concept of relative backwardness is "an operationally usable concept." ["An Approach," p. 354]

Avant-garde-ism, hero worship, being scientific, joining in the ceremonies of scientism, then, partly explained our student's youthful positivism. The certainty of its doctrines was half the rest. Eric Hoffer wrote in *The True Believer* that "The effectiveness of a doctrine does not come from its meaning but from its certitude. No doctrine however profound and sublime will be effective unless it is presented as the embodiment of the one and only truth." [1963 (1951), p. 83f]

The remaining charm was efficiency. Even to a graduate student it was clear that positivism saved effort. It was economical in ways attractive to the young and impatient. Here was a method of being an economic historian, for example, that required no tiresome involvement with "all the sources" (as the people in the Department of History kept saying so irritatingly). No. One needed merely to form an "observable implication" of one's "higher order hypothesis," then proceed to "test" it. Most of the facts of the matter could be ignored, since most could be construed as not bearing on the hypothesis under test. No tacit knowledge was necessary, no sense of the landscape, no feel for the story. A young historian of the British iron and steel industry did not have to learn broadly about the iron and steel industry. (He did in fact learn more than was required on properly positivistic grounds, but only because he was thrown into a company of historians at the London School of Economics while doing his research, and anyway he had a non-positivistic father, also an academic, who from time to time would remark mildly to his technocratic son that one needs to know something to write about it.) Nothing could be simpler than the positivistic formula. In fact, nothing was: the proliferation of normal science in economics has shown how simple it is.

The simplicity of positivism has great appeal to the young. To put it harshly, it is a 3" x 5" card philosophy of science. Its doctrines can be stated briefly and understood shortly thereafter. Once understood they can be applied to everything, and most particularly they can be applied by the young and ignorant. The young can be forgiven, having few enough weapons against the old. Game theory has such charm these days; econometrics once had it; tomorrow it will be computer simulations.

Positivism avowedly and from its beginnings tried to narrow the grounds on which scholars could converse to the observable, to the numerical, to the non-tacit. The physicist Ernst Mach famously attacked the very idea of the electron, as a non-observable figment. His slogan was "the observable." The economic slogans are equally unargued: "macro-economics must be expressed as microeconomics"; "ethical discussions are meaningless." Positivism is one of the great sloganeering movements. So it is with movements attractive to young intellectuals. The German classicist, Ulrich von Wilamowitz-Moellendorff, wrote of his own youthful fascination with the Method of his age:

> *Philology had [in 1870] the highest opinion of itself, because it taught method, and was the only perfect way of teaching it. Method, via ac ratio, was the watchword. It seemed the magic art, which opened all closed doors; it was all important, knowledge was a secondary consideration.*

He remarked ruefully fifty years on, "Gradually the unity of science ["inquiry" in German] has dawned on me . . . . Let each do what he can, . . . and not despise what he himself cannot do." [1928 (1930), p. 115; cf. 1927 (1982), p. 136]

The Harvard graduate student's attitude towards the *via ac ratio* in 1964 is best illustrated by the motto he affixed a couple of years later over the doorway of the Economic History Workshop, in the attic of a building just off Harvard Square: "Give us the data and we will finish the job." It seemed clever at the time. Economists would not need to be concerned with the mundanities of *collecting* the data. And there was nothing beyond quantifiable, observable implications to be known from a phenomenon.

By way of contrast, consider the great biologist Barbara McClintock, who approached Nature with the idea, as Evelyn Fox Keller puts it in her account of McClintock's career, that

> *Organisms have a life and an order of their own that scientists can only begin to fathom.... [McClintock said] "there's no such thing as a central dogma into which everything will fit." ... The need to "listen to the material" follows from her sense of the order of things ... [T]he complexity of nature exceeds our own imaginative possibilities.... Her major criticism of contemporary research is based on what she sees as inadequate humility.... [The usual] dichotomies of subject-object, mind-matter, feeling-reason, disorder-law ... are directed towards a cosmic unity typically excluding or devouring one of the pair [1985, pp. 162-63]*

Perhaps positivism is a male method. The style of empirical inquiry that spends six years on the aberrant pigmentation of a few kernels of corn is rare in economics. Yet no one is surprised to find it disproportionately among female economists: Margaret Reid of Chicago, for example, or Dorothy Brady of Pennsylvania and of the Women's Bureau at the Department of Labor, or Anna Jacobson Schwartz of New York University and the National Bureau of Economic Research. "The thing is dear to you for a period of time: you really [have] an affection for it," said McClintock. [Keller, 1985, p. 164] What is dear to male economists, by contrast, is quick fits to models. "Testing hypothesis," after all, is easier than thinking and much easier than making the thing "dear to you for a period of time."

One could reverse the old calumny on socialism: Anyone who is not a positivist before 25 has no brain; anyone who is still a positivist after age 40 has no heart. But that is not quite right. The brain/heart distinction is itself a piece of positivism, dividing up the world into what we know and what we feel, science and passion. Positivism is a young man's passion about what he feels positively he knows.

Einstein wrote to his friend Michele Angelo Besso about Ernst Mach's positivism: "I do not inveigh against Mach's little horse; but you know what I think about it. It cannot give birth to anything living; it can only exterminate harmful vermin." [13 May 1917, cited in Jeremy Bernstein's book on Einstein; self-cited in his essay on Besso in the *New Yorker* Feb. 27, 1989, p. 86f] That seems about right. Positivism was a reaction to German idealism. Harmful or not, idealism was exterminated in the English-speaking world for fifty or sixty years. It is coming back as something more grown-up, as pragmatism or rhetoric or other projects after virtue, finding its reality in social discourse rather than in the transcendental spirit or in data seen clearly and distinctly by a lone observer. In the meantime positivism did not give birth to anything living. Our theories of the economy are more precise than they were before positivism and claim to be more observable, at least by a narrow standard of observability. But our living understanding of the economy has not much advanced. In some brains it has retrogressed.

The graduate student of 1964 went on to get his Ph.D. from Harvard, becoming there a Chicago economist in method and in politics, and in 1968 began twelve years teaching at the University of Chicago. Gradually, very gradually, his student positivism faded. Such intellectual growth will come as a surprise to people who cannot think of the Chicago School of Economics as anything but the incarnation of all evil (such people are surprisingly common, though it turns out that they do not know the Good Old Chicago School of Frank Knight, T. W. Schultz, Margaret Reid, and Ronald Coase).

The positivism faded when the method talk of other Chicago economists stopped sounding fresh and new. It took ten years. At Chicago the positivism was laid on thick, and conversations with George Stigler were likely to be terminated abruptly by a positivist ukase and a sneer.

One conversation with Stigler was especially eye opening to an associate professor beginning at last in 1978 to doubt the epistemological claims of positivism. George was holding forth on the merits of behaviorist theories of voting in which people are said to vote their pocketbooks. His younger colleague, who had just read Brian Barry's devastating attack on such models [1978] and for ten years had been teaching first-year graduate students about the small man in a large market, following George's exposition in *The Theory of Price,* noted that people would be irrational to go to the polls in any case. Since the people were nuts to begin with, it would be strange if they voted their pocketbooks when they got inside the booth. The argument struck a nerve, and Stigler became as was his custom abusively positivistic, declaring loudly that all that mattered were the observable implications. To the doubting positivist, though, the argument seemed to throw away some of the evidence we have. That did not seem right to him: throw away some of the evidence and then proceed to examine the evidence. He noticed, too, that Stigler refused to talk any more about the matter. By 1978 Milton Friedman had left Chicago for the Hoover Institution, Harry Johnson was dead, Robert Fogel was at Harvard, and T. W. Schultz was long retired. The ethics of conversation at Chicago was being governed by Stigler. One began to wonder whether a method that resulted in such irrational ends to conversations was all that it was cracked up to be.

A conversation with Gary Becker a year or so later opened the eyes of the apostate positivist still further. The Lord works in mysterious ways, and it may be significant that the conversation took place at the regular Economics luncheon in the cafeteria of the Episcopal Theological Seminary. The Chicago economists were talking about the economics of capital punishment (conversations at Chicago were always about economics, which is why it was the best place to be an assistant or associate professor, though maybe not such a good place to be a full professor, if you wanted to grow intellectually). Gary was explaining the result from his colleague and student Isaac Erlich that from a cross-section of states one execution appeared to deter seven murders. The now definitely apostate colleague (he was reading philosophy of science again) remarked that an execution was not the same as a murder. He did not express it very clearly at the time, and Gary may not have followed the point (Becker was more open-minded than Stigler on such matters). The point was that an execution is an elevation of the state to life-and-death power, whereas a murder is an individual's act. The two are not morally comparable. It would be like deterring truancy by shooting the parents: shooting, would work, no doubt, probably in a ratio about seven to one, but would not, therefore, be morally desirable. Becker was greatly annoyed (again that conversation rupturing feature of positivism). In a positivistic and utilitarian spirit he broke off the discussion, muttering repeatedly, "Seven to one! Seven to one!"

And so it went, quickly. At about this time (the end of the 1970s) the former positivist picked up a copy of Feyerabend's *Against Method* at the Chicago bookstore, found Stephen Toulmin's book *The Uses of Argument* [1958] in a New Orleans second-hand shop, and finally in 1980 was asked by the English professor Wayne Booth to give a talk on "The Rhetoric of Economics," whatever that was. The invitation probably came on the strength of a reputation for knowing more people outside economics than most economists at Chicago did and being marginally less inclined to sneer at non-economists than the rest of the Department. The economist read hurriedly Booth's *Modern Dogma and the Rhetoric of Assent* and Michael Polanyi's *Personal Knowledge* in his mother-in-law's house in Vermont over Christmas 1980. He gave the lecture and wondered what he was talking about.

In the spring came the final break with Chicago's version of positivism. An otherwise excellent graduate student gave a thesis seminar consisting of "observable implications" which massively ignored evidence and reasoning that did not fit into a positivistic mold. The associate professor, having by this time declared that he was going to leave Chicago, made himself a pain in the neck at the seminar, grilling the candidate and the faculty supervisor on why they did not want to look at all the evidence.

* * * * *

Later the other arguments against positivism became important. Positivism has long claimed to be a sword and buckler against totalitarianism. The Demarcation Criterion was taken to demarcate civilization from the darkness. As Terence Hutchison expressed the notion in 1938:

> The most sinister phenomenon of recent decades for the true scientist, and indeed to Western civilization as a whole, may be said to be the growth of Pseudo-Sciences no longer confined to hole-in-corner cranks.... [Testability is] the only principle or distinction practically adoptable which will keep science separate from pseudoscience. [pp. 10-11]

This rhetorical turn has been popular since the 1930s. It was the convention of the 1950s to associate fascism, somehow, with Hegel and Neitzsche and even with the anti-fascist Croce. The turn is still in use - witness the use of the late

Yale critic Paul de Man's fascist past (the fact of it is in dispute) as a way of attacking recent trends in literary criticism. Think of it as intellectual McCarthyism. I hold in my hand a list of intellectuals with plain connections to the enemies of civilization.

The turn has parallels in many fields. Peter Novick in *That Noble Dream: The "Objectivity Question" and the American Historical Profession* discusses its use in academic history and observes that "as early as 1923 Bertrand Russell [consider the source] had made a connection between the pragmatic theory of truth and rigged trials in the Soviet Union. In a 1935 discussion of the ancestry of fascism he made it clear that doubts about the existence of objective truth [or Objective Truth, McC.] figured prominently in that genealogy." [1988, p. 289]

The viciousness of the assaults on "relativism," and the willingness to tar people of good will with fascism or Stalinism, conceals a weakness in the case. The weakness is that totalitarianism can be more plausibly connected with positivism than with relativism. One can reply, in other words, *tu quoque*. Hutchison was attacking, of course, the pseudoscience of racism. What he failed to notice was that this particular pseudoscience was itself a product of early positivism. The political analysis here, echoed even now in rearguard actions by neo-positivists, was always weak. Especially so it was weak, I am saying, because the positivists themselves (for example, Karl Pearson) devised the pseudosciences of which Hutchison speaks - eugenics, for example, and racial anthropology, the sciences of the extermination camps. A day at Auschwitz does not put one in mind of Hegel or Nietzsche. It puts one in mind of factories and laboratories and record-keeping, the measuring of skulls and the testing of human tolerance for freezing water.

I am not claiming that positivists are fascists. I am suggesting merely that they cannot in all fairness claim that their opponents are. The trick of saying that anyone who does not agree with a particularly narrow version of French rationalism or British empiricism is an "irrationalist" [Stove 1982] and is, therefore, in cahoots with Hitler needs to be dropped. One of many awful truths about Nazism and the Holocaust is that they came from Western civilization, from its best as from its worst, from positivism itself as much as from Valley-girl irrationalism. The positivists have long been accustomed to shouting angrily that open discourse leads to totalitarianism. Perhaps their anger defends them from a wordless guilt.

Positivism, then, claims to contribute to human freedom. I must say I have not noticed such results. The narrowing of argument down to a nub of first-order predicate logic and the results of controlled experiments makes people more not less intolerant and more not less willing to use violence in support of their ideas. One is reminded of the sometime chief rabbi of the British Empire of whom it was said he never used reasoning until he had exhausted violence. The violence with which economists outside the mainstream excluded from the conversation is one example (though our Nation Science Foundation has in fact been admirably tolerant, to its cost). A physicist who works on the paranormal (that is, works on it, not "believes in it") is instantly ostracized from science. [Collins and Pinch, 1982]

A case can be made, in fact, that positivism is a denial of human freedom, a step beyond freedom and dignity. It is a subordination of individuals to the rare systematic genius. John Ruskin, the 19th-century critic of architecture, noted that the search for a crystalline ideal has been an incubus on classical and Renaissance (and now modernist) architecture. He attacked the tyranny of the lonely genius, seeking by contemplation in his warm room a universal system to impose upon us all. Of the Renaissance he wrote:

> [I]ts main mistake ... was the unwholesome demand for perfection at any cost.... Men like Verrocchio and Ghiberti [try Marx or Samuelson] were not to be had every day.... Their strength was great enough to enable them to join science with invention, method with emotion, finish with fire.... Europe saw in them only the method and the finish. This was new to the minds of men, and they pursued it to the neglect of everything else. "This," they cried "we must have in our work henceforward:" and they were obeyed. The lower workman secured method and finish, and lost, in exchange for them, his soul. [1853 (1960), pp. 228-229]

Consider whether Ruskin's argument does not apply to positivism in economics, seeking an all-embracing, testable Theory quite apart from the practical skills of the statesman, the craftsman, or, indeed, the economic scientist. An "interpretative economics," as Arjo Klamer and Don Lavoie are calling it, would turn the other way, as economists really do in most of their work. It is in Ruskin's terms "Gothic economics," an end to searching for a Grail of a unified field theory, an awakening from Descartes' Dream. As Ruskin said again,

> [I]t requires a strong effort of common sense to shake ourselves quit of all that we have been taught for the last two centuries, and wake to the perception of a truth ... : that great art ... does not say the same thing over and over again.... [T]he Gothic spirit ... not only dared, but delighted in, the infringement of every servile principle. [1853 (1960), pp. 166-167]

Positivism has the young man's willingness to enslave himself to a 3"x 5" card principle and the corresponding intolerance. A few years ago A. J. Ayer, the importer of a simplified form of Vienna positivism into the English-speaking world, gave a speech at the University of York. His subject, astonishingly, was tolerance (it was a series, not his own choice of topic). He used religion as the example of intolerance, as befits the condition of the West that positivism helped cure. At the reception after the talk he was asked if he had been tolerant of non-positivists in the 1930s. He did not seem startled by the question: "No," he said, "I was not tolerant."

Toleration is not the strong point of positivism. The philosopher Clark Glymour amused many of his colleagues by beginning his *Theory and Evidence* with the following: "If it is true that there are but two kinds of people in the world - the logical positivists and the god-damned English professors - then I suppose I am a logical positivist." [1980, p. ix] That most philosophers find this funny is a measure of how far they have wandered from the love of truth. Another philosopher, Stanley Rosen, noted that "the typical practitioner of analytic philosophy" succumbs "to the temptation of confusing irony for a refutation of opposing views." [1980, p. xiii] To Glymour I say in reply that if there are but two such kinds of scholars, and one loftily scornful of what can be learned from the other, then I suppose I am a goddamn English professor.

Many economists I admire talk in positivist terms - Friedman, Armen Alchian, Harold Demsetz, Robert Fogel. But I think this only suggests that it is possible to be a good economist and a poor philosopher. My habit is to avoid picking fights with such people on their philosophy, sticking to the economics. The philosophy may be pretty weak, but it seems to give them the strength to go on. We need inspiriting in academic life because the rewards come so late. If an illogical philosophy makes an economist courageous in collecting facts and ideas about the economy, then no one should object. The other English professors and I are willing to be more tolerant of the positivists than they were of others.

If some good economists espouse positivism, the question arises how economics would be different without it. Not much [see Klamer *et al.* 1988]. An economist without the 3"x5" card would take questionnaires more seriously. Right now a confused argument that people sometimes (shockingly) do not tell the whole truth suffices to kill questionnaires in economics. He would be more serious about analysing his introspection. Right now the introspection comes in by the back door. He would recognize his metaphors and his stories [McCloskey, 1988b]. Right now he calls them models and time series, thinking himself superior to the humanists. He would reassess his devotion to value-freedom, without abandoning the distinction entirely. Right now the values run the wizard's show from behind the curtain. He would be less enamoured of utilitarianism. Right now utilitarianism seems to most economists to be the same as thinking. He would look at all the evidence. Right now his positivism allows him to narrow the evidence to certain mismeasured numbers and certain misspecified techniques. [McCloseky, 1989] Economics would become less rigidly childish in its method. I do not know what changes in conclusions would follow. If I did I would be rich. [McCloskey, 1988a]

Positivism, in short, is not a philosophy for an adult in science. Young men - especially young *men* - can believe it because they can believe any crazy thing. Recall the title. Why am I no longer a positivist? Because finally the graduate student of 1964, in this one matter at any rate, was able to put away his childish toys.

REFERENCES

Ayer, A. J., ed. *Logical Positivism*. New York: Free Press, 1959.

Barry, Brian. *Sociologists, Economists and Democracy*. Chicago: University of Chicago Press (London: Collier-Macmillan, 1970), 1978.

Braithwaite, Richard B. *Scientific Explanation*. Cambridge: Cambridge University, Press, 1953.

Colander, David and Arjo Klamer. "The Making of an Economist." *Journal of Economic Perspectives* (Fall 1987).

Collins, Harry and Trevor Pinch. *Frames of Meaning: The Social Construction of Extraordinary Science*. London: Routledge and Kegan Paul, 1982.

Conrad, Alfred H. and John R. Meyer. *"The Economics of Slavery and Other Studies in Econometric History*. Chicago: Aldine, 1964.

Friedman, Milton. "The Methodology of Positive Economics." In his *Essays in Positive Economics*. Chicago: University of Chicago Press, 1953.

Gerschenkron, Alexander. "Economic Backwardness in Historical Perspective." Reprinted pp. 5-30 in *Economic Backwardness in Historical Perspective: A Book of Essays*. Cambridge: Harvard University Press, 1953 (1962).

_____ "The Approach to European Industrialization: A Postscript." In *Economic Backwardness*, (1962), pp. 353-366.

Glymour, Clark. *Theory and Evidence*. Princeton: Princeton University 1980.

Hempel, Carl G. "The Function of General Laws in History." In P. Gardiner, ed., *Theories of History* (New York: Free Press, 1959), 1942.

Hoffer, Eric. *The True Believer: Thoughts on the Nature of Mass Movements*. New York: Time, Inc., 1963 (1951).

Hutchison, Terence. *The Significance and Basic Postulates of Economic Theory*, 2nd ed. New York: Kelley, 1960 (1938).

Keller, Evelyn Fox. *Reflections on Gender and Science*. New Haven: Yale University Press, 1985.

Klamer, Arjo, Donald N. McCloskey, Robert M. Solow (eds.). *The Consequences of Economic Rhetoric*. New York: Cambridge University Press, 1988.

Klamer, Arjo. *Conversations with Economists: New Classical Economists and Opponents Speak Out on the Current Controversy in Macroeconomics*. Totawa, N.J.: Rowman and Allanheld, 1983.

_____ "The Advent of Modernism in Economics." MS, University of Iowa, 1987.

Klamer Arjo, D. N. McCloskey, and Robert Solow, eds. The *Consequences of Rhetoric.* Cambridge: Cambridge University Press, 1988.

McCloskey, D. N. "The Limits of Expertise: If You're So Smart, Why Ain't You Rich?" *The American Scholar,* 57 (Summer 1988a), pp. 393-406.

_____ "The Storied Character of Economics." *Tijdschrift voor Geschiedenis, 101* (4,1988b), pp. 643-654.

_____ "Formalism in Economics, Rhetorically Speaking." *Ricerche Economiche,* forthcoming, March, 1989.

Marchi, Neil de and Abraham Hersh. "Milton Friedman's Pragmatism." Unpublished paper.

Novick, Peter. *That Noble Dream: The 'Objectivity Question' and the American Historical Profession.* Cambridge: Cambridge University Press, 1988.

Passmore, John. "Logical Positivism." art. P. Edwards, ed. *The Encyclopedia of Philosophy.* New York and London: Macmillan and Collier Macmillan, 1967.

Popper, Karl. *Unended Quest: An Intellectual Autobiography.* London: Fontana. (First published in *The Philosophy of Karl Popper,* 1974), 1976.

Rosen, Stanley. The *Limits of Analysis.* New York: Basic, 1980.

Ruskin, John. *The Stones of Venice.* Abridged by J. G. Links. New York: Farrar, Strauss & Giroux, paperback edition of 1983 (New York: Da Capo Press), 1863 (1960).

Stove, David. *Popper and After. Four Modern Irrationalists.* Oxford: Pergamon, 1982.

Wilamowitz-Moellendorff, Ulrich von. *My Recollections,* trans. G. C. Richards. London: Chatto & Windus, 1930 (1928).

The History of Art and the Art in Economics

Rick Szostak*

Philip Mirowski has recently written about the influence of physics on the history of economics.[1] Society, however, has been done a great disservice by existing studies of the evolution of economics which treat it as if it were (entirely) a scientific discipline. Our purpose here is to right this wrong and highlight the evolution of economics as an art form.[2] It is, to be sure, a complex art form, but any student of art will tell you that a true appreciation of painting or music or literature only comes after lengthy study of underlying principles. So it is with econ-art. Some pieces are of an easily comprehended beauty, while others will to the novice appear to have no artistic merit whatsoever. This is perhaps why society, and even the practitioners of the art itself, have been largely unaware of the existence of econ-art. This situation should be remedied at once, for just as music is able to evoke elements of the human spirit which the sculptor cannot reach, econ-art explores territories which none of the traditional art forms can venture into.

Econ-art is only beginning to show its great potential. Music, art and literature can all uplift the soul of humanity and transport it far away from the grime and toil of everyday existence. But such journeys are only temporary. The soul inevitably snaps back to earth. Econ-art is capable of so much more than mere momentary refreshment. The true aficionado can be carried permanently away from the cares of this earth, to run carefree through a world far more well-behaved than our own. The beatific smiles of the foremost practitioners can be observed at conferences. Despite - or perhaps because of - their lack of recognition as an artistic elite, they seem untroubled by the legendary traumas of the artist. It is the most peaceful of arts, the most contemplative, the most sublime. Having long pursued recognition as queen of the social sciences, it may soon recognise a higher role as the queen of the arts.

One advantage econ-art has is its use of multiple media. Rooted in a literary tradition, its use of diagrams (which while only rarely featured in formal works, play a crucial role in undergraduate education and thus the shaping of the economist's world view) renders it also a visual art. More novel is the use of mathematic formulation to achieve purity of both insight and expression; this, we shall see, has emerged as the key element in modern econ-art.

"There is not a generally recognised definition of art" (Kung 1981, 10). We might all think we know what art is, but cannot agree on a verbal formulation of the concept. This could provide a huge stumbling block to an attempt such as this to establish the existence of a heretofore unrecognised art form. There will be many who object to the very existence of econ-art. Indeed even the artists themselves in their ignorance may object to such a classification (though we will try to show in what follows that art is a loftier aim than science). I have long thought that the most useful - if tautological - definition of art is that which someone perceives as being art. The conundrum of whether econ-art exists is thus solved; the very perception of artistic value in the work of economists makes it art, and no amount of denigration by others can make it otherwise.

Greater 'proof' is clearly desirable if econ-art is to gain the full light of society's understanding and criticism. The obvious path to follow is to draw comparisons with the traditional arts. We are aided here by advances in the discipline of art history. While still a highly disputatious field, there is now a large body of work which describes the evolution of art forms as resulting from changes in society at large. We form a simple hypothesis: if econ-art is art, its evolution will have been shaped by the same forces which have shaped the evolution of painting, sculpture, film, literature and music. Clear parallels should exist.

Ideally, we would be able to draw on the work of historians of economic thought; we could then juxtapose their words with those of art historians to show that the same forces have been perceived to have been at work in both areas. With a couple of notable exceptions, though, such works have eschewed the placement of the evolution of economic ideas in any sort of socio-cultural context. Fortunately, the parallels are generally quite obvious. Indeed, we will limit our attention to only a handful of the most important concepts in modem economics; many more connections will leap to the minds of readers familiar with economic theory and practice. Even those who reject the sobriquet of econ-art may still recognise the value in reprising the cultural influences which art historians have identified as having conditioned the evolution of modern art, and discerning the effects these forces had upon the evolution of economics. This alone fills a notable gap in the literature.

The Question of Purpose

But surely art must be purposeful, and the artist self-aware of his role as artist? If thousands of economists believe themselves to be solely pursuing the goals of science, then surely this must be so? We need not pause here to note that many have in fact recognised non-scientific motives, for even if the whole discipline revelled in the mistaken self-perception of themselves as scientists, it would not mean that they could not also be artists. We do, after all, admire the beauty of, and display in museums, many artifacts of the past which were designed primarily for their utility. Pottery is the clearest example. Generally, those distant craftsmen would not have called themselves artists; many would have taken a narrowly utilitarian view and considered the term derogatory. Not all would even have been conscious of the aesthetic sensibilities which their craft serves. The modern economist, then, would be in good company if they were to unknowingly produce works of art. Indeed, Meakin (1976 135-41) has forcefully argued that the dichotomy the modern mind draws between works of utility and art is mistaken (and elitist).

It might be thought odd that the pursuit of art could for so long be misinterpreted as the pursuit of science. Recent developments in the philosophy of science tell us that we can not know with certainty whether we are right or wrong.[3] Moreover, economists can not, in general, run experiments, and when we do we can not control them as exactly as the chemist or physicist. This does not mean that inquiry is useless. It does mean that knowledge advances through the collective evaluation of new information. Therein lies the danger. With no objective criteria, it is quite possible that subjective decision-making may serve goals unrecognised. Thus art may be rewarded, even though both rewarded and rewarder never use the word.

The work of Meakin implies that the goals of art and science need not be incompatible.[4] This point, at least, has recently been recognised by Dasgupta and Stoneman [both economists]; "Knowledge all too frequently is both a consumption and a capital good. A mathematical theorem is often valued for its beauty, as well as for its potential for the generation of other theorems" (1987, 2). Art, after all, is a different medium for understanding the world we live in; it could well be imagined that a symbiotic relationship could emerge between the pursuit of artistic and scientific understanding. A problem only arises when the artistic motive is not recognised, for while the two goals may not be incompatible they are hardly similar.

The Purpose of Art

If art involved the realistic portrayal of the world around us, there would be no reason why the cause of econ-science could not be served by the pursuit of art. Art, though, is anything but realism. Even those works of art which seem at first glance to be realistic portrayals of the world around us in fact capture our hearts through subtle misrepresentation. "Distortion of some kind is present in a very general and perhaps paradoxical way in all art. Even classical Greek sculpture was distorted in the interests of the ideal. The line of brow and nose was never in reality so straight, the face so oval, the breasts so round ..." (Read 1968, 29). To comprehend art at all we must recognise that people derive pleasure from certain sensory stimuli. Even without knowing exactly what these preferences are, we can see that the purpose of art is to transform the world about us into a more pleasing form.

We must be careful to distinguish distortion from simplification, for the latter is a valid scientific exercise, designed to impose order on a complex world (though only a very misguided science would casually forget the simplifying assumptions it had originally made). The artist's distortions are not designed merely to simplify. Indeed the artist often adds complexity to their image: splashes of colour that were not there; the cubist representation of figures from many angles at once; the novelist's juxtaposition of unrelated events.

The very subtlety of much artistic distortion makes it possible that econ-art could go unrecognised for so long and poses the greatest danger to econ-science. The work of the econ-artist, which must involve the transformation of the world we actually live in into one of superior aesthetic form, *must* inevitably distort the pursuit of econ-science. This is undoubtedly a lesser sin than the perversion through ignorance of the art form itself, but provides a further motivation for the present inquiry.

Art versus Science

Perhaps, though, econ-art and econ-science merely cohabit in economics departments, without either perverting the other? Such can not be the case. Just as the image of science hangs over all economists, the urge to create art must infect them all. Not all are blessed with equal amounts of either scientific acumen or artistic sensitivity, to be sure, and thus left to their own devices would pursue the two divergent goals to different degrees. But economics is a community, with its own standards of what is good and what is bad. These standards affect the individual practitioner in two ways. First, they provide her with important personal incentives; hiring, tenure, and promotion all depend on publication, and the latter depends on satisfying community standards.[5] The psychic benefits of scholarship also depend in large degree on meeting these standards. As Paul Samuelson has said, "In the long run the economics scholar works for the only coin worth having, our own applause" (in Breit 1982,107). Only the most heroic of scholars can be expected to battle against standards they consider to be misguided. The second effect is more subtle. Lacking objective criteria, the community decides which ideas are correct, and the emerging scholar can not help but be conditioned by the community values which she inherits.

Our focus here is on econ-art, so we can leave to others, at least for now, the question of what, if any, scientific standards guide the discipline. While much of the work to follow will highlight the role of artistic ideals in the evolution of economic thought, it is useful at this point to make some general observations about this pervasive influence.

McCloskey, and others have in recent years stressed the role of rhetoric in economic discourse. Economists do not simply put forth new ideas unadorned to prosper or die in the cold light of truth but use a variety of argumentative devices to present their case. Recognition of this fact must at least raise the possibility that science need not be the only arbiter of quality. "Shakespeare used 200 rhetorical devices; economists do with less, using mainly metaphors but also analogy and appeal to authority, to a person, a mathematical procedure, or whatever else might please a reader by its order or beauty" (Spiegel 1991, vii). The use of the word 'beauty' by Spiegel can hardly be viewed as a slip of the pen. Nor for that matter should the frequent use of the word 'elegant' to praise this model or that. If scientific understanding of the world we live in were the only purpose of economics, there would be no place for such language in economic discourse. It is well known that econometric techniques are generally incapable of showing that one model describes reality better than another. How then do we choose one over another? The appeal to beauty and elegance must be a powerful influence when scientific criteria are difficult to establish. The futile attachment of econ-science to a methodology which purports to be capable of precision and conclusive proof, when such are not possible, merely opens the door to the ascendancy of artistic values.

Of course, scientific merit alone is rarely if ever the sole reason for the ascendancy of a new view of reality in any field. Romain Rolland has stated this best: "Ideas have never conquered the world as ideas but by the force they represent. They do not grip men by their intellectual contents but by the radiant vitality which is given off by them at certain periods in history.... The loftiest and most sublime idea remains ineffective until the day when it becomes contagious, not by its own merits, but by the merits of the groups of men in whom it becomes incarnate by the transfusion of their blood" (in Fleming 1970). Ideas must always win through by appealing to more than man's intellect. Man is not a computer but a being constrained to respond to feeling and intuition as well as logical thought.

It might be thought that the lack of willingness to eschew a model simply because an alternative explanation appears to provide a better description of reality represents false scientific values rather than artistic values. It must be an incredible perversion of scientific method, however, to disregard the clear implication that reality does not accord at all well with theory.[6] Who that has ever taught international trade - drawn the Edgeworth box diagram, derived offer curves, illustrated the effects of tariffs with production possibility frontiers and indifference curves - who can have done that, that would not shed a tear if this elegant mass of theory had to be pushed to the background for the mere crime of only being a residual claimant on truth. We should not lose heart, though. If econ-science only has place for such diagrams in the footnotes, they will always have a prominent place in the annals of econ-art, for they are exquisite. The world need not work that way for us to treasure them.

We now take a slight excursion into biography to ask how the conflict is worked out at the level of the individual economist. Breit and Ransom (1982) asked Abba Lerner why he had chosen to be an economist. He spoke first of his concern with improving the condition of mankind, but also of the "keen enjoyment I have always felt, and still do, in the mental exercise involved in the achievement of elegant proofs and diagrams" (137). He noted that he could have satisfied the latter desire more fully by pursuing mathematics or chess (the authors later note Lerner's skill at constructing wire mobiles of animals, "a task that Lerner takes with the same seriousness that he does the elucidation of his most abstruse arguments on economic theory" (142)); it was thus the former desire which drew him to economics. It was perhaps the self-awareness of the aesthetic pleasure he derived from his work that allowed Lerner to shine as an econ-scientist; he moved freely from prose to diagrams to mathematics as the occasion suited.

Culture and Economics

As we shall soon see, art historians have made great strides in relating the evolution of art to broader cultural forces. As Kung says, "Art is related to society and every work of art is actually action on and reaction to socio-political conditions" (1981, 23). Historians of art have gone beyond such general observations to relate particular art movements to particular social forces. While this has only rarely been done in the history of economics, it is still worthwhile before proceeding to make note of the recognition which socio-cultural forces have achieved.

Blaug typifies the attitude of most historians of economic thought. He notes the possibility that, "shifts in emphasis within economics are due to changes in philosophical attitudes or dominant modes of reasoning", dismisses some attempts to do exactly that and then decides to largely ignore questions of social milieu and philosophical currents in order to focus on the momentum of economic ideas themselves (1985, 3-7). It is of course no mistake to recognise that economic theories have a life of their own, and that today's theories must represent some evolution of theories of the past. Historians of technology have recognised the interplay of social and technical considerations in the process of technological innovation and have struggled in recent years to overcome their natural tendency to focus on the latter. Academic specialisation is not to be criticised lightly, but when both expertise and ease of exposition lead to an unnatural emphasis on one set of criteria, scholars must attempt to achieve greater balance. The standard portrayal of economic theory as developing of its own accord gives an undeserved paean of scientific validity to the entire enterprise.

We should emphasise that we would not want the pendulum of analysis to shift entirely in the other direction. The existing body of theory at any point in time creates a mind set which conditions the future research agenda. We will see that many schools of modern art - surrealism for example - had great difficulty in becoming established because the audience had to adjust their mode of appreciation. Likewise, new economic concepts can fail because they fly in the face of received wisdom:

> "a good deal of received doctrines is metaphysics [unverifiable]. There is nothing wrong with this, provided it is not mistaken for science. Alas, the history of economics reveals that economists are as prone as anyone else to mistake chaff for wheat and to claim possession of the truth when all they possess are intricate series of definition or value Judgements disguised as scientific rules" (Blaug 1985, 711).

Ideas which originally achieved currency due to their artistic merit may thus exert a continuing influence on the direction of both scientific inquiry and artistic expression. We will want to remain cognizant of this influence, while attempting to discern the artistic motives at work in the first place.

Roll (1956), Spiegel (1991), and Fusfeld (1977) are among those who have attempted to discern environmental influences on economic theory. "Economic thought reflects specific social or economic[7] conditions, or the spirit of the age; this is confirmed by the observation that many advances in thought were made in the form of multiples - that is, independently by more than one author" (Spiegel 1991, 21). Yet while the emergence, for example, of marginal utility theory contemporaneously in three countries with quite different intellectual traditions points strongly toward some common philosophical movement, it is not easy to discern what this movement might be (Blaug 1985, 300).

We can safely say, then, that while the potential role for cultural determinants has been recognised, the actual role these may have played at particular times has been scarcely elucidated. We will not be misguided, then, if we attempt to uncover first what influences have conditioned the evolution of the traditional arts in the twentieth century, and secondly to see whether the same forces appear to have been at work in economics.

Modern Art

It is common in works of art history to speak of two broad movements which encompass most of twentieth century art. Without at all denigrating those who prefer to concentrate on the commonality in modern art, it will suit our purposes to discuss these two broad movements separately, focussing in each case on the best-known sub-category. The first movement to be discussed is expressionism, which Fleming (1970) describes as art which looks within to the world of emotion and psychology. One common characteristic of such work is the use of bright colours to illustrate emotion, a technique which can be traced to at least Van Gogh. Expressionism includes such traditions as surrealism, dadaism, social realism, and primitivism. We will focus on the first of these, for it is not only the best known but the most pervasive. Indeed, Hauser (1956) has claimed that surrealism is the dominant art form of the twentieth century.

The second broad movement is abstractionism, which "implies analysing, deriving, detaching, selecting, simplifying, geometrising, before distilling the essence from nature and sense experience" (Fleming 1970, 506). Examples include cubism, futurism, and nonobjectivism. We will look at the first of these later. Expressionism and abstractionism can be perceived as speaking to different aspects of the modern soul. Fleming feels the former expresses the heat of psychological and political revolutions, while the latter transmits the light of new intellectual points of view. We will find in what follows that it is easier to feel the heat than the light.

Surrealism

Precursors of surrealism can be found in the works of artists such as Chagall and de Chirico in the immediate pre-World War 1 period, and, of course, elements of surrealism can be found in works of previous centuries. But it is generally accepted that it is the horror of the First World War which gives birth to the movement. The previous sense that civilization was progressing was shattered during those four years, and many began to search for alternative philosophies. To a number of artists it appeared that if the outcome of rationalism was war, "the only cure for man was irrationality" (Hedges 1983, xii). Spurred on by Freudian psychology, they turned to the exploration of man's inner self, in the belief that only there could the basis of a superior civilisation be found.

The first postwar reaction was Dadaism. This short-lived phenomenon focused on denouncing previous artistic sensibilities. Dadaist exhibits were designed purposely to shock the audience into a new world view by failing to fulfil their expectations. Poetry emphasised circular word games. Typical of dada activity was the issuance of manifestos denouncing manifestos. Never popular with either critics or public, this art form could on its own in any case have had little effect on econ-art, for it was only capable of destroying that which had gone before, and could not imagine what to replace it with. Its importance lies in illustrating the extreme disapproval of society which characterised the artistic avant-garde of the period. Moreover, dada provided the necessary dissolution preliminary to the recombination of elements into a new vision in surrealism (Hedges 1983, 33).

Two elements can be discerned as the driving forces behind surrealism. The first is "an unrelenting revolt against a civilisation that reduces all human aspirations to market values, religious impostures, universal boredom, and misery" (Rosemount 1978, 1). Surrealists described themselves as specialists in revolt. We must be careful, though not to conceive of this attitude in the narrowly political sense in which the word 'revolution' is normally used. To be sure, many surrealists and historians of surrealism had left-wing tendencies, and there were notable interactions between major surrealist figures and, for example, Trotsky. On the other hand, many saw surrealist irrationalism as supportive of fascism, and Stalin viewed it as decadent (Rosemount 1978, 6).

While we can not ignore ideological overtones, surrealists were artists, not politicians. Their antagonism to the existing society was much less narrowly focussed than that of political activists. In such a world view, capitalism was at most a symptom, rather than the root cause, of the failure of western civilisation. The problem was with man himself, his attitudes, the way in which he perceived himself and his universe. Unlike dada, surrealism had an answer, and this answer was rooted in psychological rather than political theory.

This brings us to the second key element in surrealism. It was Freud, not Marx, that held out hope to surrealists. The problems of mankind were due to man's lack of understanding of his own subconscious. This was the mission of the artist in modern society, then, to reintegrate the conscious and subconscious minds, to bring the audience in touch with their own inner selves. "Members of the group believed in the superior reality of the dream to the waking state, of fantasy to reason, of the subconscious to the conscious" (Fleming 1970, 521).

Surrealists, quite simply, aimed to portray a world different from the one in which we live. They attempted to describe a higher reality, the reality of our inner rather than outer beings:

"In their relentless pursuit of another world, the surrealists carefully avoid traditional forms of representation that in one way or another favour a mechanical adherence to the tangible world of experience .... Artistic manipulation and dream activity provide necessary mediations that encourage them to transform recognisable or descriptive reality into otherness. This does not mean that allusions to everyday existence cannot be traced in surrealist works in general and books in particular" (Hubert 1988, 343).

While all art involves distortion, surrealism went a step further and purposely tried to create a world different from our own. While their limitations as human beings meant that reality often intruded, and at other times reality and unreality were intentionally juxtaposed, the overriding goal was to create a new and better world, totally cut off from reality. They responded to a "longing" for the unattainable" (Fleming 1970, 519). The world we live in was the basis only for flights of fancy. Hubert speaks of surrealist book illustrators: rather than taking the traditional view of the text as a model for which they were to provide a graphic equivalent, they viewed it only as a stimulus to their imagination (1988, 344). Never before had art been so detached from reality.

While surrealism was born and prospered in the France of the 1920s, its effect on twentieth century art was pervasive. The turmoil of Depression and Second World War could only encourage the international spread of the movement (in particular, various French surrealists were forced to take refuge in the United States during the war). Often under different names, the surrealist vision grew from inauspicious counter-cultural beginnings to influence almost all modem art: "Surrealists adopted ideas which seemed perverse.... Today, many of its principles, artistic, political, and moral have begun to appear more significant than the orthodox ideas which emerged during the period between the two World Wars" (Haslam 1978, 6)."During the 1960s and 1970s artists throughout the world have acknowledged the influence of the movement" (Haslam 1978, 237). Effects were felt in all fields of art: Joyce, Prokofiev, and Ravel were inspired by surrealism (Fleming 1970, 523). We must conclude from its pervasive and lasting influence that surrealism has captured important elements of the modern psyche, and can therefore suspect that similar influences should have been at work in econ-art. As Rosemount has noted, "Surrealism never has ceased to expand its researches into every form of human expression" (1978, 2).

Surrealism in Econ-Art

While most of the classic works of economics were written in the 18th and 19th centuries, which Bertrand Russell characterised as "a brief interlude in the normal savagery of man", twentieth century theory has had to respond to world wars, mass unemployment, and barbaric despotism, all of which posed a threat to liberal philosophy (Spiegel 1991, 599). While Spiegel focussed on the implications for economic ideology, we can now see that economists were part of a larger culture in which reality was being attacked on a much wider front.

Hauser defined surrealism as the discovery of a 'second reality' which, although fused with ordinary reality, is nevertheless so different from it that we are only able to make negative statements about it (1956, 223). Our minds are so accustomed to this reality that they can only consciously understand the other in terms of its differentness. Yet when we are truly struck by a surrealist work it speaks to us directly and transports us into that other reality. Since that other reality is in fact superior to our own, we should accept it; to denigrate its lack of correspondence to everyday reality is to entirely miss the point.

Lacking this insight, much criticism of modern economic theory has done exactly that. Of course it doesn't accurately depict the world we live in: consumers don't really rationally maximise utility, corporate managers certainly don't maximise profits, perfect competition (and thus supply curves) never exists, the economy is never ever in general equilibrium, any natural tendencies toward full employment are sluggish at best. The list could be extended almost indefinitely. What might once have been dismissed as simplifying assumptions serving scientific principles of investigation have long since coalesced into a body of unreal theory. Economists casually forget the original assumptions and apply the verdicts of the theory of competition to a very uncompetitive world. Experiments show that people don't behave at all the way our theory presumes: the results are ignored.

We need not rehash the standard criticism here; writers as diverse as Galbraith, Thurow, and Mirowski have made these points before us. Some have attributed nefarious ideological motives to economists; some of these have conceded that such motives are not consciously held. None of the critics, blinded by the illusion of economics as only a science, have been able to see that the humble econ-artist has been doing exactly what society wanted of them. Like surrealists in other media, they have created a world to replace the one we must live in. Econ-art has transcended reality, created order out of chaos, invented a world that works, that overcomes human greed, power-lust, vanity, and incompetence. It is not just real; it is much better than that: it is surreal. Walk into the garden of econ-theory for a moment, and free your mind from the troubles of the day. What bothers you? Labour market discrimination? Not in this garden, for if some workers of equal ability are shunned by some firms, the competitive environment ensures that others will not only hire the discriminated, but beat the discriminators in the market place. Perhaps nasty trade wars in this world make you fear for the future? The garden is peaceful; everyone accepts the free trade verdict of the theory of comparative advantage. Do you worry about unemployment? Involuntary unemployment, beyond some trivial transitory job search component, doesn't exist in the garden. Do you fear that modern man has lost touch with basic human values and is buffeted wildly by advertising and fads? All in the garden are rational independent utility maximisers. Does the onward march of technology cause trepidation? Relax; technological change occurs in the background in the garden; productivity increases virtually of its own accord.

Not all of the elements of economic theory are superior to reality. Indeed, *homo economicus* would be a rather boring species. However, it would be a serious error to conceive the purpose of surrealism as the creation of perfection. One does not consciously create the other world, after all. It must emerge from the subconscious. "The dream becomes ... in broad sense the paradigm of the whole world picture" (Hauser 1956, 224). Dreams give only a partial insight. Just as dreams combine meticulous details in arbitrary fashion, so also must the surrealist artist. The subconscious world may be superior, but not every detail it yields will be wonderful. The artist, as unconsciously as possible, builds a picture of jumbled details. This is what gives surrealist art the appearance but not the substance of reality. It is what gives econ-art the appearance but not the substance of science.

One last side-effect should be noted. The essence of works of art, and especially surrealist works, is that they attempt to illuminate that higher reality by describing in detail some small aspect of that reality, and only sketching the broader picture. Unlike the economics of its predecessors, twentieth century econ-art has totally embraced this approach. From the late nineteenth century, "economics had ceased to be the proliferation of world views which ... seemed to illuminate the whole avenue down which society was marching. It became instead the special province of professors whose investigations threw out pinpoint beams rather than the wide-searching beacons of the earlier economists" (Heilbroner 1968, 156). Econ-art did not need to fill in the big picture in order to create the illusion of completeness. It could shy away from questions of economic growth with which its constructs could not deal. Not only was this possible but the very methodology of the artist made it imperative. The intellectual may conceptualise the big picture; the artist must focus on the particular.

Before proceeding to examine in greater detail the elements of the surreal world, we are advised to meet again the criticism that economics is just bad science, not art. The continued refinement of abstruse unverifiable models proceeds on many fronts in a manner which hardly serves scientific goals. Clower dismisses the work on general equilibrium models since the time of Edgeworth in the nineteenth century as footnoting (1989, 28). We have in recent years seen a rash of rational expectations models. Such meticulous attention to detail in the construction of an unreal picture is more characteristic of surrealist art than positive science.

Toward a Better World?

Philosophers of art have suggested that art does not simply point to a better world but a world which may yet actually arise:

> "The work of art proceeds from the longing for that perfect existence which is not yet, but which man, despite all disappointments, thinks must come to be when the existent has reached its full truth and reality has been subordinated to actual entities. The tree on the canvas is not like that outside in the field .... The tree, however, is not sealed in its unreality, but rouses the hope - if it really exists - that the world as it ought to be will at some time actually arise. Thus art projects in advance something that does not yet exist. It cannot say how it will come to be; nevertheless it provides a consoling assurance that it will come ... we feel its promise" (Guardini, in Kung 1981, 51-2).

Kung himself echoes these sentiments, though leaving alive the possibility that perhaps the second reality is more a dream than a realistic expectation:

"Its [art] particular service to man consists in symbolising, without cold comfort or false solemnity, what is not yet, how man and society might be, what man's yearning awaits: in this world of purposes and constraints, a free space for the element of play which leaves open all possibilities. For a great work of art is ... more than a downright lie .... It is - particularly when it is aesthetically immanently perfected - more than a hint and anticipation of a world still awaiting its consummation" (1981, 51).

Surrealists certainly saw themselves in this light. The goal of surrealism was to lead to alterations in perceptions of reality which would carry over into life (Hedges 1982, 58). Surrealist art was viewed not as an end in itself but as part of a social revolution (Rosemount 1978, 43-4). We must understand, though, that they felt that society would only be changed if man was changed. To the extent that people were put in touch with their true inner selves they would be able to fashion a society without conflict.

Marxists generally shared a somewhat similar hope of changing man. They felt, however, that it was possible to change social institutions first and man's basic impulses thereafter. Some might be transformed by philosophy alone; the rest would change if they lived in a communist world. This was the long cherished dream; that mankind's tendencies toward non-selfish, collectively-oriented behaviour could be brought about by political revolution. If possible, this would be a much quicker path to utopia. Changing man is no simple task, and doing so through the subtle medium of art is certain not to happen overnight. "[Visual] art can indeed make its mark on consciousness and thus, indirectly, change society, but this cannot be brought about instantaneously, only as a long-term effect" (Kung 1981, 24). We can not yet judge the success of surrealist art in changing man, though its continued popularity is indicative.

A generation of Marxists was scorned in the west for the belief that man's attitudes could be transformed by institutions. Economists of the mainstream chased their own dream in more subtle fashion. Perhaps the *homo economicus* of the textbooks could be created if we just collectively believed in him, if we shut ourselves off from the polluting thoughts of psychologists and sociologists who suggested not just that mankind was needlessly complex but - heresy of heresies -that this was somehow important. If businessmen could be convinced of the inevitable return to full employment, perhaps investment wouldn't fluctuate so much in the first place. If politicians were convinced that tariffs were bad, perhaps we could get rid of them. If those with market power imbibed the notion of contestability they would satisfy themselves with normal profits.

We cannot be sure to what degree a greater dedication to the principles of science might by now have bequeathed to us a discipline capable of providing helpful advice to governments on the crucial issues of the day: encouraging growth, reducing unemployment, controlling inflation, improving the income distribution etc. Given the pitiful record to date of econ-science in improving the state of society, we must be relieved that so much effort has been devoted to the artistic goal of changing man instead. Econ-science holds out hope for the quick fix, the blazing insight which allows farsighted political leaders to recraft our institutions in miraculous fashion to create a kinder, gentler tomorrow. Econ-art must pursue the slower path of fashioning a world toward which we might aim, and urging mankind to transform itself to suit the image.

The above comparison was biased against econ-art, for it took as its benchmark the ostensible goal of econ-science: the refashioning of society. We must never lose sight of the fact that art serves a loftier goal than science. If civilisation is tending toward any goal, it must be the realisation of man's true potential. Institutional restructuring is just a means; the goal is self-actualisation. Seen in this truer light, it is econ-science which pursues the indirect path, while econ-art speaks directly to the heart and soul of man.

Econ-science still has a role to play: the release from unnecessary toil and discomfort is a prerequisite for the widespread discovery of man's inner spirit. But we would err greatly were we to exalt the piano tuner above the concert pianist or composer.

This leads us back to the question of whether the reality portrayed in econ-art must be the future which we actually wish to achieve. The answer, surely, is no. Elements of the picture may be exactly that, but other elements may merely represent a purposely idealised version of that which should be but never could be. The goal, after all, is to transform man; if man's reach did not always exceed his grasp there would be no place for curiosity, or hope, or striving, for much of what is best in the human spirit. Art must, in the end, hold out an unreachable goal; man grows and evolves and achieves some of the possibilities which lay before him, but it is not in man to achieve perfection.

Econ-art evokes the future in order to free man from the present. Writers as diverse as Tolstoy and Wadsworth had argued that artists transmit feeling and emotion in their work. While the artist expresses feeling, that which is transmitted is understanding, and such understanding takes the heat out of our emotional problems (Read 1968, 262-7). Only by recognising how art inspires the best part of the human spirit, can we understand the ancient Greek equation of beauty with moral goodness (or simple truth). A man who absorbs the image of the econ-art world, of a world without discrimination or exploitation and where people get what they deserve, is free. The best of worlds, after all, exists only in our hearts.

At one level, *homo economicus* must seem to be quite a departure from the Freudian construct which inspired surrealism. Yet he reflects the constraints of the new art form. The painter, the novelist, and the sculptor can readily capture the neurotic conflicts of the inner being. The economist has difficulty dealing with conflicting desires. Elaborate models of elegance and beauty can not easily be created unless people behave in predictable fashion.

At a deeper level, Freudian and economic man are one and the same. Haslam describes the surrealist discovery as the recognition that modern man was still driven by primitive instincts (1978:7). This, again, was a reaction to the received philosophical tradition in which civilised man was driven by higher virtues - philanthropy, good taste, philosophical introspection. Freud pointed to a different set of impulses. Econ-art echoes the return to emphasis on selfish motives (always, to be sure, an important element in the discipline). It echoes the desire to put the unmasked individual at the centre of artistic expression. It is, in its own way, a rebellion against the naivete of nineteenth century philosophy.

An Orderly World

Read describes art as an attempt to create pleasing forms (1968,18). We can thus go beyond our discussion of the yearning for a better world to look at particular characteristics of that other reality. The first essential characteristic is order. "Art is an escape from chaos." (Read 1968, 42-3). Surreal art has much of its impact through the very precision with which unreal elements are juxtaposed. Art cannot be a jumble; every element has its place. Ideally, one should be able to say; "Ah yes, every piece fits. There are no loose ends". Only then can understanding be complete. In the real world there are loose ends. Moreover, there are always caveats. A may cause B most of the time, but not always, and it may be difficult to enumerate much less explain the various situations in which this causal link does not hold. In the higher reality of the artist, A can cause B all of the time. Indeed, in any work of art A must cause B all of the time. Understanding in art may be deep but must be simple.

We have, then, our first limited insight into the preference for mathematical discourse in econ-art. If scientific goals alone were to be pursued, one would imagine that it would soon be recognised that the precision of mathematics is ill-suited to our present highly imperfect knowledge of the functioning of the economy.[9] Maths has its place to be sure, but we would be well advised to devote more attention to uncovering the caveats than working out the mathematical niceties of a world in which A always causes B. For econ-art, though, mathematics is an unmixed blessing (ignoring the unfortunate side-effect of reducing the potential audience).[10] It guarantees order. Every element of the model is related exactly to every other. If one wishes cerebrally to work out the exact role of any element, this may take some time. But while the art historian may want to examine every paint stroke (or not), the connoisseur appreciates the work as a whole. So it is with econ-art. One does not have to recreate the work of the artist to appreciate the message. A model expressed in precise prose must inevitably encourage intellectualisation, and the subtler the message the more difficult it will be to by-pass the conscious mind and appeal to the intuition of the subconscious. Since we know a mathematical model must not defy logical rules, we are able to accept it as a whole. Unless we wish to use it as an input into further artistic exploration, we can accept the message without feeling any need to analyse the details. Elegance, simplicity, beauty, order: we are transported immediately to that other world.

We should not neglect the possibility that some of this appeal is misplaced. Philosophers as diverse as Socrates and Kierkegaard have argued that we should not choose order, but accept the inherent difficulty and complexity of life (learning that it is difficult but not impossible). We can be tyrannised by order, as when the laws of economics become excuses for the horrors of economic life (Arrington 1990, 92). The difficulty here lies in the confusion of econ-art with econ-science. As art, economics serves a valuable function in transporting the audience into a better world. Only when art is mistaken for science does it limit our ability to cope with the world we live in.

The Quest For Understanding

Precision serves not just the aesthetic requirements of all art, but also responds to the desperate desire of modern man for hard answers in a world of uncertainty. The tight cultural net which bound our forefathers has been cut. Unprecedented rates of change in the world around us serve to cause further disorientation. "To be modern is to find ourselves in an environment that promises us adventure, power, joy, growth, transformation of ourselves and the world - and at the same time, that threatens to destroy everything we have, everything we know, everything we are". In the nineteenth century, writers struggled to deal with the complexities of the world they lived in; in the twentieth century they have tended to the extremes of admiration or condemnation. Postwar attempts to achieve some synthesis between these two extremes have failed (Berman 1982:15,24 and 32). Seen in this light, the failure of dada and the success of surrealism can be attributed to the fact that the latter provided an answer whereas the former was anarchic.

While mankind can still revel in the subtle discourses of the great philosophers, we can not deny that there is a *taste* for the closed system, the feeling that, "this is *the* answer; we need look no further". Econ-artists, then, by the order and completeness of their creation, satisfy a basic human need. At its best, this can aid the ability of the recipient to cope with reality. The danger of course is that one must be able to separate reality from surreality. Art fails in its mission of understanding if its message is misinterpreted. The problem is not so much that econ-science and econ-art are interwoven, but that econ-art is badly presented. Nevertheless, the confusion of art and science must increase the possibility that econ-art is misunderstood.

We cannot speak of the understanding which is the aim of art in the same way that we speak of the understanding which comes from science. Still, just as scientific speculation can be erroneous, so too can art be misleading. Art should increase our capability to cope, to prosper, to grow. "Art is rehearsal for those real situations in which it is vital for our survival to endure cognitive tension" (Peckham 1967, 314). While the critics may be right when they claim that economics is cut off from reality, econ-art ironically fails in its mission because it does not always *appear* to be divorced from reality. It thus unintentionally enters the dangerous arena of demagogues and religious charlatans, and provides false succour by acting as if easy answers existed to life's harder questions. Economics has a valuable role to play but cannot do so as long as she is unable to face reality herself.

An Antidote to Nationalism

Surrealism arose as an antidote to nationalism and militarism (Haslam 1978, 237). From the outset, surrealist artists strove to achieve a worldwide movement, confident (at least hopeful) of the power of art to unite mankind. Visual art, especially, could easily cross national boundaries. And if humanity could share the surrealist vision nationalist tensions must be eased.

The implications for econ-art were far-reaching. International trade theory concluded that trade barriers were bad policy (in a world of free trade, much if not all of the economic pseudo-rationales for military adventures would disappear) and this could not help but strike a responsive chord in a profession and populace both weary and fearful of war. It would not just be in international trade but across the discipline that the reaction to nationalism would be felt. In a time of ethnic turmoil there was a natural attraction of a 'science' that focussed on what mankind had in common rather than its diversity (Spiegel 1991, 650). Tastes could be ignored in favour of identical utility-maximising consumers. Differences in cultures, institutions, and technologies could be ignored in product and labour markets with homogeneous labour and capital. The all-important question of why some countries grew faster than others, or had lower unemployment rates, could be pushed to the background; pure deduction of the driving mechanism of the typical economy would be pursued instead.

"Only during the past fifty years has there emerged a worldwide homogenised mass culture and, in conjunction with other factors, the acceptance of a mathematical economics world wide in its sweep that abstracts from the specifics of time, place, and national differences" (Spiegel 1991, xii). Through the nineteenth century, different economic traditions were pursued in different countries; e.g. the German Historical School,[11] the Austrian School. Even into the interwar period, it was common for major developments in theory to remain unknown outside the country of origin for years. Mathematics provided an answer to that. Both by facilitating communication and glossing over national differences, it created one theory for all. It can be no coincidence that Von Neumann, one of the earliest popularisers of mathematical economics, was, like Freud before him, a product of the protracted breakup of the Hapsburg Empire, nor that mathematical economics first caught on in the ethnic melting pot of the United States (Spiegel 1991, 640 and 661). Econ-art brought the world closer together.

Suspicion of Authority

The First World War could not help but cause people to question the wisdom of those in charge. The later rise of totalitarian governments encouraged an even greater suspicion of power. Not only was the state losing its credibility, but the natural authority of the church was in serious decline. Surrealism was in large part a reaction to the loss of legitimacy by both church and state; its goal to shock society into a new world view (Haslam 1978, 7). In the cauldron of Depression, when much of the intelligentsia, especially in Europe, sided with authoritarianism, surrealists retained their suspicion (Hauser 1956). While conscious thought could not always see any alternative, the subconscious yearned for images of a world in which the horrors which resulted from the abuse of power would not be possible.

The free market orientation of mainstream economics is often attributed by its detractors to ideological motives. Yet a deeper and less hostile interpretation is clearly possible. Econ-artists merely reflected the temper of their times: the clearest antidote to the abuse of power was the assertion that the world would function perfectly well on its own. Man did not have to consciously rule his own affairs, as the invisible hand would do this for him. Practical considerations might force politicians and some economists to argue for, and achieve, a haphazard accretion of government powers. This could not lessen the attraction of works of theory which argued that such intervention was unnecessary.

The University of Chicago has long been the central outpost of the idea that state interference is generally counterproductive. The two leading scholars there during the Depression were Knight and Simons. Simons, like Keynes himself, was only too conscious of the justification which the latter's theories could provide to totalitarian regimes (Breit 1982, 209). Knight has left us a clear statement of his views on the matter:

> "I mistrust reformers. When a man or group asks for power to do good, my impulse is to say, 'Oh yeah, who ever wanted power for any other reason? And what have they done when they got it?' So I instinctively want to cancel the last three words, leaving simply 'I want power'; that is easy to believe. And, a further confession: I am reluctant to believe in doing good with power anyway" (in Breit 1982 198).

It is not a belief in the market, or even of the rights of private individuals that provides the starting point of his philosophy but a justified fear of the abuse of power which encouraged him to look for other mechanisms which could mediate men's lives. Both Knight and Simons were willing to recognise some role for government. The latter even suggested that natural monopolies should be operated by government, and that other corporations should be limited in size to prevent the exercise of market power. These are hardly the suggestions to be expected of an ideological lackey. They express rather a fear of power in all forms, and the hope that market forces could discipline man. We might feel that hope to be misguided or even naive, but can hardly be surprised that it strikes a chord in the soul of modern man.

The Deification of Technique

The role of artistic motives in economics helps us to comprehend one of the puzzles of the modern profession: the focus on technique rather than results.[12] This is a source of much hilarity among our brethren in mathematics and statistics departments who marvel at how a group of academics supposedly devoted to understanding how the world works can pride themselves instead on the mastery of techniques taught daily to graduate students, if not undergraduate majors, in mathematics.

The economist retort is, of course, that the real challenge is the application of these techniques: the subtle manipulations required to bend the precise tools of the mathematician to the explication of the complex world we live in. The initiated, however, know only too well that approximation to reality is not a standard which developments in theory are required to satisfy.[13] Perhaps it is inevitable that with thousands upon thousands of economists pressured to publish a steady stream of articles and books, all of which are supposed to contain something 'new', that the profession must evolve a standard less demanding than that each article actually contains some net addition to our understanding of how the world works. Yet one can't shake the feeling that chemists and biologists, and hopefully physicists as well, are more focussed on the results, and less fixated on the means used to derive them.

Painters are often known by their brushstrokes, composers by their innovative use of various instruments, and novelists by their vocabulary or manipulation of grammar. While there is much debate on the issue, the style of an artist is still considered an important focus for the art historian. Jackson Pollock, and other modern artists, have indeed gone so far as to raise the process of creating art above the finished work, and invited their audience to participate with them in the creative process. Technique, then, while just the means to an end for the true scientist, is more than that for the artist. It must be a part of the latter's view of self. The novelist is ever-conscious of their flair with words, or peculiar skill in characterisation. The self-image of the econ-artist is likewise tied up with their ability to make mathematical symbols dance.

Two criticisms of the analogy can be raised, which on further inspection arise from the same source. The first is that while economists have undue pride in their mastery of the basics of mathematics, the musician makes no mention of his ability to read music and the novelist of her ability to read and write. The second is that true artists never entirely dissociate their technique from their purpose. An artist's virtuosity with the paint brush is only hailed when they are perceived to evoke some aspect of the human spirit. Nimbleness on the piano keyboard might be recognised in its own right, but the true artist is deified only for their ability to make the music come alive. The economist too is hailed on occasion for their view of reality, but are much more likely to be hailed for technical virtuosity alone (note, for example, the difficulty the Nobel Prize committee had in discerning any real-world application of the life work of Debreu).

Why do econ-artists go overboard relative to other artists in their focus on technique? Is it not simply because they deny their artistic side? Technique has a place in both art and science, and therefore putting it on centre stage does not require any discussion of the higher purpose of economics. Yet mathematics, which sometimes does and other times does not service the interests of economics as a science, is admirably suited to the pursuit of economics as art. While econ-artists have thus successfully blended technique and artistic sensibility, they have only generally been conscious of the former.

Automatic Writing

Mathematics is more than just a tool with which the econ-artist can achieve elegance of creation. Art is intuitive rather than intellectual. This is why econ-artists are never able to visualise more than small parts of that other reality. Only through intellectual activity can the big picture be imagined, and if the merely intuitive is lost the result is no longer art.

Surrealist artists had to struggle with this dilemma as well, but to differing degrees. Most difficult was the work of the novelist or poet, for writing must of necessity require some conscious thought. The technique devised to overcome this was called automatic writing. Rather than consciously deciding what he wished to put on paper, the author was required to concentrate as little as possible, simply to put down words as they emerged in his mind, and try to let the words take on a life of their own. Through this stream of consciousness approach it was hoped that some of the true inner being would be transferred to the page. The surrealist manifesto of 1925 described the method as "pure psychic automatism by means of which one sets out to express, verbally, in writing or in any other manner, the real functioning of thought without any control by reason or any aesthetic or moral preoccupation" (Fleming 1970, 521). Revolutionary at the time, such an approach to writing is now a staple of writing courses and how-to-write books worldwide.

Economists are not unaware of the appeal to intuition involved in mathematical formulation. An economist working out a theory in words must consciously conceive of each step. A mathematician can write down a set of equations and be surprised by the result the solution of the system throws out. The economist may attribute such moments to the fortuitous intervention of the gods. In the very form in which the original equations are set down on paper, the subconscious mind is able to work its magic. The conscious mind may receive a shock at the end, but this is only because it is not in better touch with the true inner self. Thus elements of unreality, which the conscious mind could never imagine, are craftily imbedded in innocent-looking symbols, and fused into a system which captures some aspect of the other world. Most of what passes for modern economic theory could never have been crafted consciously. It thus owes not just its widespread acceptance but its very existence to mathematisation.

Maths as Science?

We should digress again to deal with the contention that mathematics serves primarily scientific goals within economics. In 1972, Phelps-Brown could assert that economic theory was still not ripe for mathematisation (Spiegel 1991, 666). Surely, nobody can doubt that there are still wide areas in which our understanding of economic processes is so limited that the employment of the precision of mathematics as an explanatory device is laughable. If economics were just a science, maths would be employed selectively.[14] It is only in economics as an art form that one technique could come to so dominate the discipline to the virtual exclusion of other forms of discourse.[15] Keynes used mathematics sometimes, but was well aware of the danger of losing track of the complexity of the real world in the use of symbols (Spiegel 1991, 667). The fact that he therefore moved from one form of exposition to another to explain different elements of his theory was a source of confusion to his readers even in the 1930s. Since that time, of course, the mass of economists has only come in contact with those elements of his work which were or could be highly formalised.

Scientists are critical not of the use of maths, but of the use only of maths, of the view, "that the only scientific method worth the name is quantitative measurement; and consequently that complex phenomena must be reduced to simple elements accessible to such treatment, without undue worry whether the specific characteristics of a complex phenomenon, for instance man, may be lost in the process" (Spiegel 1991, 646). "Mathematics is a language that can impose its own limits and structuring on our perception of reality" (Samuels 1990, 6). The far-reaching speculations of the classical economists could not be translated into the new language. "Obviously, the purification of the utility concept, the opportunity-cost doctrine, and the marginal-productivity theory of productive shares are more appropriate to the neutral language of functional equations than were the doctrines of John Stuart Mill" (Roll 1956, 463). The use of maths can of course be defended on scientific grounds. Its complete domination of the discipline cannot. "The process of translation [into mathematics] required the abandonment of that tension-fraught world of the earlier economists, but it yielded in return a world of such neat precision and lovely exactness that the loss seemed amply compensated" (Heilbroner 1968, 25).[16] It is due to its artistic virtues that mathematics was able to achieve total dominion.

Cubism

While surrealists focussed on the unconscious, cubists were concerned with form and colour (Haslam 1978, 6). [As with surrealism, cubism had influences not just on painting but sculpture, architecture, literature, and music - (Fleming 1970, 513)]. It would be a mistake, though, to dismiss cubism as less important simply because it seems to emphasise style over substance. While the structure of a work of art is not always obvious, it is very important in the making of any work, even if it is not necessarily the deliberate choice of the artist (Read 1968, 69). Cubists explored the meaning of form and colour. Their discoveries were often borrowed by artists in other traditions. Thus, the boundaries between expressionist and abstractionist art often become blurred. While it is less easy to describe the cultural influences behind cubism, its popularity indicates that it strikes some chord in the soul of modern man.

One way in which it did so has been suggested by Berman (1982, 30). He describes twentieth century modernism in art as the "quest for pure self-referential art"; it was felt that, "the proper relation of modern art to modern social life is no relation at all". The painter, for example, should focus merely on the flatness of the canvas before her. Berman may be extreme in crediting this desire to all of modern art, but we shall see that cubism followed a natural progression away from depictions of the world around us toward simple arrangements of lines and colours on canvas. It reflected, then, a desire to escape from reality in art. We have already had much occasion to note how successfully econ-art has responded to that yearning.

Progression in Abstractionist Art

Fleming (1970) provides a synopsis of the development of abstractionist art. For the early cubist, "Natural appearances play little part in his design that reduces a landscape or a group of objects to a system of geometrical shapes, patterns, lines, angles, and swirls of colour which achieve his desired abstract imagery". Reality, though, is still the starting point, no matter how seriously distorted it may become. Over the next decades there was a natural progression toward pure abstraction, "in which a work of art has no representational, literary, or associational meaning outside itself, and the picture becomes its own referent" (506). By the 1960s at the latest, abstractionist art no longer took reality as its starting point:

"Abstractionism was carried to its logical geometrical conclusion by Piet Mondrian just as expressionism had reached its point of pure abstraction in the work of Kandinsky .... Both artists are nonobjective in that they are nonfigurative and nonrepresentational, and that the pictorial content of their canvases bears no reference to recognisable objects or to anything outside the actual pictures.... The picture with its lines, shapes, and colours is its own referent" (Fleming 1970, 530-1).

This was not the only progression. The early cubists took their inspiration from Cezanne. It was he who had first suggested that art not represent nature in the usual sense but rather impose upon nature geometric forms derived from the human mind (Fleming 1970, 513). But Cezanne never mentioned cubes, and his works emphasised curves. Cubist art from the beginning was largely rectilinear. Again, Mondrian would represent the logical outcome; his art contained only straight lines, either vertical or horizontal. It was the guiding principle of his art that, "All references to the 'primitive animal nature of man' should be rigidly excluded in order to reveal 'true human nature' through an art of 'balance, unity, and stability'". This he could only achieve through using rectilinear forms (Fleming 1970, 531).

It is no coincidence, then, that abstractionist art is characterised by both a move toward straight lines, and a move away from reality. The two were the same. Only through rigid linearisation could the abstractionist artist totally tear free (at least consciously) from the world around her and create completely self-referential art.

Progression in Econ-Art

The phrase 'self-referential' leaps from the pen of any historian of abstractionist art. So in econ-art, we value models not for their relationship to reality but for their own internal logic. Despite the emphasis on self-reference, expressionist artists created a body of work which evolved over time. Insights into form by one artist were built on by the next. So in econ-art, models evolve over time. Roy Weintraub's (1988) history of general equilibrium analysis is an excellent case study in this respect. Each work takes the preceding as given. One would search in vain for Cezanne's models in Mondrian. The lack of artistic purpose has perhaps prevented the total eclipse of reality in econ-art, but who could deny the trend?

Then there is the related matter of linearity. The artistic value of straight lines could only have supported the decision by mathematical economists to focus on linear relationships. I am told that earlier in this century, much greater care was taken in indicating the curved nature of demand and supply curves, even in undergraduate lectures. It is now commonplace to draw these 'curves' as straight lines (students, indeed, often ask why we call them curves). A small sin perhaps, though it does encourage the belief that supply and demand determine one unique price, whereas in the real world the forces of supply and demand usually determine only a range of prices over which bargaining can occur.

The Phillips Curve, grounded in decades of British data though it might be, is another example. The long run Phillips Curve is now assumed to be a vertical line. A science could hardly have embraced the natural rate of unemployment so quickly. As a work of econ-art, though, it is perhaps the single greatest creation of the twentieth century. It is simple; with only one or two unrealistic assumptions it serves the cubist goal of replacing the curves which depict reality with the straight lines of true art. But this is not all. It also serves the surrealist goal of depicting a better world in which public interference is self-defeating. And, like any classic work, it spawned whole schools of imitation. Once one stops mistakenly searching for reality in it, one cannot help but be struck by its beauty.

The Cubist View of Time

"The cubist theory of vision took into account the breaking up and discontinuity of the contemporary world view in which objects are perceived more hastily in parts rather than more leisurely as wholes. The world, as a consequence, was seen fragmentarily and simultaneously from many points of view rather than entirely from a single viewpoint" (Fleming 1970, 513). The cubist realisation that side and front (and back) views could be presented at the same time is, indeed, one of the signatures of that art form. The fragmentation of time was not unique to cubism. From the late nineteenth century, art had increasingly focussed on, "the momentary, the fragmentary, the everyday occurrence" in, for example, novels which comprised a series of fragments rather than a logical whole (Fleming 1970, 499). Hauser (1956, 230) attributes the abruptness with which modern art describes life to the time experience of the modern age which is focussed on the present.[17]

Econ-art thus turned its back both on history and on dynamic processes. The historical tradition, which had argued the sensible and correct position that the present could only be understood as a result of the past, was forgotten. Economic historians still argue for path dependence - that economies don't naturally tend toward any one position of rest, but rather decisions made in the distant past may influence the course of events to this day - but this message is only weakly noted by theorists who continue to focus on ahistorical models with unique equilibria. The lengthy discourses of classical economists on the dynamic forces of growth have been forsaken for the minute inspection of short run allocative decisions. This last was Marshall's major contribution to economic discourse.

Heilbroner (1990, 190-1) notes that he changed economists' view of time, and ignored the sudden changes (the motto of his 'Principles' was that 'Nature makes no sudden leaps') and dynamics which are the key to economic life. Perhaps this is unjust to Marshall, but economics has never looked back. Econ-science has thus lost much of its purpose in order that econ-art could prosper.

Ideally, in art, the focus on the momentary fragment of the present was not at all incompatible with the comprehension of change. Bergson a philosopher of art, "ranked intuition as a higher faculty than reason, because through it the perception of the flow of duration was possible, and through it the static quantitative facts were quickened into the dynamic qualitative values of motion and change. Existence is never static but a transition between states and between moments of duration" (Fleming 1970, 500). The moment would be transmitted, but the consciousness of the audience would comprehend motion. It would fill in the gaps in the music of Debussy, and join together the fragments in poems and paintings.

Such at least is the principle, and we might question how well the artist generally succeeds in transmitting true understanding of the broader reality of motion. In econ-art, as well, it is often claimed that dynamic processes can be understood through static portrayals. That is, we start with a supposed equilibrium. We then change one or more elements and calculate the new equilibrium. In so doing we purport to describe a dynamic process of action. But we can only do so by assuming that dynamics don't matter, that the process of change itself has no effect on where the system ends up. There is no place for the path-dependence (or disequilibrium) of the real world here.

But of course art isn't about the real world. It is about a better world. Change in the real world, at least with our present degree of scientific understanding is unpredictable, and therefore both exciting and frightening. Society, Berman notes, has contradictory desires for growth and stability. Modern people, "are moved at once by a will to change - to transform both themselves and their world - and by a terror of disorientation and dissent, of life falling apart" (1982, 35 and 13). We would not want to turn our backs on economic growth but we would wish that economic change did not throw innocent people out of work, impoverish whole cities and regions, upset international trade and financial links, or jeopardise our savings.

Econ-art reflects these contradictory desires by describing growth as obeying simple rules. There is no danger that mistakes made today will deflect us from our pursuit of that better world, for we assume away path-dependence. Disembodied technological change gives us productivity advance without structural change. The fragments we focus on in econ-art are already idealised, and thus the vision of change which they evoke is naturally of a benevolent force for good. If econ-art were to actually devote itself to dynamic portrayal, it could only with great difficulty achieve such an advantageous result.

Technological Incursions

The development of motion pictures provided a new medium in which the emerging conception of time and place could be handled as never before. We speak here not of the simple fact that the eye is fooled into thinking a rapid series of still photographs represents motion. Rather, it is the way in which one scene is presumed to naturally follow from the other, or that inter-splicing of separate scenes could create the impression of simultaneity. No other art form had ever been able to bridge the gaps of space and time so freely (though novelists could aspire to doing so). As such, the advent of this new technology could not help but give further impetus to the fragmentation of time.

The computer plays an analogous role in econ-art, for it allows the complex economic evolution of decades to be reduced to a handful of numerical series representing economic aggregates. Computers not only allow the compilation of the necessary statistics, but seemingly create the possibility of discerning the causal relations contained within. This both depends on and reinforces the view that the process of growth follows a regular and unchanging course. It is now widely recognised that econometric analysis of time series is incapable of solving questions of historical causality. The effort provides its own reward, however. The combined efforts of the mathematical modeller and econometrician gave witness to a belief in a simple world of straightforward, unchanging unidirectional causal links. (Hume, or even Hicks' work on *Causality in Economics,* were quickly ignored). This would have been only barely possible without the development of the computer. It freed the econ-artist from the complexity that is reality and allowed her imagination to soar.[18]

Return to the Classics

Cubism, as well as surrealism, had precursors from the nineteenth century which were recognised by the artists in these later traditions. One of the best characteristics of modern art is in fact the willingness of artists to combine elements from previous (even primitive) art forms (Fleming1970, 544). In this way, the best of the past is retained, while the artist tries to improve upon it, and tries also to reflect modem desires. The twentieth century, and especially the 1920s, also sees a classical revival; numerous artists tried to reproduce works in the classical tradition (Fleming 1970, 531). While not necessarily a negative development, we should note the false legitimacy which an appeal to the classics can give to a work of art. Hadjinicalaou (1978), indeed, views this as one of the major ways in which emerging social classes seek to justify both their artistic tastes and position in society.

Econ-art has often referred to the classics to buttress its legitimacy. Indeed it uses the word 'neoclassical' to refer to the main body of modern theory, even though it has jettisoned the concern with growth that formed the core of classical theory. From the point of view of econ-science, we could scarcely hope for a better example of misplaced reverence. Economists have not kept the best of the former traditions, but have selectively maintained those tenets of the faith which are supportive of modem theory. From the standpoint of econ-art, of course, it is highly desirable to ascribe the legitimacy of the past to works which achieve so many artistic goals.

Ideology in Art

Haslam characterizes the early surrealists as feeling that art was only valid if it denied middle class values and morals (1978,11). Fleming (1970, 526-30) recognizes that many artists used their work to protest against economic exploitation and war (e.g. Picasso's 'Guernica'). Even the casual observer must note that mainstream economics has borrowed not at all from this tradition of protest. This raises the question of why econ-art appears so different from other arts in this regard. In this context, it is worth noting, as Rosemount (1978, 57-8) does, that surrealism as transferred to the American market was largely sanitized of its revolutionary content; it was not Breton but Salvador Dali, who replaced revolutionary fervour with whimsy, who was identified with surrealism across the Atlantic. Since the United States increasingly became the centre of the world of economics as the century progressed, this could go some way towards explaining the less revolutionary orientation of economics, at least after the demise of American institutionalist thought. We have not in this work, though, suggested in the main that economists absorbed cultural influences from the world of traditional arts, though this is certainly possible, but rather that all art forms naturally reacted to the same evolution of underlying cultural influences. It could still be that American culture was much less hostile to the existing economic order, and this could explain both why surrealism was 'sanitized' and econ-art was developed in a very non-revolutionary fashion.

We have seen, though, that artists need not be conscious of the goals which their art serves. The intellectual predispositions of the artist may not be captured in their exposition of their intuitive side. The ideology which the conscious mind espouses may not at all be the ideology which the subconscious mind transmits.

Hadjinicalaou (1978) has forcefully argued that art (and art history) always reflects the ideology of the dominant social class. He rejects the idea that art transmits true understanding; rather it serves to legitimize the existing social order. The purpose of ideology "is not to provide people with a real understanding of the structure of society, but to give them a motive for continuing the practical activities which support that structure" (1978, 10). Since ideology of necessity provides a misleading view of the world, so must the art which represents it (100). The values of the ruling class permeate those of other classes; when we see a struggle between different artistic styles this generally represents differing views within the ruling class rather than the struggle between classes (102). Most importantly, artists who consider themselves radical may still produce works that unwittingly support the status quo (ch. 6). The subtle and intuitive nature of art can easily defy the revolutionary intent of the artist. Thus, Hadjinicalaou argues, David during the early years of the French Revolution painted pictures with a classicist composition and naturalistic figures, which reflected the views of the rising middle class. Later, during the Directory, he painted in the style of a return to antiquity which appealed to the upper middle class and aristocracy (116-20). Rembrandt also at times painted in the style of the aristocracy and at others in the style of the bourgeoisie (125-38).

While it is folly to deny the importance of other influences than class ideology - philosophers of art after all constantly refer to the influence of general social and intellectual conditions - it is also folly to ignore the effect such ideologies are likely to have on the artistic community. As Kung (1981, 12) notes, even art 'revolutionaries' are funded by the establishment. We thus have good reason for suspecting that the revolutionary sentiments of artists were not always translated into their work, and that econ-art as well may to a large degree reflect ideological values.

Ideology in Econ-Art

We must approach gingerly the question of ideology in economics. Economists, if they serve the ruling interest, must do so subconsciously or they would feel that they had to dissociate themselves from it (Ayres 1978, 8). Ideology, in order to operate, must do so subconsciously. If we are bending our thoughts in order to accept the existing social order we can not be aware that we are doing so.

Spiegel (1991, xix) provides a fairly standard definition of ideology: "the claiming of scientific validity for propositions that in truth are derived from one's philosophical preferences, subjective valuations, or material interests." Heilbroner argues, though, that the word need not have pejorative connotations. Since ideology is a framework by which order and legitimacy are imposed on social understanding the analysis of ideology is simply another way (like the work of rhetoricians) of reflecting the fact that economists cannot approach their subject objectively but carry a host of cultural perceptions with them (1990, 102). "Economics ... is thus intrinsically normative in the sense of embodying, whether it will or not, the constitutive beliefs of the parent society." His key point is that ideology is not knowingly misrepresentative. In this way, his analysis is quite similar to our own, excepting that he, like Hadjinicolaou, emphasizes just one sort of cultural influence.

We have had many occasions in this work to recognize that the pursuits of artistic and scientific goals have clashed. That which is pleasing to the subconscious need not always serve the interests of the conscious mind (as legions of psychoanalysts will attest). It is bizarre to suspect that the purposes of econ-science at least, if not econ-art, would not be furthered by economists becoming aware of their biases. It seems entirely possible that their hidden subconscious desires may prevent the profession from achieving key insights, either within the existing paradigm or by overturning it.

Ideological bias is easier to detect in the works of the past, for we can approach these with some historical detachment. The Iron Law of Wages, and the wages fund doctrine, both key concepts in nineteenth century economics, clearly served the interests of those in power by asserting that real wages could not permanently be raised (Spiegel 1991, xviii). Yet it would be sheer folly to doubt that ideology is not still an important determinant of economic ideas. Even ideas which might appear 'radical' may still serve an ideological function. The surrealists, while talking revolution, may have unwittingly provided a release which helped prevent revolution from occurring. Keynes, while on the one hand seeming to propose a degree of governmental involvement antithetical to the interests of the business class, provided an answer to the problems of the 1930s which was much less threatening (if at all) to their interests than the interventions proposed by others.[19] Despite his eccentric and disrespectful behaviour, Keynes was quite clear on where his loyalties lay, saying in 1925: "How can I adopt a creed which, preferring the mud to the fish, exalts the boorish proletariat above the bourgeois and the intelligentsia who, with whatever faults, are the quality in life and surely carry the seeds of all human advancement" (in Spiegel 1991, 599).

The Existence of Econ-Art

The work of numerous art historians has established that cultural influences affect artistic practice. The purpose of the artist is to express society's inner feelings; the successful artist will be one whose vision strikes a chord with a wider audience. It would be naive to expect that these social desires which manifest themselves in the arts would not also influence scientific endeavours which cannot possess objective standards of evaluation.

Art historians have gone beyond the general to point to specific cultural influences which have had particular effects on artistic evolution. We have been able, by comparison, to detect numerous influences on econ-art: the depiction of a better world, the desire for order, the reaction to nationalism, the fear of authority, the elevation of technique, the pursuit of a methodology which would allow the intuitive to dominate the intellectual, the quest for linearity (abstraction), the fragmentation of time, the fear of change, the appeal to the classics, and ideological bias. There may be some readers who accept the role of (some of) these cultural influences in the development of economics, but still object to the label of art. But one implies the other. If economists aren't using scientific standards to judge their work, what are they doing? They are creating works which satisfy some other faculties of appreciation, at least among themselves.

Econ-Art/Econ-Science

We must now turn our attention to the effects which econ-art and econ-science have had on each other through cohabitation. Since our concern has been with econ-art we will first suggest ways in which econ-art might be improved by shedding its scientific pretensions. As we have seen earlier, art and science need not be completely antithetical. Positive fertilization of the arts by science has been noted in the literature. From the late nineteenth century:

"Artists in all fields were aware of the extraordinary success of the scientific method. Realism and impressionism brought a new objective attitude into the arts, together with an emphasis on the technical side of the crafts and a tendency for artists to become specialists pursuing a single aspect of their various media .... A painting for an impressionist was a kind of experiment, an adventure in problem solving .... The literary realists were cultivating a scientific detachment in their writing and developing a technique that would enable them to record the details of their observations of everyday life with accuracy and precision" (Fleming 1970, 498).

While art is intuitive, the intellectual side is not completely ignored. The greater the understanding the artist has of the world she lives in, the greater her ability to transcend that reality. As well, the technical apparatus designed to serve science can be of great value to the artist. Similarly, most of that which the modern economist knows aids naturally the work of the econ-artist. Indeed, we have seen that mathematical techniques serve the goals of art to a greater degree than they serve the goals of science.

The conscious pursuit of scientific goals must act to limit artistic expression however. A parallel can be found in the world of architecture. "Experimental architecture is possible, but the discipline of sound engineering has kept architects from some of the wilder flights of fancy seen in painting, sculpture, literature, and music" (Fleming 1970, 532). The parallel can only be extended so far. Architects must obey physical laws or their buildings will collapse. Econ-artists only think that they have to maintain ties with reality. As we have hinted many times before, the only factor holding back econ-art is the lack of self-awareness.

If poets were told that their purpose was to unravel the laws of physics, we should have been bequeathed huge masses of stilted and argumentative verse. Artistic temperament must win out often enough we must suspect, to ensure that we would inherit some works which are truly sublime. Econ-artists, labouring for some decades under the misapprehension that they were actually scientists, have naturally fallen into a similar trap. While the artistic strain has thankfully dominated, the field is littered with works of no artistic merit.

If we wish to separate econ-art from econ-science (a difficult task as most work combines both elements), we could first sort works by this criterion. To be a scientist, one must focus on the world we live in, and thus turn one's back on the whole focus of art. The result can scarcely be beautiful, at least to, modern eyes. This does not mean, of course, that all work which fails as art should be viewed as science. Failure is necessary, but not sufficient. There is work which fails to meet either standard.

What must econ-art do to achieve its true potential? It must turn its back on reality in at least four major ways. It must cease to worry about the realism of its basic assumptions; indeed, it must come to revel in their un-reality. It must forego attempts to test its theories against the world we live in; any 'testing' which goes on should be based on elegant techniques incapable of determining whether the theory has any relationship to the real world. It should value economic models for their elegance and pursuit of artistic values alone. It should eschew questions which do not lend themselves to elegant expression (or which raise public fears), for artistic understanding does not require that each stone be uncovered. It is amazing how much of this has already been achieved under the false banner of science.

The Quest for Econ-Science

There will be those who will eschew the lofty heights of econ-art in order to tread the narrow path of econ-science. They will see economics as a vocation. The world needs the advice of scientific economists. Science, they will claim, is more valuable than Art. What can one say to such as these? Does not Art represent the highest achievement of our species? When one thinks of the most glorious accomplishments of the human spirit does one think of Newton or Beethoven, of Galileo or Michaelangelo? The case could hardly be clearer. Econ-science must forever live in the shadow of Econ-art.

Some will continue to follow the narrow path of science, to explain the world as it exists, not as it could have been. The contradictory details which the true artist brushes over are their focus. If theory and fact are in disagreement, they try to adjust the theory. Perhaps they quest for power and influence, the seductive embrace of the politician needing advice. The true artist never consciously panders to popular acclaim. Or they may be driven by some sense of social duty to try to make the world a better place through understanding it.

The critics of economic methodology might also be cautioned. Economics was in error, they have cried. The assumptions made and the techniques used were inappropriate for understanding the world we live in. But now we know what should have been obvious long ago: describing the world was not the point. Economists had been pursuing a much loftier goal. They could not, and did not, consciously respond to their critics, but knew in their hearts that they were right. Art provides its own reward to the artist.

While art is a much more valuable pursuit than science, it is nevertheless true that Art can have deleterious side effects if it is confused with science, if the audience mistakenly feels that art is in fact describing reality. The best antidote to this misperception would be for there to be a strong scientific tradition alongside econ-art. Since we will never be rid of econ-science, we must strive to delineate its boundaries clearly, so that art is no longer misconstrued as science.

As hinted above, the cleansing of art is not the sole justification for the pursuit of econ-science. If we can separate econ-art from econ-science, the public will be much better served. Those with aesthetic tastes will peruse the works of the former genre with enhanced appreciation. Those of less heightened sensibilities can provide an audience for the econ-scientist. The present skepticism of the public can, in a narrow sense, be attributed to the fact that economists are generally seen in the public eye doing what they do worst - forecasting the future, or to the predilection of journalists for finding diametrically opposed opinions on every issue. In a broader view, the recognition that economists have lost touch with reality - albeit in pursuit of a higher purpose - makes skepticism of their policy prescriptions much more comprehensible. One would not, after all, engage a creator of modern sculpture to fix one's plumbing. The separation of art and science cannot guarantee public support but must encourage it.

The Existence of Econ-Science

Has science actually progressed behind the scene-stealing activity of econ-art? We have seen that all economists have both scientific and artistic motives, but suggested that the internal reward structure has tended to emphasize the latter. The fact that economists perceived themselves to be performing science is no guarantee that they in fact did so. Certainly, much of the research output of this century has enhanced our understanding of reality not at all. McCloskey (1988, 290), for example, argues that there have been no big advances in trade theory since 1965, success in deciding between alternative explanations of important issues since 1940, and no additional insight gained from the reworking of general equilibrium theory since 1950. He recognizes that some advances have occurred in some areas, though, arguing that economic history and labour economics have been most successful in this regard because they are forced to face facts more so than other areas.

Our purpose here is not to catalogue the failures of econ-science but to note the existence of some signs of hope. The 'birth' of macroeconomics in the cauldron of Depression must be considered a scientific advance. We might regret that the classical focus on economic growth was not regained, but at least the profession was shaken from its undue emphasis on what would come to be called microeconomics. The contemporaneous elucidation of the theory of imperfect competition must also be considered an important advance (even if Friedman considered it irrelevant). On a lesser plane, we could note the important role econ-science has come to play in debates about such key issues as regulation and pollution control. Econ-science is still far from having all the answers even in these areas, but it would be a mistake to think that econ-art has so dominated the discipline that it has entirely ceased to be of any practical use.

Improving Econ-Science

While it has not been our purpose to do so, our analysis points to a number of ways in which econ-science can be improved merely by shedding characteristics imported from econ-art. First, it must face up to reality; it must both recognize and constantly strive to overcome the temptation to distort reality. Of course, this requires that economists become self-aware of the conflicting impulses which act upon them. Second, economists have to realize that the real world is complicated, and thus that economic theory must become less beautiful the closer it comes to approximating reality. Third, they must return their attention to aspects of the economic question which had no appeal to the econ-artist. More effort must be expended on describing the big picture. Narrowly focussed studies must always have their place, but the discipline is destined to advance slowly if at all if continual efforts are not undertaken to tie the pieces together. In particular, the stress upon dynamics and growth which characterized the work of the classical economists must be regained. Fourth, and necessarily related to all of the above, economists must recognize that their present methodological biases are not firmly rooted in scientific principles, and open their minds to a greater variety of methodological approaches. Style and substance are not easily separable, and the insistence on one form of argument needlessly limits the scope of economic inquiry. These conclusions are supported by recent work in both the philosophy of science and in the analysis of the rhetoric of economics.

Reality

Art historians and psychologists are both aware of the fact that we perceive reality only in terms of our preexisting view of the world. People develop frames of reference which allow them to impose some order on the complex events occurring around them. In the world of art, this means that the audience naturally expects new works of art to conform to the principles of previous works (e.g. novels will have plot, theme, continuous characterization). New genres, such as surrealism, will at first seem alien, and thus the reader/viewer will be forced to work harder until the new genre has become the norm (Hedges 1983, 38-9).

In economics as well, once economists have come to accept mainstream theory as the norm, they must have a natural tendency to evaluate any new theory primarily by its violation of the norms of the existing theory, rather than its approximation to reality. Even though many of the tenets of mainstream theory are merely beliefs that have never been tested (Blaug 1985, 701), they have a captivating effect on the minds of economists. While logical abstraction is necessary for the advance of science, there is a danger of this becoming the normative standard (Whitehead 1985). For example, once the idea of self-adjusting equilibrium is accepted, then any real-world deviations from this are either ignored or attributed to institutional malfunction. Reality can only slowly, if at all, overcome such a belief system.

Ricardo's predictions as to the effect of the Corn Laws were entirely mistaken because his theory neglected the possibility of technological advance. Yet his theory survived for decades unchallenged. "Had the classical economists acted on Mill's urging to 'carefully endeavour to verify our theory' such weaknesses in the structure would have come to light and led to analytic improvements" (Blaug 1985, 699). Later in the nineteenth century civil servants started collecting statistics which showed that investment was highly volatile, and thus a likely cause of business cycles, but economists stuck with Say's Law and continued to blame cycles exclusively on monetary policy (Fusfeld 1977, 86-7). It would be hopelessly naive to think that modern economists are any less likely to choose theory over reality when faced with cognitive dissonance.

The answer can only be that we must constantly strive to confront theory with reality. The pursuit of artistic goals severely exacerbates the tendency to focus on self-referential theory. We must recognize that our present methods of 'testing' serve artistic goals, and are at best an imperfect guide to the relevance of theory. We must open ourselves to other sorts of observation. Economic history, while far from immune from artistic temptation, has always been held in check by the fact that it must deal with particular historical events; this has meant both greater methodological diversity and more realistic explanations. Economics in general has much to gain by paying similar attention to real-world events. Biology appears to advance through the working out of observation; Solow suggests that economics could well behave more like biology (1989, 39-40). To continue to devote the vast bulk of our efforts to refinement of theory and technique is to guarantee disaster.[20]

We can impose simple rules, such as that authors of articles indicate the practical relevance of their work. We can instruct our referees to rate relevance more highly than elegance. We can recognize that a partial answer to an important question is better than a precise answer to a trivial question. In the end, though we can only succeed by changing attitudes. If the bulk of the profession remains wed to existing theory then it is highly unlikely that truly new insights will emerge, no matter how much better these accord with reality. A new theory is like an infant; it will not survive unless nurtured. This fact is widely recognized among philosophers of science. "An argument becomes effective only if supported by an appropriate attitude and has no effect when the attitude is missing" (Feyerabend 1978, 8). Economists need to be more open-minded, more willing to accept the seemingly obvious fact they don't have all the answers. If those with the greatest artistic drive devote themselves to econ-art, econ-science will be left to those who exalt the merely practical.

Truth, Beauty and The Big Picture

Science isn't pretty. Elements of a theory may be elegant, but real scientific understanding of complex phenomena cannot be so. The problem with economic theory is not so much that it's wrong but that it's unimportant. Our quest for elegance has stood in the way of our quest for understanding. "As long as we're not willing to deal with the real messiness of our subject, we're going to live in a 'crisis' - not just in macroeconomics but in microeconomics. Economists are trying to say too much about things where they haven't the knowledge to improve on refined common sense" (Clower 1989, 29). The complexity of the subject matter of economics may frustrate the fainthearted, but must appeal to the noblest yearnings of the human spirit.

The classical economists tried to comprehend how the economy as a whole functioned. This naturally caused them to simplify much, but their theoretical inquiry was always guided by their quest for the big picture. Economists in this century have turned increasingly toward narrowly focussed research. We would not want all economists to turn back to the big picture, but it is essential that some do so, if we are to avoid the pursuit of mere trivialities.

It is not uncommon for economists to bemoan the narrow focus of most practitioners. Indeed, the American Economics Association founded the *Journal of Economic Perspectives* so that economists could be aware of what their colleagues were doing. Yet big thinkers such as Galbraith are marginalized. The economist may accept much of what he says, but wonders what to do with a man who discusses issues ignored by the mainstream, and which moreover do not lend themselves to the usual methodology. The answer, of course, is that you first recognize the question, and then realize that both the big picture and the exploration of new questions do not readily lend themselves to the precision of mathematical exposition. Once we choose reality over elegance, we naturally become more encouraging of those who think big thoughts.

It would be sheer folly to attempt an exhaustive list of the areas of inquiry which have been ignored by economists. Still, there are some areas in which there is a glaring deficiency in research. Economists have over the last century turned away alarmingly from the analysis of economic growth. Closely connected to this is the minimal attention paid to technological change. The result is that in a world where the man on the street could tell you that the reasons for differences across time and space in rates of economic growth must be (one of?) the most important economic questions, and that understanding technology is essential to understanding the modern economy, the modern economist has little to say about either. The methodology-constrained attempts to date to deal with either growth or technology have yielded limited insight. Even those who recognize the need for a new technology-centered theory of economic growth feel constrained to develop that theory mathematically (see Dosi 1988).[21] Economists naturally shied away from areas which they sensed would not lend themselves to mathematical exposition in the past, but the precision of mathematics is ill suited to the early exploration of any area of study. The question of scope of inquiry is thus inextricably linked to the question of methodological flexibility.

Methodological Diversity

We have seen that the methodological bias of economists serves artistic goals. It is thus only natural to suspect that this bias stands in the way of scientific inquiry. One does not have to look far to find economists who have realized that econometric testing leaves much to be desired[22]. "Econometric work often is done to demonstrate mastery of new techniques, rather than to answer questions" (Colander 1989, 33). Eichengreen, following Cagan, has concluded that time series econometrics is incapable of solving questions of historical causality. McCloskey has suggested that econometrics has not settled any major debate in economics. Leontief argued that, "in no other field of empirical inquiry has so massive and sophisticated a statistical machinery been used with such indifferent results" (in Beed 1991, 485). Solow has noted that the profession has refined econometric techniques beyond the capacity of the data; "The only possible solution that I see is to enlarge the class of eligible facts, or class of observations, that one is willing to take account of. I think you have to include anecdotal facts, impressions, and direct observation" (1989, 40).

The recognition that data does not exist with which their models can be tested often drives economists in exactly the wrong direction. A common practice is simulation, where 'plausible' values are inserted in a model in place of un-estimable parameters. Models can be 'tested' by seeing whether numbers can be chosen that will generate a result which resembles reality. The profession has no standards whatsoever for judging simulation results (McCloskey 1983, 502). Yet they are regularly used to evaluate policy proposals. In the recent Canada-United States Free Trade debate, for example, the Canadian public was justifiably bewildered by a series of general equilibrium simulations which predicted widely different impacts on incomes and employment (even though all took standard trade theory as their starting point). Notwithstanding this, some economic historians have felt that we can accurately simulate the working of eighteenth and nineteenth century economies about which we know even less. Science, it must seem, is less well served than Art by such pretense.

The development of econometrics, after all, witnessed the same confusion between the purposes of econ-art and econ-science as the rest of the profession. Some of its theory proposes solutions to real problems of statistical testing. The rest simply builds an impressive edifice of pseudo-testing. Beyond its own aesthetic values, econometric testing provides a pseudo-scientific rationale for the mathematical machinations of others.

Economists must only ask themselves how much of their belief set has ever been empirically established. Experiments after all, regularly claim to disprove the basic tenets of microeconomic theory. The shreds of wisdom which the econ-scientist possesses are generally due not to the high-powered techniques of the artist but to informed observation of the real world. To bring collective common sense to the forefront of the evaluation of economic theory is to ensure that reality cannot long be forgotten.

Methodological diversity should provide even greater gains in the long run than in the short run. We have argued that artistic and scientific capabilities are unequally distributed across the population. Solow recognized that most modern economists are ill-suited to the non-quantitative forms of observation which he recommended. Keynes spoke of the breadth of vision and knowledge required of the good economist.[23] To require that all economists be mathematically facile is to close the profession to those whose strengths lie in other areas.

Philosophy of Science

Economists are generally out of touch with recent developments in the philosophy of science, and economists have embraced the positivist point of view to a greater extent than any other discipline (Beed 1991, 475). Thus, while scientists elsewhere have moved past a naive view that scientific theories can either be proved correct or at least falsified, economists cling to the fanciful notion that research can establish undeniable truths.

Since we can not confront reality directly but only through the lens of theory, the best we can hope to do is observe a variety of facts in a variety of circumstances to see if the theory holds (see Chalmers 1976, ch.2). We can not even conclusively falsify theories; since observations depend on theory any clash between theory and observation may mean the observations are wrong (57-8). Even if difficulties with subsidiary hypotheses could be overcome, most theories have a probabilistic element which prohibits falsification (McCloskey 1983, 487). It is a mistake, then, to criticize economic theory for having moved away from the possibility of falsification (see Blaug 1985, 697), for this was a false god in any case. One can only conjecture that confusion as to the true aims of modern economic practice contribute to this unwillingness to recognize the truth.

It may seem dangerous to abandon long-held scientific beliefs and to sail out upon a murky sea where common sense is recognized as the final arbiter of truth. In fact, though, we interpret statistical results in the light of prior beliefs which we form on the basis of a variety of evidence (McCloskey 1983, 494-5). The best we can do is be honest with ourselves and accept that we as a profession have the joint responsibility of evaluating diverse pieces of information in order to arrive at our best guess as to how the world actually works. Once we recognize that we must rely on collective decision making, it is essential that we be self-aware of our biases (see Chalmers 1976, ch.12).

Rhetoric

McCloskey, Klamer, and others have recently begun to investigate the rhetorical devices used by economists. They have recognized that economic discourse is a continuous argument, and have suggested that economists would be well served by an understanding of the devices they and others use to persuade. Within this framework, the present methodological bias in the profession is seen as a collectively sanctioned set of criteria which have no inherently superior scientific validity relative to other modes of argument. Mathematics is a tool used by economists to lend scientific credibility to their ideas. McCloskey describes the present standards of consistency and prediction as "six inch hurdles over which the economist leaps with a show of athletic effort" (1988, 289). He and Klamer conclude that other rhetorical devices would serve the interests of Science just as well (1988, 17).

The rhetorical approach provides more than just a further rationale for methodological diversity. It highlights the fact that style and substance are inseparable: "What is the distinction of style and substance in ice skating or still life painting or economic analysis?" (McCloskey 1988, 286). Aesthetic appeal becomes a natural goal of the economist in her attempt to attract others to her point of view. "Rhetoric, again, gives a way to understand the persuasive power of diagrams in economics, their metaphors and symmetries, which I came like so many others to admire passionately in my second year. For the same aesthetic reasons I came in my third or forth year to admire the mathematics" (McCloskey 1988, 284). If the profession values artistic merit, then economists will naturally strive to achieve artistic value in their work.

McCloskey, though, does not recognize that the pursuit of artistic values may be antithetical to the pursuit of science. He completes the statement above with, "Its truth is its beauty, or it had better be." There is, of course, no necessity that this be the case, and we have seen at length that good art is not good science. The fact is that the profession accepts as valuable many characteristics of economic research which serve no scientific purpose.

Rhetoricians make a valuable plea for honesty. We must first of all be honest with ourselves and recognize the non-scientific motives we pursue. Then, we must be honest with others and try to present our ideas in as straightforward a manner as possible (whether ideas are expressed as words or symbols or diagrams). Rhetoricians have made a valuable first step toward both goals. We have taken matters a step further by suggesting ways in which economic practice is opposed to the pursuit of Truth.

Concluding Remarks

Only by separating art from science can we hope to achieve an honest and progressive econ-science. We must recognize that that which we admire most about works of economics is not science at all. Econ-science must take as its sole standard the ability to 'explain' the world around us. Econ-science lives forever in the shadow of econ-art. Econ-scientists must consciously eschew the goal of art in their work, and mercilessly excise it from scientific discourse in the works of others. Econ-art, after all, has a much greater role to play in this world than mere interference with the pursuit of science.

While the aficionado of econ-science may wish to throw up his hands in despair, one can discern hopeful signs in many fields - trade theory, industrial organization, and macro are the clearest cases - that a much greater understanding of dynamic processes is required. Further, the study of technological evolution has shown that research along any one trajectory naturally encounters diminishing returns.

In this article, we have striven to plant the insidious thought that much of modern economic practice is driven by societal tastes rather than an objective pursuit of Truth. We have thus questioned much of modern theory as well as the methodological bias of modern economics and made suggestions on how the profession cam positively respond.

*   Department of Economics, University of Alberta, Edmonton, Alberta, Canada, T6G 2H4. Dr. Szostak's first book was *The Role of Transportation in the Industrial Revolution* (McGill-Queen's University Press, 1991). He has recently completed a 360 page manuscript titled *Technological Innovation and the Great Depression*. The present article is adapted from a hundred page manuscript entitled "Econ-Art: A Connoisseur's Guide" (April 1992). The author would like to thank Steve Gregory, Craig Freedman, Peter Kriesler, John Perkins, Alex Blair, Frank Barry and Roberta Ryan for advice and encouragement.

Notes

1. Mirowski (1989). For a powerful critique of this view see Walker (1991).

2. Some who deny economics' role as a science, or even the existence of science itself, have used the word art, though generally pejoratively. Klamer and Amariglio have spoken of art as the paradigm of modernism, and argued that economics is modernist, but the modernism they speak of is a philosophy which predates modern art and economics by centuries (Wendt 1990). None have started with the question of what art is, and whether economics truly is art. Economists ignore the insights of their fellow social scientists, and thus, "The suggestion that the study of literature or communication or even the nonliterary arts might speak to them would be regarded by many economists as absurd' (Klamer, 1988, 4).

3. Recent works on economic methodology recognise that the best ideas need not win out (Colander 1989, 2). The lack of "timeless criteria by which to judge" economic ideas was credited by Mirowski (1989) with encouraging economists to "usurp the legitimacy of science" by imitating physics.

4. Klingender feels the bond between art and science built up in the eighteenth century was destroyed in the nineteenth when political economy abandoned humanism to protect property. Still, artists glorified the railway, Samuel Smiles glorified the engineer, and artists employed the scientific method to evaluate the new materials made possible by technological advance (1947 38 and 100).

5. Many feel that "... in economics normal science has run amok. The invisible hand of truth has lost its guiding influence" precisely because the internal reward structure does not necessarily reward truth (Colander 1989. 31-2). Colander notes that most social sciences have splintered due to an inability to define what is scientific advancement, but not economics.

6. Mirowski (1989) has argued that economics has been misled by the subconscious desire of its practitioners to mimic physics. It is entirely possible that misguided scientific values could co-exist with unrecognised artistic values.

7. Roll (1956, 14) notes that it is difficult to establish causal links between changes in the economy and changes in economic theory. This is a fact widely recognised by both economic historians and historians of economic thought. It would seem to reflect the loose connection between theory and reality.

8. "Somewhat like the romantic revolt of a century earlier, the expressionist artist reasserts the primacy of the imagination over the intellect and takes flight from reality in order to find a superior reality in the world of mystery and fantasy. The tendency is anti-intellectual in the extreme, though the symbols and vocabulary are evolved by highly rationalist procedures". It should be possible to extend our analysis back into the nineteenth century.

9. Even Solow, defending the achievements of econ-science estimates that we only understand about one-quarter of how the macroeconomy functions (1988).

10. We should note that surrealists, as well, refused to cater to public tastes or sensitivities. They, too, pursued the purity of their art form.

11. "The rise of mathematical economics meant defeat for historical economics and removed the threat that historicism had posed to the unity of science" (Spiegel 1991, 646).

12. Alfred Marshall, the father of neoclassical economics, was trained as a mathematician, and therefore likely less proud of his technical capabilities than those who were to follow. He asserted that, "The right place for mathematics in a treatise on economics is in the background", and he left the equations in the appendices in his *Principles*. The high moral purpose he brought to political economy caused him to relinquish with regret purely speculative exercises which smacked of 'l'art pour l'art' (Spiegel 1991, 553 and 563).

13. Robert Clower, former editor of the *American Economic Review*, has noted that most models are presented without any indication of what real world phenomena they might actually explain. Most economics, he concludes, serves simply to make common sense difficult. Economists are more concerned with techniques and game-playing than ideas. Thus most of the papers he received while editor should not (from a scientific standpoint) have been written, much less published (1989, 24-7).

14. The critics of mathematical economics all recognise that it has its place. Only its proponents often fail to see the advantage of using diverse methodologies. More cynical motives can be discerned. Mirowski (1989) speaks of an influx of mathematicians and engineers into the discipline in the 1930s. It was easy for them to produce papers which translated mathematical physics into economics. It is also easier for academic referees to judge techniques than ideas.

15. Rosenberg (1983) went so far as to claim that economics was no longer a science (due to its inability to make predictions) but merely a branch of mathematics devoted to examining the formal properties of a set of assumptions just like geometry.

16. "It was not all foolishness, though certainly much of it was" (Roll 1956, 160). Colander suggests that "Economics is tied together not by a common set of questions but by a common set of techniques" (Colander 1989, 32). He notes that a survey of graduate students found that while 90% felt knowledge of maths and modelling was important, 68% felt knowledge of the economy was not. Heilbroner (1990) has argued that if maths provides economics with rigor, it also provides it with mortis.

17. Other explanations are possible. While Fleming (1970, 542) recognises that "it is both impossible and undesirable to make any precise analogy between cubist principles and the mathematics of space-time", he suspects a causal link from the theory of relativity to artistic perception.

18. Kaldor argued that neither mathematical economics or econometrics were leading anywhere. He felt that economics was at a pre-scientific stage; since we do not understand the economy, we keep trying the same things over because we can not reject anything (in Spiegal 1991, 665).

19. The Interwar years had strangely little effect on economic theory, despite bringing its relevance into question; they induced a split between theorists and policy-oriented economists (Roll 1956, 455). Heilbroner feels the attraction of Keynes was his non-radical response to the Depression (1968, 254).

20. Economists since at least the time of Marshall have suggested that biology provides a better model for economics than physics, but the profession has found physical theory more attractive. Samuelson "appreciates the fact that economic relationships are seldom as simple as the diagrams or equations would lead us to believe". Noting that much of his theoretical work was highly abstracted from the world of policy, he remarked that he would have to pay in heaven for the sin of stimulating so much work in mathematical economics (Breit 1982, 133 and 111).

21. In the late nineteenth century, Jevons "recognised that the only practical problem which a mathematically rigorous theory was capable of handling was the static problem of allocating given resources to produce an optimum return" (Deane 1989, 130). Modern theorists feel that advances in mathematics have facilitated the modelling of growth.

22. Blaug makes the important point that much of our knowledge is of a qualitative nature: models usually only predict the direction of change; "We must begin by disenchanting ourselves of the idea that economic predictions must be quantitative in character to qualify as scientific predictions" (1985, 701).

23. McCloskey and others have circulated the following letter which has been signed by numerous prominent economists, including at least four Nobel Laureates:
    "We the undersigned are concerned with the threat to economic science posed by intellectual monopoly. Economists today enforce a monopoly of method or core assumptions often defended on no better ground than it constitutes the 'mainstream'. Economists will advocate free competition, but will not practice it in the marketplace of ideas".
    "Consequently, we call for a new spirit of pluralism in economics involving critical conversation and tolerant communication between different approaches. Such pluralism should not undermine the standards of rigor; an economics that requires itself to face all the arguments will be a more, not a less rigorous science".
    "We believe that the new pluralism should be reflected in the character of scientific debate, in the range of contributions in its journals, and in the training and hiring of economists".

Bibliography

Arrington, C.E. "Comment" in Warren J. Samuels, ed., *Economics as Discourse*. Boston: Kluwer, 1990.

Ayres, Clarence. *The Theory of Economic Progress*. Kalamazoo: New Issues Press, (1944) 1978.

Balakian, Anne. *Literary Origins of Surrealism*. London: University of London Press, 1947.

Beed, Clive. "Philosophy of Science and Contemporary Economics: An Overview." *Journal of Post-Keynesian Economics*. 14(3): Summer, 1991.

Berman, Marshall. *All That is Solid Melts Into Air*. New York: Simon and Schuster, 1982.

Blaug, M. *Economic Theory in Retrospect*. 4th ed. Cambridge University Press, 1985.

Breit, William, and Roger Ransom. *The Academic Scribblers*. Chicago: Dryden, 1982.

Chalmers, A.F. *What Is This Thing Called Science?* St. Lucia: University of Queensland Press, 1976.

Clower, Robert. "The State of Economics: Hopeless But Not Serious?" in David Colander and A.W. Coats eds. *The Spread of Economic Ideas*. New York: Cambridge University Press, 1989.

Colander, David. "The Invisible Hand of Truth" in David Colander and A.W. Coats (eds). *The Spread of Economic Ideas*. New York: Cambridge University Press, 1989.

Dasgupta, Partha, and Paul Stoneman. "Introduction" in Dasgupta and Stoneman eds., *Economic Policy and Technological Performance*, New York: Cambridge University Press, 1987.

Deane, Phyllis. *The State and the Economic System*. New York: Oxford University Press, 1989.

Dosi, Giovanni et al eds. *Technical Change and Economic Theory*. London: Pinter Publishers, 1988.

Feyerabond, Paul. *Science in a Free Society*. London: Verso, 1978.

Fleming, William. *Arts and Ideas*. 3rd ed. New York: Holt, Rinehart, and Winston. 1970.

Fusfeld, Daniel R. *The Age of the Economist*. Glenview, IL: Scott, Foresman, and Co., 1977.

Hadjinicolaou, N. *Art History and Class Struggle*. London: Pluto Press, 1978.

Haslam, Michael. *The Real World of the Surrealists*. London: Weidenfeld and Nicholson, 1978.

Hauser, Arnold. *Social History of Art*. London: Routledge and Kegan Paul, 1956.

Hedges, Inez. *Languages of Revolt*. Durham, N.C.: Duke University Press, 1983.

Heilbroner, Robert. *The Worldly Philosophers*. 3rd ed. New York: Simon and Schuster, 1968.

Heilbroner, Robert. "Economics as Ideology" in Warren J. Samuels, ed., *Economics as Discourse*. Boston: Kluwer, 1990.

Hubert, Renee. *Surrealism and the Book*. Berkeley: University of California Press, 1988.

Kendry, Adrian. "Paul Samuelson and the Scientific Awakening of Economics" in J.R. Shackleton and G. Locksley eds. *Twelve Contemporary Economists*. London: MacMillan, 1981.

Klamer, A. and McCloskey, D.N. "Economics in the Human Conversation" in A. Klamer, D. McCloskey and R. Solow (eds.) *The Consequences of Economic Rhetoric*. Cambridge: Cambridge University Press, 1988.

Klingender, F. *Art and the Industrial Revolution*. Frogmore, St. Albans, Herts.: Paladin, (1947) 1972.

Koestler, A. and J.R. Smythies eds. *Beyond Reductionism*. New York: MacMilian, 1969.

Kung, Hans. *Art and the Question of Meaning*. London: SCM Press, 1981.

McCloskey, Donald N. "The Rhetoric of Economics" *Journal of Economic Literature,* 1983.

McCloskey, Donald N. "The Consequences of Rhetoric' in A. Klamer, D. McCloskey, and A. Solow eds. *The Consequences of Economic Rhetoric*. 21(1), 1988.

Meakin, David. *Men and Work*. New York: Holmes and Meier, 1976.

Mirowski, Philip. *More Heat than Light. Economics as Social Physics*. Cambridge: Cambridge University Press 1989

Peckham, M. *Man's Rage For Chaos: Biology, Behaviour, and the Arts*. New York: Schocken, 1967.

Read, Herbert. *The Meaning Of Art*. 4th ed. London: Faber and Faber, 1968.

Roll, Eric. *A History of Economic Thought*. London: Faber and Faber, 1956.

Rosemount, F. *What is Surrealism?* New York: Monad Press, 1978.

Rosenberg, A. "If Economics Isn't Science What Is It?' *The Philosophical Forum* 14, 1983.

Samuels, Warren J. "Introduction" in Warren J. Samuels, ed. *Economics as Discourse*. Boston: Kluwer, 1990.

Solow, Robert M. "Comments From Inside Economics" in A. Klamer, D. McCloskey, and R. Solow (eds.), *The Consequences of Economic Rhetoric*. Cambridge: Cambridge University Press, 1988.

Solow, Robert M. "Faith, Hope, and Clarity" in David Colander and A.W. Coats (eds.), *The Spread of Economic Ideas*. New York: Cambridge University Press, 1989.

Spiegel, Henry. *The Growth of Economic Thought*. 3rd ed. Durham, N.C.: Duke University Press, 1991.

Vernon, R. ed. *The Technological Factor In International Trade*. New York: Columbia University Press, 1970.

Walker, Don. "Economics as Social Physics" *The Economic Journal* 101 (406) May 1991.

Weintraub, R. *General Equilibrium Analysis: Studies in Appraisal*. New York: Cambridge University Press, 1988.

Weintraub, R. "Comment" in Warren J. Samuels, ed. *Economics as Discourse*. Boston: Kluwer, 1990.

Wendt, P. "Comment" in Warren J. Samuels, ed. *Economics as Discourse*. Boston: Kluwer, 1990.

Whitehead, A.N. *Science and the Modern World*. London: Free Association Books, 1985.

The Glass Shattered

This was the first time that her soul was charmed by the power of poetry, which shows us the lot of man so truthfully and so sympathetically and with so much love for that which is good that we ourselves become better persons and understand life more fully than before, and hope and trust that good may always prevail in the life of man (Halldòr Laxness).

CONFESSIONS OF AN EX-BEAUTY QUEEN: SOME SIMPLE LESSONS FOR THE PROFESSION

Rick Szostak
University of Alberta

Those who have seen the light must always experience some frustration in preaching to the unconverted. No matter how finely honed their arguments, they will find it nearly impossible to shake people from deeply held beliefs. This is especially so if those beliefs are an important component of the audience's sense of personal identity, or if the audience has good reason to believe that their status in the community will suffer if belief systems change. Thus those of us who recognize that the present methodological bias in economics has severely limited the advance of economic knowledge can never expect easy conversions, especially from those who have had the most success under the existing *misguidelines.*

The task is made even more difficult by the widespread belief in the discipline that it is somehow superior to all other social sciences. As Leijonhufvud (1973) suggests, contempt for other disciplines may be the major factor which maintains some sense of unity within our rancorous community. Given the sluggish state of advance in economic knowledge, our only claim to superiority can be in terms of methodology. To question that methodology, then, is tantamount to renouncing the crown. Just because we alone recognize our role as queen of the social sciences does not mean we will casually discard the title: the world is after all replete with pretenders to long defunct thrones. The mere fact that in doing so we would greatly enhance our actual success as scientists will scarcely seem to be reason enough to those who, consciously or not, value appearance above substance.

Rhetoricians well know that the mere statement of truth will not generally win the day. We must all hope (with good reason) that being right does give one an advantage in open debate; nevertheless there are a host of argumentative strategies one can pursue to win over one's adversary. The various authors in this book all point to problems in the existing practice of economics (most of them intentionally), but do so in quite different ways. Some attack the subject head on, and employ logic as their main device of persuasion. Others prefer a satirical tone. The silliness of modern economic practice is thus exposed by taking these practices to extremes. It is worth noting that the reader, familiar with the economics literature of our day, will often in these cases have some nagging doubt as to whether the author really does have tongue in cheek; alternatively, they could be forgiven for thinking that Fair (1978) must be kidding. Humor in various forms is utilized; one advantage of this is that the most determined cynics may yet be induced to read the piece, and may not be able to completely defend themselves against the implantation in their subconscious of heresy. Irony, as McCloskey has argued elsewhere, can often be the strongest of rhetorical devices. Perhaps economists can be embarrassed into changing their ways. Finally, McCloskey (1989) recounts how he himself came to see the light; this autobiographical sketch may strike some chord of recognition.

We have, then, a diversity of arguments. Moreover, our selections are well written, a quality often lacking among the works of economists. As noted above, many of these works strive to educate and entertain at the same time. This, we are constantly told, is especially important if one wants to reach the latest TV generation of young economists.

Who is our audience? In the first instance, we would expect those who share our methodological concerns to take pleasure in this work, and to find within it encouragement - both moral and intellectual - to continue their efforts. We would wish, though, to do more than preach to the converted. The battle for the minds and hearts of the economics profession will not be won overnight, but slowly economist by economist. Yet each victory paves the way for the next. While the juggernaut of excessive formalism may seem unstoppable, there are also signs afoot of an increasing recognition by at least some practitioners that all is not well in the state of Econ. Even without our efforts, we have reason to hope for change in the discipline. Insulated though it is from the thinking in other disciplines, economics is nevertheless guided by changes in the wider society, as Szostak (1992) illustrates. The post-modern world, one in which philosophers have unanimously turned away from the type of naive positivism to which many economists still cling, must inevitably have some effect on the dismal science. More immediately, the discipline faces increasing criticism from the public at large for failing to address key public policy issues; such criticism threatens both our status and our incomes. Even within the discipline, one must expect that the pleasure to be derived from arcane mathematical models divorced from reality must face seriously diminishing returns. Our job, then, is merely to accelerate a transition that should be inevitable. The future (we hope) is ours.

As Leijonhufvud (1973) notes, our profession has long since ceased to pay the respect to its elders which was once their due. As one batch of techniques is replaced by another, the young find little to learn from the old. This regrettable state is not without its opportunities. If the young come to recognize the error of their elders' ways, the profession can change more quickly than we might suspect.

Surveys of graduate students (e.g. Hansen, 1991) leave no doubt that the prevailing training fails to impress its own target audience. They could prove to be fertile ground for the message herein. They will, of course, be greatly concerned with furthering their careers, and this will encourage them to adhere to the status quo. Yet each journal editor, book editor, and referee who recognizes the value of methodological flexibility weakens the pull of this standard. Moreover, as Frank, Gilovich, and Regan (1993) note, economists are not quite as selfish as their theory suggests they should be (though they *are* much more selfish than regular people). Most of our graduate students and assistant professors would like to make a contribution to our understanding of the world, rather than engage in mental gymnastics. At present, many subconsciously subvert this selfless goal to the necessities of career advancement (McCloskey's (1989) own self-portrait shows how easy it is for the young scholar to ignore methodological concerns; the existing orthodoxy is seductively simplistic.) If we can force them to recognize the true nature of the alternatives they face, we might succeed in convincing a growing number to take the path less followed.

Not all will, of course. Excessive formalism *can* fool some of the people all of the time. Yet this is not such a great problem. Our goal, after all, is not to expel the existing methodology from the discipline. It is, rather, to argue for methodological flexibility. Our enemy is not formalism itself, but the narrow-mindedness of many mainstream economists which excludes other valuable approaches from consideration.

The reward structure will only change as the profession wills it to do so; yet one must survive within the existing reward structure in order to have any say about what this should be. While there are increasing opportunities to publish non-mainstream work, these are not always fully appreciated by hiring or tenure committees (it is a sad irony that we preach comparative advantage, but yet all economics departments strive to be the same). David Colander (1996: 49) urges the young to get tenure before exercising their heretical instincts. While this advice is important, we should also encourage the young to seek value not just in the extrinsic rewards of the profession. They should look instead for the internal reward of believing what they do to be worthwhile. Samuelson has suggested that economists work for 'the only coin worth having' the applause of their peers (in Breit and Ransom 1982:107). To be sure, economists who are completely ignored will be wasting their time. Yet we would be a much better profession if economists would take more pleasure from the intrinsic value of their work (that is, its ability to make the world a better place) than solely from the applause of their fellow travellers.

Perhaps matching the mainstream in its narrow-minded approach would make our own prescribed road easier and more attractive. A belief that only mathematical modelling and sophisticated statistical testing is scientific[1] is simple and can be casually swallowed by those focussed mainly on getting ahead. The opposite contention, that such practices have no place in the discipline, might have a similar, though smaller, appeal. But we do not wish to supplant one narrow dogma with another. Methodological flexibility is a harder sell, for it cannot be reduced to one simple rule. [It can be reduced to a non-rule, that there simply is no one right method of scientific inquiry, but that is not the same thing at all.]

The papers in this volume point the inquiring mind toward the major failings of our present practice. McCloskey (1991) makes a frontal attack on the emphasis on formalization. While economists like to tell themselves they are merely acting like genuine scientists - i.e. physicists, McCloskey (1991) shows that we are in fact more mathematical than practising physicists. This is because physicists are focussed on explaining how the world works. They are thus generally willing to leave proofs to the mathematician. Like other natural scientists, they care little about existence theorems - they want to know what specifically happens, not what is theoretically possible. The purpose of mathematics, in their minds, is to allow quantification, but existence theorems provide no quantifiable results.

The unavoidable conclusion is that we imitate mathematicians rather than physicists. Yet the former make no pretence of explaining how the world works (as portrayed in Levins' (1992) conversation with Dona Hardy). As Szostak (1992) points out, the behavior of mathematicians is actually more similar to that of artists than that of scientists (both McCloskey (1991) and Leijonhufvud (1973) also recognize an aesthetic motive for formalization in economics). This suits mathematics well, but provides a weak foundation for our own. If we really want to behave like scientists, we have to focus on important real world questions rather than on overly sophisticated techniques.

Katzner's (1991) defence of formalization is very instructive. Note first of all that he explicitly agrees with McCloskey (1991) on many key points (Lesson: orthodox economists, once drawn into methodological debate, will find that they cannot maintain some of their most cherished beliefs). Further, his argument that once a science has developed a model, it will naturally explore such issues as uniqueness and stability seems on the one hand to fly directly in the face of McCloskey's (1991) evidence drawn from physics, and on the other to confirm the hypothesis that economists will naturally be excessive in their purely mathematical inquiries. (Katzner (1991) himself recognizes that the culture of economics could encourage too much formalization.) Katzner (1991) suggests that we need to be confident of uniqueness of equilibrium before we can proceed to perform comparative statics exercises. This would come as something of a surprise to legions of economists who have performed comparative statics exercises while retaining their innocence of proofs of uniqueness.

Again we must note that the argument is not about whether formalization is good or bad but whether there is too much of it. I have always marvelled at the pride with which economists will proclaim they have designed a model which generates result X. Surely they realize that, unless there are some logical inconsistencies within result X, there *must* exist at least one model which will generate it. Unless the model they have developed serves some useful purpose (that is, it has the potential for guiding empirical estimation - not just that it provides another formal avenue down which others can putter), it serves no scientific function whatsoever.

Katzner (1991) feels that the discipline's real problems are that it asks the wrong questions and oversimplifies. Yet where can we place the blame for such sins if not on an excessive desire for formalization? As many of our essays show, economists become easy targets for satire due to their penchant for making ludicrous assumptions for no other discernable purpose than mathematical tractability. Thus we have the economics of brushing teeth and of sleeping; neither would be funny if economists could not recognize that they reflect too closely their own simplistic models. Levins' (1992) tongue-in-cheek appraisal of the agricultural economics literature (which is often felt, as he recognizes, to be one of the most down-to-earth arms of our discipline) leaves no doubt that we are all too willing to leave out the most important of potential causal factors. As he notes, our conclusions are necessarily prefaced by a lengthy series of 'ifs'. But cursed with short memories, we forget the restrictive assumptions made at the beginning when a few short pages later we write or read the conclusion. McCloskey (1989) shows how a belief in naive positivism has too often been used as a rationalizing device for assuming away some of the more important considerations. Those who propose that even ridiculous models can serve as tools of prediction (not that our predictive abilities have been much to brag about) fail to realize that prediction is a greatly inferior goal to explanation: as Levins (1992) notes, we gain little explanatory power by assuming the world away. Surveying the literature, we can but wonder how concerned the profession is with solving the world's problems, as opposed to creating a mathematically beautiful world of the imagination.

This is bad enough, for the world has such pressing problems that it deserves better than an economics profession devoted to fantasy. Worse, the realm of fantasy can intrude upon the world to the latter's detriment. Frank, Gilovich, and Regan (1993) show that economists score much worse [better, some economists might well argue] on tests of fairness, charity, cooperation, and honesty than do other people. This may in part represents self-selection - our subject simply attracts the dishonest and selfish. The authors remain convinced, though, that education must play a major role. Years of having such virtues assumed away before their eyes, and being told that markets work best without such niceties, inevitably cause students to shrink back from the common decency their parents and teachers had previously instilled. To the extent the outer world heeds us, we may do much harm, for the system works much better when trust and fairness guide it. Economists, often portrayed as defenders of the status quo, may prove to be its unintentional destroyers.

If the primary concern of economists was with the world as we know it, we would be unlikely to devote so much effort to insulating our models against corrupting outside forces. Leijonhufvud (1973) mocked this practice decades ago, but it is still with us. One advantage of ridiculous assumptions is, after all, that the events of the world can never provide an irrefutable test. How then can the economics community reach interesting conclusions? Quite easily. As Levins (1992) makes quite clear, we simply start with the conclusion we want, and fill in the necessary equations. Models which produce the wrong conclusions are thrown out on the flimsiest of complaints, while those which give the right answer can never be toppled by the evidence. It is ironic that a discipline which prides itself on its scientific approach can embrace such arbitrary decision rules.

Freedman (2003) details an even more insidious practice. By means of our refereeing practises, we refuse to allow true novelty to see the light of day. Those who shun the existing methodology will find that the insights they proffer are judged to be the product of bad science. Economists can thus claim that as bad as their theory may be, there is no obvious alternative. The alternatives have been smothered in the cradle. Each (any?) referee and editor who chooses to emphasize relevance and results over technique serves to ever so slightly change the incentives faced by the profession. As new ideas gain currency, the profession should find it increasingly difficult to defend naive formalism. Though many in the profession would raise serious doubts and objections, this paradigmatic shift may already be under way.

It is a common observation among both people on the street and professional psychologists that those who exude the greatest degree of arrogance are those with the least justification for it. Bergstrom (1976) parodies the arrogance of economists in the economics of sleeping, while Blinder (1974) playfully pokes fun at arrogance in his economics of brushing teeth. Bronfenbrenner (1991) and Freedmen (1993) both explore the characteristic arrogance of many economists in a more serious vein, and display the severe costs imposed on the discipline by the lack of open-mindedness and common civility which define it. With few accomplishments of their own to point to, economists become the playground bullies of the social sciences, and scream their superiority. If we cannot be superior in terms of the output of our theorizing, then we must save our bragging rights for the inputs.The anthropologist spending months in the jungle, or the sociologist running (inevitably flawed, unlike our own data) surveys are viewed as scientific Lilliputians when compared to economists producing mathematical models. Even the psychologist running experiments - once thought the very essence of the scientific method in certain circles - is snubbed. Of course, any economist who borrows the methods of these other disciplines must receive similar contempt.

It is no coincidence that some of our authors speak of the advantage which the discipline might gain from a more open attitude to interdisciplinary work. Once we abandon our insistence on one and only one methodology, then we are able to admit the possibility that we might have something to learn from our colleagues in other disciplines. Leijonhufvud (1973) notes that development economics lost status because its practitioners often consorted with those denizens of lesser disciplines. The mere fact that they were trying to improve the miserable economic condition of the bulk of the world's population was not enough to spare them from disdain. (I would argue that the study of economic growth in general has been slighted to this day because it is less amenable to formal analysis; see Szostak, 1999). Yet most - if not all - of what we do involves us intrinsically with the concerns of other disciplines. The economics of brushing teeth admirably displays the ease with which an economist willingly ignores the role of cultural norms and medical advice in determining personal behavior. We do not ignore only the social sciences. Bronfenbrenner (1991) agrees that we lose much from ignoring history as well. Yet even economic historians - incredibly - have been guilty of this sin. McCloskey (1989) notes that economic historians found naive positivism attractive because it spared them from the mastery of historical fact that so burdened real historians; one needed only a hypothesis and some data.[2]

As a result, it becomes easy to point to an obvious paradox in economic practice. We shun the surveys[3] or the interviews of others because we feel that what agents think they are doing is not that important: we *know* that they are maximizing utility (at least the representative agent by definition must be) so why ask them? We not only ignore the fact that altruism may motivate them to a greater degree than is convenient for our models, but sidestep behavior constraints like the cost of obtaining information (recent exceptions aside). It is easier to assume that they operate in accordance with a true model of the economy. But if they do that already without our help (they, to their credit, care as little about our thoughts as we about theirs), then what is the use of us developing better theories? We have casually assumed away our own usefulness. Perhaps, faced with this challenge, economists may decide inter-disciplinarity has something to offer.

In the meantime the best defence is a good offence. Instead of opening our minds to the insights of other social sciences, we invade their domains with our own well-worn bag of tricks. In an ideal world of intellectual co-operation, we would naturally both have much to learn from each other. Yet, as Bergstrom (1976) and Blinder (1974) make clear, the one-sided excursions of economists into other domains are notable mainly for showcasing our excessive willingness to ignore the non-economic motives in human behavior. As Bronfenbrenner (1991) points out, our arrogance has earned us a great deal of enmity from those who should be our allies.

Perhaps, our disdain of outsiders is due in part to the fact that the denizens of math/stats departments scoff at our feeble efforts. Ignorance of other disciplines is preferable to facing the risk that they may be able to do some things better than we can. The root of this problem also lies in excessive formalism. As Levins (1992) makes clear, if our articles bristle with mindless mathematics then we deserve our unfortunate reputation as second-rate mathematicians. It is, indeed, a pitiful sight when economists have nothing more to boast about than the mastery of techniques which humble students in math departments consider to be old hat. If we were to focus instead on practical questions and use whatever methods were best suited to their exploration, we might just get the respect from mathematicians (and physicists) that mindless imitation can never earn.

The proof is in the pudding, as our grandmothers like to say, and we must face the simple fact that economists have had few breakthroughs in understanding to which they can point (and even fewer decent puddings). Not surprisingly, dedication to pseudo-scientific principles has severely limited our success as scientists (not entirely of course; McCloskey (1991) and Szostak (1992) both detail how some of our colleagues have nevertheless produced good science - but even these could have done better by following more appropriate guidelines). If honest, we would all admit that even the greatest accomplishments of our Nobel Laureates look simplistic when viewed by the general public. These shining lights have won their general acclaim by essentially embedding common-sense conclusions in complex mathematical analysis. I remember a talk James Tobin gave when I was a graduate student. He spoke of being interviewed by reporters after his Nobel win. When trying to explain portfolio theory in a few words proved difficult, he gave them the old proverb: 'don't put all of your eggs in one basket'. The next day, a local newspaper ran a cartoon with a Nobel medalist in medicine saying, "It's quite simple. An apple a day..." Without at all deprecating Tobin's accomplishments - especially as he seemed lacking in the arrogance one generally expects, and has in fact used mathematics for its proper purpose of quantification - we should still be able to understand from whence comes the bemusement of the outside world. They, after all, evaluate us by quite different standards than our own.

McCloskey (1991:7) recounts the story of Robert Solow complaining to a physicist (Nobel laureate Victor Weisskopf) about the lack of really bright economists compared to the situation in physics. The physicist responded with a handy bit of economic analysis. We should expect marginally bright physics students to migrate toward fields where they would have a greater chance to shine. In the long run, the marginal student in both fields would be equally bright.[4] While this analysis ignores the possibility that the intrinsic interest of fields may vary, and that scientists may not be driven solely by a desire for fame, it still contains a valuable kernel of truth. Why is it easier to point to physicists making real breakthroughs in their science than to find the same in economics? The fault, alas, lies not in us but in our methodological blinders. If physicists were constrained to behave in the same narrow fashion that we are, they would scarcely shine so bright (as any biography of their most successful practitioners will show).

We need not just speculate about the costs to the discipline of narrow-mindedness. It is clear that we lose excellent people and excellent ideas. Bronfenbrenner (1991) tells us that he is unlikely to have prospered (or even survived) if he had come on the scene a generation later. Why is there almost no space in our discipline for those who care more about relevance than technique, and do not wish to arbitrarily limit their methods of inquiry? Surveys of graduate students bear witness to Bronfenbrenner's (1991) fear. Who can deny that those who wish to play formalistic games will fare better in graduate school than those who wish to understand how the world works? Even if the latter survive, Leamer (1991) notes that the necessity of mastering so much mathematics must squeeze out the intellectual growth which should occur in graduate school. If W.W. Rostow (1990) is correct in thinking (and anything is possible) that great economists (like mathematicians) develop their best ideas in their 20s, what hope is there? What do we think we are selecting for if we teach nothing but techniques for the first year or more?

Some competition for resources is inevitable, of course (see Bronfenbrenner 1991). The theorist must always have a personal interest in his or her department hiring a like kind rather than some fuzzy historian (and vice versa). In economics, this process has gone to extremes. Bad economists have surely chased out good. Who can really believe that the ten-thousandth mathematical tinkerer adds more to our community's product than one who dares to use some other methodology? We are ridiculously far from equating marginal products. Some redress is surely desirable before we can reach Bronfenbrenner's (1991) 'golden mean'. I share with McCloskey the optimist's view that a balanced profession is possible. What force can drive us more surely toward equalizing our marginal product than the focus of a true scientific community bent on results and their relevance?

Our focus on means rather than ends, our adulation of techniques, our arrogance, our unwillingness to listen to others: these naturally combine to limit communication between the profession and the public. Our internal nastiness, as Freedman (1993) documents, forces us to retreat even further into obfuscation. Since we have little to say, and will be slammed for being non-orthodox, we can only dazzle each other with ever-more-complicated techniques (much like special effects in big-budget action films - all surface, no depth). Our self-satisfaction ensures that we do not try to interpret these works for the masses (except in return for a fat consulting fee, in which case we prove willing to say whatever is desired). Economic journalists thus march to their own tune; not surprisingly their writings contain psychological, sociological, and even ethical concerns alien to academic economists. A scientific discipline which should have much to offer the public deliberately cuts off its main lines of communication instead.

How could science come to turn its back so firmly on open-mindedness? McCloskey (1991) should not have to make a plea for understanding to a community of scholars. We can hope that his words do cause some twang of conscience in the discipline. Naive positivism may have done some good in its day, but has latterly become the enemy of freedom. There is simply no excuse for this behavior. Philosophy cannot justify it; nor can our track record. If the economics mainstream will not willingly accept open-mindedness as a virtue on its own merits, then the only remaining option is to embarrass them into doing so.

References

Bergstrom, Theodore (1976) "Toward a Deeper Economics of Sleeping," *Journal of Political Economy.* 84(2): 411-412.

Blinder, Allan (1974) "The Economics of Brushing Teeth," *The Journal of Political Economy.* 82(4): 887-892.

Breit, William and Roger Ransom (1982) *The Academic Scribblers.* Chicago: Dryden.

Bronfenbrenner, Martin (1991) "Economics as Dentistry," *The Southern Economic Journal.* 57(3): 599-605.

Colander, David (1996) "Surviving as a Slightly Out of Sync Economist," in Stephen J. Medema and Warren J. Samuels (eds.) *Foundations of Research in Economics: How Do Economists Do Economics?* Cheltenham: Edward Elgar.

Fair, Ray (1978) "A Theory of Extramarital Affairs," *The Journal of Political Economy.* 86(1): 45-61.

Frank, Robert, Thomas Gilovich and Dennis Regan (1993) "Does Studying Economics Inhibit Cooperation," *The Journal of Economic Perspectives.* 7(2): 159-171.

Freedman, Craig (1993) "Why Economists Can't Read", *Methodus.* 5(1): 6-23.

Freedman, Craig (2003) "Economic Nostrums and Economic Practices- Accountability in Economic Journals", in Freedman, Craig and Rick Szostak (eds.) *Tales of Narcissus - A Journey Through the Soul of an Economist.* Armonk New York: Nova Science Publishers.

Hansen, W. Lee "The Education and Training of Economists: Major Findings of the AEA's COGEE". *Journal of Economic Literature*, September 1991, 1054-87.

Katzner, Donald (1991) "In Defense of Formalization in Economics," *Methodus* 3(1): 17-24.

Klamer, Arjo and David Colander (1990) *The Making of an Economist*. Boulder: Westview Press.

Leamer, Edward (1991) "Comment: Has Formalization Gone Too Far?" *Methodus* 3(1): 25-26.

Leijonhufvud, Axel (1973) "Life Among the Econ," *Western Economic Journal* 15(2): 327-337.

Levins, Richard (1992) "The Whimsical Science," *Review of Agricultural Economics*. 14(3): 139-151.

McCloskey, Donald (1989) "Why I Am No Longer a Positivist," *Review of Social Economy*. 47(3): 225-239.

McCloskey, Donald (1991) "Economics Science: A Search Through the Hyperspace of Assumptions?" *Methodus* 3(1): 6-16.

Rostow, W.W. *Theorists of Economic Growth From David Hume to the Present*. New York: Oxford University Press, 1990.

Samuelson, Paul (1962) "Economists and The History of Ideas," *The American Economic Review*. 52(1): 1-18.

Szostak, Rick (1992) "The History of Art and the Art in Economics," *History of Economics Review*. 18(Summer): 70-107.

Szostak, Rick *Econ-Art: Divorcing Art From Science in Modern Economics*. London: Pluto Press, 1999.

Notes

[1] McCloskey (1989) makes the interesting observation that the word 'science' has a different connotation in English than most other languages. Most of these treat science as any sort of systematic inquiry. English, however, invests it with a measure of superiority due to supposedly greater objectivity. Our discipline might not have become so close-minded in a different linguistic environment.

[2] It is not just in economic history that this sin is detrimental. While economists think only in terms of models, the agent on the street is all too aware that their economic environment is a historical construct.

[3] A pet project of mine is that the AEA regularly survey its own membership on their views about key economic questions, and report the results in the *Journal of Economic Perspectives*. (This has admittedly been done in the past, though only in a rather sporadic fashion.) Once we recognize that science advances not through conclusive proof but by the collective judgement of the scientific community, it seems a logical step. We could then see what effect the latest generation of models has had, if any. Such a survey would also give us a quantitative response to the journalistic complaint that we never agree on anything. (Most surveys have shown remarkable agreement.) Our belief that surveys aren't science, and our refusal to accept the fact that science advances through the collective judgement of a community of scholars, holds us back.

[4] This is reminiscent of a remark attributed to a former prime minister of New Zealand. Commenting on the heavy migration from New Zealand to Australia, he claimed that this managed to raise the average IQ of both countries.

INDEX

A

absolution, 116
academic journal, 132, 133
accountability, vi, 11, 131, 132, 135, 136, 147, 244
achievement, 10, 206, 225
adolescence, 190
agriculture, 62, 176, 178, 179, 180, 181
altruism, 145, 150, 157, 242
amnesty, 100
anger, 198
anthropology, 32, 198
apathy, 153
application, 11, 77, 79, 80, 89, 100, 135, 163, 178, 187, 192, 216, 217
applied microeconomics, 127
argument, 59, 73, 74, 77, 81, 85, 86, 88, 89, 93, 108, 111, 116, 120, 123, 127, 128, 129, 144, 151, 161, 165, 170, 181, 185, 186, 190, 196, 198, 199, 200, 227, 228, 230, 239, 240
Aristotle, 15
assumptions, 6, 7, 34, 76, 77, 78, 81, 82, 86, 87, 88, 89, 90, 93, 118, 140, 175, 179, 182, 183, 186, 205, 210, 220, 225, 226, 232, 233, 240, 241
astronomy, 38, 39, 46, 98
attachment, 17, 206
attention, 5, 54, 87, 108, 118, 131, 162, 165, 181, 204, 211, 214, 224, 227, 228, 229
attitudes, 207, 209, 212, 228
attribution, 48
Australia, ix, 245
authoritarianism, 215
automatic writing, 217
awareness, 3, 108, 117, 206, 225

B

bankers, 100, 101
banking, 120
banking system, 120
behavior, 18, 29, 30, 31, 32, 33, 37, 38, 40, 47, 48, 59, 60, 75, 86, 87, 88, 90, 113, 116, 127, 145, 179, 182, 186, 192, 239, 242, 244
behavioral sciences, 101
Bessel function, 74
bonds, 69
bourgeoisie, 10, 223
Britain, 101, 118, 192
Buchanan, James, 79
bugs, 176
bureaucracy, 154
bureaucrats, 154

C

cabinet ministers, 96
calculators, 7, 83
California, 17, 83, 118, 123, 149, 181, 182, 233
Canada, 229, 231
capital, 79, 85, 168, 191
capitalism, 75, 76, 82, 209
career choice, 98
caste, 17, 18, 19, 20, 23, 25
causality, 91, 222
central planning, 97, 105
chaos, 80, 210, 213
chaos, 83, 121, 234
chaos theory, 80
China, 38

choice, 23, 33, 34, 35, 87, 90, 93, 94, 95, 113, 118, 120, 127, 128, 145, 154, 157, 160, 161, 162, 163, 165, 166, 169, 170, 171, 180, 200, 218
Chrysler, 171
citations, 132, 140, 141, 152
coding, 63
cognition, 7
cognitive dissonance, 228
cohabitation, 224
coherence, 127
colleges, 169
commodities, 5, 83, 113
common sense, 127, 187, 199, 228, 230, 232
communication, 112
communities, 135, 153
compensation, 138
competency, 154, 155
competition, 13, 73, 81, 100, 118, 119, 147, 152, 165, 166, 168, 171, 210, 227, 233, 243
competitiveness, 101
complexity, 88, 176, 194, 205, 214, 218, 222, 228
comprehension, 221
computer program, 98
computer simulation, 75, 100, 193
concept, 20, 85, 116, 124, 193, 203, 218
concreteness, 91
conflict(s), 21, 93, 96, 111, 125, 132, 136, 140,160, 206, 212, 213
conformity, 93
conscience, 114, 244
conscious, 10, 107, 109, 125, 204, 209, 214, 215, 216, 217, 218, 223, 225
consciousness, 117, 212, 217, 221
conservation, 123, 124, 125, 126, 127, 128, 180
conservation laws, 127, 128
conservation of energy, 124
consumer demand, 134
consumers, 4, 106, 107, 114, 115, 160, 163, 169, 210, 215
consumption, 45, 57, 175, 204
consumption taxes, 175
continuity, 177, 178
control, 30, 34, 36, 38, 39, 106, 108, 133, 134, 135, 136, 144, 151, 153, 190, 204, 217, 227
control group, 30, 38, 39
cooperation, 34, 35, 38, 40, 112, 240
coping, 27
core, 6, 106, 108, 110, 154, 222, 233
correlation, 63, 183
cosmology, 25
cottage industry, 115
credit, 129
criterion, 81, 131, 225

crop production, 181, 182
cultural differences, 74

D

Darwin, Charles, 109
decay, 19, 27
denial, 113, 199
dependent variable, 34, 35, 50, 60, 63, 64, 65, 67
depression, 98, 116
Descartes, Rene, 191, 199
determinism, 95
development, 86, 88, 89, 98, 105, 123, 124, 125, 131, 219, 221, 222, 224, 230, 241
deviation, 8, 46, 106, 107, 109, 113, 117, 119
diet, 13, 110, 111
discrimination, 152, 210, 213
displacement, 27
dissonance, 113
diversity, 4, 8, 215, 228, 230, 231, 238
dominance, 13
double blind, 140
dreaming, 186
drive, 93, 100, 109, 124, 186, 228, 243

E

$E = mc^2$, 124
earth, 79, 203, 240
eclipse, 220
econometric tests, 75
economic activity, 105
economic development, 38
economic growth, 73, 82, 211, 221, 226, 229, 241, 245
economic journals, 97, 105, 119, 132, 133
economic model, 78, 86, 111, 150, 225
Economic Policy, 233
Economic Regulation, 150
economic system, 115, 143
economics of sleeping, 45, 241
economists, v, vi, vii, ix, 3, 4, 7, 8, 10, 11, 12, 14, 15, 29, 31, 32, 33, 37, 41, 43, 71, 73, 74, 75, 77, 78, 83, 103, 105, 108, 109, 110, 111, 112, 114, 116, 117, 118, 119, 120, 146, 148, 149, 150, 153, 157, 186, 190, 194, 201, 206, 210, 212, 217, 222, 223, 226, 228, 229, 230, 232, 233, 241, 244, 245
editorial boards, 101, 136, 137, 147, 153
education, 9, 13, 23, 32, 61, 62, 64, 67, 68, 82, 83, 114, 120, 157, 159, 168, 170, 171, 178, 203, 240, 244
efficiency, 149

ego, 153
Einstein, Albert, 86
elaboration, 124, 126, 147
elections, 33, 40, 153
electron, 194
emergence, 207
emotion, 41, 173, 199, 208, 213
empathy, 156
empiricism, 85, 170, 189, 198
employment, 12, 121
encouragement, 175, 231, 238
England, 20, 128, 178, 186
environmental influences, 207
equilibrium, 83, 91, 234
etiquette, 13
Euclid, 74
Euripides, 118
Europe, 106, 199, 215
evaluation, 127, 156, 204, 224, 230
exclusion, 33, 89, 135, 152, 218
excuse, 109, 116, 142, 214, 244
exercise, 11, 32, 57, 111, 134, 205, 206, 216
expectation, 37, 211
experimental design, 31
exploitation, 213, 222

F

formalization, 81, 82, 85, 86, 87, 88, 89, 90, 93, 190,
   239, 240
frustration, 237
fundamental, 80, 112, 125, 138, 146, 159, 175

G

gene, 193
generalization, 87

H

Hamiltonian dynamics, 127
Hapsburg Empire, 215
hate, 118
heuristic, 3, 125
Hobson, John A., 97
honesty, 108, 170, 178, 231, 240
human behavior, 47, 242
human capital, 47, 48, 50, 159, 168
Hume, 191, 222, 245
hypothesis, 21, 22, 32, 34, 38, 40, 170, 183, 193,
   195, 204, 240, 242

I

idealism, 17, 195
Illinois, 96, 168
illusion, vii, 210, 211
imitation, 77, 82, 123, 220, 242
imperialism, 101
Implementarists, 23
incentive, 81, 105, 117, 135, 136, 144, 155, 166, 167
inclusion, 32, 55
income distribution, 97, 100, 212
income, labor, 46
income, nonlabor, 50, 54, 56, 58, 64, 68
independent variable, 35
India, 175
Industrial Revolution, 186, 231, 233
industrialization, 23
inertia, 105
inference, 126
infinite, 24, 66, 183
inflation, 98, 212
initial conditions, 127
inputs, 140, 159, 160, 181, 185, 241
insight, 3, 86, 120, 132, 156, 176, 203, 210, 211,
   212, 213, 226, 229
insomnia, 180
instability, 114
integrity, 133
interest rates, 114
interference, 133, 147, 152, 216, 220, 231
interleukine, 233
international trade, 77, 206, 215, 221
interpretation, 24, 25, 39, 87, 97, 109, 110, 113, 119,
   126, 140, 216
intervention, 216, 218
introspection, 3, 4, 200, 213
intuition, 166, 169, 206, 214, 217, 221
invasion, 98
inversion, 8
investment, 30, 50, 76, 97, 114, 115, 160, 164, 212,
   228
Iowa, 73, 82, 152, 189, 202
irrationalism, 198, 209
irrationality, 208
irrigation, 175, 181, 182

J

Japan, 95, 101
Japanese, 146, 148, 161, 172
job training, 47

journals, 3, 9, 78, 81, 98, 101, 105, 106, 107, 108, 113, 117, 118, 131, 132, 133, 134, 135, 136, 137, 138, 139, 140, 141, 144, 146, 147, 151, 152, 153, 154, 155, 156, 157, 175, 176, 177, 179, 233

justification, 55, 110, 161, 165, 187, 216, 226, 241

K

Kansas, 46, 187

kinetic energy, 124

knowledge, 3, 7, 81, 82, 83, 88, 89, 99, 110, 114, 115, 131, 134, 138, 145, 151, 153, 157, 161, 162, 171, 176, 193, 194, 204, 214, 228, 230, 232, 233, 237

L

labor force, 45, 46, 50, 73

labor force participation, 73

leadership, 116, 187

learning, 96, 163, 165, 177, 180, 183, 191, 214

leisure time, 53, 54, 59, 68

lens, 151, 230

likelihood, 13, 38, 99, 115, 141

liquidity, 114

literary tradition, 82, 203

loyalty, 142

M

manufacturing, 20

market economy, 115

market forces, 216

marketplace, 170, 233

marriage, 47, 53, 54, 57, 58, 59, 60, 61, 62, 64, 65, 66, 68

Marx, Karl, 100, 113

Marxism, 91, 97, 120

Maryland, 184

Massachusetts, 83, 85

mastery, 93, 216, 217, 229, 242

materialism, 89

Math-Econ, 19, 23, 24, 25

matrix, 34, 74

mean, vii, viii, 10, 33, 36, 59, 66, 74, 81, 99, 113, 115, 119, 120, 126, 138, 140, 145, 163, 178, 183, 184, 204, 209, 225, 230, 237, 243

measurement, 79, 86, 218

median, 32

metaphor, 7, 73, 87, 88, 93, 100, 111, 123, 124, 125, 126, 127, 128, 129, 159, 160

metaphysics, 125, 127, 191, 207

methodology, 8, 80, 85, 120, 123, 140, 151, 156, 165, 171, 175, 179, 184, 206, 211, 224, 226, 229, 232, 237, 238, 241, 243

microeconomics, 39

migration, 26, 245

Mill, John Stuart, 95, 105, 169, 218

mining, 25

Minnesota, 79, 175, 180, 181

Mississippi, 96, 179

Missouri, 96

mode, 4, 8, 90, 107, 113, 126, 207

model(s), 3, 4, 6, 7, 10, 13, 29, 31, 33, 34, 37, 40, 47, 48, 49, 50, 53, 54, 55, 56, 59, 60, 63, 65, 66, 68, 77, 78, 79, 80, 86, 87, 88, 89, 90, 91, 93, 110, 111, 113, 116, 117, 119, 120, 124, 126, 127, 128, 150, 164, 166, 172, 175, 177, 179, 181, 183, 184, 187, 191, 192, 195, 196, 200, 206, 209, 211, 213, 214, 220, 225, 229, 232, 233, 238, 239, 240, 241, 242, 245

model-building, 86, 88

modeling, 87, 100, 187, 232, 233, 239

momentum, 207

monetary policy, 228

money, 30, 31, 32, 34, 38, 90, 96, 98, 114, 115, 120, 123, 126, 132, 160, 170, 182, 184, 186

morality, 25

motivation, 24, 40, 55, 68, 95, 145, 205

mutual, 153, 160

N

narcissism, 11, 151

national income, 46, 76

nationalism, 215, 224

natural, 10, 23, 25, 32, 39, 75, 80, 96, 97, 98, 99, 109, 112, 113, 123, 135, 146, 170, 207, 210, 215, 216, 219, 220, 227, 229, 231, 239

natural resources, 25

natural science, 23, 32, 75, 96, 99, 112, 123

neoclassical economics, 8, 83, 120, 123, 124, 125, 126, 127, 128, 129, 232

neutral, 157, 218

New Deal, 97, 99

new technology, 163, 167, 221, 229

New Zealand, 245

Nietzsche, 198

nitrogen, 176

North Carolina, 95

O

objectivity, 88, 133, 138, 245

offspring, 47, 118, 152
opportunity costs, 139, 167
optimism, 25, 27, 76
organic, 89
organisational structures, 136
organization, 26, 38, 134, 231
originality, 99, 157
output, 95, 97, 105, 106, 115, 117, 132, 133, 136, 140, 144, 152, 162, 185, 226, 241

P

perception, 20, 25, 199, 204, 212, 218, 22, 2231, 232
performance, 9, 31, 37, 136, 143, 144, 147, 153, 157, 159
personal goals, 109
personal identity, 237
personality, 120
persuasion, 81, 112, 114, 237
pessimism, 19
pitch, 161
Plato, vii, 117
pluralism, 233
Poland, 98
police, 186
politicians, 100, 101, 169, 209, 212, 216
pollution, 19, 181, 182, 227
pollution control, 227
population, 25, 60, 98, 152, 154, 230, 241
population growth, 25
population growth rate, 25
positivism, 10, 189, 190, 191, 192, 193, 194, 195, 196, 197, 198, 199, 200, 238, 240, 242, 244
potential energy, 124
poverty, 5, 18, 23, 25, 26
power struggle, 169
pragmatism, 195
prediction, 40, 49, 175, 190, 231, 240
price level, 54
prices, 121, 150
prime minister, 245
principle, 25, 113, 118, 141, 145, 154, 164, 197, 199, 219, 221
private enterprise, 160
probe, 3
problem solving, 165, 225
production, 50, 55, 73, 113, 120, 139, 159, 160, 163, 177, 179, 181, 182, 206
productivity, 31, 82, 83, 89, 140, 211, 218, 221
program, 77, 81, 100, 125, 184, 192
proliferation, 117, 154, 193, 211
property rights, 132, 133
proposition, 49, 74, 80, 159

protective, 111, 154
pseudoscience, 197, 198
public finance, 37, 97
public policy, 238
public support, 226
publishers, iv, ix, x, 133, 136, 137, 152, 160, 161, 163, 164, 168, 169, 170, 171
punishment, 47, 196

Q

quantum mechanics, 125

R

racism, 198
radical, 117, 126, 169, 223, 224, 233
rationalism, 85, 198, 208
rationality, 113, 145, 163
rationalization, 23, 90, 119
reasoning, 75, 85, 88, 110, 125, 127, 151, 164, 166, 175, 179, 182, 197, 199, 207
recalling, 83
recession, 116
recognition, 90, 99, 107, 108, 118, 134, 136, 146, 153, 203, 207, 213, 226, 229, 238
recombination, 208
reconstruction, 91
refereeing, 9, 131, 132, 138, 139, 140, 141, 143, 144, 145, 146, 147, 151, 155, 156, 157, 241
referees, 9, 110, 132, 135, 136, 137, 138, 139, 140, 141, 142, 143, 144, 145, 146, 147, 151, 154, 155, 156, 157, 228, 232
regression, 34, 38, 50, 183
rehearsal, 215
reincarnation, 8
relationships, 17, 18, 20, 55, 135, 193, 220, 233
relativity, 124, 125, 232
reliability, 157
religion, 24, 32, 115, 191, 200
Renaissance, 199
repetition, 128
reputations, 39, 106, 151
resistance, 105, 169
resolution, 46
response, 5, 9, 25, 26, 34, 38, 40, 108, 142, 143, 154, 165, 184, 233, 245
revolutions, 136
reward, 90, 138, 139, 147, 151, 154, 222, 226, 232, 239
rhetoric, 8, 12, 76, 78, 80, 81, 101, 105, 109, 110, 111, 112, 116, 117, 118, 195, 206, 227

risk factors, 184
robustness, 78

S

sample, 32, 33, 34, 35, 36, 37, 45, 48, 50, 60, 63, 162
scientific inquiry, 207, 229, 239
scientific method, 184, 206, 218, 224, 232, 241
self, viii, 3, 4, 5, 6, 7, 8, 9, 10, 11, 18, 29, 31, 33, 34, 36, 37, 40, 43, 63, 74, 75, 80, 82, 106, 108, 110, 111, 112, 114, 116, 117, 119, 127, 128, 131, 134, 135, 136, 137, 142, 145, 146, 147, 153, 157, 162, 163, 164, 168, 170, 171, 182, 195, 204, 206, 208, 212, 217, 218, 219, 220, 225, 227, 228, 230, 238, 240, 244
self-esteem, 131
self-image, 18, 217
self-interest, 29, 31, 33, 34, 36, 37, 40, 131, 136, 137, 145, 157
self-perception, 204
sensitivity, 205
sex differences, 35
Siberia, 96, 99
simulation, 75, 100, 229
Slovenia, 97
small business, 38
smog, 36
social life, 17, 219
social relationships, 20
social stratification, 148
social structure, 17, 19, 20, 25
social theory, 123
social work, 62
socialism, 195
Socialists, 113
sociology, 7, 32, 74, 81, 83, 90, 91, 101, 151, 190, 192
sovereignty, 9, 114
Soviet Union, 153, 198
space-time, 232
specialization, 178
specific knowledge, 7, 110
stability, 76, 86, 87, 88, 89, 91, 94, 115, 117, 219, 221, 239
stages, 89
Stalin, Joseph, 97, 209
statistical significance, 34
statistics, 9, 79, 82, 97, 183, 216, 221, 228
stress, 40, 118, 165, 227
supply and demand, 87, 186, 220
Supreme Court, 97
surrealism, 207, 208, 209, 210, 211, 212, 213, 214, 218, 222, 227

survival of the fittest, 109
symbol, 124, 125
symmetry, 124
sympathy, 157
symptoms, 26, 82

T

tax burden, 182
taxes, 97, 175, 182
technological change, 211, 221, 229
temperament, 225
textbooks, 13, 77, 79, 114, 116, 159, 160, 161, 162, 163, 165, 166, 167, 168, 169, 170, 212
theory, 6, 10, 11, 31, 38, 45, 46, 47, 48, 49, 50, 54, 55, 59, 66, 68, 74, 75, 76, 77, 78, 79, 80, 81, 82, 83, 85, 89, 97, 98, 109, 113, 116, 117, 119, 120, 123, 124, 125, 126, 127, 128, 150, 151, 154, 157, 159, 178, 180, 184, 185, 191, 192, 193, 198, 199, 204, 206, 207, 209, 210, 211, 215, 216, 217, 218, 220, 222, 225, 226, 227, 228, 229, 230, 231, 232, 233, 238, 241, 243
thermodynamics, 124, 128
thinking, 82, 83, 91, 93, 109, 132, 154, 157, 161, 163, 164, 165, 166, 170, 171, 175, 178, 180, 190, 191, 195, 200, 221, 237, 238, 243
third parties, 19
tobacco industry, 5
tolerance, 81, 117, 198, 199
totalitarianism, 197, 198
trade barriers, 215
traits, viii, 43
transformation, 205, 214
transport, 203
troops, 9
tyranny, 199

U

unconscious, 10, 218
unemployment, 98, 210, 212, 215, 220
unemployment rate, 215
United States, iv, 167, 209, 215, 222
universities, 31, 169
university presses, 133, 148, 153

V

validity, 7, 207, 223, 230
value of goods, 54, 64, 68
variable, 35, 50, 55, 56, 57, 58, 63, 64, 65, 66, 67, 68, 86, 183

variance, 108
vector, 55, 56, 124, 125
Vietnam War, 191
violence, 117, 198, 199
voting, 33, 196

W

wage rate, 45, 48, 54, 56, 63, 64, 68
water supply, 50
wealth, 91, 147
Western civilization, 197, 198

Wisconsin, 83, 98, 121, 151, 189
word processing, 166
words, 1, 9, 11, 18, 21, 25, 29, 38, 49, 73, 79, 85, 87,
    89, 112, 116, 118, 123, 125, 126, 128, 140, 168,
    198, 204, 216, 217, 231, 243, 244
workers, 74, 210
World Wide Web, 162

X

xenophobia, 17